A different school of thought.^{SM}

KAPLAN UNIVERSITY

Investment Planning

Second Edition

by Keith R. Fevurly and Harold F. Lenhart

ISBN: 978-0-9796762-5-3

TABLE OF CONTENTS

Chapter 1: Cash and Cash Equivalents

Chapter 2: Bonds and Debt Securities

Chapter 3: Stocks and Stock Attributes

Chapter 4: Mutual Funds and Managed Investments

Chapter 5: Insurance-Based Investments

Chapter 6: Real Estate and Real Estate Investment Trusts (REITs)

Chapter 7: Alternative Investments

Chapter 8: Sources of Investment Risk

Chapter 9: Measurements of Investment Risk

Chapter 10: Portfolio Management Theory and Behavioral Finance

Chapter 11: Measures of Investment Return

Chapter 12: Valuing Equity Securities

Chapter 13: Valuing Debt Securities

Chapter 18: Taxation of Investment Vehicles

PREFACE

In the financial planning process, investment planning is likely the most important subject matter area since it is the "engine" behind the process. Specifically, investment planning (if done properly) *builds investor wealth*. As such, it provides the lump sum capital needed to accomplish other common investment and/or financial planning goals, such as a comfortable retirement and distribution of one's wealth to other family members at death.

Since this book addresses only those topics in CFP Board's 2004 Job Analysis Study relating to investments (specifically, topic numbers 34-43), it may not discuss some concepts historically considered in traditional college or university investment courses. In addition, the book covers numerous theoretical concepts (such as the underpinnings of modern portfolio theory or "MPT") that the investment practitioner may or may not use when constructing a portfolio for his or her client. Nevertheless, the subject matter covered throughout the course is both informative and useful to readers preparing to take and successfully complete the CFP® Certification Examination.

This book is designed to serve primarily as the textbook for the second or third course of a personal financial planning program registered with Certified Financial Planner Board of Standards Inc. (CFP Board) and satisfying the educational component of CFP Board's requirements for earning the CERTIFIED FINANCIAL PLANNER™ certification*. The book has been written at the upper undergraduate (junior and senior) levels and may also be successfully used in introductory investment courses at traditional colleges and universities. Each of the 18 chapters opens with an introduction of the chapter subject and a list of learning objectives. At the end of each chapter, there is a list of important concepts, questions for review, and suggested additional readings.

Finally, this book is also used as the sole textbook for Investment Planning, the third course in Kaplan University's Online Certificate in Financial Planning Education Program and in Kaplan University's accelerated classroom education program. In the online course, the book is supplemented by brief online readings, exercises, quizzes at the end of each of the 10 units, and a Final Examination consisting of 50 multiple choice questions similar to those appearing on CFP Board's Certification Examination. Students in Kaplan University's online financial planning education program also have the use of a message board where they can pose questions online to qualified practitioners/instructors.

---

*CFP®, CERTIFIED FINANCIAL PLANNER™ and CFP® are marks owned by Certified Financial Planner Board of Standards, Inc. These marks are awarded to individuals who successfully complete CFP Board's initial and ongoing certification requirements.

Kaplan University does not certify individuals to use the CFP®, CERTIFIED FINANCIAL PLANNER™ and CFP® marks. CFP certification is granted only by Certified Financial Planner Board of Standards to those persons who, in addition to completing an educational requirement such as this CFP Board-Registered Program, have met its ethics, experience and examination requirements.

ACKNOWLEDGMENTS

The authors are indebted to all the academicians and personal financial planning practitioners who have created the body of knowledge covered in this text. These individuals have not only taught or practiced investments in an exemplary manner, but have also participated in several CERTIFIED FINANCIAL PLANNER^{TM} job analysis studies conducted by CFP Board of Standards Inc. delineating the investment topics that are the basis of examination.

We particularly thank Jeffrey B. Mershon, MBA, CPA/PFS, CFP®, Kaplan's Chair for Financial Planning, who conducted a very thorough proofing of the manuscript for this second edition and who helped to identify items in the first edition needing improvement or correction in this second edition. His efforts have helped to create a substantially improved textbook.

In addition, we wish to thank Kaplan University's Kelly Landy and John Howard who endured several rounds of revisions and produced the final document in a highly professional manner.

Keith R. Fevurly
MBA, JD, L.L.M (Taxation), CFP®, RFC

Harold F. Lenhart
MBA, MS, CFA

ABOUT THE AUTHORS

Keith R. Fevurly, MBA, JD, L.L.M. (Taxation), CFP®, RFC is currently the online instructor for the Estate Planning course of Kaplan University's Certificate in Financial Planning education program. The Certificate in Financial Planning education program is part of Kaplan Continuing Education (KCE) at Kaplan University, a subsidiary of Kaplan Higher Education Corporation, which in turn is wholly-owned by Kaplan, Inc. Kaplan, Inc. is a wholly-owned subsidiary of The Washington Post Company. Mr. Fevurly was co-developer and formerly Assistant Dean of Kaplan's online Certificate in Financial Planning education program. Prior to this position, Mr. Fevurly served as Chief Operating Officer for a private business as well as holding the Academic Director and Vice President of Education positions at the College for Financial Planning, Denver, Colorado. He has also served on CFP Board of Standards' Board of Examiners (1994-1996). He has been involved in traditional and distance education for over 25 years.

Mr. Fevurly holds graduate degrees in law, business, and taxation as well as the CFP® financial planning certification. He has written numerous articles and books in the field of financial and estate planning as well as presenting seminars and keynote presentations before many financial services firms. He is the author of *Estate Planning*, used in the last course of Kaplan University's Certificate in Financial Planning online and accelerated program, and is the co-author of *Individual Income Tax Planning* (2nd edition), used in Kaplan University's Income Tax Planning course. He also currently serves on the Board of Editors for the *Journal of Financial Planning*, the major professional journal for practicing financial planners. He is recognized in both *Who's Who in American Law* and *Who's Who in American Education*.

Mr. Fevurly lives in Centennial, Colorado with his wife, Peggy, and two children, Rebecca Dawn and Grant.

Harold F. Lenhart, MBA, MS, CFA is currently the online instructor for the Investment Planning course of Kaplan University's Certificate in Financial Planning education program. Mr. Lenhart is a lecturer in finance and investments at Regis University and the University of Colorado at Denver. Mr. Lenhart also develops courses (online and classroom) for accredited graduate degree programs in the areas of corporate finance, quantitative analysis, debt and equity analysis, derivative securities/risk management, and portfolio management. Mr. Lenhart holds the Chartered Financial Analyst (CFA®) designation and is an active member in the CFA Institute. Mr. Lenhart has authored numerous technical papers on the term structure of interest rates, technical analysis, derivative securities, and attribution analysis.

Mr. Lenhart lives in Lakewood, Colorado with his wife and daughter.

SAMPLE INVESTMENT FORMULAS

CERTIFIED FINANCIAL PLANNER
BOARD OF STANDARDS, INC.

Provided Formulas

These formulas are provided with the exam booklets when taking the CFP® Certification Examination:

$$V = \frac{D_1}{r-g}$$

$$r_i = r_f + (r_m - r_f)\beta_i$$

$$r = \frac{D_1}{P} + g$$

$$r_p = r_f + \sigma_p\left(\frac{r_m - r_f}{\sigma_m}\right)$$

$$COV_{ij} = \rho_{ij}\sigma_i\sigma_j$$

$$S_p = \frac{\overline{r}_p - \overline{r}_f}{\sigma_p}$$

$$\sigma_p = \sqrt{W_i^2\sigma_i^2 + W_j^2\sigma_j^2 + 2W_iW_j COV_{ij}}$$

$$\alpha_p = \overline{r}_p - \left[\overline{r}_f + \left(\overline{r}_m - \overline{r}_f\right)\beta_p\right]$$

$$\beta_i = \frac{COV_{im}}{\sigma_m^2} = \frac{\rho_{im}\sigma_i}{\sigma_m}$$

$$T_p = \frac{\overline{r}_p - \overline{r}_f}{\beta_p}$$

$$\sigma_r = \sqrt{\frac{\sum\limits_{t=1}^{n}(r_t - \overline{r})^2}{n}}$$

$$D = \frac{\sum\limits_{t=1}^{n}\frac{c_t(t)}{(1+i)^t}}{\sum\limits_{t=1}^{n}\frac{c_t}{(1+i)^t}}$$

$$S_r = \sqrt{\frac{\sum\limits_{t=1}^{n}(r_t - \overline{r})^2}{n-1}}$$

$$D = \frac{1+y}{y} - \frac{(1+y)+t(c-y)}{c\left[(1+y)^t - 1\right]+y}$$

$$CV = \frac{Par}{CP} \times P_s$$

$$\frac{\Delta P}{P} = -D\left[\frac{\Delta y}{1+y}\right]$$

$$IR = \frac{R_P - R_B}{\sigma_A}$$

SAMPLE INVESTMENT FORMULAS

(Note: These formulas will be provided to all candidates taking the CFP® Certification Examination, although *without titles* (as on page xii) specifying the meaning and use of each formula.)

Constant Growth Dividend Discount Model

$$V = \frac{D_1}{r-g}$$

Expected Return Form of Dividend Discount Model

$$r = \frac{D_1}{P} + g$$

Covariance Between Two Sample Assets

$$COV_{ij} = \rho_{ij}\,\sigma_i\,\sigma_j$$

Standard Deviation of a Two Asset Portfolio

$$\sigma_p = \sqrt{W_i^2\sigma_i^2 + W_j^2\sigma_j^2 + 2W_iW_jCOV_{ij}}$$

Beta Coefficient of Sample Asset

$$\beta_i = \frac{COV_{im}}{\sigma_m^2} = \frac{\rho_{im}\sigma_i}{\sigma_m}$$

Population for Standard Deviation of a Single Asset

$$\sigma_r = \sqrt{\frac{\sum_{t=1}^{n}(r_t - \bar{r})^2}{n}}$$

Sample for Standard Deviation of a Single Asset

$$S_r = \sqrt{\frac{\sum_{t=1}^{n}(r_t - \bar{r})^2}{n-1}}$$

Conversion Value of a Convertible Bond

$$CV = \frac{Par}{CP} \times P_s$$

Capital Asset Pricing Model

$$r_i = r_f + \left(r_m - r_f\right)B_i$$

Capital Market Line

$$r_p = r_f + \sigma_p\left[\frac{r_m - r_f}{\sigma_m}\right]$$

Sharpe Index of Portfolio Performance

$$S_p = \frac{\bar{r}_p - \bar{r}_f}{\sigma_p}$$

Jensen Index of Portfolio Performance

$$\alpha_p = \bar{r}_p - \left[\bar{r}_f + \left(\bar{r}_m - \bar{r}_f\right)\beta_p\right]$$

Treynor Index of Portfolio Performance

$$T_p = \frac{\bar{r}_p - \bar{r}_f}{\beta_p}$$

Macauley Duration/Duration

$$D = \frac{\sum_{t=1}^{n}\frac{c_t(t)}{(1+i)^t}}{\sum_{t=1}^{n}\frac{c_t}{(1+i)^t}}$$

Macauley Duration/Duration

$$D = \frac{1+y}{y} - \frac{(1+y)+t(c-y)}{c\left[(1+y)^t - 1\right]+y}$$

Estimate Change in Price of a Bond

$$\frac{\Delta P}{P} = -D\left[\frac{\Delta y}{1+y}\right]$$

Information Ratio

$$IR = \frac{R_P - R_B}{\sigma_A}$$

Meaning of Symbols used by CFP Board in Sample Formulas Sheet:

V = Intrinsic Value of Stock as used in Constant Growth Dividend Discount Model

D_1 = Next Year's Dividend payable by Stock in Constant Growth Dividend Discount Model

r = Required Rate of Return in Constant Growth Dividend Discount Model; also used to mean Expected Rate of Return in Expected Return Form of Dividend Discount Model

g= Growth Rate of Dividends in Constant Growth Dividend Discount Model

P= Purchase Price of Targeted Stock using Expected Return Form of Dividend Discount Model

COV_{ij} or COV_{im} = Covariance between Two Sample Assets ($_{ij}$) or Covariance between One Sample Asset and Market or Market Index ($_{im}$)

p_{ij} or p_{im} = Correlation Coefficient between Two Sample Assets ($_{ij}$) or Correlation Coefficient between One Sample Index and Market or Market Index ($_{im}$)

σ_i = Standard Deviation of First Sample Asset (i)

σ_j = Standard Deviation of Second Sample Asset (j)

σ_p = Standard Deviation of a Portfolio

W_i = Weighting Percentage of First Sample Asset in Standard Deviation of a Portfolio Formula

W_j = Weighting Percentage of Second Sample Asset in Standard Deviation of a Portfolio Formula

2 = Number in Standard Deviation of a Portfolio Formula to Represent Correlation Paired Sequences of (a,b) and (b,a)

β_i = Beta Coefficient of Sample Asset

σ_m = Standard Deviation of Market or Market Index

σ_r = Population Standard Deviation for Single Asset

$\sum$ = Greek Sigma meaning summation number (n) of actual returns

$\bar{X}$ = Average, Mean, or Expected return among a multiple number of actual or possible returns.

s_r = Sample for Standard Deviation for Single Asset

CV = Conversion Value of a Convertible Bond and also Coefficient of Variation in relative risk measurement.

Par= Par Value of Bond (normally $1,000)

CP= Conversion Price of a Convertible Bond

P_s = Current Market Price of Underlying Stock used in Conversion Value of a Convertible Bond Formula

r_i = Required Rate of Return in Capital Asset Pricing Model

r_f = Risk Free Rate of Return in Capital Asset Pricing Model, Capital Market Line Theory, Sharpe, Jensen, and Treynor index measures of portfolio performance

r_m = Market Rate of Return in Capital Asset Pricing Model

β_i = Beta Coefficient of Sample Stock or Asset in Capital Asset Pricing Model or Slope of the Security Market Line (SML)

r_p = Portfolio Rate of Return in Capital Market Line Theory, Sharpe, Jensen, and Treynor index measures of portfolio performance

S_p = Sharpe index measure of portfolio performance

a_p = Jensen index measure of portfolio performance; also known as "alpha"

β_p = Beta Coefficient of Sample Portfolio in Jensen and Treynor index measures

T_p = Treynor index measure of portfolio performance

D = Macauley Duration of a Bond

D_{Mod} = Modified Duration of a Bond

D_{Eff} = Effective Duration of a Bond

ΔP = Change in Bond Price given a respective change in market interest rates (Δy)

r_B = The realized rate of return of the benchmark.

σ_A = The difference between the standard deviation of the portfolio and the standard deviation of the benchmark.

σ_B = The standard deviation of the benchmark.

CHAPTER ONE

Cash and Cash Equivalents

• • •

This is the first of seven chapters describing the characteristics of various investment vehicles or assets. This chapter considers the most fundamental of these vehicles, cash, although it also addresses those assets that may easily be converted into cash without any significant loss of the amount invested (also known as the investor's "principal").

Upon completing this chapter, you should be able to:

- Describe the use of cash and cash equivalents in the financial planning process
- Explain investment assets primarily offered by banks, such as certificates of deposit (CDs), money market deposit accounts, and passbook savings accounts
- Explain cash equivalents offered by the U.S. Treasury, including Treasury bills and U.S. "savings bonds"
- Describe the use of corporate commercial paper and bankers' acceptances
- Define *Eurodollars*
- Explain the features and use of the investment policy statement in the financial planning process

CASH AND CASH EQUIVALENTS IN THE FINANCIAL PLANNING PROCESS

Most individuals believe that they have a clear understanding of what is meant by the term *cash*. In financial planning, cash has a very specific meaning. It refers to cash equivalents and bank instruments of deposit that have a high level of *liquidity*.

By definition, an investment is *marketable* if it can be sold relatively quickly. In contrast, an investment is *liquid* if can be sold or redeemed quickly, at or near its market price. Marketability and liquidity are not the same. Assets may be marketable but finding a ready buyer or seller may be difficult, therefore decreasing its liquidity. Houses are marketable but depending on the market, they may not be very liquid. Conversely, while a savings account is very liquid, since it may be converted to cash without loss of principal, it is *not* marketable. In fact, a savings account is *redeemable*, meaning it must be converted to cash only by the issuer of the investment, in this case, the bank. There really is no market for savings accounts.

All cash and cash equivalent investments share the same characteristic of liquidity. Accordingly, since little, if any, risk (via loss of principal) is assumed, the return on these investments is relatively small. Since their ultimate return of principal is ensured, cash and cash equivalents are most suited to the satisfaction of short-term investment and emergency needs. Indeed, when establishing an *emergency fund* for a client, you should advise him or her that only cash and cash equivalents should be used for this purpose. The cash investments that clients most often use to constitute such a fund are checking accounts (preferably interest-bearing), passbook savings accounts, money market deposit accounts, money market mutual funds, and certificates of deposit (CDs) with a maturity of one year or less. Regardless, all of these investments are also part of what is known in the investment marketplace as the "cash" or "money market" (as contrasted to the "investment" or "capital market") since the maturity date, if any, is *one year or less*.

All individuals need some amount of liquid assets, if for no other reason than to pay current expenses and for aforementioned emergency funds. However, some individuals, by virtue of an extreme risk-averse temperament, may tend to overemphasize them. If you have such a person as a client, it is important to acknowledge their concern over losing a portion of their principal, but it is imperative to educate them concerning the investment risk inherent in holding a great amount of cash and cash equivalents in an inflationary economy. One of the most damaging financial mistakes that senior citizens make is to put too much of their investment portfolio in cash and cash equivalents only to find, not so many years later, that their capacity to buy necessities of living (purchasing power) is eroding. This is what financial planners refer to as *purchasing power* or *inflation risk*.

If inflation is 4 percent per year and savings account interest is 2 percent per year, one dollar one year from now is worth 98 cents $\left(\frac{1.02}{1.04} \times \$1.00 = \$0.98\right)$. After five years the dollar is worth only $0.91 $\left[\left(\frac{1.02}{1.04}\right)^5 \times \$1.00 = \$0.91\right]$ in purchasing power and, after 10 years, it is only worth $0.82 $\left[\left(\frac{1.02}{1.04}\right)^{10} \times \$1.00 = \$0.82\right]$.

HB 10Bii calculator keystrokes: First, make sure the calculator default setting is one period per year. To do so, hit [Orange][C ALL]. If the display reads 12 P/Yr, you need to change the default. Hit [1][Orange][P/YR]. Check by repeating [Orange][C ALL]. The display should now read 1 P_Yr. Also, set the display to four places. This is done by hitting [Orange][DISP][4].

    1.02[÷]1.04[=] Display: 0.9808 or $0.98

    1.02[÷]1.04[=][Orange][y^x]5[=] Display: 0.9075 or $0.91

    1.02[÷]1.04[=][Orange][y^x]10[=] Display: 0.8235 or $0.82

It should be recognized in the above example that the senior citizen's financial situation may be made even more dire when the effect of income taxes is taken into account. Nonetheless, the overall point is clear: *All investors*, with the possible exception of those that are terminally ill or those that have more monthly income than they could possibly spend, *need a growth component in their portfolio.*

PASSBOOK SAVINGS ACCOUNT

A passbook savings account is established with a commercial bank or savings and loan (S&L) and is a *redeemable* investment. The account usually has no minimum balance and features a penalty-free withdrawal of funds at any time. The account generally does not include (or has only very limited) check-writing privileges and returns a relatively low rate of interest.

CERTIFICATES OF DEPOSIT (CDs)

Certificates of deposit or CDs (also sometimes known as *time deposits*) are deposits made with a bank or S&L for a specified period of time, usually a minimum of three to six months. The financial institution generally pays a fixed rate of interest for the term of the certificate, with rates increasing the longer the term. Usually, an investor who wants to redeem (liquidate) a CD prior to its stated expiration date must pay a substantial penalty in the form of either a one-time fee or a lower overall interest rate. The practical effect of this penalty for early withdrawal is somewhat mitigated by the availability of an *above-the-line* income tax deduction (a deduction from an individual's *gross income* to reach his or her *adjusted gross income*), but it still lowers one's investment return.

It is usually recommended that investors with a relatively large amount of money to invest in CDs purchase *multiple* certificates rather than investing in only *one* certificate. This makes it possible to redeem part of the investment without accessing the other certificates or paying the penalty for early withdrawal on the total amount. In addition, a viable investment strategy is to *ladder* the maturity dates of the multiple certificates in order to more effectively manage interest-rate risk. For example, if interest rates increase, dividing an investment in CDs into 6-month, 12-month, 18-month, and 24-month maturities will yield a higher overall interest rate than investing all of the individual's money in the 6-month maturity CD. Then, as each CD matures every six months, it may be reinvested at the then-higher interest rate and, if so desired, extended further by another 6 months, beyond the 24-month original ending date maturity of the total investment.

Finally, not all CDs are insured by the federal government (specifically, the Federal Deposit Insurance Corporation or FDIC) and, even if they are insured, amounts in excess of the insured limit per account are *not* covered. FDIC coverage was increased from $100,000 to $250,000 only through December 31, 2009 by the Emergency Economic Stabilization Act of 2008. Accordingly, if the investor wishes to ensure that a large investment is covered, he or she should invest in CDs offered by different financial institutions, and in no more than the amount of the insured limit in any one institution. An alternative strategy is for the investor to purchase certificates in the names of a spouse or children so that no one certificate exceeds the insured limit. Fortunately, these investments may also be made jointly with others or using the other investor's name.

Negotiable CDs

Issued in exchange for a deposit of funds by most American banks, the *negotiable CD* is a marketable deposit of the issuer, who also stands ready to sell new CDs on demand. The deposit is maintained in the bank until maturity, at which time the investor receives his or her deposit back plus interest. However, these CDs are *negotiable* since they may be sold in the secondary market before maturity. Broker/dealers in securities make a market in negotiable CDs.

MONEY MARKET FUNDS AND DEPOSIT ACCOUNTS

A money market mutual fund is a fund offered by an open-end investment company (mutual fund) that invests in high quality, short-term investments, such as Treasury Bills, commercial paper from various corporations, and large or *jumbo CDs* from large commercial banks. All of these investments will mature within one year and generally have an average maturity of 30 to 90 days. The typical minimum investment is $1,000 and funds may be withdrawn from the account at any time without penalty by writing a check on the account. Most funds also offer shareholders the ability to wire transfer money from the fund to the investor's bank account. The rate of return paid by the fund is highly sensitive to changes in short-term rates due to the short maturity of the investments within the fund.

There are also money market funds that specialize in short-term, *tax-exempt* investments. The payments received by investors from these funds retain their federal income-tax-free status, although the payments may be taxable for alternative minimum tax purposes. National tax-exempt funds are diversified across many state obligations and are exempt from federal tax, but subject to state tax. Other funds that are invested in a single state's obligations are exempt from federal and state tax for investors who reside in the state that issued the security.

Many commercial banks and S&Ls offer *money market deposit accounts (MMDAs)*. The interest paid on these accounts is normally *less* than that paid by money market mutual funds for the simple reason that the MMDA is federally insured subject to the per account insured limit (accordingly, the investor assumes less risk). MMDAs are essentially a variation of the passbook savings account offered by banks, with the investor paying a service fee if his or her balance falls below a minimum amount. Still, MMDAs are a popular cash-equivalent alternative since they are convenient and the balance may be obtained at the same location where the investor banks. Typically, six pre-authorized transfers are permitted from the account each month, up to three of which may be by personal check.

TREASURY BILLS

A Treasury bill (T-Bill) is a short-term debt security offered by the federal government with a maturity of either 4, 13, 26, or 52 weeks. The Treasury Department discontinued the 52-week T-Bill in July, 2001. However, beginning in June 2008, the Treasury started issuing 52-week T-bills again. T-Bills are purchased in a minimum amount of $100 (reduced from $1,000 in June 2008) and are issued "at a full discount," meaning that they are sold at *less* than their par or face value. At the time of maturity, the investor collects the face value and reports the difference between the discounted purchase price and the value of the T-Bill at maturity as accrued interest (ordinary income). The interest earned, however, is income-tax free at the state and local level under the *doctrine of reciprocity* of federal tax law.

Because of their lack of default risk, high degree of marketability, and low exposure to interest rate risk, T-Bills are often used as the proxy for a risk-free investment in modern portfolio theory (see chapter 10). Specifically, the 13-week (90-day) T-Bill is frequently cited as the risk-free rate. T-Bills are offered by the Treasury Department according to a regular schedule, with 13- and 26-week bills offered every week. Every Thursday the offering is announced publicly in *The Wall Street Journal* and any investor who wants to purchase a new-issue T-Bill directly from the U.S. Treasury submits a standardized form known as a "tender", either by mail or in person, at the appropriate Federal Reserve Bank. The bills are auctioned on the following Monday. In addition, individual investors may purchase a T-Bill from their local bank or brokerage firm, although a commission will be charged as well as a premium on purchases under $100,000.

(Note that the other predominant forms of Treasury Department securities, the Treasury note and Treasury bond, will be discussed in chapter 2 of this textbook.)

SERIES EE AND SERIES HH SAVINGS BONDS

Also known as *savings bonds*, Series EE bonds are cash investments that, with recent changes, may provide a relatively high interest rate and, sometimes, a tax advantage. EE paper bonds are purchased at 50% of their face amount and range in face value from $50 to $10,000 (therefore, they may be purchased for as little as $25). Savings bonds continue to accrue interest after the stated maturity date until the Treasury announces discontinuance of payments, generally after 30 years. The investor may defer payment of any federal income tax until he or she redeems the EE bond or may choose to accrue and pay this interest annually on his or her IRS Form 1040 (or similar form). The interest earned on the bond is exempt from state and local income tax and there are special tax benefits available for bonds used in payment of higher education expenses for the taxpayer, his or her spouse, or any dependent of the taxpayer (below specified adjusted gross income limits at the time of redemption) for whom the taxpayer is allowed a dependency exemption.

EE bonds that are issued from May 1, 1997 through April 30, 2005 pay interest based on a *floating rate* equal to 90% of the average return on the five year Treasury note. They increase in value every month, instead of every six months, and interest is compounded semi-annually. Series EE savings bonds bearing issue dates prior to February 1, 2003 cannot be redeemed within the first six months from date of purchase and a three month interest penalty applies to any bond that is cashed in prior to five years from the purchase date. This rewards longer term bond holders who then benefit from the higher 5-year interest rates over the remaining term of the bond. Issues dated on or after February 1, 2003 bear a minimum holding period of 12 months.

EE bonds that are issued on or after May 1, 2005 earn a *fixed rate* of interest, with this fixed rate applying for the life of the bond, including an extended maturity period. Interest accrues monthly and is compounded semi-annually. The EE bond must be held a minimum of one year from date of purchase and a three-month interest penalty applies to bonds that are held less than five years from the issue date. The Treasury Department also guarantees that the bond's value will double after 20 years.

Series HH bonds, which are no longer offered but may be otherwise encountered in a financial planning practice, pay interest every six months at a fixed rate established when the investor purchased the bonds. (Note that HH bonds issued from January, 1980 through August 31, 2004 [when they ceased being offered to the public] have a 20 year maturity date.) Unlike EE bonds, the investor who purchases HH bonds has *no* tax deferral election and must report the interest annually on his or her income tax return. However, prior to September 1, 2004, upon redemption, the investor in EE bonds could exchange at least $500 of the bonds for Series HH bonds and continue the tax deferral on the EE bond interest until the year in which the HH bond reached final maturity or was redeemed. Beginning September 1, 2004, this option is no longer available (that is, the investor must separately redeem his or her EE bonds and pay the income tax due on the accrued interest at that time).

COMMERCIAL PAPER

Commercial paper is a negotiable, short-term, unsecured promissory note issued by large, well-known, and financially strong companies to finance their short term operating needs. The name refers to the actual piece of paper on which the borrower's (the corporation's) obligation of repayment is printed. Denominations start at $100,000, with a maturity date of 270 days or less. Such paper is normally sold at a discount and is rated by a rating service (such as Standard & Poor's) with respect to the paper's quality. Because it has a somewhat greater risk than Treasury bills and other government securities, commercial paper normally offers higher interest rates.

BANKER'S ACCEPTANCES

Banker's acceptances are short-term (30- to 360-day maturities) drafts that are drawn by a non-financial firm on a major bank used to finance imports and exports. Before a foreign exporter will ship goods to the United States, it normally wants assurances that the funds are ready for payment when the goods arrive. Accordingly, the exporter often requests that a banker's acceptance be drawn on its behalf in the currency of choice.

> **Example 1-1:** XYZ Foreign Cars is purchasing three German automobiles for sale in its showroom. Since it cannot pay for the automobiles in advance, XYZ goes to its bank and arranges for a draft made payable to the German manufacturer one week from receipt of the autos (thereby providing for sufficient time to inspect the quality of the delivery). XYZ's bank knows from past experience (or from XYZ's account on file at the bank) that it is "good for the money" so therefore it honors the draft (in the form of a banker's acceptance) and sends it on to the German manufacturer. The exporter/manufacturer now knows that it will be paid for the automobiles.

Banker's acceptances are typically traded at a discount from their face value on the secondary market. The trading values of such financial instruments may easily be tracked by referring to the *Wall Street Journal* or other financial newspapers or periodicals.

REPURCHASE AGREEMENTS (REPOs)

Dealers in government securities use repurchase agreements (also known as *repos*). In order to improve liquidity (get cash), such a dealer will *sell* some of those securities to another dealer with an agreement to buy them back at a later date at an agreed-upon price. The buyer of the repurchase agreement then receives the equivalent of a fixed yield or return on its investment. Such repurchase agreements are included in the context of money market securities since the term of the agreement is typically less than one year. Indeed, the standard repo may only have an *overnight* maturity. The short-term maturity and government backing means that repos provide lenders with extremely low risk.

The opposite of the repo is the *reverse repurchase agreement (or reverse repo)*. In a reverse repo, the dealer *buys* government securities from an investor and then sells them back at a later date at a higher price.

Repos and reverse repos also have importance in open market operations conducted by the Federal Reserve Bank *(the Fed)*. The Fed manages interest rates (federal funds rate) through open market operations, selling securities to increase interest rates and buying securities to lower interest rates.

EURODOLLARS

Contrary to its name, Eurodollars are not dollar-denominated deposits in European countries. Rather, Eurodollars are simply U.S. dollar-denominated deposits at banks *outside* of the United States. The average Eurodollar deposit is very large (in the millions) and has a maturity of less than six months. Therefore, the market is obviously way out of reach for all but the largest financial institutions and the only way for individuals to invest is indirectly through a money market mutual fund.

A variation on the Eurodollar time deposit is the Eurodollar certificate of deposit (Euro CD). A Eurodollar CD shares the same characteristics with its U.S. counterpart, except that the Eurodollar obligation is a liability of a *non-U.S. bank*. Accordingly, it is less liquid (due to the exchange-rate risk assumed by the investor) and, thus, offers a slightly higher yield than that of the obligation of the domestic bank. In addition, the Eurodollar market is relatively free of government regulation, thereby potentially lessening the safety of the obligation.

AUCTION-RATE PREFERRED STOCK

Auction-rate preferred stock is a money market instrument in which the dividend is reset every seven weeks through a Dutch auction process. In a Dutch auction, the bid price is gradually lowered until a ready buyer emerges. Treasury bills are sold through Dutch auction. A Dutch auction is a one-sided trading system as opposed to a double auction or two-sided trading system (bid – ask) reflected in major stock and commodity exchanges.

Auction-rate preferred stock is also known as money market preferred stock and under such proprietary acronyms as DARTS. Auction-rate preferred stock gained notoriety in 2008 when investors were sold the securities on the basis of cash management/money market liquidity, yet the accounts were frozen as no bidders emerged. The Federal Reserve stepped in as buyer of last resort.

THE INVESTMENT POLICY STATEMENT IN THE FINANCIAL PLANNING PROCESS

The *investment policy statement* has three purposes in the financial and investment planning process:
1) To articulate and confirm the investor's policy objectives and tolerance for risk
2) To define how the portfolio will be monitored and how progress toward the stated investment objectives will be measured
3) To define the investor's target asset allocation, which studies have confirmed to be the single most important component in whether the client actually meets his or her investment planning goals

An investment policy statement will normally include the facts of the client's financial situation. It will also include information not unlike the following:

- The client's investment objectives, in order of priority
- The client's time horizons for meeting these objectives
- The client's risk tolerance level
- A preferable *expected* rate of return on any investments that are made
- The client's projected cash flow needs (or surplus)
- An investment strategy or asset allocation guidelines reflective of the investor's life cycle
- Standards or *benchmarks* for the performance measurement of the portfolio

The statement will eventually arrive at a suggested or recommended portfolio of investment assets, of which cash and cash equivalents may be a part. However, cash equivalents (most notably, money market mutual funds) are typically used only as a *sweep account* to deposit monies until a more productive use (namely, a higher yielding investment) for them may be found. While an investment policy statement is *not* a required element in sound investment planning, most investment advisors do prepare such a statement and refer to it often as the guideline for managing the portfolio of an investor. (Alternatively, you should note that the preparation of an investment policy statement is a legal prerequisite for trustees investing qualified retirement plan monies.)

IMPORTANT CONCEPTS

Cash equivalent	Series HH bond
Passbook savings account	Commercial paper
Certificate of deposit (CD)	Banker's acceptance
Negotiable certificate of deposit	Repurchase agreement (repo)
Money market mutual fund	Reverse repurchase agreement (reverse repo)
Money market deposit account (MMDA)	Eurodollar
Treasury bill	Auction-rate preferred stock
Series EE savings bond	Investment policy statement

QUESTIONS FOR REVIEW

1. What is the importance of cash and cash equivalents in the financial planning process?

2. Define the following three terms:
    - Liquidity
    - Marketability
    - Redeemable

3. Explain the *laddered* CD investment strategy.

4. What is a negotiable certificate of deposit (CD) and what attribute does it possess that is not present with a CD issued by a bank or savings and loan (S&L)?

5. What is the primary purpose of the money market mutual fund in the investment planning process?

6. What is meant by the term *money market* in finance and investments?

7. Contrast a money market mutual fund to a money market deposit account (MMDA). Which one is insured by the FDIC and up to what amount?

8. How is interest paid on a U.S. Treasury bill?

9. What are the maturities of a U.S Treasury bill? Which maturity date is typically used as the proxy for the risk-free rate of return in modern portfolio theory?

10. How is the interest rate computed on Series EE savings bonds for those issued prior to May 1, 2005? How is this rate computed on such bonds issued on or after May 1, 2005?

11. Who issues commercial paper and what is its maturity date?

12. What is the primary use of a banker's acceptance?

13. Contrast a repurchase agreement (repo) to that of a reverse repurchase agreement (reverse repo). In what context are both of these obligations used by the Federal Reserve Bank (the Fed)?

14. What is a Eurodollar and how does an individual investor purchase this obligation?

15. Describe a Dutch auction. How is it different from a double auction? Where are the two types of auctions found?

16. What are three purposes of the investment policy statement in portfolio management? How are cash equivalents reported on this statement and how do most financial planners and/or money managers use them?

SUGGESTIONS FOR ADDITIONAL READING

Tools and Techniques of Investment Planning, 2nd edition, Stephen R. Leimberg, Robert T. LeClair, Robert J. Doyle, Jr., and Thomas R. Robinson, The National Underwriter Company, 2006.

Investments: An Introduction, 9th edition, Herbert B. Mayo, Thomson/ South-Western, 2008.

Investment Analysis and Portfolio Management, 9th edition, Frank K. Reilly, and Keith C. Brown, Thomson/South-Western, 2009.

The Wall Street Journal Guide to Money and Investing, 3rd edition, Kenneth M. Morris, and Virginia B. Morris, Fireside Publishing, 2004.

Dictionary of Finance and Investment Terms, 6th edition, Barron's Financial Guides, 2003.

CHAPTER TWO

Bonds and Debt Securities

• • •

A bond is a loan that an investor makes to corporations or governments. The obligation pays interest over a fixed term (or *maturity*), at the end of which the *principal* of the bond, or original investment amount, is also repaid to the lender or bond holder.

Typically, the rate at which interest is paid and the amount of each payment is *fixed* at the time the bond is offered for sale. The percentage rate specifying this amount of interest (as computed on the original issue or *par value* of the bond) is known as its *coupon rate*. Since the amount of each payment and percentage rate of interest is fixed, bonds are sometimes referred to as *fixed income securities*. A bond's interest rate must be competitive when issued, which means that the rate it pays must be comparable to what other bonds being issued of similar quality and maturity are paying.

Bond prices move inversely to interest rates. This is because the coupon interest is generally fixed and changes in market interest rates must be reflected in the price of the bond. When market interest rates increase, the price of a bond decreases and vice versa. Therefore, if the investor sells the bond in the secondary market prior to the bond's maturity, he or she will realize a capital gain or loss on the bond if the prevailing interest rate at the time of the sale differs from the bond's coupon rate.

Upon completing this chapter, you should be able to:
- Explain the characteristics and uses of U.S. Treasury notes and bonds in investment planning
- Identify the types of bonds issued by state and local governments (also known as *municipalities*)
- Describe each of the various forms of corporate bonds, including convertible and callable issues
- Describe the suitability of foreign bonds as a possible investment
- Explain the features of zero coupon bonds

There are essentially three types of bonds or *debt securities*. There are securities offered by the U.S. government through the Treasury Department (known as *Treasury bills, notes or bonds*), those issued by municipalities (known as *municipal bonds, munis, or tax-exempt bonds*), and those issued by private corporations or businesses (*corporate bonds*).

U.S. GOVERNMENT SECURITIES

The U.S. government issues five major types of securities, one of which, the *Treasury bill* (T-Bill) is discussed in chapter 1. The other major types of securities are:

1) The Treasury bill
2) The Treasury note/bond
3) The Treasury STRIP
4) Treasury Inflation Protection Securities (*TIPS*)

They differ from each other in their maturities, in the interest they pay, and in the manner in which this interest is paid. However, unlike (for example) corporate debt securities, government securities all share the characteristic of safety. That is, as is often said, only the government may "print more money," meaning that it can always reimburse the investor for any debt obligation incurred. Accordingly, since the investor here assumes comparatively less risk, U.S. government securities also offer less return than comparable debt securities issued by a private corporation.

Treasury Bills

Treasury bills (T-bills) are short-term (one year or less), full-discount securities sold through competitive bidding on a weekly and monthly basis in a minimum denomination of $100. T-bills are the most widely used of all government securities and are the primary instrument in setting Federal Reserve fiscal policy.

T-bills are openly traded in the secondary market on a bank discount yield basis of 360 days. For example, a dealer may quote a bid/ask price of 3.03 – 01. The bid price (dealer's buy price) is a discount of 3.03 percent and the ask price (dealer's sell price) is a discount of 3.01 percent. On a $100,000 dollar trade for a six-month T-bill (181 days to maturity), the dealer would buy at a price of $98,476.58:

$$\text{Discount} = \$100,000 \times 0.0303 \times \frac{181}{360} = \$1,523.42$$

$$\text{Price} = \$100,000 - \$1,523.42 = \$98,476.58$$

The dealer would sell at a price of $98,486.64:

$$\text{Discount} = \$100,000 \times 0.0301 \times \frac{181}{360} = \$1,513.36$$

$$\text{Price} = \$100,000 - \$1,513.36 = \$98,486.64$$

The discount yield understates the effective yield. The asking yield of 3.01 percent actually has a bond equivalent yield (BEY) of

$$BEY = \frac{365(dy)}{360 - (t_{sm})(dy)} = \frac{365(0.0301)}{360 - 181(0.0301)} = 0.0310 = 3.10\%$$

dy = discount yield
t_{sm} = time from settlement to maturity, in this example 181 days

Treasury Notes and Bonds

Treasury notes and bonds are similar in all aspects except maturity. The "long bond" is the Treasury 30-year bond and the "benchmark security" (used as a reference point in reflecting long term interest rates) is the Treasury 10-year note. Notes are also sold with two-year and five-year maturities.

Notes and bonds are coupon-bearing securities with a minimum face or par value of $100. Coupons are paid semiannually. They are quoted on a market basis of 365 days. Unlike T-bills, notes and bonds are quoted as a percent of par in 32nds.

For example, a dealer states a bid quote of 103-12 and an ask quote of 103-14. These quotes are 103 and 12/32 percent of par (103.375) and 103 and 14/32 percent of par (103.4375) respectively. On a $1,000 par bond, the dealer will buy at $1,033.75 ($1,000 x 1.03375) and will sell at $1,034.375 ($1,000 x 1.034375). You may see a quote such as 103-145. This is 103-14 positive tick. The positive tick is 1/64th. The quote is 103 and 14.5/32nds percent of par or 103.4531 ($1034.531).

Treasury STRIP

A Treasury STRIP (standing for *Separate Trading of Registered Interest and Principal of Securities*) is the U.S. Treasury form of a *zero coupon bond*. Stripped bonds are created when investment bankers buy large blocks of coupon-paying bonds (typically U.S. Treasury issues) and separate them into the coupon and principal portions. Each component is then sold separately, with the principal (or *stripped bond*) sold at an adequate-enough discount to provide a competitive market yield until the date of the bond's maturity. An investor who wants to eliminate any risk associated with the reinvestment of the coupon payments from a regular bond will be interested in a stripped bond since the reinvestment rate is guaranteed. (In other words, reinvestment rate risk is eliminated with the purchase of a Treasury STRIP or any other form of zero-coupon bond).

STRIP prices are always *less than par*, since they are issued at a deep discount. Those closest to maturity trade at higher prices since they can be redeemed at par value relatively soon (that is, at their date of maturity). However, prices of STRIPs (as with any zero coupon bond) are more sensitive to interest rate changes than prices of coupon-paying bonds of the same quality and maturity. This is because of a concept known as *bond duration* that we will discuss in chapter 13 of this text. Since the *duration* of a zero coupon bond (including a Treasury STRIP) is equal to its maturity, and interest rate sensitivity is measured by duration, the *greater* the maturity of the bond, the *greater* the price change of a zero coupon bond, given a corresponding change in market interest rates. (Note that we will discuss other forms of zero coupon bonds, specifically those issued by municipalities and corporations, later in this chapter).

How are STRIPS created? The Treasury does not issue zero-coupon notes and bonds (only T-bills) but does allow the owner, usually primary dealers in Treasury securities, to strip the coupon and re-package as a series of full discount instruments maturing every six months (corresponding to semiannual coupon payments). Suppose a dealer purchases a 10-year T-note and wishes to create a series of STRIPs. The dealer would create 20 coupon STRIPS (20 semiannual periods in 10 years) and one principal STRIP for a total of 21 STRIPS.

Finally, the income tax consequences of an investment in STRIPs (and zero coupon bonds generally) are very important. The discount on STRIPs is treated as taxable income and *earned annually*. This is the case even though the investor in a STRIP does *not* receive any cash interest at the same time. Therefore, a cash flow problem arises: specifically, the investor must pay taxes on interest for which he has not received any cash. This is known in the financial planning world as *phantom income* and leads to an important investment conclusion: Taxable STRIPs are very suitable investments to be placed in a retirement plan or any tax-deferred type of account, but, under most circumstances, they should *not* be part of a taxable portfolio. The exception to this rule is where a tax-exempt STRIP is purchased by the investor. Tax-exempt STRIPs are excellent vehicles for children under age 19 who are subject to their parent's tax rate on unearned income (that is, where the *kiddie tax* applies and the child pays only very little tax on the accrual of STRIP interest).

Treasury Inflation Protection Securities (TIPS)

A unique group of securities issued by the U.S. Treasury are Treasury Inflation Indexed or Protection Securities, often simply referred to as *TIPS*. These securities were first issued in early 1997 and are now auctioned by Treasury four times each year. As the name indicates, TIPS are designed to offer protection against the effects of inflation. They are marketable securities and are traded on the secondary market subsequent to issue. The face value of TIPS is adjusted semiannually to keep pace with inflation as measured by the Consumer Price Index (CPI) over the previous six-month period. Like other Treasury securities, TIPS pay a fixed rate of interest; however, this rate is not applied to the par value, but rather to the inflation-adjusted principal. Therefore, the higher the inflation rate, the higher the face value of the bond and the higher the semiannual interest payment.

> **Example 2-1:** John pays $1,000 for a TIPS security (10 year inflation-indexed note) that carries a 3% coupon (paid semiannually) on January 2, 200X. At mid year, the Consumer Price Index (CPI) measured an inflation increase of 1 percent during the first six months of the year and 1.5 percent increase during the last six months of the year. During the year, John receives two coupon payments of $15 each ($1,000 x 0.03/2). In addition, John's principal balance on the

bond is $1,010 ($1,000 × 0.01) after six months and $1,025.15 ($1,010 × 1.015) at the end of the year. John would report $30 of interest income and $25.15 of phantom income for a total of $55.15 on his tax return.

Of course, as may be anticipated, TIPS are very useful when an investor is particularly concerned with the effects of inflation (loss of purchasing power) on his initial investment.

The investor is taxed annually on the interest payment *plus* the appreciation in face value. However, only federal tax applies since TIPS, like other Treasury securities, are exempt from state and local taxes. In Example 2-1 above, the $30 in interest income (received in cash) plus the $25.15 increase in principal would each be taxed at the investor's ordinary income tax rate. Further, the $25.15 increase in face value constitutes *phantom income* (like the Treasury STRIP interest accrual) that is not collectible until the bond is sold or matures. Also, like the STRIP bond, this income is taxable in the year that it is *accrued* since the Internal Revenue Code makes *no* distinction between real and phantom income. Therefore, TIPS are also best positioned in a tax-deferred or tax-advantaged account.

I Bonds

Series I Bonds are a new type of inflation-indexed security issued by the U.S. Treasury for the individual investor who does not have a great deal of money to invest. They are essentially the TIPS equivalent of the Series EE savings bond (see chapter 1) and generally share the taxable consequences of TIPS. They are sold at face value, starting in denominations as low as $50, and earn interest for up to 30 years. An individual may buy up to $10,000 of I bonds in any one calendar year, with separate purchases of Series EE bonds unaffected. While Series EE bonds cannot be exchanged for Series I bonds, an investor may cash in (redeem) the EE bonds and use the proceeds to buy I bonds. The interest earned, however, on the EE bonds must be reported on the investor's federal income tax return for the year in which such bonds are redeemed.

The interest on a Series I bond is determined by two rates. One, set by the Treasury Department at time of issuance remains constant over the life of the bond. The second is a variable inflation rate announced each May and November based on corresponding CPI index changes.

Mortgage Backed Securities

The U.S. Treasury also directly guarantees or implicitly backs (indirectly guarantees) debt-type securities that are secured by a pool of mortgage obligations. In the financial world, these are sometimes collectively known as *asset-backed securities*, although the term "asset-backed" can also include securities that are secured by obligations other than home mortgages, such as credit card receipts, car loans, etc.

Three of the best known mortgage backed securities are obligations (*certificates*) issued by the Government National Mortgage Association (GNMA, Ginnie Mae), the Federal National Mortgage Association (FNMA, Fannie Mae), and the Federal Home Loan Mortgage Corporation (FHLMC, Freddie Mac). GNMA is a wholly-owned U.S. government corporation that buys Federal Housing

Administration (FHA) and Veterans Administration (VA) insured mortgages from banks and places them into mortgage pools and then issues pass-through certificates representing an individual interest in the pool. Each investor receives monthly interest and principal payments generated by the pool of underlying mortgages.

Ginnie Maes are a *direct guarantee* of the U.S. Treasury. The minimum size of an individual GNMA sold to an individual investor is $25,000. While there is no default risk (such issue is, after all, backed by the U.S. government), an investor does assume interest rate risk given that the obligation is a type of fixed income security. A GNMA certificate also carries reinvestment rate risk, since the investor has to assume a reduced certainty of monthly payments due to homeowners who have financed their purchases with FHA and VA mortgages repaying those loans early when market interest declines. Still, an investor who desires a relatively high rate of return with a commensurate high level of liquidity may strongly consider the purchase of a GNMA pass-through certificate either directly or by investing in mutual funds that specialize in such securities.

Fannie Mae and Freddie Mac were federal government-sponsored agencies but, due to the mortgage meltdown in 2008, the federal government fully nationalized both agencies due to their impending insolvency from "toxic assets" of mortgage pass-through derivatives known as collateralized debt obligations (CDOs).

CDO securities are derivatives, based on the underlying value of the mortgage pass-through securities, which in turn are based on the value of the underlying pool of mortgages. CDO securities come in a variety of "flavors" or what is referred to as "tranches" (*French for slice*). Some tranches are high quality, engineered to receive a stable cash flow (and lower risk). Lower tranches must assume the risk shed from these higher-quality tranches. This continues down to what we call the junk tranches with such names as inverse floaters (which caused the bankruptcy of Orange County, Calif.), IOs (interest only), and POs (principal only).

MUNICIPAL BONDS

A municipal bond, also known as a *muni bond*, is a debt instrument issued by a state, county (or parish), city, special districts, or other non-federal governmental agency. Generally, any municipal bond shares the characteristic of generating *tax-free income* to the investor for federal income tax purposes. Some municipal bonds are also insured by either the American Municipal Bond Assurance Corporation (AMBAC) or by the Municipal Bond Insurance Association Corporation (MBIA). The reason that an issuer would also incur the cost of insuring its bond is to achieve a higher quality rating by a rating agency (such as Standard & Poor's), thereby increasing the attractiveness of the issue in the open market. Of course, the insurers guarantee payment of the bond's interest and principal should the issuer let the bond default.

As noted above, the interest earned on a municipal bond is exempt from *federal* income tax. However, this interest is subject to state and local tax (unless the bond is purchased by a resident of the state that has also issued the bond-- also referred to as a *double barreled bond*). Capital gains (or losses) realized on the sale of a municipal bond are subject to normal capital gain (or loss) tax treatment. Special rules apply to municipal bonds issued at a discount and that are known as *original issue discount* (OID) bonds (see chapter 18 of this textbook). Compared to an alternative investment generating taxable income, municipal bonds should be compared on a tax equivalent yield basis (or taxable bonds on an after-tax yield basis).

$$\text{Tax Equivalent Yield (TEY)} = \frac{\text{Tax - exempt yield}}{1 \text{ - Tax rate}}$$

Or,

$$\text{After - Tax Yield} = \text{Taxable yield} \times (1 \text{ - Tax rate})$$

Example 2-2: Richard owns a municipal bond that features a tax-exempt yield of 5%. He is in the 35% federal marginal income tax bracket. Accordingly, the tax-equivalent yield (T.E.Y.) on a taxable investment is 7.69% [or .05 divided by (1-0.35)]. This means that Richard would need to purchase a taxable investment returning him at least 7.69% annually to exceed the equivalent 5% tax-free return generated by the municipal bond.

The *higher* an investor's marginal income tax bracket, the *greater* the advantage of investing in an asset that returns federally tax-exempt income. Conversely, if an investment already features tax-exempt income (such as a qualified retirement trust), a municipal bond investment providing an additional exemption is generally unwise since the investor will unnecessarily suffer a reduction of possible return.

There are three types of municipal bonds—*general obligation (G.O.) bonds*, *revenue bonds*, and *private purpose bonds*.

General Obligation (G.O.) Bonds

General obligation (G.O.) bonds are normally issued to finance the general operations, functions, and programs of the issuer (municipality).

A general obligation municipal bond is backed by the full faith, credit, and taxing power of the municipality. This means that the municipality promises to increase taxes on its citizenry without any limit if needed to pay off the bondholders. In the unlikely event of default, G.O. bondholders have the right to force a tax levy or legislative appropriation to make payment on the debt. Because of this, G.O. bonds are generally considered to be the *safest* type of municipal bond (and, accordingly, will reflect the *lowest* stated or nominal yield).

Revenue Bonds

Revenue bonds are normally issued to finance public capital projects (such as an airport, bridge, or toll road) or public services (such as a sewage treatment plant) where user fees or specific assessments are intended to repay the debt.

A revenue bond is one that is backed by a specific source of revenue to which the full faith, credit, and taxing authority of the municipality is *not* pledged. Therefore, bondholders must rely on the adequacy of the fees or tolls received by the municipality to pay interest on the bonds. Revenue bonds are usually junior to the municipality's general obligation bonds (meaning that they are paid only after the G.O. bonds are paid), so revenue bondholders assume a greater amount of credit risk. Revenue bonds generally have longer terms of maturity. Accordingly, they trade at higher yields than do general obligation bonds.

Private Purpose Bonds

Private purpose bonds are issued to finance certain activities that do *not* constitute the normal functions of a municipal government (such as the development of an industrial park). Typically, the bonds are used in the trade or business of individuals or entities other than the state or local government (municipality).

The important feature to note about a private purpose bond is that its interest is *not* tax-exempt for federal income tax purposes (although it may be from the issuing municipality's income tax). Such interest is also a *tax preference* item for alternative minimum tax purposes, meaning that it is added back in the computation of alternative minimum taxable income (AMTI) under that system of taxation. As a result, the yield quoted on the bond is higher still than either a general obligation or revenue bond, so as to take into account the generally disadvantageous tax consequences to the investor.

Finally, rather than purchasing all of these types of municipal bonds separately, some investors prefer the greater diversification available in a *municipal bond unit trust*. Such a trust is a fixed, unmanaged portfolio, meaning that there is no *active management* (trading) of the assets. A unit trust is also *self-liquidating*, which means that when its asset values drop below a certain point (normally 20% of the initial investment), the fund terminates and unit holders receive their proportionate share of the current value of the portfolio. Therefore, unit trusts are best for long-term bondholders who wish to receive a certain amount of *fixed* income. As the trust's holdings reach their maturity date, the bondholders are paid on a pro-rata basis.

CORPORATE BONDS

Corporate bonds are public offerings of debt by private companies. Coupons are paid semiannually (U.S. bonds) and the coupon interest paid to investors is taxable. Corporate bonds usually carry a face or par value of $1,000, have a term maturity (principal due all at once generally from a sinking fund), and are traded on major exchanges. Finally, corporate bonds may be "straight bonds" (option-free, the cash flow pattern is constant) or contain embedded options (the cash flow pattern may change if the embedded option is exercised).

Following are definitions of various types of corporate bonds:

Investment Grade Bond: A bond that is rated BBB or higher by the Standard and Poor's rating agency; generally, a high-quality bond with little risk of default by the issuer.

High Yield Bond: A bond that is rated BB or below by the Standard and Poor's rating agency; generally, of lower quality with a greater risk of default by the issuer than an investment grade bond; also known as a *speculative grade* or *junk bond.*

Mortgage Bond: A bond that pledges specific assets such as buildings or equipment; generally, a secured bond where the assets pledged are used to pay off the bondholders in the event of default.

Debenture: A bond that promises payments of interest and principal but pledges no specific assets; generally, an *unsecured bond.*

Discount Bond: A bond sells at a discount when its par value exceeds the bond's purchase price on the secondary market; also known as a *market discount bond*; contrast to an *original issue discount bond* (OID bond) where the bond is *issued* at a discount or reduction to its stated par value.

Premium Bond: A bond sells at a premium when the bond's market price exceeds the bond's par value.

Zero Coupon Bond: A bond that pays its par value at maturity but has *no* periodic interest payments (i.e. pays a 0% coupon rate); offered by both corporate and government issuers.

An investor purchasing zeros must generally include the accrued interest on the bond in his or her taxable income annually, even though no cash is received until the bond matures, is sold, or is called. This leads to the conclusion that taxable zeros are usually appropriate if positioned within a retirement plan or other tax-deferred account. Tax-exempt zeros are suitable investments for high-income-tax-bracket taxpayers who want to accumulate wealth, have little need of immediate cash, or are not concerned about reinvestment of cash flows. Although investors in a zero-coupon bond are guaranteed that they will receive a reinvestment rate equal to the bond's yield to maturity (assuming that they do not sell the bond or the bond is not called prior to that date), they achieve this advantage at the expense of sacrificing the opportunity to reinvest earlier cash flows if market interest rates increase during the term of the bond. Conversely, of course, the investor will be very pleased if he or she is locked into a high *implicit* rate of return during a time of declining interest rates.

Bond issuers like zeros because they have an extended period to use the money they have raised *without* paying periodic interest. Thus, they can be an effective cash flow management instrument for the issuer. Investors like zeros because the heavily discounted price means that they can purchase more bonds with the same amount of investment monies, and that they can purchase bonds of different maturities, timed to coincide with anticipated expenses. In reading the bond quotes as published in financial newspapers, the investor will recognize that the bond being traded is a zero by the inclusion of the symbol "zr" next to the bond issuer, whose symbol is immediately followed by the scheduled maturity date of the bond.

Foreign Bond: A foreign bond has three distinct characteristics:
- The bond is issued by a foreign entity (such as a government, municipality, or foreign corporation; note that if the bond is issued by a foreign corporation, but is denominated in U.S. dollars, it is referred to as a *Yankee bond*)
- The bond is traded on a foreign financial market; and/or
- The bond is denominated in a foreign currency

Of these three characteristics, the major risk to a domestic investor is that of the denomination of the security in a foreign (non-U.S dollar) currency. As such, the domestic investor is subject to *currency* (or *exchange rate*) risk. Simply defined, currency risk is the potential for loss due to fluctuations in currency exchange rates. Accordingly, this risk may turn a profit on a foreign investment into a loss or vice-versa.

> **Example 2-3:** Sharon, a U.S. citizen, purchases a 1,000 U.K. pound par value bond with a 5 percent coupon rate. At the time that she made the investment, the currency exchange rate was 1.50 U.S. dollars to 1.00 U.K. pounds. This means that Sharon paid $1,500 in U.S. currency for the U.K. bond. Several years later, the bond matured and Sharon was issued a check for 1,000 U.K pounds (the par value of the foreign bond). Unfortunately, when she goes to convert the pounds to U.S. dollars, Sharon finds that the currency exchange rate has adjusted to a standard of 1.40 U.S. dollars to 1.00 U.K. pounds (or the dollar has "strengthened" against the pound). As a result, Sharon incurs a loss of $100 due entirely to the currency risk fluctuation (that is, she only receives $1,400 for a bond that she purchased for $1,500).
>
> Of course, it is also possible to *profit* from currency risk. In the example above, if the dollar had "fallen" against the pound (for example, the exchange rate adjusted to 1.80 U.S. dollars to 1.00 U.K. pounds), Sharon would have received $1,800, or $300 more than she had paid for the foreign bond.

Eurobond: A Eurobond is one that is issued and traded in a country *other than* the one in which the currency is denominated. An example is General Electric (G.E.) issuing a bond denominated in U.S. dollars in the German financial markets. Therefore, a Eurobond does not necessarily have to originate or end up in Europe, although most debt instruments of this type are issued to European investors by non-European entities.

Promissory Note: Promissory notes are *private transactions* between a lender and borrower primarily used to finance business operations or expansion. Since these notes are private and are not marketable, they are not really "investments" in the meaning attributed to them here. Nevertheless, at times, a financial planner is asked by a client to assess the quality and/or terms of such note and should generally be aware of its characteristics and importance as a financing mechanism for the small business owner client.

The written execution of a promissory note may be very helpful in avoiding the treatment of the transaction as a gift, subject to federal gift taxation. While the interpretation of a gift in lieu of what was intended to be a loan is not a significant issue in non-family transactions, it is a potential pitfall where family members are the only parties to the transaction. Moreover, in the event that the note fails to provide for interest or provides for interest below certain market rates, interest may be imputed to the lender and considered paid by the borrower under the so-called *below market loan rules*. These rules (unless a *de-minimis rule* applies) re-characterize a transaction as an *arms length* loan, requiring payment of interest at the applicable federal rate (APR) as published by the Treasury Department on a monthly basis. All of the interest from a promissory note (whether imputed or stated) is fully taxable to the investor at ordinary income tax rates.

Promissory notes tend to be highly customized to reflect the intent of the parties to the agreement; however, most include one of the following types of repayment schedules:

- Equal monthly payments
- Equal monthly payments with a final *balloon* payment (which must be paid off in a final lump sum usually reflecting a shorter time period than that of a month)
- Interest-only payments (this type of note is becoming more popular in real estate/home mortgage financing as a means of permitting a first-time homebuyer to enter the market; of course, the significant disadvantage of the interest-only note or loan is the fact that little to no equity is accumulated in the property purchased); or
- A single payment of interest and principal (this type of repayment schedule is normally only for loans that are due within one year)

A promissory note should also specify whether the borrower has the right of prepayment on the note and, if so, whether a penalty is in effect. Such a provision may be a valuable inducement for the borrower to execute the note and substantially lower the total interest cost of the loan. You should note that, in the context of home mortgage financing, pursuant to the provisions of the Truth in Lending Act, the lender is *required* to provide to the borrower a written statement indicating the total amount of interest that is paid over the term of the loan, in addition to informing the borrower of any pre-payment penalty associated with paying off the note before its stated term of expiration.

Bonds with Embedded Options:

Callable Bond: A callable bond consists of the straight bond component and an embedded call option to the issuer. The bondholder is "long" (has bought) the straight bond component and is "short" (has sold) the embedded call option. The implied price of the embedded option is realized in a higher interest rate (as opposed to a comparable option-free bond) and in the premium paid to the bondholder at the time the bond is called. The issuer may "call" or redeem the bonds after a grace period. This is done when interest rates fall to the level where the issuer re-finances the outstanding issue with a lower-rate issue.

Putable Bond: A putable bond also consists of the straight bond component and an embedded put option. The bondholder is long both the straight bond component and the embedded put option (the right of the bondholder to sell the bond back to the issuer prior to maturity). The implied price of the put option is, therefore, realized in a lower interest rate compared to an option-free bond. The bondholder may redeem the bond when interest rates rise.

Convertible Bond: A bond with the added feature that the bondholder has the option to turn the bond back into the issuer in exchange for a specified number of common stock shares of the issuer. If the bondholder converts the bond to stock, the bond issuer (corporation) replaces the debt liability with equity on the balance sheet. The bondholder is long the straight bond component and long the conversion option.

Bond With Warrants: A bond with warrants is a combination of debt and equity financing for the issuer. The issuer receives debt financing from the sale of the bond and equity financing if the warrants are exercised. Warrants are essentially call options on the issuer's stock. A bondholder can strip the warrants from the bond and sell them separately on the secondary options market. The bondholder is long the straight bond and long the stock call option.

Mortgage-Backed (Mortgage Pass-Through) Bond: The holder of a mortgage-backed security is long the straight bond component and short the embedded call option. The call option is the underlying right of the homeowner to refinance his or her home.

Characteristics of Bonds

Par Value: This is the stated value of the bond at date of issuance and the amount that is returned to the investor when redeemed; usually a $1,000 minimum; also referred to as the bond *principal*.

Coupon Rate: This is the stated rate of interest on the debt obligation (bond); the interest paid by the corporation on the bond (unlike a dividend declared on stock) is income tax deductible as an "ordinary and necessary" business expense. The coupon rate on a fixed rate bond does *not* change. Finally, be aware that a bond's coupon rate is sometimes confused with its yield. The former *never* changes, but the latter frequently does, as will subsequently be shown.

Indenture: The formal written agreement between the issuer of the bond and the trustee of the bond acting on behalf of the bondholders; also called a *deed of trust*.

Sinking Fund: A bond provision that requires the issuer to either:

- Redeem some or all of the bond systematically over its term rather than in full at maturity, or
- Set aside sufficient capital in a separate account, over the life of the bond issue, which will ultimately pay off the total bond principal at the bond's maturity.

Priced at Par: A bond is priced at par when the market-required yield is equal to the bond's coupon rate.

Priced at Premium: A bond is priced at premium to par when the market-required yield is less than the bond's coupon rate.

Priced at Discount: A bond is priced at discount to par when the market-required yield is greater than the bond's coupon rate.

Promised Yield-to-Maturity (YTM): The YTM is the internal rate of return on the bond if held to maturity and is a function of the bond price and coupon rate.

Yield-to-Call (YTC): YTC is associated with callable bonds and is the yield realized if the bond is called on the first available call date.

In most corporate bond issues, coupon income and principal repayment are relatively safe. Bonds normally pay interest income on a semi-annual basis and, once begun, cannot be changed in either amount or timing regardless of the financial condition of the issuer. In other words, unlike the payment of dividends on stock that is made only at the discretion of the corporation's board of directors, interest payments on bonds are a *fixed legal obligation* of the issuer. This also means, as a creditor of the corporation, a bondholder may force the bond issuer into bankruptcy proceedings. Accordingly, where the investor's objective is a secure and consistent cash flow of income, the purchase of investment-grade corporate bonds may be warranted.

Bonds are exposed to a variety of risks. Common types of risk include:
1. Default risk,
2. Purchasing power risk (inflation risk),
3. Interest rate risk,
4. Re-investment rate risk,
5. Country risk, and
6. Currency risk

Default risk is the risk that the issuer becomes unable to meet the indenture obligations of the bond. As a result, both the remaining interest and principal payments on the bond may be forfeited. Treasury securities are risk-free from a default risk perspective.

Purchasing power risk is the risk of inflationary devaluation of the remaining coupon and principal payments.

Interest rate risk is the risk of falling bond prices resulting from an increase in market interest rates.

Re-investment rate risk is the risk of re-investing coupon and principal cash flows at lower market interest rates.

Country risk is the risk of default on foreign sovereign bonds.

Finally, *currency risk* is the exchange rate risk of foreign bonds paying coupons and principal in their home currency, which may subsequently depreciate against the investor's domestic currency.

Bond prices move *inversely* to market interest rates. Because coupon payments are fixed, fluctuation in market interest rates must be reflected in bond prices. For example, an investor would not purchase a previously issued bond paying $80 a year in interest at par if she could buy a comparable new issue at par earning $100 a year in interest. However, if the previously issued bond is selling at a sufficient discount to drive the yield up to equal the new issue, she is indifferent to buying either one. Conversely, an investor would not sell a bond paying $100 a year in interest at par if comparable new issues are selling at par paying only $80 a year in interest. She would, however be indifferent in selling the bond if the price is at a sufficient premium over par to drive the yield down to the level of the new issue.

Most corporate bonds are issued as *debentures*, meaning they are an unsecured credit obligation of the issuing corporation. Further, most bonds offered in this form are *subordinated* in security (safety) to all other corporate creditors, including its general creditors. Because of the greater risk associated with *subordinated debentures,* these types of bonds pay a higher interest rate than those of either comparable mortgage bonds or non-subordinated debentures. Still, as debt obligations, even subordinated debentures have a security preference over any equity shares (common and preferred stock) issued by the corporation and, therefore, carry *less* investor risk than common and/or preferred stock.

The taxation of bonds will be covered in chapter 18 of this textbook when discussing the "Taxation of Investment Vehicles."

BOND VALUATION

Bond valuation models and examples will be discussed in detail in Chapter 13 of this text. Following is a general overview of valuation for different types of bonds.

Straight (Option-Free) Bonds

The cash flows of a straight (option-free) bond can be shown on a time line as follows:

The traditional bond valuation model is the sum of the present value of the coupon annuity and the present value of the principal lump sum at maturity.

Convertible Bonds

An investor who is interested in combining the certainty of semi-annual income payments with the opportunity for significant capital gains may be interested in a *convertible bond*. Convertible bonds offer *two* opportunities for capital appreciation. The first is through the conversion of the bond into ownership of the common stock of the issuing corporation. The second is through the appreciation in the market value of the convertible bond that occurs as the market price of the underlying common stock increases.

The *conversion ratio* of a convertible bond is the number of common stock shares received if the bond's conversion option is exercised. This ratio is changed to reflect any stock splits to protect the convertible bondholder from dilution.

The *conversion premium* associated with the bond is the amount by which the convertible bond exceeds the market price of the underlying shares of stock. If the premium is *high*, the convertible trades like any fixed-income bond. If the premium is *low*, the convertible begins to trade like the underlying stock.

Conversion parity occurs when the convertible bond value equals the conversion value. The conversion value is the market price of the underlying stock times the conversion ratio.

> **Example 2-4:** A convertible bond has a conversion ratio of 40 shares of common stock. The underlying stock sells for $20. If the convertible bond is issued at par ($1,000), the initial conversion premium is $200 ($1,000 bond value versus $800 conversion value) or $5/share. Conversion parity would occur when the stock price is $25 (considering the bond is selling at par).
>
> There is a separate formula for calculating the conversion value of the convertible bond if the conversion price of the stock is given in the indenture agreement rather than the conversion ratio. This formula is as follows:
>
> $$CV = (PAR/CP) \times P_s$$
>
> where PAR is the par value of the bond, CP is the conversion price and P_s is equal to the current market price of the underlying stock.
>
> **Example 2-5:** Calculate the conversion value of a $1,000 par value convertible bond if the conversion price of the stock is $40 and the stock is currently selling at $35.
>
> $$CV = [\$1,000 / \$40] \times \$35 = \$875$$

Another important characteristic when evaluating convertible bonds is the *payback period* (sometimes also known as the *break-even time*). This period measures how long the interest income from the convertible bond (compared to the dividend income from the common stock) must continue to make up for the difference between the price of the bond and its conversion value. The formula used to compute this period is as follows:

$$\text{Payback} = \frac{\text{Bond Price less Conversion Value}}{\text{Coupon Payment less Dividends from Equal Investment in Common Stock}}$$

Example 2-6: Debbie's ABC Company convertible bond has a conversion ratio of 27.5 shares, coupon of 6 percent, and sells for $1,200.00. ABC stock sells for $35 and pays a dividend (annual) of $1.50 per share. Calculate the payback period for her convertible bond.

Bond price = $1,200
Conversion value = 27.5 x $35 = $962.50
Coupon payment (annual) = $1,000 x 0.06 = $60
Dividends = $1,200/$35 = 34.2857 x $1.50 = $51.4286

$$\text{Payback} = \frac{\$1,200 - \$962.50}{\$60 - 51.4286} = 27.71 \text{ years}$$

Finally, rating agencies such as Standard & Poor's evaluate convertible bond issues and assign quality ratings in much the same manner as regular corporate bonds. However, there are very few convertible bonds with ratings of A or higher. This is because the rating agencies tend to award ratings to convertible bonds (given its convertibility to higher risk equity) that are one level *below* that of the issuer's non-convertible debt. As a result, most convertibles have a rating in the BBB or even BB range. The BB or below rating equates the convertible issue with that of high-yield bonds generally.

Callable Bonds

Callable bonds require the valuation of both the straight bond component and the embedded option component. Exercising the embedded call option by the issuer results in a change in cash flows to the bondholder.

Value of callable bond = Value of straight bond component – Value of embedded call option (Note that the embedded call option is subtracted because the holder of the option is the issuer.)

The appreciation of a callable bond in a decreasing interest rate environment is limited to the call price. If interest rates are rising, the callable bond is valued more as an option-free bond. Binomial option pricing models are often used to value the embedded call option.

FOREIGN BONDS

Foreign bonds are valued using the same models as U.S. bonds with some adjustments. First, European bonds generally pay annual interest as opposed to semiannual interest and second, currency exchange rate fluctuations require adjustments in translation to domestic currency.

Example 2-7: A European bond has a 10 percent coupon, paid annually, while a U.S. bond pays a semiannual coupon. Assuming all other features of the two bonds are the same, calculate the corresponding U.S. coupon rate.

This is really nothing more than a periodic interest rate problem:

$$(1 + \text{ European rate}) = \left(1 + \frac{\text{U.S. rate}}{2}\right)^2$$

$$1.10 = \left(1 + \frac{\text{U.S. rate}}{2}\right)^2$$

$$\sqrt{1.10} = \left(1 + \frac{\text{U.S. rate}}{2}\right)$$

$$1.0488 = \left(1 + \frac{\text{U.S. rate}}{2}\right)$$

$$0.0488 = \frac{\text{U.S. rate}}{2}$$

$$0.0976 = \text{U.S. rate} = 9.76\%$$

ZERO COUPON BONDS

Zero coupon bonds (zeros) are valued using the traditional bond valuation model. Even though there is no semiannual coupon, the principal must still be discounted on a bond equivalent yield semiannual basis.

IMPORTANT CONCEPTS

Debt security

Treasury note

Treasury bond

Treasury STRIP

Treasury Inflation Protection Security (TIPS)

Series I bond

Mortgage-backed security

Government National Mortgage Association Certificate *(Ginnie Mae)*

Federal National Mortgage Association Certificate *(Fannie Mae)*

Federal Home Loan Mortgage Corporation Certificate *(Freddie Mac)*

Municipal bond

Tax equivalent yield (T.E.Y.)

General obligation (G.O.) bond

Revenue bond

Private purpose bond

Par value

Coupon rate

Mortgage bond

Debenture

Investment grade bond

High yield bond

Convertible bond

Conversion value

Payback period

Callable bond

Foreign bond

Yankee bond

Zero coupon bond

Promissory note

Bond valuation

Yield-to-Maturity (YTM)

Yield-to-Call (YTC)

QUESTIONS FOR REVIEW

1. What is the most common example of a *debt security* that is issued by a corporation or government?

2. Why might the *floating* of a debt security by a corporation be a more preferable financing mechanism than merely issuing stock?

3. What is the term of maturity of a Treasury note? What is the term of maturity for a Treasury bond?

4. A Treasury STRIP is what type of debt security? If purchased, where should it be positioned within an individual's portfolio?

5. What is the major advantage of an investment in U.S. Treasury securities (from the standpoint of the individual or institutional investor)?

6. What characteristics are important to an investor who is considering an investment in Treasury Inflation Protection Securities (TIPS)?

7. What is a Series I bond?

8. Which government or quasi-governmental agency issues each of the following *pass-through* certificates?

    - Ginnie Mae
    - Fannie Mae
    - Freddie Mac

    Which one of these is a direct guarantee of the U.S Treasury? (Ignore the current conservatorship of Fannie Mae and Freddie Mac in explaining your answer.)

9. Explain what is meant by the term *mortgage-backed security*? What is the primary investment risk associated with such security?

10. There are three primary types of municipal bonds. What are they and which has the least amount of investor risk? Why?

11. Who (what type of taxpayer) is most suited to make an investment in municipal bonds? Why?

12. What is the measure used to compare the yield from a municipal bond with its taxable equivalent?

13. What is a major disadvantage of purchasing a private purpose or private activity municipal bond?

14. Define the following terms:

    - Par value of a bond
    - Coupon rate
    - Indenture
    - Sinking fund
    - Investment grade bond
    - High yield bond

15. In what form are most corporate bonds issued today?

16. If a bond investor is primarily interested in safety, would she purchase a mortgage bond or debenture? Why?

17. What are the two advantages of investing in a convertible security?

18. Give an example of how to compute the conversion value of a convertible security. Why is determining this value important?

19. Why does an investor pay a premium when he or she purchases a convertible security?

20. If you are a potential investor, everything else being equal, would you prefer to purchase a callable or non-callable corporate bond? Why?

21. What are three distinct characteristics of a foreign bond? Which one is likely the most important to an investor?

22. How is a *zero coupon bond* (a *zero*) different than a regular corporate bond? Where should a zero be positioned within an investor's portfolio and why?

23. What is a *Eurobond*?

24. Why might it be advantageous to execute a promissory note between family members?

25. If no interest or a below-market interest rate is charged in executing a promissory note among family members, what tax consequence is likely to occur? Explain.

26. What is a *balloon payment*?

SUGGESTIONS FOR ADDITIONAL READING

Tools and Techniques of Investment Planning, 2nd edition, Stephen R. Leimberg, Robert T. LeClair, Robert J. Doyle, Jr., and Thomas R. Robinson, The National Underwriter Company, 2006.

Investments: An Introduction, 9th edition, Herbert B. Mayo, Thomson/ South-Western, 2008.

Investment Analysis and Portfolio Management, 9th edition, Frank K. Reilly and Keith C. Brown, Thomson/South-Western, 2009.

The Wall Street Journal Guide to Money and Investing, 3rd edition, Kenneth M. Morris and Virginia B. Morris, Fireside Publishing, 2004.

Dictionary of Finance and Investment Terms, 6th edition, Barron's Financial Guides, 2003.

CHAPTER THREE

Stocks and Stock Attributes

• • •

Stocks are what most individuals think of when considering the possibility of a financial asset that may generate a significant return. However, as we shall learn, with the possibility of increased return, there is also increased investor risk.

Upon completing this chapter, you should be able to:

- Analyze the advantages and disadvantages of an investment consisting of equity ownership in a corporation (stock) versus that of debt ownership (bonds)
- Describe the characteristics and uses of common stock in investment planning
- Describe the characteristics and uses of preferred stock in investment planning
- Distinguish various forms of stock attributes, such as warrants, stock rights, and/or stock options
- Discuss when it may be appropriate to use stock or stock attributes as equity-based compensation for executives or other valued corporate employees
- Identify the use of American Depository Receipts (ADRs) in the financial marketplace
- Identify stock valuation models

EQUITY VS. DEBT

The term that is most frequently used to refer to a stock issue in the primary marketplace is *equity*. Accordingly, each equity owner (referred to as a *shareholder*) is entitled to a proportionate share of the assets and profits (dividends) of a corporation. As an added incentive to become such an owner, shareholders are given voting rights associated with their stock whereby they exercise control. While most shareholders are only a small minority of the total number of shareholders, they nonetheless are entitled to "vote their shares," most often in the form of a proxy sent to them by the corporate secretary prior to the shareholder's annual meeting.

As a comparison to debt issued by a corporation, equity has one major advantage: it does not become an ongoing liability of the business (requiring periodic payment of interest and re-payment of principal). However, equity has one major disadvantage: Unlike interest paid on debt, the corporation does *not* get an income tax deduction for any dividends declared and paid on shares of stock (both preferred stock and common stock). Therefore, it is more expensive to the corporation to issue stock than debt (at least from an income tax perspective). In addition, dividends on stock are generally taxed as ordinary income, thereby leading to a *double taxation* effect on distributions of corporate profits. While, under tax legislation passed in 2003, certain *qualifying dividends* (generally those paid by domestic corporations and corporations incorporated in a territory of the U.S., such as Puerto Rico) are entitled to a tax-favored rate similar to capital gains, other dividends are subject to much higher ordinary income tax rates.

Finally, there may be a distinct dislike of additional equity ownership (stocks) where a corporation is *closely held* (not publicly traded). In these corporations, i.e. small businesses, stock is held among a small number of shareholders, typically family members. Normally, the owners of these entities do not desire additional shareholders with their attendant voting rights and to whom the original owners, often including the founder, are ultimately responsible. As a result, to reward existing owners/employees for their efforts in growing the business and making it successful, closely held corporations will often structure executive compensation arrangements that are payable in *cash*, rather than in stock or stock rights. An alternative financing mechanism to stock for a closely held corporate owner is, of course, debt in the form of a bank loan, although usually a *personal guarantee* of repayment is a condition of the loan.

COMMON STOCK

Common stock represents units of ownership in a publicly traded corporation. Owners are entitled to vote on the selection of the Board of Directors of the corporation, and other important matters, as well as to receive any dividends that are declared on their shares. In the event that the corporation is *liquidated* (terminates business with its assets converted to cash) the claims of secured and unsecured creditors and owners of bonds and preferred stockholders take precedence over the common stockholders.

Common stocks are typically purchased through a stock brokerage firm, often referred to as a *broker/dealer*. This term is appropriate because not only may the firm purchase stock for other investors, but it also purchases shares for its own account and, therefore, acts as a "dealer" in those stocks. Once an account is established for the investor, brokers purchase or sell common shares through a variety of orders, the most common of which is a so-called *market order*. Such order is a direction by the investor/customer to buy or sell securities at the best obtainable price during the market activity of that day. In other words, in a market order, the price is basically determined by the market. Conversely, a *limit order* is a direction by the customer to buy or sell securities at a specified price (or better) determined by the customer (not the market). It is increasingly common for these orders to be placed using personal computers via online brokerage accounts.

Many investors, however, prefer to own common stocks *indirectly* as part of a *mutual fund* or *open end investment company*. Such a fund provides a number of advantages, but most notably diversification of risk and the professional management of assets. Mutual funds and managed accounts are the subject of chapter 4, in this textbook.

Dividends are external distributions of corporate profits to shareholders. Profits that are not paid out in dividends are retained earnings to the corporation. A number of growth companies (for example, Apple) have historically not paid a dividend and have reinvested profits back into the corporation for future capital appreciation. Therefore, an investor who is considering an investment in an individual common stock (or a stock mutual fund) is likely to be more interested in the possibility of appreciation in the underlying value of the shares of stock rather than regular income from the payment of dividends. This motivation is further encouraged by two consequences of income taxation: first, the shareholder may choose when to *recognize* his or her gain for tax purposes and second, once recognized (the stock is sold or otherwise disposed of), and assuming a requisite holding period is met, any gain is taxable at preferential long term capital gain rates, currently no higher than 15 percent. See Chapter 18 for more on the taxation of common shares.

Finally, common stocks are highly *marketable*. This means that they may easily be converted to cash, if necessary, as there are usually a substantial number of interested buyers. However, the market price of common stock shares may change significantly throughout the course of a trading day or series of days. It is also possible that the investor could lose *all* of his or her initial investment. The risk that an investor takes in purchasing common shares is collectively referred to as *market risk*, which may be minimized (but not entirely eliminated) by proper asset allocation and diversification of the investor's portfolio of securities.

Stock Dividends and Stock Splits

A *stock dividend* is a dividend paid in additional shares of company stock, rather than in cash. Since all common shareholders receive their proportionate share of the dividend, the total value of all the common stock of the company is unchanged. However, when such a dividend is declared and paid, the value of each common stockholder's shares is proportionally reduced. Unless the stockholder has the option to receive the declared dividend in cash rather than stock, which would entail *constructive receipt* of income (meaning that the dividend is taxable), a stock dividend is generally *not* taxable for federal income tax purposes.

Recipients of forthcoming dividends are determined by referencing those who are listed as stockholders on the corporate books as a *holder of record* as of the *date of record* when the dividend is declared. The date of record is the second business day after the *ex-dividend date*. Accordingly, for an investor to be entitled to a dividend, he or she must purchase the stock *before* the ex-dividend date.

> **Example 3-1:** If Friday, August 19, 2009 is the date of record of the corporation, when must the investor purchase the stock of XYZ Company in order to be entitled to its stock dividend? Answer: Count back two business days from August 19, 2009 to determine that the ex-dividend date is Wednesday, August 17, 2009. This means that the investor must purchase the stock of XYZ Company no later than Tuesday, August 16, 2009 to be entitled to its stock dividend declared by the corporate board of directors.

A *stock split* is defined as a distribution of more than 25 percent of the outstanding common shares of the corporation designed to lower the stock's price per share (and, thereby, make it more attractive for purchase by new investors). In a split, the par value of each share of stock is reduced and the number of common shares is increased proportionately. For example, if a stock were selling for $120 per share before a 2 for 1 split, then after the split, each shareholder would have twice the number of shares held previously, but the price per share would be $60. Unsophisticated investors typically love stock splits since they believe they now own more of the corporation for no more investment money expended. However, you should note that the investor owns *exactly* the same percentage of the corporation as before; all that has happened is that each share now represents a correspondingly smaller percentage of the company. Nonetheless, stock trading may increase due to a lower price and this could be bullish for investors owning stocks that recently split. Because of this mere "shuffling of the ownership cards," stock splits are *never* taxable to the shareholder.

The opposite of a stock split is a *reverse split*. In a reverse split, the company reduces (rather than increases) the number of shares outstanding. Such a variation of the normal split is usually initiated by companies wanting to increase the price per share of each outstanding share because the company is about to be acquired. In this manner, the company may "fend off" an interested, but unwanted, acquirer. Alternatively, a reverse stock split may be declared by a company to raise its stock price to avoid possible stock exchange de-listing.

Book Value vs. Fair Market Value

The *book value* of a corporation will be further considered in chapter 12 of this textbook when discussing how to value equity securities (stocks). Such value is defined as the accounting value of the equity as shown on the corporate balance sheet and is the sum of the common stock outstanding, any capital in excess of par, and any retained earnings. It is similar to the *net worth* computation performed in preparing a statement of personal financial position. Generally, a *low* book value may indicate that the company's assets are underestimated, and that its stock is a potentially good value for prospective investors.

Book value is frequently used when analyzing certain ratios that may aid in determining a proper amount to be paid for a stock as well as by appraisers in estimating at what multiple a closely held corporation should be purchased. However, it should be noted that such value is rarely, if ever, the single most appropriate method to value a corporation that features a number of individual security investments on its balance sheet. Rather, that corporation should be valued after adjusting those investments to their current *fair market value* as determined by the market price for the date of valuation. Since book value, by its very nature, reflects only a historical cost approach, it is only one of several factors to consider in valuing any business.

Return on Equity (ROE)

Stock analysts oftentimes examine the components of a company's profitability in order to determine whether the stock should be purchased. A primary component or ratio that analysts evaluate is that of a company's *return on equity* (ROE). Indeed, this ratio is the key component in determining the earnings growth of a company (and, therefore, the expected price increase in the value of its common stock). ROE is calculated with use of the following formula:

$$ROE = \frac{\text{Net Income}}{\text{Common Equity}}$$

Example 3-2: Assume that you have determined that a company has a book value of $100 per share. It has earnings for the year of $2.0 million and has 500,000 common shares outstanding. All of its earnings are distributed to the shareholders in the form of dividends. Therefore, the earnings per share (EPS) is $4.00 ($2 million divided by 500,000 shares). Thus, the company has a return on equity (ROE) of 4% ($4.00 divided by $100).

The three-stage DuPont ROE incorporates a firm's profit margin (how well operations are managed), the total asset turnover (how efficient the assets are utilized), and financial leverage (how optimal is the capital structure). DuPont ROE is expressed as:

$$ROE = \frac{\text{Net Income}}{\text{Sales}} \times \frac{\text{Sales}}{\text{Total Assets}} \times \frac{\text{Total Assets}}{\text{Common Equity}}$$

The three-stage DuPont ROE reduces to net income divided by common equity but provides considerably more insight into the factors that impact the ROE of any publicly-traded company.

Of course, the *higher* the return on equity of a company, the *better* it is as an indicator of the company's financial strength. However, the more important analysis is the *direction* of this ratio; in other words, if it is increasing in percentage, it usually means that the company's earnings per share (EPS) are growing and, accordingly, so are the prospects for the future market value of its stock.

Dividend Payout Ratio

A corollary ratio to that of return on equity (ROE) is the *dividend payout ratio* (DPR) of a company. This ratio is the percentage of earnings per share that a company uses to pay a dividend to its common shareholders and is computed as follows:

$$DPR = \frac{\text{Common dividends paid per share}}{\text{Earnings available for common shares (EPS)}}$$

The normal range for this ratio is 25% to 50% of a company's earnings per share, although this range may be increasing given the legislative incentive to pay out dividends under the 2003 Tax Act (JGTRRA). In general the *higher* the dividend payout ratio, the *more constant* the company's earnings growth and, thus, the dividend payout. By contrast, younger companies or particularly profitable companies with good growth prospects (and thus a great need for cash) will tend to retain most, if not all, of their earnings.

Initial Public Offerings (IPOs) and Secondary Offerings

If a small business finds that its product or service is in great demand, the owners may decide to *go public* and undertake an *initial public offering* (IPO) of its stock. To do this, the owners engage an investment banking firm to *underwrite* the stock offering; that is, to purchase all the public shares at a pre-established price and then resell them to the public (presumably at a significant profit). The proposed stock sale is publicized in the financial press with ads commonly known as *tombstones* since they are in heavy print with a notable black border. The day before the actual sale of the company's shares to the public, the underwriter typically *prices the issue*, or establishes the price that it will pay for each share. This may be done either on a *firm commitment* basis (the underwriter will purchase any shares that remain unsold) or using the underwriter's *best efforts* (the underwriter will make every effort to sell all the shares, but the company does not receive any money for unsold shares). Technically, when the investment banker agrees to sell the company's stock using best efforts, the banker does not underwrite the securities since it does not buy any securities. Rather, the banker acts only as a broker to sell whatever stock it can at the stipulated price.

With an IPO, there is a general expectation of underpricing of the newly offered shares. Therefore, there may be an investment opportunity for sophisticated investors. How great is the underpricing on average and how fast does the market adjust the price for the underpricing? Studies have tried to answer both these questions. With respect to the first, there is an average underpricing of approximately 18 percent, but it varies according to the year in which the IPO occurred and other factors. The major variables that tend to cause differential underpricing seem to be risk measures associated with the company or industry; the size of the company; the prestige of the lead underwriter; and the status of the company's accounting firm. In answer to the second question, studies indicate that the market adjusts to the underpricing within *one day* after the offering. Accordingly, this leaves a very short period of time for either an individual or institutional investor to take advantage of any market inefficiencies.

If a company has already issued shares, but wants to raise additional capital through the sale of more stock, it does so by what is called a *secondary* or *seasoned offering*. Companies are often resistant to issue more stock, since the larger the supply of stock outstanding, the less valuable each share is that has already been issued (not to mention the commensurate reduction in earnings per share). This is called *dilution*. For this reason, a company typically issues new shares *only* if its capital structure of debt and equity needs re-balancing to comply with debt covenants. If the stock price is considered to be too high in the secondary marketplace, the company may declare a stock split.

Private Placements

Instead of incurring the time and expense of an IPO, some small businesses choose to sell stock privately. In such an arrangement, referred to as a *private placement*, the company designs an issue and sells it to a small group of institutions or sophisticated individual investors. Since the transaction is exempt from registration with the SEC, the company enjoys lower issuing costs. In addition, the institution that purchases the issue typically benefits because the company passes some of these cost savings on to the institution in the form of a higher investment return. In fact, the purchasing institution or individual investor should require a higher rate of return since there is no secondary market for the stock, thereby resulting in greater market risk.

A private placement may also be offered to certain individual investors after disclosure through an *offering circular* (instead of a *prospectus*, which technically is only relevant for a public offering). Specifically, the placement may be sold to a maximum of 35 non-accredited investors and an unlimited number of *accredited investors*. An accredited investor is currently defined as a purchaser who has a net worth of $1.0 million or an individual with an annual income of $200,000. If an investor does not satisfy any of these criteria (in other words, he or she is a *non-accredited investor*), the investor must be sophisticated (experienced) and sign an investment letter acknowledging that he or she is aware of the investment risks associated with purchasing a non-registered security. Further, if the individual investor cannot evaluate the offering independently, Regulation D of the Securities Act of 1933 requires the use of a knowledgeable agent, such as a securities lawyer or tax accountant.

PREFERRED STOCK

Preferred stock is really a type of hybrid security since it combines features of both debt (bonds) and equity (common stock). As its name implies, preferred stock carries a preference with respect to the earnings of the corporation. Dividends on such stock must be paid *before* any dividends can be paid to holders of common stock. However, like common stock, there is no requirement that a dividend be declared on preferred stock at any time. Nevertheless, preferred stock differs from common stock in that it pays a *fixed* rate once a dividend is declared and that these dividends are *cumulative* in nature (meaning that any preferred dividends that are not paid as scheduled must subsequently be accumulated and paid at some future date before any dividends are paid on common stock). Finally, owners of preferred stock have precedence over common stockholders if a corporation liquidates its assets.

Like a bond, preferred stock is issued at a par value, although instead of $1,000 par value as in the case of a bond, preferred stock normally carries a par of $100. Then, as noted, preferred stocks pay a fixed dividend rate based on a stated percentage of the stock's par value. This fixed percentage is normally higher than that of bonds, however. This is because preferred stock dividends are only paid *after* the company satisfies its bond interest obligations. Since this reduced legal obligation increases the uncertainty of returns, preferred stock investors demand a higher rate of return for this enhanced risk.

The typical purchaser of preferred stock is *not* the individual investor. Rather, it is a corporate treasurer with excess funds to invest. If the treasurer were to buy bonds, all of this interest is taxable to the corporation. However, a favorable tax privilege is available if the treasurer buys preferred stock instead. Generally, a corporation is entitled to deduct 70% of the dividends it receives from other domestic corporations from its taxable income. Therefore, only 30% of the dividends received by the corporate purchaser are subject to federal income tax. This tax advantage stimulates the demand for preferred stocks by corporations as purchasers. Generally, no voting rights are assigned to preferred stockholders.

Preferred stock is a *perpetuity* because, unlike a bond, it has *no* specified maturity date. Accordingly, to recover their initial investment, investors must sell their preferred shares. In addition, because of the perpetual time frame of the security, the prices of preferred stocks are extremely sensitive to changes in interest rates. When market interest rates increase, the prices of preferred shares tend to decline, irrespective of any corporate quarterly earnings results that primarily impact common stock issues. Obviously, the inverse relationship between interest rates and the preferred share price also holds when rates decrease Preferred stocks generally exhibit the price volatility characteristic of long term bonds rather than shorter term fixed income investments.

Some preferred stocks are also *convertible* into common stock. This means that they may be exchanged at a specified rate for the common stock of the corporation at a time chosen by the preferred stockholder. Usually, it will be advantageous to convert when the price of the common shares is increasing relative to the fixed rate of exchange. However, once converted, the preferred stockholder sacrifices the preference in dividends and corporation liquation that are the hallmarks of the security form.

Perpetuity Valuation

Because preferred stock is a *perpetuity*, an investor may compute its proper value simply by dividing the stated annual dividend by the investor's *required rate of return* (see chapter 10 of this textbook) on the preferred stock. In formula terms, this is written as follows:

$$V_p = \frac{D}{k_p}$$

Where,
V_p = value of perpetuity (preferred stock)
D = dividend
k_p = required return on preferred

How can perpetuities (infinite cash streams) be valued? As time approaches infinity, the present value of a dollar approaches zero.

> **Example 3-3:** Assume that a preferred stock has a par value of $100 and has a stated dividend rate of 7 percent (or, in this case, $7 per year). Because of the expected rate of inflation and the uncertainty of the dividend payment, the investor's required rate of return on the stock is 9 percent. Therefore, the proper or "intrinsic" value of the preferred stock to the investor is $77.78 (or $7 divided by .09) on a discounted cash flow basis. Given this intrinsic value, if the stock's current market price is $80, the investor would likely not purchase the stock.
>
> Conversely, if the stock's current market price is $70, the stock is probably a good buy.

WARRANTS

A stock warrant is essentially a long-term *call option* (see chapter 7 of this textbook) to purchase the stock of the corporation issuing the warrant. That is, like a call option (or *call*), warrants give the owner the right to purchase a specified number of common stock shares for a specified period of time at a specified price. However, unlike a call where the owner has the right to purchase a *round lot* of shares (100 shares), warrants generally do not give the owner the right to buy nearly as many shares. In addition, there are other important differences between a call and a warrant. These are as follows:

- A warrant is issued by a corporation, whereas a call is created by an individual.
- A warrant is *customized* to fit the needs of the issuer and owner, whereas a call includes standardized terms as required by the Options Clearing Corporation (OCC).
- A warrant typically has a maturity date (or date by which it may be exercised) of up to several years, whereas a call normally expires at the end of nine months if not exercised before that date.
- Warrants are often attached to a debt security, typically a corporation's bond or preferred stock.

Warrants guarantee, for a small premium, the opportunity to buy stock at a fixed price during a particular period of time. In essence, they are a bet that the future price of the issuer's stock is going to increase. Thus, investors buy warrants if they are optimistic or *bullish* regarding the prospects for the stock.

> **Example 3-4:** David purchases a warrant for $1 per share that gives him the right to buy 50 shares of KRF stock at $10 per share for a period of five years from date of purchase. Assume that KRF stock goes up to $14 per share after three years and David exercises the warrant. Accordingly, he makes a profit of $150 on the 50 shares.

Profit = (Gain on stock – Cost of warrant) x Number of shares
Profit = ($4/share - $1/share) x 50 shares = $150

If the price of the warrant is *below* the specified price when the warrant expires, the warrant is worthless. However, since not much money has been expended for the warrant (in the above example, only $50), and because it has a longer right of exercise than a regular option, warrants are actively traded in the secondary market.

If corporations issue warrants at all, they usually do so in conjunction with new bond issues or preferred stock issues. These warrants give the bond or stock purchaser what is known as an *equity kicker,* making the particular issue more attractive to buyers. In addition, issuing the bonds or preferred stock with a warrant will usually *lower* the coupon or dividend rate necessary to sell the issue. Why? Because the purchaser is willing to accept a lower rate, given the opportunity to buy appreciated common stock (or an implied premium on the embedded call). In turn, the corporation's cost of debt service is reduced. Therefore, the use of warrants is especially useful for a younger company that anticipates rapid growth, but needs to hold onto as much cash as possible to finance future expansion.

When acquired as other than an employment incentive, and in lieu of compensation, warrants are taxed under the same general rules as options. Specifically, no gain or loss is recognized when the warrant is acquired and the owner does not incur a taxable event until: a) the time that the warrant period ends and the warrant expires unexercised or b) the time the option is sold. When a warrant is sold or expires unexercised, the character of the gain or loss is generally that of a capital asset with a preference for gains if the warrant is held for more than a year from date of purchase. If the warrant is exercised, there is usually no taxable event until the sale of the underlying stock that is acquired. Warrants received as an employment incentive (in lieu of compensation) are generally taxable as ordinary income at their fair market value on the date of receipt.

STOCK RIGHTS

A stock right, sometimes called a *subscription right,* is issued by a corporation that plans to raise funds by issuing new stock to the public. Each current shareholder is usually given one right for each share of stock that he or she owns. These rights give the current shareholders the opportunity to buy new shares of the new stock issue, thereby maintaining their overall percentage ownership of the corporation. Shareholders who do not wish to exercise their rights may sell them for cash before they expire. If the shareholders do not sell them before they expire and do not exercise them, the rights expire worthless.

Like a warrant, a stock right gives the owner the right to purchase common shares. However, in contrast to the warrant, the life of a stock right is *very short,* usually for only a few weeks, and thus equates to a short-term call option. Since the time until expiration is generally very short, a stock right typically has little or no speculative premium like other options. Accordingly, the value of the right may be determined with use of the following formula:

$$V = \frac{\text{Market price of current share} - \text{Subscription price of the new shares}}{\text{Number of rights required to purchase one new share of stock} + 1}$$

Example 3-5: Assume that the current market price of ABC common stock is $50 and that the subscription price of the new shares is $44. Further assume that, under the terms of the rights offering, it takes seven rights in addition to a set price for the stock to buy one share of any newly issued common stock. The current value of each right is:

$$V = \frac{\$50 - \$44}{7 + 1} = \frac{\$6}{8} = \$0.75$$

For each seven rights that the investor has, he or she can contribute an additional $44 and buy a share of stock currently worth $50.

The financial marketplace occasionally confuses the terms *warrant* and *stock right*. However, in actuality, the controlling difference is how the option to purchase shares of common stock was obtained. If the option was received as part of the purchase of a bond or preferred stock and for the purpose of purchasing existing shares, it is a *warrant*. If the option was distributed to a current shareholder as an opportunity to purchase additional shares, it is a *stock right*. Sometimes investors receive a stock right designated as a warrant. Nonetheless, to most investors, the distinction between warrants and stock rights is a distinction without a difference.

STOCK OPTIONS

Stock options are of two basic types: 1) those options that are purchased for investment (or sometimes speculative) purposes and 2) options used as an executive compensation benefit to reward performance. The first of these types will be considered when discussing derivative investments in Chapter 7 of this text and the second has already been addressed in the second course, *Insurance and Employee Benefits*, of Kaplan University's Certificate in Financial Planning Program. You should also note that options purchased for investment purposes may be written and traded on any *listed* stock of a recognized exchange, whereas options granted in lieu of executive cash compensation is usually in the form of *employer* stock.

With respect to the first (or investment) type of stock option, several points need to be made. First, options are a form of *derivative* investment vehicle; that is, their value is derived from the value of the underlying stock on which the option is written. There are both options to buy the underlying stock (known as a *call*) and to sell such stock (known as a *put*). Of course, which of these options the investor purchases depends on his or her expectation of what direction the underlying stock is likely to take. If there is an expectation that the price of the stock is likely to *increase,* he or she would purchase a *call* option and, conversely, if there is an expectation that the price of the stock is likely to *fall*, a *put* option. Regardless, many investors use stock options only for purposes of *hedging*, broadly defined as an investment strategy that aims to reduce the risk of loss associated with price movements in the underlying stock. In addition, some investors use stock options as a short-term investment strategy designed to produce income, such as the writing of what is known as a *covered call* (see Chapter 7 of this text).

Some individuals also *speculate* with stock options. Specifically, *Barrons* defines speculation as "an activity that offers the possibility of a significant reward (rate of return) but with the assumption of a higher than average possibility of a significant loss." Practically, speculation is also accomplished over a very short time frame, often mere hours or days. If recommending stock options as a possible strategy for their clients, financial planners should de-emphasize (indeed, *discourage*) the speculative aspects of the strategy and, instead, focus on options as a method of risk management (hedging). In other words, stock options as a financial planning technique should be understood as an *alternative investment*, taking into account the possibility of measurable return only in the context of measurable risk assumed by the investor. Only then will the financial planner (and, specifically, the CFP® certificant) comply with his or her *fiduciary duty* to the client.

STOCK AS EQUITY-BASED COMPENSATION

Like stock options used for executive compensation, employer stock shares (or a variation thereof) may also be used as an equity-based incentive for performance. Again, the use of employer stock for this purpose has been previously discussed in the *Insurance and Employee Benefits* course. However, you should be aware that a company's stock may not only be traded on an exchange, but also offered as an employee benefit.

There are three major types of stock used as equity-based compensation. They are:
  1) Restricted stock
  2) Phantom stock
  3) Stock appreciation rights (SARs) (Note: These should not be confused with stock rights or stock *subscription rights* discussed earlier in this chapter.)

A *restricted stock* plan is an arrangement to compensate employees (almost always executives of the company) by awarding them shares of employer stock subject to certain restrictions. Such a plan permits the employer to grant the executive an equity interest in the company, but withdraw it if the executive leaves before a certain period of time or goes to work for a competitor (this restriction is known for tax purposes as a *substantial risk of forfeiture*). If the executive satisfies the terms of the restriction, and becomes *substantially vested* in the stock, a taxable event occurs at the time of the removal of the restriction. When the executive becomes substantially vested in the restricted stock, its fair market value at that time (less any amount that the executive has paid for the stock, which is usually nothing or very little) is taxed as compensation income. Gain on any subsequent sale of the stock is generally taxable as capital gain income, at preferential long-term capital gain rates if the stock is owned for more than one year. Alternatively, an executive may elect to recognize income as of the date he receives the restricted stock, rather than waiting to become substantially vested. Any subsequent appreciation in the stock is then taxable at long-term capital gain rates. This election, known as a *Section 83(b) election* under the Internal Revenue Code Section number that provides for the same, must be made within 30 days of receiving the restricted stock or it is not effective.

Because of recent Financial Accounting Standards Board (FASB) rules, it is anticipated that the use of restricted employer stock as a compensation technique, in lieu of stock options, will significantly increase. Specifically, FASB has ruled that the value of any unexercised compensatory stock options must be shown as an expense on the corporation's income statement. Accordingly, there will be a reduction in earnings generated by the corporation, which in turn is likely to temporarily depress the trading value of its stock. Since the restricted stock alternative does not have this same accounting disadvantage, while still providing much the same employment incentive, it is likely to be increasingly used as a deferred compensation technique.

Phantom stock and *stock appreciation rights* (SARs) use different benefit formulas to accomplish the same objective of rewarding an executive for superior performance. In both, no actual stock is set aside, nor are any shares of stock actually distributed. The value of the employer stock is simply the measure that is used to determine the amount of executive benefit awarded. A *phantom stock* benefit generally refers to a plan formula based on a number of shares of hypothetical stock, whereby the employee receives a cash amount equal to the difference in the value of that stock when the agreement is entered into and when the benefit is payable. A *stock appreciation right* (SAR) formula provides that the executive's future benefits are to be determined by a formula based on the appreciated value of the company's stock over the period between adoption of the plan and the date of payment. Both of these compensation techniques are used where the company does not wish to have additional shareholders (for example, in a closely held corporation among family members).

AMERICAN DEPOSITORY RECEIPTS (ADRs)

American Depository Receipts (ADRs) are receipts for the stock of a foreign-based corporation held in the vault of a U.S. bank and entitling the shareholder to all dividends and capital gains. Therefore, instead of buying shares of foreign-based companies in overseas markets, Americans can buy shares in the form of an ADR. Indeed, such receipts were introduced as a result of the difficulties involved in buying shares in foreign countries and, particularly, the difficulties associated with trading at different market prices and with different currency values.

ADRs are priced in U.S. dollars and investors can buy or sell them in the same way that they trade American stocks. Any dividends paid on the foreign stock are also paid in U.S. dollars. ADRs are listed on all the major U.S. exchanges, including the New York Stock Exchange (NYSE), but may also be the subject of a private placement. The concept of ADRs has also been extended to other geographical markets, including the European exchanges, where foreign stocks to that region are traded in the form of European Depository Receipts (and denominated in the Euro currency).

Foreign taxes on any declared dividends are generally withheld before being passed through to the ADR holder. The holder will then receive a foreign tax credit on his or her U.S. income tax return (IRS Form 1040) for income tax paid to the foreign country. The 15% maximum tax rate for *qualified dividends* is generally applicable to U.S. individual investors in ADRs that are issued by entities that satisfy the definition of a *qualified foreign corporation*. Such corporation includes any foreign corporation that a) is eligible for the benefits of a comprehensive income tax treaty with the United States or b) has issued stock that is readily tradeable on an established securities market in the United States.

Typically, investing in ADRs is the simplest way in which a U.S. investor may engage in international investing. However, alternatives to ADRs, for the purpose of achieving international diversification of an investor's portfolio, include investing in international or global mutual funds, international exchange-traded funds (see the upcoming chapter 4 of this textbook), or investing in multi-national corporations listed on the U.S. stock exchanges.

IMPORTANT CONCEPTS

Equity	Secondary offering
Common stock	Private placement
Cash dividend	Preferred stock
Stock dividend	Perpetuity
Ex-dividend date	Warrant
Stock split	Stock (subscription) right
Reverse split	Stock option
Book value	Restricted stock
Return on equity (ROE)	Phantom stock
Dividend payout ratio	Stock appreciation right (SAR)
Initial public offering	American Depository Receipt (ADR)

QUESTIONS FOR REVIEW

1. What is one major advantage in financing future business expansion through equity ownership rather than debt obligations? What is a major disadvantage of equity ownership?

2. What does the purchase of common stock represent? How is this type of stock typically purchased?

3. Contrast a *market order* to purchase stock to that of a *limit order* for the same.

4. Why does an investor typically purchase common stock?

5. Are common stocks both *marketable* and *liquid*? Explain.

6. What is the difference between a stock dividend and a stock split? Which one is *never* taxable?

7. How does a corporation determine which stockholders are eligible to receive a dividend?

8. What is a *reverse split*? Why would a corporation do this?

9. Define the term *book value* of a corporation.

10. If a company has an EPS of $23.50 and a book value of $150 per share, what is the company's *return on equity* (ROE)?

11. What is the normal range of DPR for a company? If a company has a high DPR, what is this likely to represent?

12. Explain the difference if an investment banker uses a *firm commitment* agreement in an IPO versus that of its *best efforts*. If you are the issuer of the stock, which do you prefer and why?

13. How long have studies shown that the market takes to adjust to the general expectation of underpricing of shares offered as part of an IPO?

14. What is a *secondary offering* of a company's stock?

15. Which individuals are permitted to purchase stock that is sold as part of a private placement?

16. How does preferred stock differ from common stock?

17. Why is the coupon rate that is stated on preferred stock normally higher than that of bonds?

18. Who is the typical purchaser of preferred stock and why is this the case?

19. What formula is used to determine the proper value of preferred stock?

20. What is a *warrant* and why is it typically offered by a corporation?

21. Specify three differences between a warrant and a call option.

22. A stock right is also sometimes known as a *subscription right*. Why is this term appropriate?

23. Warrants and stock rights are sometimes confused in the financial marketplace. How can an investor tell the difference?

24. Stock options are of two basic types. What are they?

25. Should a financial planner *speculate* with stock options? Why or why not?

26. Explain each of the three major types of stock that are used as equity-based compensation.

27. Why is restricted stock expected to increase in importance in future years as a preferable method of executive deferred compensation?

28. What is an American depository receipt (ADR)? Why would an investor be interested in purchasing an ADR?

29. Which types of foreign corporations issuing dividends qualify for the favorable tax rates established under the 2003 Tax Act (JGTRRA)?

SUGGESTIONS FOR ADDITIONAL READING

Tools and Techniques of Investment Planning, 2nd edition, Stephen R. Leimberg, Robert T. LeClair, Robert J. Doyle, Jr., and Thomas R. Robinson, The National Underwriter Company, 2006.

Investments: An Introduction, 9th edition, Herbert B. Mayo, Thomson/ South-Western, 2008.

Investment Analysis and Portfolio Management, 9th edition, Frank K. Reilly and Keith C. Brown, Thomson/South-Western, 2009.

The Wall Street Journal Guide to Money and Investing, 3rd edition, Kenneth M. Morris and Virginia B. Morris, Fireside Publishing, 2004.

Dictionary of Finance and Investment Terms, 6th edition, Barron's Financial Guides, 2003.

CHAPTER FOUR

Mutual Funds and Managed Investments

• • •

A n open-end investment company (popularly referred to as a *mutual fund*) is likely the most favored form of investment asset for the small or individual investor. It provides both the advantage of diversification as well as access to professional management. However, there are several other forms of managed investment vehicles. The purpose of this chapter is to describe such vehicles and identify their appropriate use for the potential investor.

Upon completing this chapter, you should be able to:

- Describe the types of mutual funds and their use in investment planning for the individual investor
- Identify the characteristics of closed-end investment companies and/or unit investment trusts (UITs)
- Explain the recent innovation of exchange traded funds (ETFs) and/or hedge funds in the secondary marketplace
- Distinguish privately managed accounts from separately managed accounts and identify the characteristics of investors who may be interested in either type of account
- Explain what types of investments have been traditionally structured as a limited partnership investment and why this is the case

OPEN-END INVESTMENT COMPANIES (MUTUAL FUNDS)

Open-end investment companies are most frequently referred to as *mutual funds*. These funds continue to sell shares to investors after the initial sale of shares that first capitalizes the offering (thus, the term *open-end*). The make-up of the fund then continuously changes as new investors buy shares, while other existing investors or shareholders cash in by selling their shares back to the company (*redeeming* the shares). However, the shares are otherwise non-negotiable and may only be liquidated by the company offering the fund. As a result of the constant redemption and cashing out of existing shareholders, the fund must be prepared to raise cash as needed to meet redemption requests.

Mutual funds are an excellent investment vehicle for the *small investor*. They provide instant diversification and permit the investor to take advantage of a skilled, professional investment manager that the investor could otherwise likely not afford. In addition, due to the very large number of mutual funds available to the investor (over 15,000 at last count), there are many options available to satisfy the investor's financial goals at a reasonable cost.

Mutual funds may be purchased directly by the investor (for example, by telephone or over the Internet) or indirectly through a broker-dealer. They also may be purchased net of a sales charge, known as a *load*, or without a sales charge, a *no load fund*. In both instances, annual management fees and administrative charges imposed by the fund apply. These management fees typically equal anywhere from 1% to 3% of net assets under management by the fund. In addition, for those funds that are professionally managed by broker-dealers and positioned in a so-called *wrap account*, sales charges that may typically be imposed are waived in lieu of an asset management fee, normally expressed as a percentage of assets managed. In broker-dealer language, this percentage is expressed in a number of *basis points*, which is 1/100th of a percentage point. For example, a million dollar managed portfolio that carries a 100 basis point management fee (1%) would incur an annual charge of $10,000. Investors should generally search for those funds with solid past performance records (as evaluated against the performance benchmark index) on a consistent basis, as well as those that charge relatively low management fees and administrative charges (or *expense ratios*). The reader should note, however, that there are relatively few mutual funds with long-term performance records that are consistently above the benchmark index. This fact gives credence to the *efficient market hypothesis*, as subsequently discussed in chapter 9 of this textbook.

Finally, all mutual funds are priced according to their *Net Asset Value* (NAV) per share as determined at the end of market trading for that particular day. Specifically, this value is computed by dividing the total market value of all holdings in the fund (stocks or bonds) by the number of shares of the fund outstanding. Further, unlike *exchange traded funds* (ETFs) that are discussed later, open-end mutual funds may only be redeemed at the end of the trading day and *not* throughout the day. This means that the mutual fund investor may experience significant fluctuation in the value of his or her shares during the course of a trading day. In addition, mutual fund managers must make redemption of shares in cash and not with additional stock or property in-kind.

Types of Mutual Funds

As noted earlier, today there are over 15,000 different mutual funds that are available to investors. All may be segregated according to the investment objective of the fund as well as the size of companies in whose securities the funds invest (for example, small, midsize, or large market capitalization stocks). The most common types of mutual funds based on their respective investment objectives are:

1. **Growth Fund:** A fund that primarily invests in securities that, in turn, offer potentially significant capital appreciation (that is, an increasing share price that is in excess of other securities). A subcategory of this type of fund is an *aggressive growth fund* investing in securities of considerable risk, but also offering the possibility of maximum capital appreciation.

2. **Income Fund:** A fund that specializes in securities that pay higher-than-average dividends (if investing in stocks) or frequently invest a high percentage of their assets in bonds.

3. **Growth and Income Fund:** A fund that invests in securities offering potentially increasing value. You should note that this type of fund is primarily interested in *value stocks* or stocks that are underpriced relative to a stock that exhibits similar risk and return characteristics.

4. **Balanced Fund:** A fund that is relatively conservative when it comes to investing in common stock; accordingly, the fund has as its primary objective the preservation of an investor's capital and moderate growth of income and principal. Usually, a balanced fund diversifies its investments among both stocks and bonds and may provide its investors with greater protection during market downturns.

5. **Tax Exempt (or Municipal Bond) Fund:** A fund that operates principally to provide high income tax bracket taxpayers with significant after-tax returns. Such fund generally limits its investments to municipal securities or other types of issues providing tax-sheltered income.

6. **Money Market Fund:** A (typically) no load fund that invests exclusively in short-term (money market) investments such as Treasury bills, corporate commercial paper, and high-grade certificates of deposit (CDs). Money market funds are known for their relative safety and ability to provide immediate liquidity to the investor.

7. **Bond Fund:** A fund that invests only in (typically) investment grade bonds. The fund possesses several advantages over a direct investment in bonds, most notably that fund investors have a greater chance of optimizing their rate of return due to their ability to reinvest any distributions as they are received. In addition, a bond mutual fund offers greater liquidity since an investor may take money out of a no load fund without incurring excessive unfavorable bond price changes. It should be noted that investors own shares in the fund and not the underlying bonds in the fund. Share value reflects total return and is subject to greater fluctuation than a buy-and-hold strategy of owning the bonds outright.

8. **High Yield Fund:** A bond fund that invests in non-investment grade bonds (BBB or lower). There is greater potential income associated with such a fund, but also an assumption of greater risk. Usually, this type of fund is easily identified since the term "high yield" is in the name of the fund. The fund can also invest in international bonds if so permitted by the fund's prospectus.

9. **Sector Fund:** A fund that restricts its investments to a particular sector of the market, such as energy or health care. Such a fund tends to be more volatile than a more diversified fund and/or portfolio.

10. **Asset Allocation Fund:** A fund that is created to provide diversification in asset categories not traditionally offered by conventional mutual funds. Specifically, the fund invests not only in the traditional asset categories of stocks and bonds, but also the nontraditional asset categories of foreign stocks and bonds, real estate securities, and commodities. Also, an asset allocation fund may invest in money market securities to manage investor risk.

11. **Commodity Fund:** A fund that is designed to allow the small investor to invest in the commodities market, such as oil and gas. Usually, this type of fund is organized as a limited partnership, a type of professionally managed asset that will be discussed later in this chapter.

12. **Global Equity Fund:** A fund that invests in securities that are traded worldwide, including those of U.S. issue.

13. **International Equity Fund:** A fund that invests in securities of companies that are located outside the U.S. (in other words, unlike a global equity fund, securities of companies based in the U.S. are *not* included.)

14. **Hedge Fund:** A fund (currently unregulated for the most part) that uses the most aggressive investment techniques, including high leverage and *selling short* (selling assets not held, with the intent of buying them back in the future at a lower price to cover the short position). In addition, options may be used to achieve the maximum growth of principal. Such a fund is usually restricted to wealthy investors and institutions, and for those investors who are willing to assume some amount of speculative risk. Because of the growing importance of hedge funds, they are given additional attention later in this chapter.

Index Funds

Index funds are mutual funds that try to replicate (or match) the performance of a particular market index (such as the Russell 2000 index of small capitalization growth stocks). For example, the Vanguard 500 Index Fund (currently the largest mutual fund in terms of invested dollars) seeks to provide investment results that track or correspond to the price performance of publicly traded stocks as represented by the Standard & Poor's index of 500 stocks. There are approximately 700 index funds in the marketplace today.

Index funds implement what is known as a *passive management* or *passive investor* technique, since the investor only wants to achieve the same rate of return as the market index that is used as a benchmark (less trading and management fees). As such, they differ from the majority of other mutual funds, which employ *active management* in an attempt to outperform the benchmark index or broader secondary market. Studies have shown, however, that, on average, approximately 75 percent of all actively managed, common stock growth mutual funds fail to outperform the Standard & Poor's index of 500 stocks. According to market experts, this is due primarily to four factors:

1) Management costs that are associated with the traditional mutual fund

2) The *turnover* of assets that occur with the buying and selling of securities in a mutual fund, thereby adding to transaction and tax costs that the investor must assume

3) A failure to be positioned within the correct market sector at the correct time and

4) The necessary amount of cash reserves that are to be kept by the traditional mutual fund manager to fulfill investor redemptions.

Index funds also possess several disadvantages. First, the investor cannot diversify away the same market risk that bedevils all publicly traded securities. This risk is, of course, magnified if the index fund attempts to track a benchmark index that is currently out of favor with investors. Second, some of the newer market entries into the index fund market are misleading in that some active management techniques are followed. Third, and probably most important, the investor in a mutual fund sacrifices all potential for a return in excess of the benchmark index that an excellent professional money manager may be able to achieve.

Mutual Funds vs. Variable Annuities

A long-running controversy among investment professionals is to answer the question: Which are preferable, mutual funds or variable annuities?

A *variable annuity* (VA) is an insurance product that permits the owner to invest in a family of mutual funds with the purpose of accumulating (usually) tax-deferred savings, typically for retirement. The amount available for distribution is, in turn, contingent on the performance of the mutual funds selected. Normally, as an insurance product, variable annuities guarantee that the owner's beneficiary will never receive less than the sum of the periodic contributions, should the owner die before the annuity starting date. In addition, variable annuities may exhibit lower levels of stock market and total risk than the market as a whole, given their minimum guarantee.

Specifically, let us compare variable annuities (VAs) to mutual funds (MFs) with respect to a number of important issues:

1) **Fees:** VAs normally charge higher maintenance fees than a mutual fund. This is in part because VAs must provide for the risk of the owner's death in the form of mortality charges.

2) **Liquidity:** The VA is usually less liquid than the MF since it includes surrender expenses that are charged in the first few years of the contract. These surrender charges are

presumably there to encourage the owner of the VA to treat the annuity as a longer term investment and to recover the initial costs of marketing the investment (similar to the *load* sales charge that exists with some mutual funds).

3) **Death Benefit:** As an insurance product, the VA usually offers a guaranteed death benefit,to the designated beneficiary of the contract.

4) **Annuitization Option:** Only the VA can offer this distribution option, which essentially guarantees that the owner cannot outlive his or her invested funds. A mutual fund does not offer this contract advantage.

5) **Income Taxes:** The VA features, in most instances, tax-deferred earnings. However, once these earnings are withdrawn, they are taxable at ordinary income tax rates and, if taken before the owner attains age 59.5, a 10 percent penalty is also imposed. In contrast, the MF does not afford a deferral of taxes on earnings (taxes on dividends and capital gains are imposed annually), but when the MF shares are sold, any profits are taxable as capital gains. Additionally, since passage of the 2003 Tax Act (JGTRRA), dividends from MFs are likely to be *qualified*, thus enjoying a taxable rate preference, an opportunity that is not available to earnings generated from a VA.

6) **Estate Implications:** Finally, MF shares are permitted a step-up in basis at the shareholder's death. This means that the estate's heirs will receive the MF shares as if they had been purchased on the date of death of the deceased shareholder, a fact that can substantially reduce any income tax bill on the subsequent sale of any appreciated shares. VAs do *not* provide a basis step-up and, rather, constitute *income in respect of a decedent* (IRD) resulting in a lower inherited basis and, potentially, more income taxes to be paid by the heirs of the estate.

In summary, variable annuities likely provide a more favorable investment opportunity for an investor who intends to use the investment vehicle for retirement and who expects to be in a *lower* marginal income tax bracket during the distribution phase than when accumulating the savings. In contrast, mutual funds provide an effective savings and diversification vehicle for the small investor and particularly one who anticipates part-time employment during retirement and/or the same or *higher* tax bracket during retirement. Mutual funds may also be preferable for someone who is not interested in providing a death benefit to heirs or for someone who wants to provide his or her heirs with potentially significant income tax benefits.

CLOSED-END INVESTMENT COMPANIES

Closed-end investment companies stand in marked contrast to open-end mutual funds. Closed-end funds do not buy and sell (or redeem) their own shares. Rather, these funds have a one-time stock issuance and then close their books. *No* new shares are issued. The shares that are the subject of the initial capitalization then trade on the secondary market at a discount or premium to net asset value

(NAV) similar to any other negotiable security. The funds may be listed on the organized stock exchanges (such as the New York Stock Exchange) or traded in the over-the-counter market among broker-dealers. The assets are professionally managed in accordance with the fund's investment objectives and policies.

Closed-end fund structures are often used for portfolios of *illiquid* securities (for example, bonds). If these illiquid securities were purchased by an open-end mutual fund, and if investors sought to redeem those shares, then the mutual fund would be forced to liquidate the holdings of the portfolio, possibly at an unfavorable time. This is avoided with a closed-end fund, which can more easily structure when the illiquid securities are to be sold, since the request for investor redemption is not an issue. In addition, if the investor in a closed-end fund wishes to liquidate his or her shares, they must be sold in the open market, just like any other stock, at the prevailing price.

The market value of closed-end company shares is closely related to the potential return on the investment. However, as noted, this market value typically is *not* the net asset value (NAV) per share, but may be above or below this value, depending on the demand and the supply of shares in the secondary market. If the market price is *below* the net asset value of the shares, the shares are selling at a *discount* (similar to the market price of a bond that is selling below par), whereas if the market price is *above* the net asset value, the shares are selling at a *premium*.

UNIT INVESTMENT TRUSTS (UITs)

A variation on the closed-end investment company is the fixed unit investment trust, also known as a *unit investment trust* (UIT). These trusts are unmanaged and are funded with fixed income securities (such as bonds) put together by a broker-dealer and titled in the name (usually) of an independent trustee. An example of such a trust is Merrill Lynch's Government Securities Income Fund, which invests solely in U.S. Treasury securities that are a direct guarantee of the federal government.

A unit investment trust is a *passive* investment, since its assets are not actively traded but are held within the trust. Like a closed-end fund, no new securities are purchased and the securities that are originally bought are rarely sold. The trust collects income (for example, interest income on its bond portfolio) and, eventually, the repayment of principal. The trust is self-liquidating because as the income and principal is received from the trust's investments, they are *not* reinvested but are distributed to the unit holders. Such trust is particularly attractive to retiree investors who seek a steady, predictable flow of income. Further, if the investor needs additional monies, the units may be sold back to (redeemed by) the trust at their current net asset value (NAV). It is also possible to find a secondary market for UITs among other broker-dealers.

UITs do have several disadvantages, however. First, the investor must pay a rather sizeable up-front fee of 3 to 5 percent when the trust is formed and then pay for trustee fees out of trust earnings. In addition, while the trust may acquire high-quality securities (such as investment grade bonds), these securities (other than Treasury securities) are not without default risk. Finally, there is also the risk that the realized return on the fixed income security may be less than anticipated by the investor.

Participating UITs

A *participating unit investment trust* (PUIT) invests in the shares of a management company—specifically mutual fund shares. This is in contrast to the normal form of UIT that invests only in fixed income assets. Participating trust structures are frequently used when investors buy variable annuity contracts.

EXCHANGE TRADED FUNDS (ETFs)

As a preliminary note, *exchange traded funds* (ETFs) should be distinguished from *exchange funds* that are used in managing concentrated stock portfolios. Exchange funds allow investors to achieve greater diversification and lower the risk of holding a significant investment in a single security, often employer stock. As a result, if investors own securities with a low tax basis, exchange funds permit an exchange of these securities for shares in a limited partnership or limited liability company (LLC) *without* causing a taxable event. In an exchange fund, the minimum investment is usually $1.0 million and investors must be *accredited* (see previous discussion on private placements).

In contrast to an exchange fund, an *exchange traded fund* (ETF) is simply a security representing a basket of stocks or bonds and is more like a mutual fund. However, unlike a mutual fund and like an individual stock, ETFs are priced and traded throughout the day using market or limit orders. Further, like an index fund, ETFs also attempt to track a broad group of stocks from different industries and market sectors. They bear brand names such as SPDRs (*spiders*), HOLDRs, Ishares, and VIPERs. *All* of them are *passively managed,* correlating to a wide variety of sector-specific and broad-market indexes. Finally, unlike mutual funds, *stocks* may be distributed to ETF shareholders for redemption (instead of selling the securities), thus minimizing any taxable gains. This benefit also applies when stocks are removed from the particular index.

Another advantage of ETFs is their lower expense ratios and lack of an up-front sales load. They generally do not have a manager or analyst actively managing the portfolio; thus, their management fees are less. According to Morningstar, Inc., the average ETF has an expense ratio of 0.42% of assets annually, compared with an average expense ratio of 0.86% for index funds and 1.41% for actively managed mutual funds. However, as with stocks, investors must pay a commission to buy and sell ETF shares, which may be a disadvantage for those with small sums of money to invest. In such cases, the savings on ETF's management costs may quickly be erased by the trading costs, making mutual funds a potentially preferable option.

Who should use ETFs as part of their investment portfolio? Specifically, those investors who want to invest in an industry sector or index and do not wish to manage a multitude of stocks or mutual funds. ETFs will also be of interest to investors who want a low cost, tax-efficient portfolio or fund since they have greater control over when a taxable event will be recognized. Finally, investors in, for example, self-directed 401(k) plans may find ETFs attractive because of their low cost. However, this last advantage should be balanced against the possibility of *dollar cost averaging* that is used by many investors (see Chapter 15). Such investors, who make periodic regular investments, are likely to favor plain vanilla mutual funds over ETFs since investors avoid the commissions that add up quickly with ETF purchases. For example, if a broker charges $10 per transaction in an ETF and an investor is periodically purchasing $300 of shares per month, the commissions alone will cost the investor 3 percent of the investment. This is much greater than the cost of investing periodically in a mutual fund.

HEDGE FUNDS

According to Barron's *Dictionary of Investment and Financial Terms*, hedge funds are "Private investment partnerships (for U.S. investors) or offshore investment corporations (for non-U.S. or tax-exempt investors) in which the general partner has made a considerable private investment, and whose offering memorandum allows for the fund to take both long and short positions, use leverage and derivatives, and invest in many markets."

Hedge funds significantly weight fund managers' compensation towards performance incentives, whereas mutual fund managers are typically remunerated according to the volume of assets managed, regardless of performance. In addition, unlike many mutual fund managers, hedge fund managers are also usually heavily invested in a substantial portion of the funds that they manage and share the rewards as well as the risks with the investors. As a result, hedge funds tend to attract highly skilled and experienced portfolio managers and investors of some experience and considerable net worth. For example, many endowments and pension funds (*institutions*) currently allocate considerable assets to hedge funds.

In recent years, the number of hedge funds has increased considerably as has the number of dollars invested in such funds. As the number of funds has risen, so have the investment strategies that are used. Some hedge funds today use considerable leverage and derivatives, while others are more conservative and employ little or no leverage. The performance of many hedge fund strategies is not dependent at all on the direction of the stock (equity) or bond markets, but rather only on the result of the investment strategy that is pursued. This, of course, is unlike conventional mutual funds or even exchange traded funds (ETFs), which are generally 100 percent exposed to market risk. However, some hedge fund strategies are limited with respect to how much investors' capital they can successfully employ before the rates of return diminish. As a result, many successful hedge fund managers *limit* the amount of capital (invested dollars) that they will accept.

An investor of considerable means who is most interested in managing the risk of possible loss from his or her (its) investment is the most likely type of investor in a hedge fund. In addition, an investor who is very concerned about the skill and expertise of the portfolio manager should strongly consider contributing to a hedge fund. Conversely, such a fund is usually beyond the financial means of the smaller investor who is looking for capital growth or current income, the two primary investment objectives of mutual fund shareholders.

PRIVATELY MANAGED ACCOUNTS

A privately managed account is an account comprised of a diversified portfolio of individual securities managed by an institutional portfolio manager. In such an account, the investor owns 100 percent of the securities in the portfolio, rather than only a small percentage of the total as in a mutual fund. Investment restrictions may be added to avoid duplicating securities held in other managed accounts or to avoid certain stocks or industries for so-called *socially conscious investors* (for example, tobacco or gambling stocks). Large investment minimums have also historically applied to the establishment of a privately managed account.

There are both tax and management advantages associated with a privately managed account. From a tax standpoint, tax-sensitive investors (normally higher income tax bracket taxpayers) benefit from a portfolio manager who utilizes strategies designed for maximum after-tax performance. In addition, since the investor determines when the securities in the portfolio are sold, he or she controls when a taxable event will be incurred. In the typical mutual fund, since all capital gain distributions are passed through to the shareholders, the portfolio manager makes the taxable event determination.

There also is no "herd effect" associated with a privately managed account. That is, a longer term investor (sometimes referred to as a *buy and hold* investor) will *not* be affected by the redemptions of shorter term investors during a volatile market period. Thus, the portfolio manager in a private account does not have to maintain or "hold back" any cash in reserve to meet the short term redemptions frequently demanded by the "herd" in the standard mutual fund offering.

Privately managed accounts are also used in transitioning an investor with large concentrated stock holdings in one company or industry to a better-rounded, diversified portfolio.

SEPARATELY MANAGED ACCOUNTS

In many respects, the term *separately managed account* has the same characteristics as a *privately managed account*. Indeed, both are types of fee-based, managed accounts where the investor owns 100% of the securities in the account and the investment decisions are made by a professional money manager. Different broker-dealers may have their own names for their products—though the products themselves are very similar. However, both separately managed and privately managed accounts differ from mutual funds, in that the professional manager is purchasing the securities in the portfolio on behalf of the private investor and *not* on behalf of the fund. Finally, both types of accounts provide for popular *taxable gain/loss harvesting*, which is a technique for minimizing the investor's tax liability through the selective realization of gains and losses in the individual account.

Let us review an example of how a separately managed account is structured.

> **Example 4-1:** ABC Mutual Fund holds shares of two companies: Company X and Company Y. You purchase 100 shares of ABC Mutual Fund. Therefore, in the traditional *mutual fund* purchase, you own 100 shares of ABC Mutual Fund; you do *not* own any shares of either Company X or Company Y. However, if you invest in a *separate account*, the private money (portfolio) manager for that account purchases shares of *each* of those companies on your behalf. Your account is separate and distinct from that of any other investor.

The ability to maintain an *individual cost* basis in a separate account is key to the management of one's income tax liability. This can be a significant benefit for high net worth investors. Consider, for example, a separate account where the investor has purchased two securities over time at similar prices. One of the securities has doubled in value (100 percent) while the other has fallen by 50 percent. By instructing the portfolio manager to sell both securities, the gains generated by the security that has increased in value may be offset by the losses from the security that has declined in value, thereby minimizing or even eliminating any capital gains tax liability. Conversely, this advantage is not available to the mutual fund shareholder.

LIMITED PARTNERSHIPS

A *limited partnership* is a type of partnership that limits the liability of the partner to only the amount of capital that he or she has contributed to the partnership. In the typical limited partnership, one general partner manages the business (and assumes all liability for the acts of the business), while the limited partners only contribute capital and share in the partnership's profits and losses. In other words, the general partner contributes services to the partnership and the limited partner (or partners) provides the money. As such, the form of business organization operates quite easily as a capital-raising device and opportunity for outside investors to participate in a potentially profitable business opportunity.

There are several different forms of limited partnerships, some of which (because of their tax implications and interrelationship with the so-called *passive loss* rules) are discussed again in Kaplan University's *Individual Income Tax Planning* textbook by Mershon and Fevurly. The different forms of limited partnerships include a:

1) **Public Limited Partnership** (also known as a *Public Reporting Limited Partnership*): A limited partnership that is registered with the SEC and offered to the general public through broker-dealers; such partnership does not trade on an exchange and therefore has both limited marketability and limited liquidity.

2) **Master Limited Partnership (MLP):** A limited partnership that is registered with the SEC and trades on an exchange; an investment that combines the tax benefits of a limited partnership with the marketability of publicly traded companies.

3) **Private Limited Partnership:** A limited partnership that has *not* registered with the SEC and is *not* traded on an exchange; by law, such form of partnership is limited to no more than 35 limited partners.

4) **Venture Capital Limited Partnership:** A limited partnership that is formed by a venture capital firm to invest in small start-up businesses.

Typically, two types of investment activities—commercial real estate development or rental activities and oil and gas companies—lend themselves to the limited partnership form. Therefore, the form is most suitable for an investor who wants to invest in those types of businesses, but lacks the knowledge or experience to take an active role in the management of the business. Further, the form permits a pooling of investor resources whereby investors can combine capital and obtain a level of diversification and risk reduction that they could not achieve individually. For example, a limited partnership may be able to invest in numerous commercial development properties that the individual may either not know about because of geographical limitations, or not be comfortable with, if assuming the investment risk alone.

The major disadvantage to the limited partnership form is (with the exception of an MLP) the *lack of* inherent marketability and liquidity of the underlying investment. Some partnerships have arrangements whereby investors may offer their interest for sale to the other limited partners, or general partner, but there is still no guarantee of a willing buyer. Also, if the investment activity has not developed as anticipated (for example, a commercial office building is built, but not yet fully occupied), the other partners may purchase the interest, but at a reduced price. Finally, in most instances, a limited partnership is usually highly *leveraged*, meaning that the partnership is using borrowed funds to finance its investment activities. While this leverage will magnify any capital gains if the partnership's investments have done well, it also magnifies the potential for significant losses of the limited or general partner.

In summary, limited partnership investments tend to be relatively risky and generally *unsuitable* for the average investor. Alternatively, mutual funds and/or exchange traded funds (ETFs) offer investors many of the same advantages of limited partnerships, including diversification and professional management, but without as much marketability or liquidity risk.

IMPORTANT CONCEPTS

Open-end investment company (mutual fund)

Net asset value (NAV)

Growth fund

Income fund

Growth and income fund

Balanced fund

Tax exempt fund

Money market fund

Global equity fund

International equity fund

Hedge fund

Index fund

Passive management

Variable annuity

Closed-end investment company

Unit investment trust (UIT)

Participating UIT

Exchange traded fund (ETF)

Exchange fund

Privately managed account

Separately managed account

Limited partnership

Master limited partnership (MLP)

QUESTIONS FOR REVIEW

1. Why is a *mutual fund* referred to as an open-end investment company?

2. What is the primary difference between a *no load* and a *load* mutual fund?

3. What is a *wrap account* and how does a broker-dealer (or investment advisor) normally charge for assets under management (AUM) in such an account?

4. How (at what price) does a mutual fund trade on the secondary market?

5. If a small investor is interested in a mutual fund that primarily offers the chance for significant capital appreciation, in what type of mutual fund should he or she invest?

6. What is a *balanced fund*?

7. What is the primary use of a money market mutual fund for many investors?

8. What is a notable advantage of investing in a bond fund instead of investing directly in corporate bonds?

9. What is the difference between a *global equity fund* and an *international equity fund*?

10. What is an *index fund*? What types of investors are primarily interested in such a fund?

11. Define what is meant by the term *turnover of assets* within a mutual fund. Why should a potential investor be interested in this?

12. Contrast a variable annuity (VA) to a mutual fund (MF) regarding each of the six factors noted in the chapter. In summary, when is each of these investment vehicles most likely suitable?

13. Contrast a closed-end investment company to that of an open-end investment company.

14. What types of securities are normally offered by a closed-end investment company? Why?

15. How (at what price) does a closed-end fund trade on the secondary market?

16. What is a *unit investment trust* (UIT)? What types of investors are usually interested in this form of managed asset?

17. Contrast an exchange fund with an exchange traded fund (ETF). When (in what situation) is an exchange fund used?

18. What is an exchange traded fund (ETF) and how does it compare to a traditional mutual fund? Who should use an ETF as part of his or her investment portfolio? Why?

19. What is the textbook definition of a *hedge*? How is this concept applied in a *hedge fund*?

20. What types of investment strategies do most hedge fund managers use?

21. List one tax advantage and one management advantage associated with a privately managed account.

22. Define the term *tax harvesting*. What type(s) of investment accounts provide for this?

23. What are four types of limited partnerships? Which of these is publicly traded?

24. What two types of investment activities have historically lent themselves to being operated in the limited partnership form?

25. Is a limited partnership generally suitable for the average investor and why or why not?

SUGGESTIONS FOR ADDITIONAL READING

Tools and Techniques of Investment Planning, 2nd edition, Stephen R. Leimberg, Robert T. LeClair, Robert J. Doyle, Jr., and Thomas R. Robinson, The National Underwriter Company, 2006.

Investments: An Introduction, 9th edition, Herbert B. Mayo, Thomson/ South-Western, 2008.

Investment Analysis and Portfolio Management, 9th edition, Frank K. Reilly and Keith C. Brown, Thomson/South-Western, 2009.

The Wall Street Journal Guide to Money and Investing, 3rd edition, Kenneth M. Morris and Virginia B. Morris, Fireside Publishing, 2004.

Dictionary of Finance and Investment Terms, 6th edition, Downes and Goodman, Barron's, 2003.

CHAPTER FIVE

Insurance-Based Investments

• • •

In recent years, the insurance industry has offered products that include enhanced investment features. Among these are variable products, such as variable life insurance and variable annuities that invest in the securities market. These products go beyond the traditional or standard *whole life* form of life insurance policy that has dominated the insurance market for many years.

Upon completing this chapter, you should be able to:

- Explain issues that bear on the life insurance versus investment determination and why this is important
- Describe the characteristics and uses of variable life insurance products
- Analyze when the use of an annuity may be appropriate in investment planning
- Define a *guaranteed investment contract* (GIC)

LIFE INSURANCE VS. INVESTMENTS

An ongoing question for regulators, particularly the IRS, is: When is an asset purchase considered to be an insurance contract and when is it considered to be an investment? This is important primarily because the taxation of life insurance, notably the income tax free nature of the life insurance death benefit, *differs* from that of an investment. Unfortunately, a clear answer to this question may not be gleaned from the intent of the individual when purchasing an asset or contract. Many individuals are interested in a cash value type of life insurance contract as an investment, specifically because it also provides for a tax-deferred accumulation of lifetime earnings. These earnings may subsequently be used to assist in meeting a financial planning and/or investment goal of the individual, such as retirement.

An asset purchase must satisfy a technical definition in Internal Revenue Code (IRC) Section 7702 (a) if it is to be treated, for income tax purposes, as *life insurance*. Specifically, the contract must meet either a *cash accumulation test* (normally applied to traditional whole life policies) or a *guideline premium and cash value corridor test* (normally applied to universal life contracts). A variable life insurance contract must meet either of these previous tests *plus* meet the definition of a variable life contract, including diversification requirements under IRC Section 817(h). While the particulars of any of these tests are beyond the scope of this book, it is worth noting that if they are *not* met, the policy will instead be taxed as an *investment*. What does this mean? Primarily, it means that:

1) The periodic increase in the cash value of the contract (the cash value *inside build up*), if any, is taxable *annually* at ordinary income rates

2) Any distributions made from the contract in the form of dividends to the policyholder are taxable *annually* at ordinary income rates (similar to that of a dividend from a stock or mutual fund but *without* being considered as *qualified* for preferential rates); and

3) The income tax free nature of the death benefit or face amount to the policy beneficiary (or beneficiaries) is *lost*, meaning that the death benefits are fully taxable as ordinary income to the beneficiary of the policy.

Let us look at each of these taxable consequences in a bit more detail.

Cash Value Inside Build Up

If a contract is treated as life insurance and not as an investment, the general rule is that the annual cash value increase is *not* subject to current income tax. Further, a life insurance policy holder may withdraw amounts from the contract up to his or her basis (generally premiums paid minus any dividends paid) *tax-free* before any gain is realized. This, of course, means that loans from a life insurance policy are typically *not* subject to immediate taxation (the notable exception to this being a policy that is considered to be a *modified endowment contract* or MEC).

In contrast, an investment enjoys no such preferential method of taxation. Specifically, capital appreciation in the invested asset is *realized* each year. However, whether this appreciation is *recognized* for income tax purposes depends on whether the investor sells or otherwise disposes of the asset. Whether this appreciation or capital gain is taxable as a short term or as a long term gain depends on how long the investor has owned (or *held*) the asset. If the invested asset has been held for one year or less, the gain is taxable at ordinary income tax rates; whereas, if held for more than one year, the gain enjoys a lower *long-term capital gains* rate of no more than (currently) 15 percent.

Dividends

The general rule is that dividends paid on a participating life insurance contract are a return of capital and *not includible* in gross income. (Note that a participating contract is one that has historically been underwritten by a *mutual* life insurance company—versus a *stock* life insurance company.) There are usually several different dividend options available with any whole life insurance policy, but all result in the general exclusion of life insurance dividends from current income taxation (again, the notable exception to this rule is dividends payable from a *MEC*, which are taxable upon receipt).

In contrast, the dividends from an investment (notably a stock) are currently taxable as ordinary income. Under the Tax Act of 2003 (JGTRRA), *qualified dividend income* (generally, dividends paid by domestic corporations and certain foreign corporations) is treated as net capital gain and is, therefore, subject to lower tax rates. However, such dividends, representing corporate earnings, are not only still taxable to the shareholder, but the payor corporation also does not receive an income tax deduction for the same. This, in turn, leads to the concept of *double taxation* of earnings that is so frequently noted as a disadvantage of the regular corporate form of business organization.

Death Benefit

Of course, the payment of a death benefit to the beneficiaries of the insured is the essence of a life insurance policy. Under IRC Section 101 (a) (1), this benefit is generally excludible from the taxable income of the beneficiary (or beneficiaries). Like most provisions in the income tax law, there is also an exception to this result (referred to as the *transfer for value rule*), but so long as the life insurance policy is not sold to another for more than the premiums already paid by the contract owner, the insurance proceeds are non-taxable. Finally, income taxes are never due if the life insurance policy actually matures as a death benefit and the proceeds are used to repay any lifetime loans made from the policy.

There is nothing similar in the taxation of investments. Indeed, in most cases, the tax attributes of an investment die with the owner. That is if the beneficiaries of the investor are to receive any benefit, an investment must typically first be liquidated (converted to cash) and then subsequently reinvested by the new owner/beneficiary. There is some advantage provided to the beneficiary in the form of an investment basis that is *stepped up* to the fair market value at the decedent/owner's death, but this is not the same consequence as the complete exclusion of life insurance proceeds from income taxation at the death of the insured. Accordingly, unlike life insurance that is primarily purchased for *death motivated* reasons, an investment is purchased first and foremost because of its potential for significant growth (or capital appreciation) during an individual's *lifetime*.

VARIABLE AND VARIABLE UNIVERSAL LIFE (VUL)

While there are several different types of cash value (or *permanent*) life insurance policies, only variable and variable universal life (VUL) require that the *producer* (life insurance professional) must also maintain a securities license. Variable life insurance combines traditional permanent insurance with mutual-fund type investments and allows the policy owner to direct the investment of cash values among a variety of different investments. Many companies that market variable life insurance policies offer a broad choice of investment options such as growth mutual funds, bond funds, real estate funds, and sector funds. Variable universal life (VUL) insurance takes this concept one step further and also offers owners the advantage of flexible lifetime premiums and a greater certainty of a minimum death benefit payable from the policy.

Variable life has a guaranteed minimum face amount and a fixed, level premium like traditional whole life insurance, but differs from whole life in the following ways:

1) The policy owner's funds are placed in a separate account that is segregated from that of the company's general investment fund; in turn, this means that, in the event of financial instability of the underwriting company, the policy owner achieves some level of individual creditor protection not possible in a whole life policy.

2) There is *no* minimum guaranteed cash value. The cash value in a variable policy is based on the market value of the assets in the separate account; accordingly, variable life policy owners bear *all* of the investment risk associated with the policy. This is in contrast to a whole life policy where the investment risk is borne by the insurer or insurance company.

3) The death benefit is *variable*, meaning that it may increase or decrease, but not below the guaranteed minimum, based on a specified formula relating the investment performance of the separate account to the policy's face value. Alternatively, the death benefit in a whole life policy is *fixed* in value.

A variable life insurance policy is most suitable for those individuals who desire control over the amount of cash value that is accumulated in their policy and who want the possibility of increasing life insurance protection. However, these individuals should have a basic understanding of investments and believe that they are capable of making good investment decisions. They should also be aware that the growth of the death benefit in the policy (since it is tied to a formula reflecting the performance of the underlying cash value) is by no means assured and, therefore, a temporarily depressed death benefit level when the insured dies is a distinct possibility.

Variable universal life (VUL) is a combination of a universal and variable life insurance policy. Specifically, it is possible for VUL policy owners to:

1) Determine the amount and timing of premium payments

2) Adjust the amount of the policy's death benefit in response to changing needs

3) Withdraw money from the policy without an interest charge if there is sufficient cash value to cover already-assumed mortality and expense charges

The death benefit of a VUL policy is not *variable* in the same sense as the death benefit of a variable life policy. Rather, the policy owner may typically choose between two death benefit options. Under Option A, the death benefit of the policy remains *level*, similar to a traditional whole life policy. Under Option B, the death benefit is equal to a level pure insurance (or mortality) amount *plus* a cash value portion that is determined by formula. Therefore, the death benefit *increases* as the cash value grows. Usually, the policy also permits the policy owner to increase the face value (death benefit) even further by providing subsequent evidence of insurability.

A VUL policy is especially suitable as a supplement to an existing life insurance plan that features a minimum required base level of coverage. It is less suitable, however, as a means of providing such base level coverage. Rather, term or whole life may be a better alternative as a first life insurance policy purchase. In addition, VUL is particularly attractive where an individual is a self directed investor and believes that he or she can generate a cash value in excess of that possible by the issuing company and its portfolio managers. Finally, the investor should be willing to consider accessing that cash value for the satisfaction of certain lifetime financial goals, such as retirement or the providing of higher education for the investor's children or spouse.

ANNUITIES

There are almost as many ways to classify annuities as there are annuity products. For example, annuities may be classified by: (1) the number of lives covered (single or joint); (2) when the benefit payments commence (immediate or deferred); (3) the method of premium payment (single payment or over time); (4) the settlement options offered by the annuity (pure life, pure life with a period certain, pure life with a refund provision, or joint and survivor); or (5) the type of annuity payment (fixed or variable). However, as an insurance-based investment product, we will concentrate on how the earnings within an annuity are accumulated, that is either in a specified or *fixed* amount or in a fluctuating or *variable* amount.

Annuities are the *only* investment vehicle that can guarantee investors that they will *not* outlive their income. An annuity is a contract offered by an insurance company where the investor makes an up front cash payment—either single or multiple—in return for the company agreeing to pay the owner a specified amount periodically on a specified date. The money that is paid up front to the insurance company is invested by it and is periodically credited with some type of interest or growth factor—this is known as the *accumulation phase* of the annuity. So long as the owner of the annuity is an individual (and not a non-natural person, such as a corporation), the growth or earnings portion of the annuity grows on a tax-deferred basis. Indeed, no income tax is payable on the earnings until the *earlier of:* (a) the surrender of the contract; (b) withdrawal from the contract; or (c) the time that payments under the annuity begin (commonly referred to as *annuitization*). Classification as a fixed or variable annuity refers to the underlying investments during the annuity's accumulation phase; a *fixed* annuity is invested in the general fixed account of the insurance company, whereas a *variable* annuity is invested in separately managed sub-accounts selected by the annuity owner.

Annuities grow tax-deferred during their accumulation phase, although withdrawals of invested funds by the owner during this phase are taxed on a LIFO (last in, first out) basis. This means that withdrawals are considered to come first from any growth of or earnings generated by the annuity (and are thus fully taxable), and subsequently from any non-taxable principal. Payments made from the annuity during the *distribution* or *payout phase* are considered to be split. That is, a portion of each payment is considered to be paid from non-taxable principal and another portion represents interest or growth on this principal and is income taxable. The proportion of each payment is determined by an income tax concept known as *the exclusion ratio*, with amounts distributed that are considered as interest or growth, taxable as ordinary income (not capital gains). In addition, certain withdrawals before the age of 59.5 may be subject to an additional 10 percent penalty. (You should note that the tax treatment just described applies to all annuities purchased from an insurance company that are *not* part of a qualified retirement plan or a so-called *non qualified annuity*; the tax treatment of annuities purchased by an employer/sponsor of a qualified retirement plan—a so-called *qualified annuity*—is separately discussed in Kaplan University's *Planning for Retirement* textbook by Jeffrey B. Mershon.)

Fixed Annuities

A combination insurance-and-investment product, the fixed annuity offers a guaranteed rate of return, tax-deferred growth, and a steady stream of income during the distribution phase of the annuity. The rate of return paid on current contributions to the annuity may be guaranteed for one year, up to as many as 10 years, but depends on the performance of the insurance company's general investment portfolio, which is usually invested in fixed income types of investments (for example, bonds). Similar to a savings account in a bank, once interest is credited to the contributions made to the annuity, the cash value will not decrease *even if* the market value of the insurance company's general investment portfolio decreases. In summary, in the fixed type of annuity, the insurance company (rather than the investor) bears the investment risk.

There are two basic kinds of fixed annuities—immediate and deferred. Approximately 90 percent of all outstanding annuity contracts are one of these two kinds. With an *immediate fixed* annuity, the investor makes a single up-front payment, in return for which he or she receives a regular monthly check for the remainder of his or her life. With a *deferred fixed* annuity, the investor either pays a large up-front premium or spreads payments over time; withdrawals then occur at a later date. In both kinds of fixed annuities, however, the investor usually earns a somewhat higher return than on traditional cash investments and also is provided with a guarantee that he or she will be paid not less than a specified, guaranteed minimum rate. Then, depending on the payout option that is chosen by the investor, the monthly checks typically last as long as the *annuitant* is alive, and sometimes longer, if the contract permits the naming of a designated beneficiary or survivor.

The primary disadvantage of the fixed annuity is just that: it provides for a *fixed, unchanging* rate of return. Therefore, the annuitant assumes the risk that the inflation rate will exceed the rate of return credited to the cash value of the contract. Current purchasers may also worry that they are locking themselves into lifetime payments while interest rates are at historic lows. Accordingly, prudent financial planning likely suggests that only a portion of an investor's total portfolio consists of a fixed annuity ($100,000 of a $500,000 portfolio, for example) with the rest divided among a diversified mix of stock and bond mutual (or exchange traded) funds. In this manner, the overall purchasing power of the investor/annuitant is likely to be preserved once he or she begins making distributions from the annuity contract.

A specialized type of fixed annuity is a *single premium deferred annuity* (SPDA), which provides, as the name implies, a promise that a payment will begin in the future in return for a single premium. The principal feature of such annuity is that earnings accumulate tax-free until distributed. In addition, so-called "bailout provisions" permit the owner to withdraw all of his or her money without the imposition of a contract surrender charge if the interest rate that is credited falls below a certain minimum amount (referred to as the *bailout rate*).

Variable Annuities

A variable annuity is based on a different method of investing the accumulated cash value. The investor/contract owner may select from a number of separate accounts that are similar to mutual fund investments with options including diversified stock, bond, and specialized (such as sector) funds. The funds in these accounts are invested separately from the other assets of the insurance company. Each year some money is taken out of the contract owner's premium (or deducted from the account value) to cover the expenses of the company, including the mortality expense that is charged based on the owner's life expectancy. The remaining balance is then applied to purchase so-called *units of credit* in the separate accounts. In contrast with fixed annuities, the accumulated cash value in a variable annuity depends on the market value of the underlying assets in the selected separate accounts, with the investor assuming the investment risk. If the separate accounts are invested poorly, the annuitant may receive fewer dollars than would have been paid under a fixed annuity.

Conceptually, variable annuities are simply mutual funds in an "insurance wrapper." They permit the tax on all income, whether ordinary or capital gain, to be deferred until any monies are actually distributed. Like any annuity, distributions from a variable annuity, if annuitized, are taxed according to the exclusion ratio concept, although this ratio is computed differently in the case of a variable annuity than in a fixed annuity. Also, and more importantly as compared to the underlying mutual funds, variable annuities offer a number of contractual guarantees to the contract owner. However, the owner may pay a heavy price for these guarantees, notably the imposition of both contract and tax surrender charges.

Most variable annuities impose contract surrender charges if any money is withdrawn within the first five to seven years of initial investment. Therefore, such annuities are really suitable only as *long term* investments, such as in saving for an investor's retirement. As a general rule, variable annuities are less attractive than mutual funds if there is any possibility that the money used to fund the annuity may be needed relatively soon. (Note: A comparison of mutual funds to variable annuities is included as part of chapter 4 of this textbook.) This is, in part, because the period of tax deferral will usually be insufficient to overcome the additional fees and surrender charges associated with the annuity. In addition, as previously noted, most distributions from an annuity—whether fixed or variable—made *prior to* the annuitant attaining age 59.5 are subject to a 10 percent penalty tax on the taxable amount withdrawn (plus ordinary income tax). A notable exception, however, to the imposition of this penalty is a distribution that is made as part of a *substantially equal periodic payment for the life of the annuitant* (otherwise known as a *Section 72 (q) distribution* after the Internal Revenue Code Section of the same number and subsection).

Equity-Indexed Annuities (EIAs)

An equity-indexed annuity (EIA) is a relatively recent insurance-based investment product. It is essentially a hybrid of the fixed and variable product and may appeal to an investor who wishes to participate in the equity (stock) market without bearing the full investment risk of a variable annuity.

The rate of return credited to the cash value of an EIA is linked to a stock market index, such as the Standard & Poor's 500 Index. However, the annuity is *not* actually invested in the stocks making up the index. Rather, like a fixed annuity, the return on an EIA is paid from the insurance company's general account. Further, the amount allocated to the EIA is based on a percentage of the appreciation in the referenced index (for example, 80%), which is then also often subject to an annual limitation or *cap*. If the equity index that is used as a benchmark declines in value, a minimum guaranteed amount is credited to the annuity, thereby providing investors with some of the upside potential of stocks, but also with the downside protection of an amount below which the investment cannot fall. Nonetheless, as the price to be paid for the benefit of eliminating these periodic market losses, investors in an EIA should be aware that the aforementioned cap placed on credited capital gains will, in turn, likely *limit* how much contract appreciation may be achieved.

GUARANTEED INVESTMENT CONTRACTS (GICs)

Guaranteed Investment Contracts (GICs) are similar to CDs issued by commercial banks, but instead the issuer is an insurance company. In general, a GIC will pay a rate of interest about 1 percent greater than a comparable maturity CD. However, unlike a CD, GICs are *not* federally insured and, therefore, despite the inclusion of the word *guaranteed* in their title, carry more risk than a federally insured CD.

The major purchasers of GICs are institutions, specifically companies that find such an investment vehicle attractive as an option in a 401(k) or pension plan for employees. Companies typically choose between either a participating or nonparticipating contract. A *participating* GIC provides the company with a variable rate of return based on interest rate changes. Alternatively, a *nonparticipating* GIC earns a fixed rate of return. The choice of whether the company purchases a participating or a nonparticipating GIC depends on its expectation of interest rates over the term of the contract (usually 2 to 5 years). If the company believes that interest rates are likely to *increase*, the purchase of a participating GIC is likely prudent, whereas a nonparticipating GIC is a better choice if interest rates are expected to *decline*.

The insurance company offering the GIC is contractually obligated to repay the principal and guaranteed interest on the instrument to the purchaser's 401(k) or other benefit plan. Since the purchaser knows when this principal and interest will be paid (that is, at the maturity date of the contract), a GIC can serve as a very effective funding vehicle for a benefit plan where the participant's normal retirement age is also known. In addition, the provisions of the benefit plan may permit the participant to withdraw funds as part of an *in service withdrawal* (see Kaplan University's separate text on *Planning for Retirement* by Mershon). Accordingly, the proceeds of the GIC may be accessed at a date prior to maturity, often times without penalty as would be the case with a traditional CD. The deposits paid to the insurance company used to fund the GIC are held in the insurer's general account; therefore the benefit plan does incur some default risk that the payment may not, in fact, be made. However, generally, only insurance companies of the highest quality rating (minimal default risk) issue GICs.

IMPORTANT CONCEPTS

Definition of life insurance

Taxation as investment

Cash value inside build up

Life insurance dividend

Death benefit

Variable life insurance

Variable universal life (VUL) insurance

Annuitization

Exclusion ratio

Last in, first out (LIFO) taxation

Fixed annuity

Immediate fixed annuity

Deferred fixed annuity

Single premium deferred annuity (SPDA)

Variable annuity

Equity-indexed annuity (EIA)

Guaranteed investment contract (GIC)

Participating GIC

Nonparticipating GIC

QUESTIONS FOR REVIEW

1. Why is it important to determine if an asset purchase is an investment or life insurance contract?

2. What is the taxable consequence if a life insurance contract does not meet the statutory definition of *life insurance*?

3. What is meant by the term cash value *inside build up*? Contrast this to how the annual earnings on an *investment* are taxed.

4. What is the general rule regarding the taxability of dividends from a life insurance contract? Contrast this to the taxation of dividends payable from a stock.

5. Are death benefits from a life insurance income taxable to the beneficiary? Explain.

6. How does a variable life insurance contract differ from that of traditional whole life?

7. Which individuals are most likely to consider variable life insurance as a potential investment?

8. What are three characteristics of variable universal life (VUL) insurance?

9. What is the *only* investment vehicle that can guarantee investors that they will *not* outlive their income?

10. When are the earnings generated from an annuity taxable? (Assume that the owner is an individual.)

11. Contrast the provisions of a fixed annuity to that of a variable annuity.

12. When does the *exclusion ratio* apply in the taxation of distributions from a *non qualified annuity*?

13. What is the difference between an immediate fixed annuity and a deferred fixed annuity?

14. What is a *single premium deferred annuity* (SPDA)?

15. What is the "price paid" for the contractual guarantees provided in a variable annuity?

16. Describe the characteristics of an *equity indexed annuity* (EIA).

17. Who typically purchases a *guaranteed insurance contract* (GIC) and for what purpose?

19. What is the difference between a participating and a nonparticipating GIC?

SUGGESTIONS FOR ADDITIONAL READING

Tools and Techniques of Investment Planning, 2nd edition, Stephen R. Leimberg, Robert T. LeClair, Robert J. Doyle, Jr., and Thomas R. Robinson, The National Underwriter Company, 2006.

Investments: An Introduction, 9th edition, Herbert B. Mayo, Thomson/ South-Western, 2008.

Investment Analysis and Portfolio Management, 9th edition, Frank K. Reilly and Keith C. Brown, Thomson/South-Western, 2009.

The Wall Street Journal Guide to Money and Investing, 3rd edition, Kenneth M. Morris and Virginia B. Morris, Fireside Publishing, 2004.

Dictionary of Finance and Investment Terms, 6th edition, Downes and Goodman, Barron's, 2003.

CHAPTER SIX

Real Estate and Real Estate Investment Trusts (REITs)

• • •

The focus of this chapter is on real estate as a potential investment and how an investor may take advantage of real property ownership beyond its use as a primary residence.

Upon completing this chapter, you should be able to:

- Describe the use of real estate as an investment
- Contrast and compare an investment in unimproved land to that of commercial and/or rental property and describe what attributes of each may be important to a potential investor
- Identify characteristics of real estate limited partnerships (RELPs)
- Explain the types of real estate investment trusts (REITs)
- Discuss features of a real estate mortgage investment conduit (REMIC) and its close cousin, the collateralized mortgage obligation (CMO)

REAL ESTATE AS AN INVESTMENT

Very broadly, some analysts categorize investments as consisting of *financial* and *real* assets. *Financial assets* include stocks and bonds and all assets that cannot be reduced to the direct or indirect ownership of real estate. *Real assets* include real estate, which may be further defined as land and the improvements (buildings) on that land. Real estate also includes natural resources, such as oil or natural gas, which are under that land. Sometimes these resources are referred to as *mineral rights* and are sold or conveyed separately from that of the land or improvements.

The distinction between financial and real assets is important because there is some evidence that the respective assets are *negatively correlated.* That is, as financial assets *decrease* in value (for example, the Dow Jones Industrial Average is down for the trading period that is analyzed), real assets may *increase* in value. Therefore, real assets may in some cases be an effective diversifier and inflation hedge when positioned within an investor's portfolio. However, the *location* of the subject real estate will be the single most important factor in determining both the direction and amount of any price movement; this is not the case with financial assets as they do not generally suffer from this same limitation. In addition, due to typical financing constraints, real estate purchases are usually more highly leveraged than those of financial assets; accordingly, the value of real estate in any given location is *highly sensitive* to interest rate changes, particularly those of longer term obligations (mortgage notes).

Finally, some degree of management is necessary with *all* real estate investments (that is, a real estate purchase that is made other than for use as a primary residence). The manager may be either the investor or, more often than not, a professional property manager or management firm. As a practical matter, this may make small real estate investments impractical for the average investor because of the associated reduction in the cash flow generated from the operation of the property.

USE AS A PRIMARY RESIDENCE

Most individuals, if they own real estate at all, purchase real property (land and any buildings thereon) for use as a primary residence or home for themselves and their family. As such, while they may think of their home as an investment (opportunity for profit), that is *not* the primary reason that they make the purchase. As a *use asset,* this is the reason that a home is shown as such on the statement of personal financial position. (Alternatively, if the residence is converted to a rental property, the asset would now be shown as an *investment* on the statement of personal financial position.) Of course, the exception to this motivation is those individuals who purchase residential real estate for rental purposes and to generate future cash flow. Rental income is reported on an individual's IRS Form 1040 on Schedule E and, in this case, the investor is entitled to claim operating expenses as well as tax depreciation over the useful life of the residence. An individual who purchases real estate for use as a *primary residence* is entitled only to a deduction for mortgage interest incurred (within limits) on IRS Form 1040 Schedule A, as well as real estate property taxes. In addition, that individual must also elect to *itemize* his or her income tax deductions. Finally, an individual may *not* generally claim a loss for income tax purposes if real property is used as a primary residence (even if the owner of that residence anticipated that his or her property would in fact appreciate and an offsetting gain would result).

UNIMPROVED LAND

Unimproved (or *raw*) land is truly a *passive* investment. As such, it generally does not generate income or tax depreciation (land is never depreciable since it is not considered to ever wear out or have a useful life). Raw land's primary source of return is the potential for price or capital appreciation. The investment is suitable mainly for high income and net worth investors who are able to bear the associated investment risk without realizing any immediate return. In fact, unimproved land may result in a short term *negative* cash flow for the investor due to the property taxes, insurance cost, and other expenses incurred in maintaining the investment.

When unimproved land is sold, it is subject to capital gains tax treatment so long as the owner is *not* considered to be a *dealer* in such land (so called *dealer tax treatment*). Dealer tax treatment will result in the gain being taxable at ordinary income tax rates to the investor. There are a number of factors that courts (and the IRS) use to distinguish between an investor and a dealer in unimproved land, but generally this determination depends on the extent of the active participation of the individual (or his or her agents) in future transactions involving the subject land. For example, if an individual buys and sells a number of different tracts of unimproved land, and subsequently subdivides that land, dealer tax treatment may apply.

Tax on the gain of unimproved land (or for that matter, any type of real estate that is held for investment purposes) may be deferred by using the installment sale method of tax accounting. These rules, as provided for in Internal Revenue Code (IRC) Section 453, permit an investor to delay reporting any gain until cash is received in a given year. Installment sales are often used as financing vehicles (particularly among family members) rather than obtaining a loan from a bank. However, just as a bank would charge interest if a loan were obtained, so also is there an expectation among the seller and purchaser in an installment sale that some amount of the agreed-upon payment is categorized as interest. Indeed, if interest is not charged (or if the rate charged is insufficient under tax law), IRC Section 483 will *impute* interest on a portion of the sale price. In addition, as long as at least one payment will be received after the close of the taxable year in which the sale is made, installment sale treatment is *automatic* and must be *elected out of* by the seller if he or she does not wish for such tax treatment to occur.

For more on the income tax consequences of property that is sold under the installment sale method of tax accounting, you are referred to Kaplan University's *Individual Income Tax Planning* textbook by Mershon and Fevurly.

COMMERCIAL AND RESIDENTIAL RENTAL PROPERTY

Real property with associated buildings (so-called *improved land*) that is held for rental purposes is the most common type of real estate purchased as an investment. The rental income generated may be derived from real property that is held for either commercial or residential purposes. The rental income is taxable as ordinary income, although the property itself is a capital asset qualifying for capital gain treatment upon sale or disposition. An individual will typically purchase either type of real property directly from the seller or through a real estate broker. This is referred to as the *outright* or *direct* ownership of real property. However, the investor may also hold such property *indirectly* by purchasing an interest in a *real estate investment trust (REIT)* or a *real estate limited partnership (RELP)*. Both of these indirect forms of real estate ownership will be subsequently discussed in this chapter.

The direct ownership of real estate does *not* limit the personal liability of the investor for acts associated with the operation of the property. For this reason, among others, a liability insurance policy is a must for the investor. A direct owner also has absolute management responsibility over the property, although an agent (property manager) may be hired to perform the daily management tasks, such as maintenance of the property and collection of rent. However, under agency law, a direct owner of real property is responsible for the negligent acts of his or her property manager if acting on the owner's behalf. This, of course, underscores the need for the property owner to evaluate the capabilities of any agent carefully before choosing him or her (or a corporation, if acting as the property manager) to manage the subject property.

Like the valuation of securities, arriving at a proper value to pay for an investment in commercial or residential income producing real property is an important determination. This proper value is sometimes referred to as the *intrinsic value* since it represents the discounted present value of the property's future cash flows. The intrinsic value of a real estate rental property may best be computed by using the *income approach* of real estate valuation.

Income Approach

The income approach applies a perpetuity discount to income-generating properties. The perpetuity is *net operating income* (NOI). NOI is the expected gross income adjusted for the estimated vacancy rate, collection losses, insurance, taxes, utilities, and maintenance and repairs associated with the property. Once determined, NOI is then divided by the market cap rate to arrive at the expected price. The market cap rate is the rate implied by benchmark NOI and transaction price from recent transactions. Financing costs are not included in the calculation; however, the appraised value should be independent of how the property transaction is financed.

The income approach can be modified to reflect constant growth in cash flow streams such as rentals coupled with long-term leases. Valuation with constant growth in rental cash flow parallels the constant growth dividend discount model.

Example 6-1: Assume that an apartment complex has projected annual gross rentals of $250,000. The estimated vacancy rate and uncollectables is 5 percent of these rentals. Utilities are $20,000 per year, property tax and insurance is $120,000 per year, and repairs and maintenance are $15,000 per year. The benchmark cap rate for similar investment properties is 12 percent. Thus, the estimated valuation of the property using the income approach is:

NOI = $250,000 – ($250,000 x 0.05) - $20,000 - $120,000 - $15,000 = $82,500

$82,500/0.12 = $687,500

The estimated value using the income approach for the apartment complex is $687,500.

Discounted After-Tax Cash Flow Approach

An extension of the income approach occurs if the investor can deduct interest expense and depreciation from NOI. In this case, the investor's marginal tax rate influences the appraised value of the income property. The discounted after-tax cash flow approach adjusts NOI for depreciation and interest expense.

Example 6-2: Continuing with the NOI calculated under the income approach, assume the building has a value of $687,500 and is depreciated using a straight line method over 20 years. The purchase price is financed with 80 percent debt at 8 percent annual interest for 20 years, resulting in an annual mortgage payment of $56,019. The investor's marginal tax rate is 31 percent. The first year's after-tax cash flow is determined by:

NOI	$82,500
Interest portion	($44,000)
Depreciation	($34,375)
Taxable income	$4,125
Tax @ 31%	($1,279)
Net income	$2,846
Addback depreciation	$34,375
Less principal portion	($12,019)
Free after-tax cash flow for first year	**$25,202**

To find the interest portion above ($44,000), the principal financed is $687,500(0.8) = $550,000. At 8 percent on a 20-year mortgage this is an annual mortgage payment of $56,019.

Keystokes: 20[N]; 8[I/YR]; 550000[PV];[PMT] = -56,019 or $56,019.

Amortization of the first year results in interest expense of $44,000. Without erasing the above keystrokes:

1[INPUT][orange shift][AMORT]

[=] (the display is the principal portion of $12,019)

[=] (the display is the interest portion of $44,000)

Real Estate in a Portfolio Context

Real estate returns consist of income and capital gain. Market appraisals of real estate properties exhibit considerable volatility since appraisals are performed infrequently. More current value estimates are obtained using real estate indexes such as *Frank Russell Company*, *National Council of Real Estate Investment Fiduciaries*, and *Commingled Real Estate Equity Fund*.

Reference to REITs is another method for measuring price appreciation. The total return on a REIT is the income paid to shareholders and the stock market appreciation of the REIT share price. Various REIT indexes such as the *National Association of Real Estate Investment Trusts* are used to proxy the average total return on real estate investments. REITs are discussed later in the chapter.

Example 6-3: Given the following characteristics, calculate the estimated value of the following real estate investment property using the net income approach:

- Annual gross rent (YR 1) of $4 million with an annual escalator of 5 percent thereafter. Gross rent net of vacancy allowance.
- Annual fixed expenses estimated at $250,000 with an annual escalator of 3 percent thereafter.
- Variable expenses estimated to be 20 percent of annual gross rent.
- Property taxes estimated for YR 1 to be $320,000 with an annual escalator of 3 percent thereafter.
- State and Federal combined income tax rate of 40 percent. (Property taxes are deductible for combined income tax purposes.)
- 12 percent cost of capital.

Solution: Determine the cash flows for YR 1 and then apply discounted cash flow (DCF) models to calculate the terminal cash flows:

Cash Flow	YR 1	Terminal Cash Flow (YR 1)
Gross rent	$4,000,000	$60,000,000
Fixed expenses	($250,000)	($2,861,111)
Variable expenses	($800,000)	($12,000,000)
Property taxes	($320,000)	($3,662,222)
Taxable income	$2,630,000	$41,476,667
Income tax @40%	($1,052,000)	($16,590,667)
Net income	$1,578,000	$24,886,000

Total Cash Flow (End of YR 1) = ($1,578,000 + $24,886,000) = $26,464,000

PV Total Cash Flow = $26,464,000/1.12 = $23,628,571

Terminal Cash Flow Calculations (end of YR 1):

Gross rent = $4,000,000(1.05)/(0.12 – 0.05) = $60,000,000

Fixed expenses = $250,000(1.03)/(0.12 – 0.03) = $2,861,111

Variable expenses = $60,000,000(0.20) = $12,000,000

Property taxes = $320,000(1.03)/(0.12 – 0.03) = $3,662,222

REAL ESTATE LIMITED PARTNERSHIPS (RELPs)

A popular form of indirect ownership in real estate is to invest as a limited partner, usually through an investment vehicle known as a *syndication*. A *syndicated limited partnership* consists of two types of owners--one is the syndicator or promoter of the partnership, who usually also serves as the general partner, and the second is the investor(s) or limited partner(s). The syndicator will typically acquire a tract (or tracts) of real property and then attempt to sell it (or them) to the limited partnership. In addition to charging fees for the management of the property tracts, the syndicator will retain an ownership interest in the tracts. An *offering brochure* (the equivalent of a *prospectus* in a mutual fund) is then provided to potential investors. These investors have legal liability limited to the amount of their investment in the syndication (hence, the term *limited partner*).

Real estate syndications are usually adopted as a so-called *tax shelter*. That is, historically, anticipated losses from the sale and operation of the limited partnership could be used to offset earned (and otherwise) taxable income. Since the 1986 Tax Reform Act, however, losses incurred on the sale of real estate are categorized as a *passive loss* and are subject to the so-called *passive activity tax rules*. In general, the term *passive activity* means any activity that involves the conduct of any trade or business where the investor has an interest but does not "materially participate" (as separately defined in the *Treasury Regulations*). Further, this term also specifically includes *any* rental activity of either real or tangible personal property *regardless of whether* the investor materially participates. As a result, losses attributable (or *passed through*) to a limited partner in a real estate syndication may only be: (1) offset against a corresponding type of income, known as *passive income*, in the year within which the loss is generated or (2) deducted when the passive activity is sold or otherwise disposed of (that is, the passive losses are *suspended* until the activity generating the loss is no longer operational). There are exceptions to these rules, whereby a limited portion of losses from a residential real estate activity (so long as the investor is not a limited partner) may be used against earned or *active* income, but that exception is best reserved for a discussion in an income tax text (see for example, Kaplan University's *Individual Income Tax Planning* by Mershon and Fevurly). Of course, limited partners, by definition, are *passive investors* and, indeed, do not want to become active investors for fear of incurring personal liability for their activities.

Many, if not most, real estate limited partnerships (RELPs) are heavily leveraged. This means that only the partnership entity (and specifically, the general partner) is *at risk* (incurs personal liability) if any bank loans are not repaid by the partnership. Limited partners are typically *not* at risk to pay a proportionate amount of the loan in the event that the partnership's real estate activities cannot generate enough cash to pay off the debt. Therefore, the *at risk rules* provide that losses are deductible *only* to the extent that the investor is personally liable. In turn, the investor is not able to create a tax *basis* in the real property once it is sold and recover this amount in a tax-free manner. Accordingly, not only is a limited partner in a RELP restricted by the *passive activity loss rules* from taking tax losses, but even if this tax hurdle can be overcome, he or she is also *not* usually considered to be *at risk* so that any income tax deductions for leveraging the investment are permitted.

As consistent with the business form of organization, a limited partner's right to transfer his or her interest in real estate is restricted by the terms of the partnership agreement. Typically, this interest may not be transferred without the consent of the general partner or syndicator. In addition, unlike the general partnership form, the death of a limited partner will not typically result in the termination of the partnership. Alternatively, if the sole general partner in a real estate syndication were to die, the partnership would likely dissolve (unless the written partnership agreement provided for a successor general partner). To ensure that this does not happen, frequently the general partner in a RELP is a regular C corporation, which has unlimited life under law until formally terminated.

Blind Pools

A *blind pool* is a type of real estate limited partnership (RELP) where the partnership is formed, but the properties in which the partnership will invest have yet to be identified. Accordingly, the limited partner puts even greater trust in the skills and judgment of the general partner. These pools are also sometimes used for other investments (such as an oil and gas working or royalty interest), but in all blind pools, the reputation of the general partner must precede him or her (or the corporation) to attract future investors who do not have the quality of the investment on which to rely.

REAL ESTATE INVESTMENT TRUSTS (REITs)

A real estate investment trust (REIT) is similar to a closed-end investment company (see Chapter 4 of this text) except that instead of investing in securities, it invests in a managed, diversified portfolio of real estate or real estate mortgages and construction loans. The investor achieves diversification and, more importantly, marketability in a publicly traded REIT. The shares of the REIT are either listed on an exchange (the more common situation) or traded over-the-counter among broker/dealers. Although REITs are taxed like a corporation, they are not subject to tax at the corporate level *if* they distribute at least 90% of their net annual earnings to shareholders. (Note that this is in contrast to mutual funds that must distribute 98% of their net earnings to avoid tax at the entity level.) Therefore, REIT shareholders enjoy limited liability and higher dividend payouts while avoiding the double taxation of corporate ownership. Finally, REITs must be registered with the SEC pursuant to the provisions of the Securities Act of 1933.

As income producing investments, REITs do not react substantially to daily changes in the stock market. Rather, they are more sensitive to interest rate fluctuations. Generally, the movement of REITs is *inverse* to that of interest rates; as interest rates rise, the market value of REITs declines and, as interest rates fall, the value of REITs will increase. Although REITS resemble bonds in interest rate movements, studies have shown that returns on REITs have become less correlated with that of bonds and more correlated to equities. For example, Ibbotson & Associates has shown that the correlation of REIT investment returns with those of long-term U.S. government bonds has declined in recent years, leading to the conclusion that an investor may effectively diversify a portfolio with REITs. As a result, by investing a portion of their portfolio in a REIT, in addition to stocks and bonds, an investor may experience greater returns with less risk.

Shareholders pay taxes on distributions (i.e., dividends) from the earnings of a REIT. This distributed income is taxable as ordinary income (not capital gains) to the shareholder. However, because REITs do not generally pay corporate taxes (recall the *90% of earnings distribution rule*), most dividends that are payable by a REIT do *not* qualify for the favorable tax treatment (generally, a 5 percent [0 percent in 2008-2010] or 15 percent rate depending on the individual's marginal income tax bracket) brought about by the JGTRRA legislation of 2003. A small portion of dividends paid by REITs may constitute *qualified dividend income* (for example, if the REIT fails to distribute at least 90 percent of earnings and is therefore subject to corporate income tax), but this is the rare exception and not the general rule.

REITs are available to investors in three types: (1) equity REITs; (2) mortgage REITs; and (3) hybrid REITs—the characteristics of each of which are now discussed.

Equity REITs

Equity REITs invest mainly in established income-producing properties such as office buildings and shopping centers, which then lease the property to others. Such REITs also typically use a moderate amount of leverage (debt) to finance the property purchases. Due to their portfolio of investments, equity REITs generally provide moderate income to their shareholders and opportunities for increasing cash flows and capital appreciation. Some equity REITs focus on new construction and recently completed properties that have not yet been fully rented. Accordingly, there may be low initial cash flows from proven rents, but considerable growth potential and significant capital gains when the investments are sold.

As mentioned, equity REITs also frequently take on a modest amount of leverage. Indeed, equity REIT income is derived from the difference between the net rental income generated from properties that are purchased and interest that is paid on any loans to finance the purchase of those properties. If equity REITs take on too much leverage, and, subsequently, experience a higher than expected vacancy rate from actual rentals, their cash flow may be negatively impacted, resulting in decreased dividend payments to shareholders and a decline in the net asset value of the REIT shares. This is also why, as a group, equity REITs are considered to be a *riskier* investment than that of their close cousin, the mortgage REIT.

Mortgage REITs

Mortgage REITs make loans to develop property and/or finance construction. As such, they essentially invest in real estate *indirectly* (that is, only by lending funds that are used to build properties). In contrast to equity REITs, mortgage REITs generally provide for *higher income,* but also offer less *opportunity for growth* in the net asset value of their shares. In some instances, mortgage REITs also invest in mortgage-backed securities such as *Ginnie Mae* or *Freddie Mac* obligations (see chapter 2 of this textbook). Therefore, the question arises, why might an investor purchase a mortgage REIT rather than investing in the mortgage-backed security directly? The answer is primarily one of security. An investor directly purchasing a mortgage-backed security must be concerned about reinvestment rate risk and the possibility that, as mortgages are refinanced, the pools of mortgages from which their investment income is derived decline, generating less principal and interest pass-through payments.. Alternatively, most mortgage REITs have indeterminate lives and continue to acquire additional mortgages as the older mortgages in the pool are paid down. Therefore, mortgage REITs offer a greater certainty of steady income than do mortgage-backed securities.

Mortgage REITs have investment characteristics similar to long term corporate bonds and are, therefore, not likely to be good inflation hedges. Indeed, the major type of investment risk that a mortgage REIT shareholder assumes is that of purchasing power or inflation risk. If inflation accelerates, thus causing interest rates to rise, the value of the REITs underlying mortgages and loans will typically *fall.* Accordingly, in inflationary times, share values in mortgage REITs are likely to decline. This is particularly the case if the REIT has invested in fixed rate types of mortgages. If, instead, the mortgage REIT has invested in adjustable rate mortgages (ARMs), or other types of variable rate loans, any purchasing power risk is minimized since interest rates will tend to move in concert with the direction and amount of inflation.

Finally, mortgage REITs may purchase a limited amount of investments other than real estate properties. Specifically, at least 75 percent of the income from such REITs must come from real estate investments; the remainder may come from securities, such as mortgage-backed securities or traditional stocks and bonds.

Hybrid REITs

Hybrid REITs combine the features of both equity and mortgage REITs. This means that they invest in established income-producing properties as well as mortgages and securities. Thus, a hybrid REIT provides for capital appreciation growth in addition to the possibility for higher income (although not with the same expected return as either of its separately structured cousins).

REITs vs. RELPs

As we have previously discussed, real estate limited partnerships (RELPs) offer a real estate investment alternative to a real estate investment trust (REIT). Both are indirect forms of investing in real estate without the burden of personal management by the investor. However, there are differences. The primary differences are as follows:

1) Liquidity: REITs have greater liquidity and are actively traded on national and regional stock exchanges, and the over the counter (OTC) network. RELPs, with the exception of a small number of publicly traded partnerships, are generally not readily marketable and are also relatively illiquid. In addition, a REIT shareholder may sell as few or as many shares as he or she deems appropriate, whereas a RELP investor must generally sell his or her entire interest (if there is a market for the same).

2) Tax Treatment: A REIT is a portfolio investment and is subject to taxation like a stock (that is, income dividends are generally taxable as ordinary income and dispositions are taxable as capital gains or losses). A RELP, on the other hand, is strictly a *passive activity investment* and generates *passive losses,* which may only be used when an investor also has *passive income.* Because a REIT generates so-called *portfolio income* (see *Individual Income Tax Planning* by Mershon and Fevurly), losses from a RELP may *not* be used to offset taxable income from a REIT.

3) Organizational Structure: A REIT (as a corporation) is managed by a Board of Directors whereas a RELP is managed by a general partner. Further, at the death of a REIT shareholder, the organizational structure does not automatically terminate.

4) Investor Risk: The major investment risk associated with a REIT is usually the loss of potential purchasing power over time, although this may be mitigated with certain underlying investments. A RELP (as a limited partnership) suffers from extreme liquidity and marketability risks.

REAL ESTATE MORTGAGE INVESTMENT CONDUITS (REMICs)

A *real estate mortgage investment conduit (REMIC)* is a self-liquidating, flow through entity (similar to a partnership) that invests exclusively in real estate mortgages or in mortgage-backed securities. Typically, the REMIC issues debt securities that are known as *REMIC bonds.* They may be issued either as *regular interests* that are publicly traded, or as *residual interests*, which currently are privately placed and not available to the general public. Investors who hold REMIC securities receive a specified cash flow from the underlying pool of mortgages. In this respect, REMIC bonds are very similar to *collateralized mortgage obligations (CMOs)* (to be subsequently discussed). However, REMICs may issue multiple-class real estate mortgage-backed securities separated into both maturity classes and risk classes. Most newly-issued CMOs and REMICs provide for monthly payments to the investor and are offered in denominations ranging from $1,000 to $25,000, depending on the issuer of the security.

As evident from the word *conduit* in its name, a REMIC is a pass through entity that is wholly exempt from federal income tax. Thus, it acts as a conduit and holders of REMIC bonds (not the entity itself) must report any taxable income from the underlying mortgages. However, like original issue discount (OID) bonds, the holders of REMIC bonds must use the accrual accounting method to report income on their bonds, even if they are cash-basis taxpayers. Thus, *phantom income* accrues, meaning that REMIC bonds are best positioned in a tax-deferred account (like a retirement plan). Further, a special rule requires that a part of the gain on the sale of a REMIC bond is taxable as ordinary income (contrast this to the normal rule of corporate bond taxation where any gain is taxable as capital gain). The portion of the gain on the sale of a REMIC bond that is treated as ordinary income is equal to the excess of the amount that would have been includible on the bond if its yield were 110 percent of the Applicable Federal Rate (AFR) in effect when the investor's holding period began, over the amount actually included by the investor in gross income during the time that the bond was owned. The remainder portion is taxable under the normal capital gain rules.

> **Example 6-4:** Assume that a REMIC bond with a coupon rate of 6% per year is acquired for its par value of $1,000. The AFR at the time of acquisition is 8%. In three years the bond is sold for $1,150; therefore, the total gain on the sale of the bond is $150 ($1,150 less $1,000). The amount of interest that is actually included in income during the time that the bond was owned is $180 ($60 annual interest times three years). The amount that would have been included in income if the bond's yield were 110% of the 8% AFR is $264:
>
> $$\frac{8\%(1.10)}{100} = 0.088$$
>
> $$\$1,000\,(0.088) = \$88$$
>
> $$\$88 \times 3 \text{ years} = \$264$$
>
> Therefore, $84 ($264 less $180) of the $150 gain on the sale is taxable as *ordinary income* and the remaining $66, is taxable as *long term capital gain* (since the investor owned the bond for more than the requisite one year holding period).

The price sensitivity of REMIC bonds tends to be *less* than that of corporate bonds of similar quality and maturity. This is because the velocity of the change in the price is mitigated by changes in the rates of prepayments on the underlying mortgage pools. Specifically, prepayments on the existing mortgages tend to pick up when the overall market interest rates decline and homeowners begin to refinance their debt obligations. As prepayments *increase,* the average maturity of the pool of mortgages *decreases.* As a result, the price of the REMIC bonds will not tend to rise as much as its corporate counterpart. Prepayments may also slow down when interest rates increase because there will be fewer refinancings of existing mortgages. Of course, homeowners must still make mortgage payments of interest and principal. Therefore, even as interest rates rise, the price of the REMIC bonds will tend to fall less since mortgage principal is still being repaid.

This begs the question: for what type of investor is a REMIC bond most suitable? The answer is that an investor who desires both increased liquidity and more predictability of mortgage principal repayment may find a REMIC bond attractive. Moreover, since REMICs may be structured to offer *classes* of bonds that mature over a time frame of, generally, anywhere between three and 30 years, investors may invest in classes that match their investment time horizon and avoid some bond principal repayment uncertainty. The price of this assurance is an assumption of interest rate risk by the investor as with any type of fixed-income investment. In addition, the investor must assume the reinvestment rate risk of the prepayment of existing mortgages pooled by the REMIC.

Collateralized Mortgage Obligations (CMOs)

Like a REMIC, collateralized mortgage obligations (CMOs) do not view mortgage pools as a means of passing through payments to investors in exactly the same form as received. This is also a distinction that REMICs and CMOs possess from those of mortgage-passthrough-participation certificates (like GNMA certificates), which represent a direct ownership interest in the pool. Rather, CMOs package mortgage payments received on the basis of cash flow expected over the life of the pool. They do this by issuing separate classes of securities known as *tranches* (French for *slices*). The typical CMO has A to Z tranches, representing the most accelerated form of repayment, a medium or intermediate form of repayment, and the slowest or least accelerated form of repayment, respectively. The Z tranche bears no coupon (similar to a *zero coupon bond*), but receives the cash flow from the mortgage pool *after* the other tranches are satisfied. The Z tranche thus carries the highest yield but, consequently, also carries the highest interest rate risk.

CMOs and REMICs are often used interchangeably in the marketplace, but technically real estate mortgage investment conduit (REMIC) bond is the proper term. The Tax Reform Act of 1986 allowed mortgage securities pools to elect the tax status of a REMIC (that is, a tax-exempt entity). Beginning January 1, 1987, most new CMOs have been issued in REMIC form to create tax and accounting advantages for the issuers. Issuers include government and quasi-governmental organizations, such as the Government National Mortgage Association (Ginnie Mae) and the Federal Home Loan Mortgage Company (Freddie Mac), as well as other private label, third party guarantee financial institutions. Investors include institutions of all sizes but, in recent years, individual investors have also become increasingly active in the real estate mortgage securities market. The collapse of the financial system beginning in 2007 and 2008 is partially attributed to CMOs (referred to as collateralized debt obligations, CDOs, in more recent terminology). Banks and financial institutions held high-risk tranches that could not be valued in light of the home real estate collapse (or valued at too deep a discount that would cause insolvency for many banks).

IMPORTANT CONCEPTS

Financial assets

Real assets

Use asset (real estate as primary residence)

Unimproved land

Dealer tax treatment

Commercial rental property

Net operating income (NOI)

Capitalization rate (cap rate)

Intrinsic value of real estate

Real estate limited partnership (RELP)

Passive activity tax rules

At risk rules

Blind pool

Real estate investment trust (REIT)

Equity REIT

Mortgage REIT

Hybrid REIT

Real estate mortgage investment conduit (REMIC) bond

Collateralized mortgage obligation (CMO)

QUESTIONS FOR REVIEW

1. What have past studies suggested may be the correlation between *financial* and *real assets*? Why is this important?

2. What use do most individuals make of a real estate purchase?

3. Why would an investor typically invest in unimproved or *raw* land? How may tax on any gain from the sale of such land be deferred?

4. Contrast the direct purchase of improved land to that of indirect ownership. What is the primary form of indirect ownership of real estate in the secondary marketplace today?

5. In computing *net operating income* (NOI), what should be *excluded* when analyzing the applicable amount of operating expenses? Why is this the proper way to proceed?

6. How is the *intrinsic value* of real estate improved land derived? What is meant by the term *cap rate* in deriving this value?

7. "Real estate is, by its very nature, an illiquid investment." Explain this statement.

8. What is a real estate *syndication* and in what form of business entity is such investment vehicle normally offered to the investing public?

9. There are two basic income tax implications if a loss from the sale of real estate held as an investment occurs. What are these implications?

10. Often times the general partner in a *RELP* is operated as a regular C corporation. Why is this?

11. What is a *blind pool*?

12. What requirement must be satisfied before a real estate investment trust (REIT) is *not* separately taxed?

13. What are two major advantages that an investor in a REIT enjoys that are not possible with the direct ownership of real estate?

14. Are the market values of REITs generally sensitive to daily changes in the stock market? Explain.

15. Why are most dividends payable from a REIT *not* considered to be *qualified* for favorable income tax treatment?

16. What are the three types of REITS available to investors? Which one is generally considered to have the most investor risk and why is this the case?

17. Contrast a mortgage REIT to that of an equity REIT in terms of a) potential income payout and b) opportunity for capital growth.

18. What are four primary differences between a REIT and a RELP?

19. What is a real estate mortgage investment conduit (REMIC)? Who issues such securities?

20. Where should a REMIC bond best be positioned within an investor's portfolio? Explain.

21. For what type of investor is a REMIC bond most suitable?

22. Is there any difference between a REMIC and a collateralized mortgage obligation (CMO)? Explain.

23. What is a CMO *tranche*? Which one of these tranches carries the highest yield (and corresponding investor risk)?

SUGGESTIONS FOR ADDITIONAL READING

Tools and Techniques of Investment Planning, 2nd edition, Stephen R. Leimberg, Robert T. LeClair, Robert J. Doyle, Jr., and Thomas R. Robinson, The National Underwriter Company, 2006.

Investments: An Introduction, 9th edition, Herbert B. Mayo, Thomson/ South-Western, 2008.

Investment Analysis and Portfolio Management, 9th edition, Frank K. Reilly and Keith C. Brown, Thomson/South-Western, 2009.

The Wall Street Journal Guide to Money and Investing, 3rd edition, Kenneth M. Morris and Virginia B. Morris, Fireside Publishing, 2004.

Dictionary of Finance and Investment Terms, Downes and Goodman, 6th edition, Barron's, 2003.

CHAPTER SEVEN

Alternative Investments

• • •

This chapter presents *alternative investments,* which include derivatives, tangible assets (such as collectibles), and natural resources. A derivative is an investment contract that derives its value from that of an underlying asset, such as a stock. Tangible assets are characterized by their lack of marketability, as compared with other investment assets. Finally, many natural resource investments (i.e., oil and gas, minerals) are sometimes referred to as *wasting assets,* since their supply is, by definition, limited and will eventually be depleted. Of course, this is not the case with so-called *renewable* natural resources, such as lumber and water.

Upon completing this chapter, you should be able to:

- Explain the use of derivatives, including options and futures as an alternative investment
- Describe the characteristics of stock options as investments and their use as a hedging technique
- Identify attributes of an investment in tangible assets (collectibles) and/or natural resources (oil and gas wells)
- Compare alternative investments to more traditional investments

DERIVATIVES AS AN INVESTMENT

A *derivative* is an investment contract, which has a value that is derived from the value of the underlying asset from which the contract is written The most common of these alternative investments are stock options, futures contracts, and forward agreements. For each of these three general derivative positions, an investor may enter into a transaction as either the *long position* (i.e., the buyer) or the *short position* (i.e., the seller). Institutional investors have historically used derivatives to increase overall portfolio return or to hedge portfolio risk. However, in recent years, individual investors (particularly those of higher net worth and discretionary income) have made derivatives a fundamental part of privately-managed *hedge funds*. By way of review, a *hedge*, in the financial world, is a risk management strategy incorporating both the cash market and the derivatives market. The result is to partially offset a decline of value in the cash market with an increase in value of the derivatives contract. Investing only in the cash market results in an un-hedged position. Investing only in the derivatives market is speculation. A hedge combines the two markets.

FORWARD CONTRACTS

To many investors, the *forward contract* is the most basic derivative product that is available. Generally, such a contract provides its holder with both the right and obligation to conduct a transaction involving an underlying asset (usually a security or commodity) at a predetermined future date and price. There must always be two parties to the contract: the eventual *buyer* (said to be in the *long position*), who pays the contract price and receives the underlying asset, and the eventual seller (said to be in the *short position*), who delivers the security for the fixed price. The settlement date for such contract is purposely set to be in the future. However, at times, this date is established to be executed immediately (known as a *spot market* transaction). An example of a forward contract is a variable prepaid forward contract or "VPF". A VPF usually requires the advance of funds to a shareholder in a long position with a variable number of shares delivered at the end of the contract term. As a result, the shareholder now has cash equal to the market value of the stock subject to the contract, wherein such cash can be used to hedge future market risk by subsequent reinvestment in a diversified portfolio.

Forward contracts are negotiated in the over-the-counter (OTC) market. This means that such contracts are agreements between two private parties—one of which is usually a commercial or investment bank—rather than being traded through a formal security or commodity exchange. An advantage of this private arrangement is that the terms of the contract are completely flexible between the parties; however, a distinct disadvantage is that the contract is often *not marketable*, meaning here that it is extremely difficult for one of the parties to exit the contract before it matures. This lack of marketability is really a by-product of the contract's flexibility since the more customized the forward contract becomes, the less marketable it will be to someone else. *Futures contracts (futures)* solve this problem by standardizing the terms of the agreement to the extent that it can be traded on an exchange. In contrast to the forward market, both parties in a futures contract trade through a centralized market, known as a *futures exchange*. As a result, either party may always unwind its previous commitment, prior to expiration of the contract, simply by offset, which is taking an opposite position to the one currently held.

The futures price is analogous to the forward contract price. However, rules of the futures exchange require both parties in a futures contract to post collateral, or *margin*, to protect against the possibility of default. These margin accounts are held by the exchange's clearinghouse and are *marked to market*, meaning that they are adjusted on a daily basis for contract price movements in order to ensure that both parties always maintain sufficient collateral to guarantee their future participation. All contracts are financially guaranteed by the clearinghouse that processes the transaction, thereby improving market performance by eliminating such worries as the creditworthiness of either party. The underlying subject of the futures contract is usually either financial securities, such as foreign currencies, or physical commodities, such as agricultural products, oil, coffee, or cattle. Regardless, all of these underlying assets have two common characteristics: *potentially extreme volatile price movements* and *strong participation* from both buyers and sellers.

INTRODUCTION TO FUTURES AND OPTIONS

Derivatives are highly leveraged contracts whose value is *derived* from an underlying security (stock), index (S&P 500 Index), or other asset (real estate). Derivatives are priced according to the *no-arbitrage principle*, which states that the minimal requirement of any rational price for a financial instrument must exclude *arbitrage opportunities*. An *arbitrage opportunity* is the opportunity to earn a riskless profit with no personal investment. The two major types of derivative contracts are futures and options.

FUTURES AND OPTION CONTRACTS

Futures Contract
A ***futures contract*** is a binding contract, which calls for the exchange of some good at a future date for cash, with the payment for the good to occur at that future date. The buyer of a futures contract receives delivery of the good and makes payment for it, while the seller of a futures contract promises to deliver the good and receive payment. The price of the good is determined at the initial time of contracting.

Following are significant characteristics of futures contracts:

1. Futures contracts always trade on an organized exchange.
2. Futures contracts are highly standardized, specifying the quantity of the good, the delivery date, and delivery mechanism, including point of delivery, if applicable.

3. Performance on the futures contract is guaranteed by a *clearinghouse,* which is a financial institution associated with the futures exchange that guarantees the financial integrity of the market to all traders.

4. All futures contracts require that traders post margin in order to trade. *Margin* is a good faith deposit made by the prospective trader to indicate his or her willingness and ability to fulfill all financial obligations that may arise from trading futures.

5. The futures markets are regulated by an identifiable government agency, such as the Commodities Futures Trading Commission (CFTC), along with self-regulation by the exchange where the futures contract is traded.

Options

The holder (buyer) of an *options contract* has the right, <u>but not the obligation,</u> to buy (*call option*) or sell (*put option*) a specified asset at a specified date (*European*) or within a specified time (*American*), for a specified price (*strike or exercise price*). The holder of the option pays the seller (or writer) of the option a *premium*. In exchange for this premium payment, the writer confers all rights to the holder. The option payoff is asymmetrical. This means that the holder's loss is limited to the premium paid, while his or her gain, theoretically, could be unlimited in amount. However, the holder may simply let the option expire, thus limiting the loss to the premium paid to the writer.

Options on Futures

A *futures option* is an option that takes a futures contract as its underlying good. Futures options contrast with *options on the physical,* which are options on the good itself. The structure of a futures option is very similar to an option on the physical. For both types of option, the option holder has only the *right* to exercise the contract, but the option writer has the *obligation* to perform if the holder exercises that right.

APPLICATIONS OF FINANCIAL DERIVATIVES

Market Completeness

A *complete market* is one in which any and all identifiable payoffs may be obtained by trading the securities available in the market. A complete market is idealistic and in reality, unobtainable. However, pursuit of a complete market is desirable since access to a complete market benefits both its participants and the broader economy. Financial derivatives play a valuable role in moving the market toward market completeness.

Speculation

Financial derivatives are highly leveraged (compounded when traded using considerable borrowed funds). Playing on this leverage in itself is risky. However, the precision and speculative power of derivatives supports their role in also moving the market toward market completeness.

Risk Management

Even though derivatives are highly leveraged instruments, they are powerful tools for hedging and risk management when used in conjunction with physical, spot, or cash market transactions. This is because they permit considerable financial protection for a relatively small dollar outlay by the holder of the derivative.

Trading Efficiency

Derivatives can also be used to substitute for a position in the more fundamental underlying financial instrument. For example, a portfolio manager can restructure the portfolio of assets without trading any of the underlying assets by substituting their performance with derivatives. Financial derivatives are attractive because they can mimic the profit and loss performance of the underlying asset and be transacted almost instantaneously at much lower trading costs than trading the underlying asset itself.

INTRODUCTION TO FUTURES

In futures markets, the buyer of a contract has a ***long position,*** while the seller has a ***short position*** (buy long/sell short). Therefore, ***going long*** is the act of buying a futures contract and ***going short*** is the act of selling such contract. In order for the contract to trade, there must always be a long position and a short position. Trading ***volume*** is the number of fully transacted (bought and sold) contracts for a given period over the exchange. At any given time, there is some number of contracts obligated for delivery. This number is referred to as the ***open interest***.

THE ORGANIZED EXCHANGE

The exchange is a voluntary nonprofit association of its members. Exchange memberships are ***seats*** on the exchange and may be held only by individuals. Exchange seats are traded in an active market like other assets. Exchange members have the right to trade on the exchange and to have a voice in the exchange's operation. The exchanges are recently going through various transitions related to electronic trading, consolidations, and going public to meet future market demands.

The designated trading area of the exchange is referred to as the ***pit,*** and is a physical location on the floor. Each good or commodity trades in a designated pit. Federal law and rules of the exchange mandate official trading hours. The system, by which futures contracts trade is known as ***open outcry***. A trader must make any offer to buy or sell to all other traders present in the pit. Traders also use a sophisticated system of hand signals to express their wishes to buy or sell. Again, the exchanges are undergoing transition to meet technical innovations and demand.

Traders may transact for their own account, realizing profits or losses on the trades. Traders may also act as brokers on behalf of their firm or client outside the exchange. Some traders exercise both functions simultaneously. Some traders who trade for their own account may not be full members of the exchange, having leased their seat from a full member. Also, some exchanges have created special licenses allowing nonmembers to trade on certain contracts in which the exchanges are anxious to build volume.

A trader who enters the futures market in pursuit of profit and accepting the associated risk is a **speculator**. Many traders trade futures to reduce some preexisting risk exposure. These traders are **hedgers** and are often producers or major users of a given commodity. *Hedging* is taking a position on a futures contract that is opposite the corresponding position in the cash (spot) market. For example, if a portfolio manager holds (or is long) large cap stocks in a portfolio that tracks the S&P 500, he or she would short S&P 500 index futures if concerned with a declining stock market. Conversely, if the portfolio manager was expecting a large inflow of funds in the near future to purchase stocks and the trend was upward, he or she could buy S&P index futures now to capture the upside before the funds are available. In the former example, the portfolio manager is *long* the cash market of stocks and hedges against falling stock prices with a *short* futures position. In the latter, the portfolio manager is short in the cash market (does not have the stocks) and hedges against rising stock prices with a long position in the futures.

There are two types of brokers. An **account executive** for a brokerage firm is a broker serving the retail community (also known as a financial consultant). A **floor broker** is on the floor of the exchange and executes orders for other clients.

STANDARDIZED CONTRACT TERMS

Futures contracts are highly standardized with specific contract terms as to price, delivery and settlement. The futures contract specifies the quantity and quality of the good, delivery date, point of delivery, method for closing the contract, and the permissible minimum and maximum price fluctuations permitted in trading.

Stipulation of the minimum price fluctuation is the contract's **tick** size. For example, one tick on a Treasury bond contract is 1/32 of par. Since each bond historically has had a $1,000 face value, the contract's tick size is $0.00315 times $1,000 face value, or $31.50 per bond. The contract also specifies a **daily price limit**, which restricts the price movement in a single day. When the contract is trading in its delivery month, no price limits are in effect. Also, price limits are generally expanded over successive days during periods of high commodity price volatility.

Although these rules seem overly restrictive, the high degree of standardization the rules impose actually *stimulates trading*. All participants in the market know exactly what is being offered for sale and the terms of the transactions. This uniformity helps promote liquidity. Each exchange publishes its contract terms.

THE CLEARINGHOUSE

The clearinghouse may be separate or a part of the futures exchange. Each exchange has a corresponding clearinghouse, which guarantees that all of the traders in the futures market will honor their obligations. The clearinghouse serves this role by acting as the buyer for every contract seller and as the seller for every contract buyer. Every trade on the exchange has obligations to the clearinghouse with the expectation that the clearinghouse will maintain its side of the bargain.

The clearinghouse takes no active position in the market, but rather interjects itself between all parties involved in the transaction. The number of contracts bought must always equal the number of contracts sold. Since the clearinghouse maintains no active position of its own in the futures market, the risk to the buyers and sellers is, thereby, reduced.

MARGIN AND DAILY SETTLEMENT

Another safeguard in addition to the clearinghouse, is the requirement for posting margin and daily settlement. Before trading a futures contract, the prospective trader must deposit funds with a broker. This is referred to as **margin** and serves as a good-faith deposit by the trader. Margin provides a financial safeguard that the trader will live up to his or her trading obligations. The amount of margin varies among contracts as well as by the broker. The margin may be posted in cash, a bank letter of credit, or in short-term U.S. Treasury securities. The posted margin is a security deposit in which title is retained by the trader.

Initial Margin
The amount deposited by the trader to begin trading in futures is referred to as the **initial margin**. The initial margin tracks the maximum daily price fluctuation permitted for the contract being traded. For most futures contracts, the initial margin may be five percent or less of the underlying commodity's value. The initial margin is returned to the trader upon fulfillment of all obligations associated with the trader's future position. For Treasury securities posted as margin, the trader earns interest on those securities for the time they serve as the margin.

The margin serves as collateral for **daily settlement (marking-to-market)**. Daily settlement is another safeguard requiring traders to realize any losses in cash on the day of occurrence. This process prevents the accumulation of losses to the point where the trader cannot meet the contract's obligations.

Maintenance Margin
The **maintenance margin** is the margin level that triggers the trader to replenish the margin account, bringing the balance to its initial level. This demand for restoring the margin account is known as a **margin call.** The maintenance margin is generally about 75 percent of the amount of the initial margin.

Variation Margin

The additional amount of margin the trader must deposit from a margin call is the ***variation margin***. Variation margins must always be paid in cash.

To summarize, assume a trader posts an initial margin of $1,000. The account falls by $100 the first day, $100 the second day, and $75 the third day. The third decline drops the trader's account balance below the maintenance level of $750 (75% of $1,000) to $725. To fulfill the margin call, the trader must post an additional $275 in cash, the variation margin, to restore the initial balance. If the trader would have realized <u>gains</u> of $100, $100, and $75, he or she could have withdrawn the overage, but only to the initial margin level of $1,000.

There are two ways to avoid a margin call. First, the trader can deposit securities with a value well above the initial margin. Second, a trader can deposit funds in excess of the initial margin into an interest-bearing account. The trader can also instruct the broker to make daily sweeps of any profits to the interest-bearing account and hold those funds ready for any margin calls.

If the trader is unable or unwilling to post variation margin, the broker is entitled to "close" the futures position by deducting the loss from the trader's initial margin and returning any balance, less commission costs, to the trader. Failure of the trader to post the required variation margin is a violation of the trader's agreement with the broker and constitutes closure of the trader's entire brokerage account.

Margin Cash Flows

The margin system functions through a hierarchy of market participants, from the individual trader to the clearinghouse. The members of an exchange are classified as clearing members or non-clearing members. A ***clearing member*** is a member of the exchange that is also a member of the clearinghouse. The clearinghouse deals only with clearing members. (Of course, a **non-clearing member** is simply a clearinghouse member who is not considered to be a clearing member.)

The clearinghouse demands margin deposits from clearing members to cover all futures positions executed by the clearing member. A non-clearing member must clear trades through a clearing member. Many traders who trade on their own account are non-clearing members.

CLOSING A FUTURES POSITION

A futures position may be closed through (1) delivery, (2) offset, and (3) exchange-for-physical (EFP).

Delivery

Some futures contracts are written to allow completion of the futures contract through the physical delivery of a particular good. Delivery takes place at certain locations and at certain times as specified by the exchange. Exchanges have introduced futures contracts that allow completion through *cash settlement* rather than physical delivery. In a cash settlement, traders make payments at the expiration of the contract to settle any gains or losses, instead of making physical delivery. Both physical delivery and cash settlement close the contract in the expiration period.

Financial index futures are an example of cash settlement. It would be difficult to deliver the entire S&P 500 for example. Cash settlement is based on the closing index value multiplied by $250 per value point. If the S&P 500 index closed at 1,000, the contract is valued at $250,000 ($1,000 x $250 per point). Bond futures contracts may also be settled through delivery. Each contract lists candidate bonds acceptable for delivery under the contract. The seller of the bond futures contract has discretion with respect to which bond to deliver. The bond that is delivered is referred to as the cheapest-to-deliver (CTD).

Offset

Most futures contracts are closed through **offset**, also known as **reversing trade**. To close a futures contract obligation through offset, the trader transacts, in an equal but opposite position, to bring his or her net position back to zero. The clearinghouse then recognizes this offsetting transaction and absolves the trader from any further obligation. In entering the reversing trade, it is crucial that the trader buys (sells) exactly the same contract that was originally sold (bought). If not, then the trader undertakes a new contract obligation rather than canceling the old.

Exchange-for-Physical (EFP)

In an EFP, two traders agree to a simultaneous exchange of a cash commodity contract and a futures contract based on that cash commodity. The trade is reported to the exchange, which notes their positions match and cancels their futures obligations. The result of an EFP is similar to the offset. However, the EFP differs from an offsetting trade in several ways. First, the traders actually exchange the physical good. Second, the price and terms of the obligation are privately negotiated. Third, the closing transaction does not take place on the exchange floor. Therefore, the EFP transaction is referred to as an **ex-pit** transaction and is recognized by Federal law and exchange rules as an exception to the general rule that all futures trading must take place in the pit. EFPs are also known as **against actuals** or **versus cash** transactions.

TYPES OF FUTURES CONTRACTS

There are four fundamental categories of futures contracts:

1. a physical commodity,
2. a foreign currency,
3. an interest-earning asset, and
4. a financial index, such as a stock index.

Agricultural and Metallurgical Contracts

Futures contracts are traded in grains (corn, oats, and wheat), oil and meal (soybeans, soymeal, soyoil, sunflower seed, and sunflower oil), livestock (live hogs, cattle, and pork bellies), forest products (lumber and plywood), textiles (cotton), and foodstuffs (cocoa, coffee, orange juice, rice, and sugar).

For many of these commodities, several different contracts are available for different grades or types of the commodity. For most of the goods, there are also a number of specified months for delivery. The metallurgical category includes genuine metals, such as gold or silver, and petroleum contracts.

Interest-Earning Assets
Futures contracts are also traded on interest-bearing assets, such as Treasury securities, Eurodollar deposits, and municipal bonds.

Foreign Currencies
The foreign exchange futures market represents the one case of a futures market existing in the face of a truly active forward market. The forward market for foreign exchange is many times larger than the futures market.

Indexes
Many futures contracts are for stock indexes. The main characteristic of the stock index contracts is that they do not allow the possibility of actual delivery as noted above.

PURPOSES OF FUTURES MARKETS

There are two main social functions or utilitarian purposes of futures markets: (1) price discovery and (2) hedging. Although speculation is a function of the markets, it is *not* regarded as socially useful in itself (unless you are a speculator).

Price Discovery
Price discovery reflects market expectations of future cash market prices through the futures market. There is a relationship between the futures price and the price that investors expect to prevail for the commodity at the delivery date specified in the futures contract. By using this information, price estimates or trends may be developed for future time periods. Thus, a social function of the futures markets is to assist decision-makers in making better estimates of future prices.

Hedging
Hedgers have a preexisting risk exposure of some form that leads them to use futures transactions as a substitute for a cash market transaction. This type of transaction is known as **anticipatory hedging**. The opportunity for hedgers to avoid unacceptable risk by entering the futures market also contributes to the social function of the futures markets. Some individuals would not engage in certain activities that clearly have economic benefits if they were forced to bear all the risk themselves. Therefore, the ability to transfer risk to other parties, more willing and/or able to accept such risk via the futures market, enhances economic activity in general and society as a whole.

THE OPTIONS MARKET

An option is a right, but not an obligation, to buy or sell a good, at a specified price, at expiration of or within a specified period. The right to *buy* a good is a **call option**. The right to *sell* a good is a **put option**. The specified price at which the good can be bought or sold is the **exercise** or **strike price**. An option that can be exercised only at the expiration of the option period is a **European option** and an option that can be exercised at any time within the option period is an **American option**.

The options market is used by traders to (1) speculate, (2) capture additional profits, (3) control risk (hedge), and (4) restructure assets. The options exchanges trade on a wide variety of underlying goods, such as stocks, bonds, futures contracts, and foreign currencies.

MONEYNESS

"Moneyness" is an important option concept that refers to the potential profit or loss from the immediate exercise of an option. Options have an intrinsic value and a time value. The *intrinsic value* is the value associated with immediate exercise of the option. The *time value* is a decaying variable, which moves toward zero as the contract moves toward expiration and goes to zero upon the expiration date. The intrinsic value of an option is dependent on whether the option is "***in-the-money***," "***out-of-the-money***," or "***at-the-money***".

A call option is "*in-the-money*" when the exercise price is less than the market price; "*out-of-the-money*" when the exercise price is above the market price, and "*at-the-money*" when the exercise and market prices are the same. The intrinsic value of a call at expiration is represented as:

Intrinsic value of call = $MAX[0, S_T - X]$

The value of a call is the maximum (MAX) of zero (where the holder lets the call expire worthless) or the difference of the market value of the underlying asset (S_T) less the exercise price (X).

A put option is "*in-the-money*" when the exercise price is greater than the market price; "*out-of-the-money*" when the exercise price is less than the market price. The intrinsic value of a put at expiration is represented as:

Intrinsic value of put = $MAX[0, X - S_T]$

The value of the put at expiration is the maximum of zero (where the holder lets the put expire worthless) or the difference of the exercise price less the market value of the underlying asset.

If the cash flows from immediately exercising the option would be large, puts and calls can also be **deep-in-the-money** or **deep-out-of-the-money**. Both calls and puts are "*at-the-money*" when their exercise and market prices are the same.

No taxable gain or loss is recognized upon the exercise of a call option. A capital gain or loss is recognized only when the stock, acquired through the exercise of the call, is sold. At that time, the cost of the call (or the premium charged) is added to the purchase price of the stock to compute any taxable gain or loss. The holding period is measured from the date one day *after* the call is purchased, *not* from the date that the call is purchased. If the call option is not exercised (that is, it is allowed to expire), then the option is considered sold as of the expiration date and the buyer recognizes a short term capital loss equal to the premium amount.

AMERICAN AND EUROPEAN OPTIONS

The terms "American" and "European" have no geographical implication and apply only with respect to when an option can be exercised. American and European options have the same value at expiration. However, the values differ at other times prior to expiration. The owner of an American option can elect not to exercise the option until expiration, effectively making the American option perform like a European option. Therefore, the American option cannot be worth less than a European option (all other characteristics being equal). The American option will be worth more if it is desirable to exercise the option early. However, exercising an American option early forfeits the time value associated with the option.

USES OF OPTIONS

As mentioned above, options are traded to (1) speculate, (2) capture additional profits, (3) control risk, and (4) restructure assets. Many investors trade options to speculate on price movements of the underlying asset. For example, call option premiums are always cheaper than the underlying stock and generally, so are put option premiums. Options prices are more volatile than the underlying stock, so investors can get more price action per dollar of investment. Finally, options have an asymmetric payback. Option holders can limit their downside risk to the premium paid for the option while realizing high potential on the upside. Option writers realize the opposite payoff. The gain is limited to the premium received in selling the option with the loss potential high.

Example 7-1: Payoff Diagram of a Call Option ($40 exercise price, $2.00 premium)

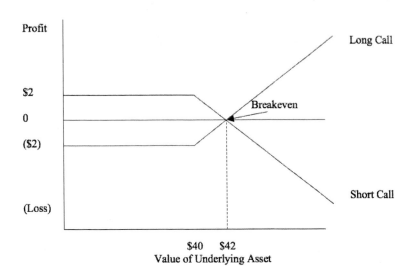

Exercise 7-2: Payoff Diagram of a Put Option ($40 exercise price, $2.00 premium)

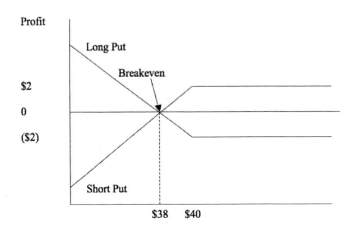

By trading options in conjunction with their stock portfolio, investors can carefully adjust the risk and return characteristics of their entire investment. *Covered calls* (where the option holder also owns the underlying stock on which the call is written) are used to capture additional profits (the call premium) on a stock portfolio. A call is written with an exercise price expected to remain above the stock price during the option period. Such a strategy is used when little market movement is anticipated.

A *collar* strategy is employed when the purchaser of stock wants to establish a range of stock values, thereby reducing the range of prices for the newly-acquired securities. The collar is created when the purchaser *sells a call option and purchases a put option* on the stock in his or her portfolio. Moreover, the collar may often be structured as a cost-free alternative for the shareholder, a so-called "cashless collar" transaction. Using this strategy, the cost of the put option purchase is funded by the option premium received on the sale of the call option.

A *straddle* strategy is employed when the underlying stock is experiencing considerable volatility. A straddle is buying a call and a put on the *same* stock. The volatility of the underlying stock adds value to both the call and the put.

A *protective* put (also known as "portfolio insurance") strategy is used to protect a stock portfolio against possible declines in stock prices. The investor buys stock and associated puts (or just puts, if he or she already owns the stock) at an exercise price that will limit any stock price decline to an acceptable loss.

Finally, investors and portfolio managers typically prefer to trade options rather than stocks in order to save on transaction costs, to avoid tax exposure, and to avoid stock market restrictions. As a result, portfolio assets may be restructured, without having to incur the additional expenses associated with trading the actual portfolio securities, by creating so-called synthetic positions with options.

OPTIONS MARKET FUNCTION

Option Contracts

Option contracts traded on the exchanges are standardized to enhance liquidity. The standardized contract has a specific size and expiration date. Trading on the exchange occurs during certain well-publicized times, so traders know when they will be able to find other traders in the marketplace. The exchange also standardizes the exercise prices at which options will trade. With fewer exercise prices available, more trading will occur at the given exercise prices. Exercise prices are also specified at certain intervals depending on the share price. In addition, every option contract has a specified expiration month and day.

Option Exchanges

Options trading on organized exchanges in the United States embrace a number of different underlying instruments. First and foremost is the *stock* option, an option on an individual share of common stock. Second, options also trade on various financial *indexes*. These indexes measure the performance of a group of stock, such as the Dow Jones Index. Third, options trade on foreign *currencies* (against a very active forward market). Finally, options trade on *futures* contracts. For an option on futures, or a futures option, the underlying asset is a position in a futures contract.

Options on individual stock trade on the Chicago Board Options Exchange (CBOE) and four other exchanges that principally trade stock themselves. The CBOE also is the major exchange for stock index options. The CBOE was formed by the Chicago Board of Trade (CBOT) in 1973.

The Philadelphia Stock Exchange (PHLX) trades options on individual foreign currencies. All prices are in US dollars and trades both American and European options. A strong forward market exists that keeps foreign currency option trading volume low.

Options on futures trading is dominated by two exchanges, the CBOT and the Chicago Mercantile Exchange (CME). The New York Mercantile Exchange (NYMEX) is the third largest exchange for futures options, largely due to its successful trading in oil-related products. Financial instruments account for the majority of futures options trading. The organization of the exchanges remains in flux to meet future demands of the trading public.

OPTION PRICING

The two major option-pricing models are the Black Scholes model and the binomial option-pricing model. Factors that influence option pricing are the:

1. Value of underlying asset, i.e., stock
2. Exercise price
3. Historic volatility (standard deviation)
4. Time to expiration, and
5. Interest rates

Example 7-3: The following table presents the factors and their corresponding influence on call and put prices (increase or decrease)

Factor	Call Value	Put Value
Increase in the underlying asset value	Increase	Decrease
Higher the exercise price	Decrease	Increase
Greater the volatility	Increase	Increase
Greater the time to expiration	Increase	Increase
Increase in interest rates	Increase	Decrease

A call approaches breakeven and generating a profit when the underlying asset increases in price. Put values move in opposite direction to the underlying asset values. (Refer to the call and put payoff diagrams.)

The greater the volatility is, the greater the values of both a call and a put, since the likelihood of the call and put being "in-the-money" increases with the underlying stock volatility. Also, the greater the time to option expiration is, the greater the values of both a call and a put, since the odds of both being "in-the-money" are improved during the period prior to expiration.

Due to the short maturities on options (typically no more than a nine month maturity date), interest rates do not have much of an effect on option values. However, rising interest rates do increase the value of a call, because the funds required to exercise the call can earn higher interest in the interim. The converse is true with a put option. The money received from exercising the put (or its exercise price) has a lower time value because of the associated increasing market interest rates.

Long-Term Equity AnticiPation Securities (LEAPS)

Long-term Equity AnticiPation Securities or LEAPS are long-term options that generally have expiration dates up to as much as 39 months (3 years and 3 months). These types of options allow investors to position themselves for market movements that are expected beyond the normal nine-month timeframe of the standard option. LEAPS that are currently traded expire in 24 months (two years) and, like a regular option, may be bought or sold at any time during this life cycle. LEAPS are only available on a limited number of securities (around 500) and indexes (around 10). Fundamentally, they operate like any other written option, but their tax treatment is unique. Although investors may have held the contract for more than 12 months (and, therefore, theoretically qualifying the contract for long term gain or loss treatment), LEAP sellers or writers must report *short term* capital gains at expiration. However, LEAP buyers or holders may report a *long term* loss at this same date.

Combinations

Investors can simultaneously buy or sell more than one option contract on opposite sides (buy and sell) of the market. The most common of these positions, known as either a *spread* or a *straddle*, may be used to limit position costs and risks (in other words, as a *hedging technique*). They will be further addressed in chapter 16 of this text when discussing *hedging and option strategies*. An investor will engage in a combination because he or she believes that there will be some future movement in the price of the underlying security. However, he or she does not know in which direction the movement will occur, so he or she buys on both sides of the market (or classes of options) and will profit, so long as either side (or class) reaches an "in-the-money" amount greater than his or her combined premium.

A *spread* is the simultaneous purchase of one option and sale of another option of the same class (call or put). For example, a *call spread* is the purchase of a call option (being *long*) and the sale of a call option (going *short*). A *put spread* is the combination of the purchase of a put option (being long) and the sale of a put option (going short). Investors can buy or sell three types of basic spreads as follows:

1. A *price spread* is one that has different exercise prices but the same expiration date:

   Long XYZ Nov *50* call at 6

   Short XYZ Nov *60* call at 4

2. A *time spread* is one that has different expiration dates but the same exercise prices:

   Long XYZ *Nov* 60 call at 4

   Short XYZ *Jan* 60 call at 6

3. A *diagonal spread* is one in which the options differ in both time and price; on an options report, a line connecting these two positions would appear as diagonal:

   Long XYZ *Nov 50* call at 6

   Short XYZ *Jan 60* call at 6

A *straddle* is composed of a call option and a put option (that is, different classes) with the same exercise price and expiration month. Investors can engage in two basic types of straddles as follows:

1. A *long straddle* is the purchase of a call and put with the same exercise price and expiration date:

   Buy 1 ABC *Jan 50* call at 3

   Buy 1 ABC *Jan 50* put at 5

2. A *short straddle* is the sale of a call and put with the same exercise price and expiration date:

   Sell 1 ABC *Jan 45* call at 4

   Sell 1 ABC *Jan 45* put at 6

SUMMARY OF FUTURES AND OPTIONS

Derivative contracts are highly leveraged financial instruments. The two main types of derivatives contracts are *futures* contracts and *option* contracts. These contracts are written on a variety of financial assets including stock indexes, Treasury securities, and physical commodities. The contracts are traded on formal exchanges.

Futures contracts require posting a security deposit known as *margin*. Gains and losses are symmetrical. Both the buyer and seller of a futures contract must post margin and are obligated to perform under the contract specifications. Option contracts are asymmetrical. The buyer of an option contract is not obligated to perform under the contract and has the right to recognize any gains from an "in-the-money" option. The buyer pays the writer a premium for the option right. The writer of an option is obligated to perform under the conditions of the option contract and posts margin. Potential losses to an option writer may be significant, whereas the gain is limited to the premium received for writing the option.

Futures and options are used in price discovery, hedging, financial structuring, and speculation.

TANGIBLE ASSETS AND NATURAL RESOURCES

Tangible assets (collectibles) as an investment are generally distinguished by their *lack of marketability*. In contrast, natural resources (particularly oil and gas investments) are characterized by their *inelasticity of demand*. Inelastic demand means that the quantity demanded of the natural resource will change by less, in percentage terms, than a given percentage in price. That is, if the resource exhibits inelasticity, a sharp increase in its price has little impact on the demand for it. This occurs primarily because there are no ready substitutes for the natural resource.

Collectibles

Collectibles are rare objects accumulated by investors. Examples are stamps, coins, oriental rugs, paintings (art), and baseball cards (among others). An activity of accumulating collectibles ceases to be a hobby and turns into an investment when the collector has a profit motive for continuing. This profit motive is not as important for investment reasons as it is for the income tax implications associated with conducting a business in the buying and selling of collectibles.

Collectibles generally provide no current income to the investor, but they do have the potential for significant long-term capital appreciation. Furthermore, they tend to vary sharply in underlying value during inflationary periods, when people are attempting to move their assets from paper currency into something more tangible. In this respect, collectibles share, with gold, the characteristic of serving as an *inflation hedge*. Finally, the returns on collectibles have historically exhibited a *negative correlation* with that of financial assets (stocks and bonds), therefore suggesting that these assets may effectively diversify an investor's portfolio and reduce overall investor risk.

A significant disadvantage of collectible investing is that most individuals are not expert enough to effectively value the item that they are collecting. Therefore, there are additional costs associated with the investment to pay independent dealers and appraisers to assist them in making a prudent choice of assets. In addition, collectibles are subject to considerable swings in popularity within a limited market. What is "hot" one calendar year may be extremely "cold" the next year. Indeed, the absence of an organized and relatively unregulated market puts *both* buyers and sellers at considerable risk; *neither* is likely to have adequate knowledge of all factors that may impact the supply of the collectible at any given point in time to be able to pinpoint a true and "fair" price for the same.

An individual who is investing in collectibles is usually purchasing a capital asset. Accordingly, any gain on the sale of a collectible is long-term capital gain, presuming it is held for the requisite period of time (more than a year from the date it is first acquired). However, the tax rate on the gain from a collectible is *not* the same as that for other capital assets. Under current law, the long-term capital gain on a collectible is taxed at a flat rate of 28% and does *not*, therefore, qualify for the preferential 5 or

15% long-term capital gain rate applicable to other investments. Like other investments, the investor may control the timing of any gain or loss on the collectible (for example, he or she simply holds onto the tangible asset for the given year and does not sell it), but this may be even more important in light of the higher tax rate applied when a taxable event does in fact occur.

Gold and Gold Mutual Funds

Gold (and other precious metals) are believed to be an *inflation hedge* in the investment marketplace. That is to say that when the investor anticipates that higher-than-average domestic inflation rates are likely to occur (or when the investor's dollars are being eroded because of international currency fluctuations), the price of gold will, therefore, tend to increase. In addition, if there is political or economic tension in the United States, or elsewhere in the world, gold is viewed as an extremely stable and secure investment. For these very same reasons, gold is also considered to be a highly *speculative* investment, since it is not as readily influenced as other investments by the normal economic factors of supply and demand.

There are various ways of participating in the market for gold, which includes gold bullion, gold coins, gold mining stocks and gold mutual funds. Bullion and coins are a direct investment in the metal, with its price fixed at various times in one of three major exchanges: London, New York, and Hong Kong. At certain points in time (for example, when inflation is high or anticipated to be high), gold-mining stocks have been very profitable. Nonetheless, these stocks also tend to follow the price of gold itself and offer primarily the convenience of not housing the metal directly. A gold mutual fund offers the investor a way of participating in the metal without the risks incurred by an unsophisticated investor dealing directly in gold or even gold-mining stocks. As with other mutual funds, the gold mutual fund provides the opportunity for diversification as well as investment management expertise not available to the typical unsophisticated investor who may be attracted to gold only for cosmetic or non-economic reasons.

Taxable gain or loss on a gold (or other precious metals) transaction is a capital gain or loss so long as the investor is not a dealer in metals. Taxable gain is realized and recognized to the extent that an investor receives more on disposition than he or she originally paid for the metal. A loss is allowable to the extent that the disposition amount is less than the original acquisition price. Similar to other capital assets, the length of time that the metal was held prior to disposition determines whether the gain or loss is short or long term in nature. However, unlike, for example, securities generally, it is possible to accomplish a non-taxable *(like kind)* exchange with gold or other precious metals. Specifically, if the metal received is of the same nature and character as the metal surrendered in the exchange, there is no immediate tax consequence. Accordingly, if one investor trades gold coins for the gold bullion of another investor, no gain or loss is recognized on the transaction.

Natural Resources/Oil and Gas

While investments in natural resources encompass more than solely oil or gas wells, for many investors they are one and the same. Therefore, oil and gas wells will be the focus of this discussion.

There are three basic types of oil and gas investments:

1. Exploratory drilling (also known by the popular term of *wildcatting*)
2. Development (or the search for oil or gas close to proven wells or after finding a proven field)
3. Income (investment in the production of proven reserves or an existing well)

Of these three basic types, the investor incurs the greatest risk with exploratory drilling. This is because, historically, only 10% of exploratory wells are successful. However, as should be expected by the risk and return relationship, if a wildcat well does "hit," the potential return is considerable. Alternatively, by participating only in proven development or income properties, investor risk is reduced considerably.

Few investors buy a direct interest in oil and gas wells. Rather, most prefer the limited partnership vehicle as the means by which to invest in natural resources. They generally perceive that the advantage of limiting their liability to the extent of their investment outweighs the disadvantage of not making operating decisions with respect to the wells. Accordingly, most invest as limited partners that are entitled only to an income or *royalty interest* in the wells that are the subject of the general partner's investments. Nevertheless, those who do invest directly do so by acquiring what is known as a *working interest* in a co-owned oil or gas well. These investors participate in every item of income and expense attributable to the operation. As a result, they are accorded certain income tax advantages, notably an exception to the *passive activity* rules that limit the amount of losses that a limited partner (or *passive investor*) may deduct against income.

There are several major tax advantages associated with an investment in oil or gas wells. Specifically, a deduction is permitted for the *depletion* of the remaining oil and gas reserves left in the ground once drilling has occurred and proven successful. There are two types of depletion and, to the extent permitted (as mentioned, generally only a direct working interest investment qualifies for tax benefits), an investor will typically use the method that generates the *largest* deduction. *Cost depletion* essentially prorates the investor's contribution in the property between the number of oil or gas units sold during the taxable year and the number of estimated units remaining. It is the theoretical equivalent of *straight line depreciation* that is applicable to direct real property investments. Alternatively, *percentage depletion* allows for a deduction of a specified percentage of the gross income derived from the property and is the functional equivalent of the *modified accelerated cost recovery* (MACRS) system used to depreciate commercial or rental real estate. Of the two types of depletion, percentage depletion is preferred by many investors since it yields the greater amount of up-front tax benefits. Thus, percentage depletion is also included as a *tax preference item* when computing an investor's potential alternative minimum tax (AMT) liability.

Intangible drilling costs (IDCs) incurred in exploratory and development oil or gas programs are also potentially income tax deductible. Accordingly, an investor may either: 1) capitalize and amortize these costs over the projected *useful life* (production period) of the well, or 2) deduct (or *expense*) them currently in the taxable year in which the expense is paid or incurred. However, as a practical matter, this choice may already be made for the investor in the limited partnership form of oil or gas investment. This is because the election to capitalize or expense IDCs is normally pre-selected by the general partner of the partnership with the decision to expense these costs immediately as the prevailing standard.

There are numerous fees that a limited partner in an oil and gas *syndication* are likely to pay. Among these are management fees, sales commissions, and broker-dealer fees. In total, these fees will generally range from 15 percent to 20 percent of the equity invested in the limited partnership. In exchange for his or her investment as a limited partner (and payment of all these fees), the investor receives the possibility of considerable income and the potential for significant capital appreciation of his or her proportionate partnership interest. In addition, an investor who desires additional diversification of his or her portfolio will likely find an oil or gas investment attractive.

IMPORTANT CONCEPTS

Derivative	Spread
Hedge	Straddle
Stock option	Forward contract
Long	Futures contract
Short	Financial futures
Option exercise price	Commodity futures
Option premium	Price inelasticity
Intrinsic value of an option	Collectible
Time value of an option	Gold
Chicago Board of Options Exchange	Gold mutual funds
Options Clearing Corporation (OCC)	Exploratory drilling
Call	Development of oil or gas wells
Put	Income from oil or gas
In-the-money	Royalty interest
Out-of-the-money	Working interest
Time premium	Cost depletion
Breakeven point of an option	Percentage depletion
Long-term equity anticipation security (LEAPs)	Intangible drilling costs (IDCs)

QUESTIONS FOR REVIEW

1. What is a *derivative* investment? Give an example.

2. In a stock option contract, who *has the right to exercise* and who *has the obligation* if this right is exercised? Explain.

3. What are the three specifications that are included in any stock option contract?

4. In options trading, what is the difference between being in a *covered* position and being in a *naked* position? Which of these two positions involves the most risk for the investor?

5. At what time is the option on a premium taxed to the seller or writer? Explain.

6. What is the difference between an *American-style* and a *European-style* option?

7. Where are stock options traded?

8. If an investor *buys* a call option, what does this entitle him or her to do? What happens if the investor *sells* this same type of option?

9. When is a call option *in-the-money*? When is it *out-of-the-money*?

10. What is meant by the term *intrinsic value* of an option and how is this computed?

11. How is the *time premium* of an option computed?

12. When is a put option *in-the-money*? When is it *out-of-the money*?

13. Assume that you read the following in the *Wall Street Journal*:

    ABC Sept 2009 45 Call at 6.

    What is the *breakeven point* of this call option? When is it likely that the option will be exercised?

14. How is the capital gain or loss of a put option computed for income tax purposes?

15. What is a LEAP? How does it differ from the standard form of stock option?

16. What is a *spread* as it is used in options trading? What is a *straddle* as it is used for this same purpose?

17. Contrast a *forward contract* to that of a *futures contract*. Which one of these is predominant in the secondary marketplace and why?

18. If a futures contract is *marked to market*, what does this mean?

19. What are the five types of financial futures in which an individual can invest? Why is an investor likely to hold any of these types of futures?

20. What is the meaning of the term *hedge* as it is practiced in the futures market?

21. What is meant by the term *closing out* a futures contract?

22. If a farmer plants wheat (and then participates in the commodity futures market), he is said to be what? If he wants to *hedge* his risk, what does he do?

23. What is meant by the term *price inelasticity* and what type of asset normally exhibits this characteristic?

24. What is the major risk associated with investing in collectibles?

25. What is the income tax rate that applies at the time of disposition or sale of a collectible?

26. Why does an investor usually make an investment in gold bullion or gold coins?

27. If gold coins are traded for gold bullion, is this a taxable transaction? Explain why or why not.

28. What are the three basic types of oil and gas investments? In which type does a potential investor incur the most risk?

29. Contrast *cost depletion* to *percentage depletion*. Which one normally provides the largest immediate income tax benefit?

30. How (in what form) do most investors make an oil or gas investment? Why?

SUGGESTIONS FOR ADDITIONAL READING

Tools and Techniques of Investment Planning, 2nd edition, Stephen R. Leimberg, Robert T. LeClair, Robert J. Doyle, Jr., and Thomas R. Robinson, The National Underwriter Company, 2006.

Investments: An Introduction, 9th edition, Herbert B. Mayo, Thomson/ South-Western, 2008.

Investment Analysis and Portfolio Management, 9th edition, Frank K. Reilly and Keith C. Brown, Thomson/South-Western, 2009.

*The Wall Street Journal Guide to Money and Investing,*3rd edition, Kenneth M. Morris and Virginia B. Morris, Fireside Publishing, 2004.

CHAPTER EIGHT

Sources of Investment Risk

• • •

The previous seven chapters of this textbook discussed the types of investment vehicles that are available in the present day primary and secondary marketplace. The remainder of this text (specifically chapters 8-18) will look at the factors that a financial planner should consider in making an investment decision, including investment strategies and asset allocation principles. The text will conclude with an analysis of certain income tax considerations that bear on the making of the proper investment decision.

Upon completing this chapter, you should be able to:

- Define investment risk
- Discuss the importance of diversification and asset allocation in minimizing investment risk
- Identify the components of total risk, including the appropriate measurement of each component
- Describe the sources of systematic risk

DEFINITION OF INVESTMENT RISK

Investment risk is the uncertainty that an investment's actual or *realized* return will not equal its *expected* return. An investment's realized returns may be tracked by its actual annual historical returns. However, the *expected return* is forward looking to the next investment horizon. This return is the sum of the products of possible outcomes multiplied by their corresponding probability of occurrence:

$$\text{Expected Return } (\overline{X}) = \sum_{t-1}^{n} X_i(P_i)$$

Where:

X_i = Outcome event

P_i = Probability of the outcome event

Number of events = 1,2,3...n

The probability of a given return occurring may be based on historic returns if the trend is expected to continue, which, of course, may or may not be relevant to actual future returns. Forecasting models, such as Monte Carlo simulation, may be used to identify possible outcome pathways with associated probabilities.

> **Example 8-1:** Assume that an investment has a 20% probability of experiencing a negative 10% annual return and that it also has this same 20% probability of encountering a negative 5% annual return. Further, assume that the investment has a 20% chance of attaining a positive 5% return and a 40% chance of achieving a positive 10% return annually. Therefore, we would *expect* an actual or realized return of a positive 2% for this investment or:
>
> Expected return = -10%(0.20) + -5%(0.20) + 5%(0.20) + 10%(0.40) = 2.0%

Investment theory is predicated on investors being risk adverse. That does not mean they shun risk by not investing in risky assets at all, but that they are adequately compensated through investment returns for the amount of risk taken. However, investors have varying degrees of risk tolerance or the level of risk that becomes unacceptable to them. In turn, an investor's risk tolerance dictates his or her range of acceptable investments.

Importance of Diversification and Asset Allocation

There are several strategies that will assist the investor in managing investment risk. Among these are portfolio diversification and asset allocation. While each of these is discussed much more fully in chapter 17 of this text, they are mentioned here because of their importance in helping the investor to achieve what should be his or her fundamental investment goal: *obtaining the highest possible investment return while assuming the lowest amount of possible investment risk.*

Diversification is structuring an individual's investment *portfolio* to maximize risk/return. In other words, an investor should attempt to realize the greatest amount of return per unit of risk. This may be pursued by: (1) structuring a portfolio that contains assets with low correlation to each other and/or (2) having a longer investment horizon. For example, an individual under age 40, who is saving for a retirement investment goal, may purchase an *aggressive investment* (defined as an investment that exhibits a wide variation of actual returns) much more safely than an individual age 65 or over. Why? Because the younger individual has a much longer time to experience the probability of significant positive returns to offset the likelihood of several negative returns. Further, as we shall see, since each asset class may not move either in the same direction as another (known as *correlation*) or in the same amount, it is possible to combine asset classes to reduce an investor's overall risk.

Asset allocation has been shown to be a very predictive determinant of a portfolio's overall realized return (the Brinson academic studies investigated this same issue). As such, before an individual selects his or her individual investments, it may be prudent to determine how much money should be allocated to each of the three traditional asset classes: (1) cash and cash equivalents; (2) stocks (*equities*); and (3) bonds (*debt*). Since each of these asset classes exhibits a different risk/return tradeoff, an effective blending is likely critical to the achievement of an investor's financial goals. In addition, some investors will want to invest in additional asset classes, such as real estate or precious metals, which have historically proven to have lower correlations to financial assets, making them particularly useful in reducing a portfolio's risk.

TOTAL RISK

The total (absolute) risk associated with any investment has two components: 1) *unsystematic*, also known as *diversifiable* risk and 2) *systematic*, also known as *nondiversifiable* risk. This relationship may also be reduced to the equation:

Total Risk = Unsystematic Risk + Systematic Risk

As we will discuss in the subsequent chapter, total risk is measured by the *standard deviation of an asset.*

Total risk is defined as the combination of all systematic and unsystematic risk that the investor assumes. In turn, as we shall learn, the investor can only *manage* systematic risk, whereas he or she can greatly *reduce* unsystematic risk through the proper diversification of assets. Unsystematic risk may be reduced significantly through proper diversification; specifically, by owning securities of companies in different industries or sectors of the market. For example, it is possible to reduce (some would say eliminate) unsystematic risk by owning 10-15 different stocks of companies involved in the different industries of energy, health care, financial services, etc. In contrast, systematic risk cannot be reduced since all investment assets are subject to this type of risk; indeed, systematic risk can only be managed and not eliminated.

Unsystematic Risk

Unsystematic risk is risk that affects only a *particular company* and its securities. Examples are the *business* or *financial risk* associated with how a company operates. Broadly, the liquidity risk that affects certain types of assets is also a type of unsystematic risk. All these types of risk are characterized by the fact that diversification (other than simply not investing in that stock or asset) may be used to protect the investor. If investing in a particular stock or asset, its risk may be offset by counter-movements in the other assets within the investor's portfolio.

Business or *company risk* is the economic or operating risk reflected in the fluctuation of the company's earnings. In turn, the variation in a company's earnings directly impacts the valuation of its stock through the price/earnings relative valuation measure that is widely adopted by financial analysts. The best defense against business risk is to invest in more than one company and in companies that are engaged in different lines of business or market sectors.

Closely related to business risk is the *financial risk* that a company incurs with respect to how it finances its business operations and/or expansion. Specifically, the more debt *(or leverage)* used by a firm to raise business capital, the greater its financial risk. This is because debt (particularly that which is secured or collateralized) must eventually be repaid to its holder (in the investment world, this is a bond owner) or the company will eventually become insolvent. An insolvency can lead to the liquidation of the business with investors in the company losing their entire investment. Financial risk is monitored by bond ratings services, such as Standard & Poor's or Moody's Investment Services.

Finally, *liquidity risk* is the possibility of not being able to sell an asset without a significant loss of principal. Generally, most cash equivalents (such as a checking or passbook savings account) are considered highly *liquid* since they can be quickly converted into cash without any loss to principal. In contrast, collectibles and real estate are characterized by their *lack* of liquidity. As we have discussed, however, the lack of liquidity of an asset should not be confused with a potential lack of marketability of that same asset. As an example, some publicly traded stocks may be relatively illiquid, but they are still marketable. Recall that liquidity is characterized by the ability to buy or sell relatively large volumes without materially affecting the price.

Investors holding illiquid assets should be mindful of liquidity risk and are well advised to have sufficient liquid assets available to offset any financial emergencies. This is also one of the main reasons that financial planners recommend maintaining three to six months of living expenses in liquid assets as an "emergency" or "contingency fund", which is readily convertible to cash prior to investing in securities.

Systematic Risk

Also known as *nondiversifiable risk*, systematic risk reflects the widespread or economy-wide uncertainty associated with an investment in *any* type of asset. This part of total risk is inescapable because, no matter how effectively an investor diversifies, the risk of the overall economy cannot be avoided. The most prominent example of systematic risk is the business cycle experienced by all businesses (and, by extension, its equity or debt offerings) in the constant ebb and flow of economic supply and demand. As long as a business is a *going concern* and contributes to the supply and demand paradigm, it cannot protect itself from systematic risk. It can only attempt to effectively manage this risk.

There are five basic components of systematic risk as follows:
1. Purchasing power (*inflation*) risk
2. Reinvestment rate risk
3. Interest rate risk
4. Market risk
5. Exchange rate (*currency*) risk

It is easy to remember these components of systematic risk by the pneumonic *PRIME*, using the first letters of each risk category.

Systematic risk is measured by the *beta coefficient (beta)* of an asset, which will be described more fully in subsequent chapters of this book.

Purchasing Power Risk

Purchasing power risk, or *inflation risk*, is the potential loss of purchasing power of an investment due to inflation. An example is the rising price of economic goods and services over time. Historically (at least since 1926), the rate of annual inflation has averaged 3 percent. This means that, using the so-called *Rule of 72*, the price of these goods and services has approximately doubled every 24 years (72 divided by 3). As a result, any investment asset that generates a specified annual income return (such as an immediate fixed annuity) is subject to a loss of real purchasing power as inflation erodes the value of the dollars received. Nonetheless, the actual risk associated with inflation is not so much with the current level of inflation (since an *inflation premium* is normally built into the purchase price of any investment asset), but with levels of *unanticipated* inflationary pressures. Indeed, some theoretical valuation models (such as the *multi-factor model* or *arbitrage pricing theory*) attempt to account for this unanticipated or unexpected rate of inflation, but it remains, at best, still an art as opposed to a science.

Reinvestment Rate Risk

Reinvestment rate risk primarily impacts fixed-income securities, particularly those that are sensitive to refinancing, such as mortgage-backed securities, like GNMA (Ginnie Mae) certificates. Specifically, reinvestment rate risk is the risk that proceeds available for reinvestment must be reinvested at a *lower* interest rate than the original investment vehicle that generated the proceeds. As an example, when mortgage interest rates fall, existing mortgage holders will rush to refinance their mortgages. Holders of these mortgage certificates will, therefore, experience, a sudden flurry of principal repayments, which puts them in the undesirable financial position of having to reinvest these repayments at now lower yields.

Interest Rate Risk

Some commentators include reinvestment rate risk as one of the two components of *interest rate risk* (the other component being the risk to the value of the principal of a fixed income asset such as a bond). However, interest rate risk is a very broad type of systematic risk stating that an increase in market interest rates will cause the market value of a fixed income security to fall. In other words, interest rates and bond prices move in *opposite directions*. When interest rates decline, bond prices increase; when interest rates increase, the price of a bond falls. A *discount bond* is one that is selling in the secondary market at a price *less* than its par value. This happens whenever the prevailing market interest rate (as reflected in any new issues of debt securities) *exceeds* the existing bond's coupon rate. Conversely, a *premium bond* is one that is selling in the secondary market at a price *more* than its par value. Bonds sell at a premium whenever interest rates fall *below* the existing bond's coupon rate. Note that when bonds sell at a premium, price change is favorable to the investor but the lower interest rate introduces reinvestment rate risk for coupon cash flows.

Interest rate risk has nothing to do with the quality of the issuer of the bond. Rather, it simply reflects the fact that (new) bonds may now be issued at a higher rate of interest than that being paid by existing bonds. Given the inverse relationship between market interest rates and bond prices, as the bond price *falls*, the current yield to an investor will *rise*. Accordingly, the price of the existing bond will have to decline sufficiently to make it more attractive to potential buyers that can now purchase a newly issued bond paying a higher interest rate. Therefore, as an investment strategy, shorter term securities are more attractive in rising interest rate environments, since holders of such securities receive their principal repayments much sooner than if they had invested in longer term securities. The price of a bond in the secondary market is a function of its coupon rate, its maturity date, and the direction market interest rates move (up or down) before the bond matures. As we shall see in chapter 13 of this text, all of these factors are succinctly captured in the concept of *bond duration*.

Market Risk

Market risk is the most fundamental type of systematic risk. In fact, CFP Board, in its latest edition of CFP® Certification Examination topics, equates market risk with systematic risk. However, more properly, market risk is a *component* of systematic risk.

Market risk is the risk of the overall securities marketplace and is sometimes simply referred to as *volatility*. It applies mainly to stocks and stock options and cannot generally be avoided by an investor in the stock market, no matter which exchange lists the stock he or she is purchasing. Volatility describes market risk because it refers to the movement of the investment rather than the reason for this movement. Such a word also implies that some reference point or *benchmark* is being used to track this movement; in this case, that benchmark is the stock market itself. The *more volatile* the movement of a stock (as represented by the term beta *coefficient* or *beta*), the *greater* its risk in comparison with other stocks included within the market index.

As is commonly understood, stocks tend to perform most favorably when economic conditions are favorable and there is an absence of unanticipated factors impacting the future growth of a company's earnings. This is commonly referred to by the popular term *bull market*. Alternatively, if economic conditions are unfavorable or deteriorating, the term *bear market* is applied to encapsulate the existence of market risk. Of course, what moves markets (or the *cause* of the resulting volatility) has been the subject of many books and articles and will not be dealt with here. Rather, it is sufficient to state that if an investor purchases *any* security (most notably, stocks) for his or her portfolio, market risk *cannot* be avoided. It can only be *managed* (which, of course, is what professional money managers are paid to do).

Exchange Rate Risk

The final component of systematic risk is *exchange rate* (or *currency) risk*. Such risk is the uncertainty associated with changes in the value of currencies and affects primarily those individuals who invest in foreign securities. As an example, assume that an American investor invests in a German stock and pays for the purchase with the euro. Even if the share value appreciates, the American investor may still lose money if the euro depreciates (or weakens) relative to the American dollar since, on the date of the conversion, the euro will buy less dollars. Conversely, the American investor may reap a double benefit (including the appreciation of the German stock) if the euro appreciates (or strengthens) with respect to the American dollar and, upon conversion, the euro will buy more dollars.

When a country intentionally changes the value of its currency relative to another country's currency (usually the American dollar), this process is known as *devaluation* or *revaluation*, depending on the directional change in the value of the currency. If a country's currency value *declines* with respect to another currency's value (in other words, it now takes more of the adjusted currency to exchange for the benchmark currency), it is referred to as *devaluing* the adjusted currency. If a country's currency value *increases* with respect to the referenced currency, it is referred to as *revaluing* the adjusted currency or appreciation against the reference currency.

> **Example 8-2:** Jay invests $10,000 U.S. in Mitsubishi stock (a Japanese company) when the exchange rate is 80 Japanese yen to the U.S. dollar. The stock of Mitsubishi then increases in value one year later by 50 percent relative to the yen. However, during this same time, the U.S. dollar has strengthened against the yen to 100 yen per dollar, meaning that the dollar will now purchase 20 more yen than when Jay bought the Mitsubishi stock. One year later, Jay sells the stock and receives 1.2 million yen. Jay's annual return on the investment is
>
> Initial investment = $10,000 x ¥80/$ = ¥800,000
> Stock appreciation (50 percent) = ¥800,000(1.50) = ¥1,200,000
> Conversion to U.S. dollars = ¥1,200,000 / $/¥100 = $12,000
> Dollar yield = ($12,000 - $10,000)/$10,000 = 0.20 or 20 percent

Alternatively, if the exchange rate had remained at 80 yen per dollar, his actual return would have been 50 percent ($5,000 divided by $10,000).

As we discussed in chapter 3 of this textbook, a popular method of investing in foreign securities while minimizing exchange rate risk is to purchase American Depository Receipts (ADRs) for those shares. An American Depository Receipt is a receipt issued by a U.S. bank on foreign securities purchased by the bank through a foreign representative and held in trust for the benefit of the ADR owner. Such a receipt is priced in American dollars and traded on all U.S. exchanges in the same manner as stocks. Further, while dividends on these foreign shares are declared in the local currency, they are paid in American dollars, subsequent to the U.S. bank withholding for any foreign taxes that are due (and for which the American investor receives an income tax credit or deduction).

Finally, a closely related risk to that of exchange rate risk is that of *political* (or *country) risk.* Political risk refers to the risk that a foreign country will not be able to honor its financial commitments, or that it is pursuing policies that are likely to be problematic for foreign investors, e.g.. nationalization or expropriation. Often it is caused by a major change in the political governance or economic system of a country. Investors or financial planners wishing to invest internationally should analyze such risk carefully as it could potentially impact the amount of future investment return.

Other Investment Risk

Two other often-overlooked types of risk that an investor should consider are *tax risk* (sometimes referred to as *tax-rate risk*) and the *risk of investment manager change* relating to his or her professionally managed assets (see chapter 4).

Tax Risk

Tax risk is the ever-present uncertainty associated with the tax laws that potentially impact the ownership and/or disposition of investment assets. For example, income and transfer tax laws in effect today may not be the same in the future. As such, it is becoming more and more difficult to effectively evaluate how long an investment asset should be held and, perhaps, when it should be sold.

Since the Tax Reform Act of 1986 (which itself was so massive as to require a renaming of the Tax Code to the *Internal Revenue Code of 1986*), there have been at least eight additional major tax bills. Further, as of this writing, the Obama administration is proposing yet another major rewriting of the Tax Code. In addition, major changes have occurred in the regulatory arena that have deregulated the financial services industry (witness the Financial Service Modernization Act of 1999 that repealed the long-standing Glass Steagall Act). Therefore, the only statement that may really be definitive about tax law and regulation is that "it never stays the same".

That being said, an investor does need to be aware that a fundamental tool of income tax planning and management is that of *income conversion*. Specifically, this means that an investor should attempt to convert or re-characterize income from that of *ordinary income* (such as salary or wages) into that of *capital gains*. Generally, any asset purchased for investment purposes will constitute a *capital asset* and, thus, qualify for a preferential rate if held for a sufficient period. This preferential rate is currently 5% (0 percent for 2008–2010) or 15%, depending on the investor's regular marginal income tax bracket and holding period of the asset. In turn, this compares to a top marginal *ordinary income* tax bracket of 35% (a potential 35% spread in applicable tax rates). Multiplied over many years and many investment dollars, this 35% spread may result in sizeable income tax savings and, ultimately, considerably more after-tax compounded dollars.

Indeed, tax management is a valuable tool in controlling investment tax risk, with the importance of effective tax management increasing the higher the individual's marginal income tax bracket and tax rate.

Investment Manager Risk

As is generally well known, the majority of actively managed funds under the management of a professional money manager *under-perform* compared to the broader market indexes. Accordingly, passively managed funds, such as an index fund, have recently increased in popularity. In addition, even if an actively managed fund does out-perform the overall market in one year, there is no guarantee that it will do so the next year. In part, this is because a professionally managed fund may lose its portfolio manager. This is particularly true if such manager is considered to be outstanding from the viewpoint of his or her peers, so that he or she is recruited away from one fund to manage another. This is what is collectively referred to as *investment manager risk*.

There is really no effective way to learn about what may be happening internally at a mutual fund or mutual fund family to avoid investment manager risk. However, the risk may be minimized by researching the historical performance of the fund or fund family. If the annual return achieved by the manager exceeds the average, it is unlikely that the manager will leave the fund in the immediate future as the fund family will likely fairly compensate him or her for his or her efforts. Additionally, some managers speak openly about what is fundamental to their investment philosophy. For example, the well-respected Peter Lynch, while running the Fidelity Magellan Fund, spoke openly about his aversion to large size mutual funds. Thus, as the Magellan Fund increased in size, it should have been of little surprise to the investors of the fund that he ultimately chose to pursue other business endeavors.

IMPORTANT CONCEPTS

Investment risk

Expected return

Total or absolute risk

Diversification

Asset allocation

Unsystematic or diversifiable risk

Systematic or nondiversifiable risk

Standard deviation

Beta coefficient

Business risk

Financial risk

Liquidity risk

Purchasing power risk

Reinvestment rate risk

Interest rate risk

Market risk

Volatility

Exchange rate risk

Devaluation

Revaluation

Political risk

Tax or tax rate risk

Investment manager risk

QUESTIONS FOR REVIEW

1. Define what is meant by the term *investment risk.*

2. What should be the fundamental investment goal of any client?

3. What have academic studies shown to be the single most important determinant of an investor's overall realized return and an effective tool in minimizing investor risk?

4. What are the two components that make up the total or absolute risk of an investment?

   Which one of these two components can be *diversified away*?

5. What is the unsystematic risk of an investment?

6. How does an investor go about effectively reducing unsystematic risk?

7. Assume that a company finances its business operations with an excessive amount of bank loans. What type of risk is experienced by an investor who invests in the stock of this company?

8. List two types of investments that are characterized by their lack of liquidity. What does this mean to a potential investor in these types of investments?

9. What is the systematic risk of an investment?

10. What are the five generally accepted components of systematic risk? Give an example of the type of investment asset most affected by each of these components.

11. What is the relationship of market interest rates and bond prices?

12. Assume that a bond is selling in the secondary market currently at a price more than its par value. Why does this occur?

13. "Market risk is sometimes simply referred to as the volatility of an investment." Explain what is meant by this statement.

14. What is an effective method of managing the exchange rate risk that is associated with the purchase of a foreign security?

15. Contrast *devaluing* a foreign currency to that of *revaluing* that same currency.

16. What is an effective tool that may be used to minimize the tax rate risk associated with an investment?

17. Explain *investment manager risk*. Where is it most commonly experienced in an investor's portfolio?

SUGGESTIONS FOR ADDITIONAL READING

Tools and Techniques of Investment Planning, 2nd edition, Stephen R. Leimberg, Robert T. LeClair, Robert J. Doyle, Jr., and Thomas R. Robinson, The National Underwriter Company, 2006.

Investments: An Introduction, 9th edition, Herbert B. Mayo, Thomson/ South-Western, 2008.

Investment Analysis and Portfolio Management, 9th edition, Frank K. Reilly and Keith C. Brown, Thomson/South-Western, 2009.

The Wall Street Journal Guide to Money and Investing, 3rd edition, Kenneth M. Morris and Virginia B. Morris, Fireside Publishing, 2004.

CHAPTER NINE

Measurements of Investment Risk

• • •

As a logical progression from the previous chapter wherein the types and sources of investment risk were discussed, this chapter considers how to quantitatively compute that risk. Accordingly, a proper understanding of certain formulas used to measure investment risk and the ability to compute the appropriate measure using a financial function calculator (for example, the Hewlett Packard, HP 10BII) is very important.

Upon completing this chapter, you should be able to:

- Identify types of probability distributions and the role that such distributions play in quantifying investment risk
- Explain and compute the standard deviation of an asset or portfolio
- Explain the concept of semi-variance and its use in quantitative analysis
- Apply and compute covariance and/or correlation coefficient as a measurement of investment risk
- Explain and compute the beta coefficient of an asset or portfolio
- Apply and compute coefficients of determination as a measurement of investment risk
- Use and interpret coefficients of determination in portfolio evaluation

MEASURES OF CENTRAL TENDENCY

A useful statistic in defining a population or a set of observations is the average of those observations. What point values represent the largest cluster of observations of a population or sample of a population? Measures of central tendency are single value estimates of the population (or sample) and include the mean, median, and mode.

Mean

The mean is the average value of the observations. This can be the arithmetic mean or the geometric mean. The arithmetic mean or simple average is the sum of the observations divided by the number of observations:

$$\overline{X} = \frac{\sum_{i=1}^{n} X_i}{n} \text{ , Where:}$$

Σ is the mathematical notation for "sum."

X_i = observation i

n = number of observations

The geometric mean is the compound average of the observations. The geometric average may be used for expressing the compounded rate of change, rate of return, etc. The formula for determining the geometric mean is:

$$\overline{X} = \left[\prod_{i=1}^{n} (1 + k_i) \right]^{1/n} - 1 \text{ , Where:}$$

Π is the mathematical notation for "product."

k_i = observation as a percentage expressed in decimal form

n = number of observations

As an example, following is a *population* of observations of portfolio returns for the last five years:

Year 1	15%
Year 2	8%
Year 3	-1.5%
Year 4	8%
Year 5	18%

The arithmetic mean is:

$$\overline{X} = \frac{15\% + 8\% - 1.5\% + 8\% + 18\%}{5} = \frac{47.5\%}{5} = 9.50\%$$

The geometric mean is:

$$\overline{X} = \left[(1.15)(1.08)(0.985)(1.08)(1.18)\right]^{1/5} - 1 = (1.5591)^{0.20} - 1 = 1.0929 - 1 = 0.0929 \text{ or } 9.29\%$$

Why is the geometric mean less than the arithmetic mean? The reason is because of compounding. The compounded average is always less than the arithmetic average unless the observations are the same. Only then does the arithmetic mean equal the geometric mean. When dealing with observations that represent rates of growth or rates of return, the geometric mean is preferable.

Median
The median is the central value of observations arranged in order of lowest to highest. From the above data of observations:

-1.5%, 8%, 8%, 15%, 18%

The median is 8 percent since two observations lie below and two observations lie above this value. If the number of observations is even, the median is the average of the two central values.

Mode
The mode is the observation value with the greatest frequency. In the data set above, the mode is 8 percent since two observations represent the greatest frequency.

Therefore, from this data set we have four different measures of central tendency:

> Arithmetic mean = 9.50%
>
> Geometric mean = 9.29%
>
> Median = 8%
>
> Mode = 8%

The mean is an absolute value and is the best indicator of central tendency of a distribution. The geometric mean is used in determining compounded rates of return.

Expected Value
The expected value is the mean of a probability distribution. A probability distribution is a distribution of *expected* observations, *not historical* observations. Since the observations are expected, a probability is associated with their possible occurrence. Assume that the five observations given above are expected observations for the upcoming year with the associated probabilities in parenthesis:

-1.5% (0.05)

8% (0.50)

15% (0.30)

18% (0.15)

Note that the probabilities sum to one.

The expected value is determined by the formula:

$$\overline{X} = \sum_{i=1}^{n}(X_i)P(X_i)$$, Where:

X_i = observation i
$P(X_i)$ = probability of occurrence of observation i

$$\overline{X} = -1.5\%(0.05) + 8\%(0.50) + 15\%(0.30) + 18\%(0.15) = -0.075\% + 4\% + 4.5\% + 2.7\% = 11.125\%$$

Therefore, the expected value for the probability distribution example is 11.125%.

MEASURES OF DISPERSION

Variance
Variance is a statistical measure of dispersion around the arithmetic mean or expected value. Dispersion represents total risk. Thus, the variance is an absolute measure of total risk. The greater the variance is, the greater the total risk since outlying outcomes may occur, i.e., large losses (as well as the possibility of large gains).

The variance, σ^2, of a *population* is determined by the formula:

$$\sigma^2 = \frac{\sum(X_i - \overline{X})^2}{n}$$

The difference between the observed value and the mean is squared to capture the total dispersion, i.e., negative observations do not offset positive observations. However, squaring results in nonsensical units, such as square percent, square dollars, etc.. Therefore, taking the square root of the variance restores the measurement process to useable units. The square root of the variance is the standard deviation, σ. or:

$$\sigma = \sqrt{\sigma^2}$$

Refer to the population of returns exhibited above. The variance of the returns is:

$$\sigma^2 = \frac{(15\% - 9.5\%)^2 + (8\% - 9.5\%)^2 + (-1.5\% - 9.5\%)^2 + (8\% - 9.5\%)^2 + (18\% - 9.5\%)^2}{5} = \frac{228}{5} = 45.6$$

$$\sigma^2 = 45.6\%^2 \text{ (nonsensical)}$$

However, the standard deviation is:

$$\sigma = \sqrt{45.6\%^2} = 6.75\%$$

If the data set was a *sample* rather than a population, the variance equation must then be adjusted to reflect the ability to find the fifth value if the average and the other four variables are known. This refers to so-called "degrees of freedom" with the resulting adjustment as "n-1" in the denominator instead of "n."

As an example, assume that the five observations are not a population of the last five years but a five-year sample from the last 30 years. Thus, the variance would be:

$$\sigma^2 = \frac{(15\% - 9.5\%)^2 + (8\% - 9.5\%)^2 + (-1.5\% - 9.5\%)^2 + (8\% - 9.5\%)^2 + (18\% - 9.5\%)^2}{5 - 1} = \frac{228}{4} = 57$$

$$\sigma^2 = 57\%^2$$

The standard deviation is:

$$\sigma = \sqrt{57\%^2} = 7.55\%$$

You should be aware that most financial function calculators default to the *sample* standard deviation and not to the *population* standard deviation.

Variance of a Probability Distribution

The variance of a probability distribution is the sum of the differences of the expected observation and the expected value squared times the probability of occurrence of the observation. This may be written in formula format as follows:

$$\sigma^2 = \sum (X_i - \overline{X})^2 P(X_i)$$

When referring to the earlier probability distribution of expected returns, the variance is:

$$\sigma^2 = (-1.5\% - 11.125\%)^2 (0.05) + (8\% - 11.125\%)^2 (0.50) + (15\% - 11.125\%)^2 (0.30) + (18\% - 11.125\%)^2 (0.15)$$
$$\sigma^2 = 7.9695 + 4.8828 + 4.5047 + 7.0898 = 24.4468\%^2$$

The standard deviation is:

$$\sigma = \sqrt{24.4468\%^2} = 4.94\%$$

When dealing with expected observations, i.e., returns, and their probabilities of occurrence, the variance formula for a probability distribution should be used.

Coefficient of Variation

Variance/standard deviation is an *absolute* measure of dispersion of a set of observations. Alternatively, the coefficient of variation is a *relative* measure of dispersion allowing comparison between two different sets of observations. The coefficient of variation is found using the formula:

$$CV = \frac{\sigma}{\overline{X}}$$

Therefore, the coefficient of variation, CV, is the standard deviation divided by the mean or expected value. For investment returns, the coefficient of variation is a measure of the *relative* amount of risk per unit of return. The coefficient of variation for the population data set above is:

$$CV = \frac{6.75\%}{9.5\%} = 0.71$$

This value may be compared to other data sets with a resulting relationship that the higher the coefficient of variation is, the greater the relative risk of the investment.

Covariance/Correlation

Covariance is an absolute measure of the association between two sets of historical observations over time. The covariance of a *population* set is calculated using the formula:

$$COV_{i,j} = \frac{\sum (X_i - \overline{X}_i)(X_j - \overline{X}_j)}{n}$$

For a *sample* set, the denominator is "n-1."

For example, assume the following population of returns of Stock A and Stock B over the last five years:

Stock A	Stock B
10%	7%
21%	12%
-3%	2%
8%	5%
15%	11%

The mean and standard deviation of Stock A is 10.2% and 8.07%, respectively, and the mean and standard deviation of Stock B is 7.4% and 3.89%, respectively.

The covariance of the returns for Stock A and Stock B is:

$$COV_{A,B} = \frac{(10\% - 10.2\%)(7\% - 7.4\%) + (21\% - 10.2\%)(12\% - 7.4\%) + (-3\% - 10.2\%)(2\% - 7.4\%) + (8\% - 10.2\%)(5\% - 7.4\%) + (15\% - 10.2\%)(11\% - 7.4\%)}{5}$$

$$COV_{A,B} = 28.72$$

As with the variance, the covariance result is, intuitively, nonsensical. Therefore, dividing the covariance by the product of the standard deviations of Stock A and Stock B gives a useful relative measure, the correlation coefficient, or ρ:

$$\rho_{A,B} = \frac{COV_{A,B}}{\sigma_A \sigma_B} = \frac{28.72}{(8.07)(3.89)} = 0.9149$$

The correlation coefficient has values between -1 and $+1$. The value -1 means that the relationship between the historical sets of returns is perfectly negatively correlated, the value $+1$ is perfectly positively correlated, and the value zero implies no correlation. There is a high correlation between Stock A and Stock B in the example.

Portfolio Mean Return and Standard Deviation

The portfolio mean return is the weighted average of the asset returns in the portfolio:

$$\overline{X}_{Portfolio} = \sum X_i Wt_i \text{ , Where:}$$

X_i = the return of asset i in the portfolio, and
Wt_i = the weight of asset i in the portfolio.

Looking at a simple two-asset portfolio with the following characteristics:

Asset A	Asset B
$1,000,000	$2,000,000
15% return	10% return
7.5% standard deviation	5.2% standard deviation
Correlation $_{A,B}$ = 0.85	

The portfolio has a total value of $3,000,000 and its mean return is:

15% (0.3333) + 10%(0.6667) = 11.67%.

Note that because of correlation between portfolio assets, the standard deviation is *not* simply the weighted average of the standard deviations of the assets in the portfolio. Rather, the equation for the standard deviation of a portfolio is:

$$\sigma^2_{Portfolio} = \sum Wt_i^2 \sigma_i^2 + \sum \sum Wt_i Wt_j \sigma_i \sigma_j \rho_{i,j} \text{ (where i} \neq \text{j)}$$
$$\sigma_{Portfolio} = \sqrt{\sigma^2_{Portfolio}}$$

This formula looks formidable, but it simply states that the standard deviation of a portfolio is the square root of the sum of the product of the asset weights and variances in the portfolio plus the sum of the product of the weights, standard deviations, and correlation of each asset pair in the portfolio. The double sigma implies that a combination of asset A and asset B is in the form of AB or BA. The double-sigma is often substituted by the number 2. Therefore, the standard deviation of the two-asset portfolio above is:

$$\sigma_{Portfolio} = \sqrt{(0.3333)^2 (0.075)^2 + (0.6667)^2 (0.052)^2 + 2(0.3333)(0.6667)(0.075)(0.052)(0.85)}$$
$$\sigma_{Portfolio} = \sqrt{0.0006 + 0.0012 + 0.0015} = \sqrt{0.0033} = 0.0574 \text{ or } 5.74\%.$$

The equation may also substitute the covariance for the product of the standard deviations and the correlation since the two are equal:

$$COV_{A,B} = \sigma_A \sigma_B \rho_{A,B}$$

$$\sigma^2_{Portfolio} = \sum Wt_i^2 \sigma_i^2 + \sum \sum Wt_i\, Wt_j COV_{i,j} \ (\text{where } i \neq j)$$

Standard Normal Distribution

A standard normal distribution has a mean of zero and a standard deviation of one. Any random variable of a normal distribution may be standardized by using the following formula:

$$Z = \frac{X - \mu}{\sigma} \text{ , Where:}$$

Z = the standardized random variable,

X = the random variable,

μ = the mean, and

σ = the standard deviation.

There can be as many normal distributions as there are random variables. To answer any probability questions about a random variable, X, we can use standardized values and probability tables for Z. Referring to our portfolio of two stocks above, the 15% return of asset A is standardized as:

$$Z = \frac{15\% - 11.67\%}{5.74\%} = 0.5801$$

Accordingly, the probability of the portfolio in the above example having a return less than or equal to 15 percent is the same as the probability of being less than or equal to the standard normal variable 0.58.

Using the cumulative probability table in Table 9-1 find 0.5 in the left-hand column and move over to 0.08 in the upper row. The value is 0.7190. Thus, the probability is 71.9 percent that the return of the portfolio is less than or equal to 15 percent. This makes sense since the mean return of the portfolio is 11.67 percent (see previous discussion), which represents a 50 percent probability.

Widely used approximations of confidence levels are: One standard deviation around the mean represents a 68 percent probability (68 percent of the area under the curve) of an observed return falling in the range; two standard deviations around the mean represents a 95 percent probability; and three standard deviations around the mean represents a 99 percent probability. Again, refer to Table

9-1 and find the value closest to 0.84. It is 0.8413, which corresponds to a Z-value of 1.0. The tables are cumulative probability tables. The value 0.8413 (round to 0.84) represents a tail area of 0.16. For a two-tailed distribution, the area in the two tails is 0.16 x 2 = 0.32. This corresponds to the area around the mean (excluding the tails) of 0.68 or 68 percent or one standard deviation around the mean. A 95 percent area around the mean corresponds to 2.5 percent in each tail. Referring to Table 9-1, the area of 0.9725 corresponds to a Z-value of 1.96, close to two standard deviations.

Table 9-1. Cumulative Normal Probability Tables (Z-Values)

Z	0.00	0.01	0.02	0.03	0.04	0.05	0.06	0.07	0.08	0.09
0.0	0.50000	0.50399	0.50798	0.51197	0.51595	0.51994	0.52392	0.52790	0.53188	0.53586
0.1	0.53983	0.54380	0.54776	0.55172	0.55567	0.55962	0.56356	0.56749	0.57142	0.57535
0.2	0.57926	0.58317	0.58706	0.59095	0.59483	0.59871	0.60257	0.60642	0.61026	0.61409
0.3	0.61791	0.62172	0.62552	0.62930	0.63307	0.63683	0.64058	0.64431	0.64803	0.65173
0.4	0.65542	0.65910	0.66276	0.66640	0.67003	0.67364	0.67724	0.68082	0.68439	0.68793
0.5	0.69146	0.69497	0.69847	0.70194	0.70540	0.70884	0.71226	0.71566	0.71904	0.72240
0.6	0.72575	0.72907	0.73237	0.73565	0.73891	0.74215	0.74537	0.74857	0.75175	0.75490
0.7	0.75804	0.76115	0.76424	0.76730	0.77035	0.77337	0.77637	0.77935	0.78230	0.78524
0.8	0.78814	0.79103	0.79389	0.79673	0.79955	0.80234	0.80511	0.80785	0.81057	0.81327
0.9	0.81594	0.81859	0.82121	0.82381	0.82639	0.82894	0.83147	0.83398	0.83646	0.83891
1.0	0.84134	0.84375	0.84614	0.84849	0.85083	0.85314	0.85543	0.85769	0.85993	0.86214
1.1	0.86433	0.86650	0.86864	0.87076	0.87286	0.87493	0.87698	0.87900	0.88100	0.88298
1.2	0.88493	0.88686	0.88877	0.89065	0.89251	0.89435	0.89617	0.89796	0.89973	0.90147
1.3	0.90320	0.90490	0.90658	0.90824	0.90988	0.91149	0.91308	0.91466	0.91621	0.91774
1.4	0.91924	0.92073	0.92220	0.92364	0.92507	0.92647	0.92785	0.92922	0.93056	0.93189
1.5	0.93319	0.93448	0.93574	0.93699	0.93822	0.93943	0.94062	0.94179	0.94295	0.94408
1.6	0.94520	0.94630	0.94738	0.94845	0.94950	0.95053	0.95154	0.95254	0.95352	0.95449
1.7	0.95543	0.95637	0.95728	0.95818	0.95907	0.95994	0.96080	0.96164	0.96246	0.96327
1.8	0.96407	0.96485	0.96562	0.96638	0.96712	0.96784	0.96856	0.96926	0.96995	0.97062
1.9	0.97128	0.97193	0.97257	0.97320	0.97381	0.97441	0.97500	0.97558	0.97615	0.97670
2.0	0.97725	0.97778	0.97831	0.97882	0.97932	0.97982	0.98030	0.98077	0.98124	0.98169
2.1	0.98214	0.98257	0.98300	0.98341	0.98382	0.98422	0.98461	0.98500	0.98537	0.98574
2.2	0.98610	0.98645	0.98679	0.98713	0.98745	0.98778	0.98809	0.98840	0.98870	0.98899
2.3	0.98928	0.98956	0.98983	0.99010	0.99036	0.99061	0.99086	0.99111	0.99134	0.99158
2.4	0.99180	0.99202	0.99224	0.99245	0.99266	0.99286	0.99305	0.99324	0.99343	0.99361
2.5	0.99379	0.99396	0.99413	0.99430	0.99446	0.99461	0.99477	0.99492	0.99506	0.99520
2.6	0.99534	0.99547	0.99560	0.99573	0.99585	0.99598	0.99609	0.99621	0.99632	0.99643
2.7	0.99653	0.99664	0.99674	0.99683	0.99693	0.99702	0.99711	0.99720	0.99728	0.99736
2.8	0.99744	0.99752	0.99760	0.99767	0.99774	0.99781	0.99788	0.99795	0.99801	0.99807
2.9	0.99813	0.99819	0.99825	0.99831	0.99836	0.99841	0.99846	0.99851	0.99856	0.99861
3.0	0.99865	0.99869	0.99874	0.99878	0.99882	0.99886	0.99889	0.99893	0.99896	0.99900
3.1	0.99903	0.99906	0.99910	0.99913	0.99916	0.99918	0.99921	0.99924	0.99926	0.99929
3.2	0.99931	0.99934	0.99936	0.99938	0.99940	0.99942	0.99944	0.99946	0.99948	0.99950
3.3	0.99952	0.99953	0.99955	0.99957	0.99958	0.99960	0.99961	0.99962	0.99964	0.99965
3.4	0.99966	0.99968	0.99969	0.99970	0.99971	0.99972	0.99973	0.99974	0.99975	0.99976
3.5	0.99977	0.99978	0.99978	0.99979	0.99980	0.99981	0.99981	0.99982	0.99983	0.99983
3.6	0.99984	0.99985	0.99985	0.99986	0.99986	0.99987	0.99987	0.99988	0.99988	0.99989
3.7	0.99989	0.99990	0.99990	0.99990	0.99991	0.99991	0.99992	0.99992	0.99992	0.99992
3.8	0.99993	0.99993	0.99993	0.99994	0.99994	0.99994	0.99994	0.99995	0.99995	0.99995
3.9	0.99995	0.99995	0.99996	0.99996	0.99996	0.99996	0.99996	0.99996	0.99997	0.99997
4.0	0.99997	0.99997	0.99997	0.99997	0.99997	0.99997	0.99998	0.99998	0.99998	0.99998

Table 9-1. Cumulative Normal Probability Tables (Z-Values) (continued)

Z	0.09	0.08	0.07	0.06	0.05	0.04	0.03	0.02	0.01	0.00
-4.0	0.00002	0.00002	0.00002	0.00002	0.00003	0.00003	0.00003	0.00003	0.00003	0.00003
-3.9	0.00003	0.00003	0.00004	0.00004	0.00004	0.00004	0.00004	0.00004	0.00005	0.00005
-3.8	0.00005	0.00005	0.00005	0.00006	0.00006	0.00006	0.00006	0.00007	0.00007	0.00007
-3.7	0.00008	0.00008	0.00008	0.00008	0.00009	0.00009	0.00010	0.00010	0.00010	0.00011
-3.6	0.00011	0.00012	0.00012	0.00013	0.00013	0.00014	0.00014	0.00015	0.00015	0.00016
-3.5	0.00017	0.00017	0.00018	0.00019	0.00019	0.00020	0.00021	0.00022	0.00022	0.00023
-3.4	0.00024	0.00025	0.00026	0.00027	0.00028	0.00029	0.00030	0.00031	0.00032	0.00034
-3.3	0.00035	0.00036	0.00038	0.00039	0.00040	0.00042	0.00043	0.00045	0.00047	0.00048
-3.2	0.00050	0.00052	0.00054	0.00056	0.00058	0.00060	0.00062	0.00064	0.00066	0.00069
-3.1	0.00071	0.00074	0.00076	0.00079	0.00082	0.00084	0.00087	0.00090	0.00094	0.00097
-3.0	0.00100	0.00104	0.00107	0.00111	0.00114	0.00118	0.00122	0.00126	0.00131	0.00135
-2.9	0.00139	0.00144	0.00149	0.00154	0.00159	0.00164	0.00169	0.00175	0.00181	0.00187
-2.8	0.00193	0.00199	0.00205	0.00212	0.00219	0.00226	0.00233	0.00240	0.00248	0.00256
-2.7	0.00264	0.00272	0.00280	0.00289	0.00298	0.00307	0.00317	0.00326	0.00336	0.00347
-2.6	0.00357	0.00368	0.00379	0.00391	0.00402	0.00415	0.00427	0.00440	0.00453	0.00466
-2.5	0.00480	0.00494	0.00508	0.00523	0.00539	0.00554	0.00570	0.00587	0.00604	0.00621
-2.4	0.00639	0.00657	0.00676	0.00695	0.00714	0.00734	0.00755	0.00776	0.00798	0.00820
-2.3	0.00842	0.00866	0.00889	0.00914	0.00939	0.00964	0.00990	0.01017	0.01044	0.01072
-2.2	0.01101	0.01130	0.01160	0.01191	0.01222	0.01255	0.01287	0.01321	0.01355	0.01390
-2.1	0.01426	0.01463	0.01500	0.01539	0.01578	0.01618	0.01659	0.01700	0.01743	0.01786
-2.0	0.01831	0.01876	0.01923	0.01970	0.02018	0.02068	0.02118	0.02169	0.02222	0.02275
-1.9	0.02330	0.02385	0.02442	0.02500	0.02559	0.02619	0.02680	0.02743	0.02807	0.02872
-1.8	0.02938	0.03005	0.03074	0.03144	0.03216	0.03288	0.03362	0.03438	0.03515	0.03593
-1.7	0.03673	0.03754	0.03836	0.03920	0.04006	0.04093	0.04182	0.04272	0.04363	0.04457
-1.6	0.04551	0.04648	0.04746	0.04846	0.04947	0.05050	0.05155	0.05262	0.05370	0.05480
-1.5	0.05592	0.05705	0.05821	0.05938	0.06057	0.06178	0.06301	0.06426	0.06552	0.06681
-1.4	0.06811	0.06944	0.07078	0.07215	0.07353	0.07493	0.07636	0.07780	0.07927	0.08076
-1.3	0.08226	0.08379	0.08534	0.08692	0.08851	0.09012	0.09176	0.09342	0.09510	0.09680
-1.2	0.09853	0.10027	0.10204	0.10383	0.10565	0.10749	0.10935	0.11123	0.11314	0.11507
-1.1	0.11702	0.11900	0.12100	0.12302	0.12507	0.12714	0.12924	0.13136	0.13350	0.13567
-1.0	0.13786	0.14007	0.14231	0.14457	0.14686	0.14917	0.15151	0.15386	0.15625	0.15866
-0.9	0.16109	0.16354	0.16602	0.16853	0.17106	0.17361	0.17619	0.17879	0.18141	0.18406
-0.8	0.18673	0.18943	0.19215	0.19489	0.19766	0.20045	0.20327	0.20611	0.20897	0.21186
-0.7	0.21476	0.21770	0.22065	0.22363	0.22663	0.22965	0.23270	0.23576	0.23885	0.24196
-0.6	0.24510	0.24825	0.25143	0.25463	0.25785	0.26109	0.26435	0.26763	0.27093	0.27425
-0.5	0.27760	0.28096	0.28434	0.28774	0.29116	0.29460	0.29806	0.30153	0.30503	0.30854
-0.4	0.31207	0.31561	0.31918	0.32276	0.32636	0.32997	0.33360	0.33724	0.34090	0.34458
-0.3	0.34827	0.35197	0.35569	0.35942	0.36317	0.36693	0.37070	0.37448	0.37828	0.38209
-0.2	0.38591	0.38974	0.39358	0.39743	0.40129	0.40517	0.40905	0.41294	0.41683	0.42074
-0.1	0.42465	0.42858	0.43251	0.43644	0.44038	0.44433	0.44828	0.45224	0.45620	0.46017
0.0	0.46414	0.46812	0.47210	0.47608	0.48006	0.48405	0.48803	0.49202	0.49601	0.50000

Linear Regression

Investment analysis often incorporates the assumption of "linearity". This means that the correlation between an independent variable, such as the market, and a dependent variable, such as an individual stock, can be expressed as a straight line (the regression line):

$y = a + bx + \varepsilon$ Where:

y = the dependent variable,

a = the Y-intercept,

b = the slope,

x = the independent variable, and

ε = an error term. (A distribution of the error terms would have a mean of zero; so, oftentimes, the linear regression is expressed without the error term.)

Coefficient of Determination and Correlation
The degree of association between the dependent variable and the independent variable, as explained by the regression line, is referred to as the coefficient of determination or R^2. For example, an R^2 of 0.85 implies that 85 percent of the association between the dependent variable and the independent variable is explained by the linear regression. The correlation between the dependent and independent variables is the square root of the coefficient of determination:

$$\rho_{y,x} = \sqrt{R^2}$$

A regression with an R^2 of 0.85 implies a correlation between the regression variables of:

$$\sqrt{0.85} = 0.922$$

Capital Asset Pricing Model (CAPM)
The Capital Asset Pricing Model, or CAPM is derived from regressing the returns of an individual stock against the returns on the market portfolio. The slope of the regression line is the stock's beta (β_k). The intercept is fitted to the risk-free rate r_f). The independent variable is the market risk premium ($r_{mkg} - r_f$) and the dependent variable is the expected stock return (r_k).

$$r_s = r_f + \beta(r_m - r_f)$$
$$(y = a + b_x)$$

Graphing the x-axis to beta results in the Security Market Line (SML):

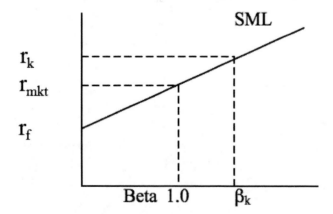

Beta

Regressing returns of an individual stock against returns of the market portfolio results in a regression line that best fits the plot of returns. The slope of this regression line is the stock's beta. Beta is a measurement of an investment's *systematic risk* or risk that cannot be diversified by assembling a portfolio of securities.

Betas may also be used in developing correlation matrices. The correlation between two stocks can be estimated by observing how each stock moves against the market portfolio. The resulting equation is:

$$\rho_{A,B} = \frac{\beta_A \beta_B \sigma_{Mkt}^2}{\sigma_A \sigma_B}$$

Regressing each stock against the market portfolio and finding the slope of the respective regression lines provides the beta for each stock. Incorporating the betas of Stock A and Stock B with their respective standard deviations and the market variance results in the correlation estimate between Stock A and Stock B *based on their relative movement to the market.*

Semivariance

Semivariance is a measure that focuses on the downside risk of an expected return and is described as the average square deviation below the mean. The formula for semivariance is:

$$\text{Semivariance} = \frac{\sum_{\text{for all } X_i \triangleleft \overline{X}} (X_k - \overline{X})^2}{n^* - 1} \quad \text{Where:}$$

n^* = number of observations, X_i are the returns below the mean return, and $\overline{X}$ is the mean return.

Example 9-1: Assume that the following is a population of observations of portfolio returns for the last five years:

Year 1	15%
Year 2	8%
Year 3	-1.5%
Year 4	8%
Year 5	18%

The arithmetic mean is:

$$\overline{X} = \frac{15\% + 8\% - 1.5\% + 8\% + 18\%}{5} = \frac{47.5\%}{5} = 9.50\%$$

The standard deviation is:

$$\sigma = \sqrt{\frac{(15\% - 9.5\%)^2 + (8\% - 9.5\%)^2 + (-1.5\% - 9.5\%)^2 + (8\% - 9.5\%)^2 + (18\% - 9.5\%)^2}{5}}$$

$$\sigma = \sqrt{\frac{228\%^2}{5}}$$

$$\sigma = \sqrt{45.6\%^2} = 6.75\%$$

Since the arithmetic mean return is 9.50% and is in the population observations, three returns are below the mean: the Year 2 return of 8%, Year 3 return of -1.5%, and Year 4 return of 8%. The semivariance is, therefore:

$$\text{Semivariance} = \frac{(8\% - 9.5\%)^2 + (-1.5\% - 9.5\%)^2 + (8\% - 9.5\%)^2}{3 - 1} = \frac{125.5}{2} = 62.75\%^2$$

$$\text{Semideviation} = \sqrt{62.75\%^2} = 7.92\%$$

Again, this has nonsensical units. The semideviation is:

The semideviation of 7.92% is greater than the standard deviation of 6.75% implying that the standard deviation understates the downside risk.

SKEWNESS

A distribution that is *not* symmetrical not a normal distribution, is a *skewed distribution*. The tails in a skewed distribution have different areas. A distribution that is skewed to the *right* (positively skewed) has a longer right tail. Conversely, a distribution that is skewed to the *left* (negatively skewed) has a longer left tail.

Positively Skewed
(Right-tailed)

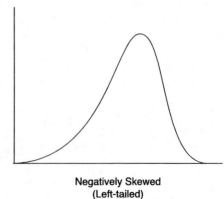

Negatively Skewed
(Left-tailed)

LOGNORMAL DISTRIBUTION

A random variable, X, is lognormal if the natural log of X is normally distributed. Lognormal distributions are bounded by zero and, thus, are positively skewed (long right tail). This has an important application to stock prices since stock prices are bounded by zero (no negative stock prices). For example, consider a single period, t, and the beginning price and the ending price relationship as follows:

$$\frac{\text{Ending Price - Beginning Price}}{\text{Beginning price}} = \frac{P_{t+1} - P_t}{P_t} \approx \ln\left(\frac{P_{t+1}}{P_t}\right)$$

If the natural log of the t period return is normally distributed, then the t-price level is log-normally distributed. Periodic natural log returns reflect a normal (or near-normal) distribution (symmetrical); however, price levels do not (are positively skewed).

KURTOSIS

Another measure of deviation from a normal distribution is *kurtosis*. Distributions with more observations clustered around the mean display a greater peak than distributions with observations more dispersed around the mean. Another way to look at this cluster is that distributions with higher peaks have fatter tails, as opposed to narrow tails associated with more rounded peaks. As a result, distributions with narrow tails have the potential for greater surprise events.

Normal distributions have a kurtosis value of three. Distributions with a kurtosis measure *less than* three have more rounded peaks and narrower tails than a normal distribution. Distributions with a kurtosis measure *greater than* three have higher peaks and fatter tails than a normal distribution. Most equity return series do, in fact, exhibit positive excess kurtosis. Therefore, if statistical models not accounting for the fatter tails are used, the likelihood of estimating very bad or very good outcomes is reduced.

MONTE CARLO SIMULATION AND BLACK SWANS

Monte Carlo Simulation (MCS) is an analytic and risk management tool widely used in finance. MCS incorporates computer programming to generate stochastic (probability) random value inputs in simulating thousands of iterations. The steps in the Monte Carlo simulation process include:

1. Identify a domain of inputs
2. Create a deterministic computation of the dependent variable (Y) as a function of the independent inputs $(X_{1, 2\,n})$

$$Y = f(X_1, X_2, ..X_n)$$

3. Generate random inputs for a defined probability distribution, i.e. normal distribution, etc., using MCS

4. Repeat for several (thousands of) iterations; and

5. Aggregate the results of the iterations into a final value.

MCS is used in valuing complex securities such as mortgage-backed securities and options. The process is also used in risk management, particularly Value at Risk (VaR) computations. However, the risk management models used by several banking and investment firms have recently failed to assess the implications of a so-called "Black Swan event". A Black Swan event is a rare event that is unpredicted and results in a major impact (both positive and negative) of historical proportions. When a Black Swan does appear, it is usually explained only by hindsight.

The current mortgage market and financial meltdown is an example of a Black Swan event. Even with the "risk management" systems in place, the impact was, nevertheless, unexpected as predicted (or ignored) by the models. The result, as traders say, was a "blow-up" in the mortgage securities market of unprecedented proportions.

IMPORTANT CONCEPTS

Standard deviation

Variability

Total risk

Beta coefficient

Volatility

Systematic risk

Probability distribution

Simulation

Monte Carlo Simulation

Normal distribution (bell curve)

Lognormal distribution

Skewness

Kurtosis

Standard deviation of single asset

Standard deviation of a two asset portfolio

Coefficient of variation

Semi-variance

Covariance

Correlation coefficient (R)

Coefficient of determination (R^2)

Weighted beta

QUESTIONS FOR REVIEW

1. What is the relevant measure of the *total* risk of an asset or portfolio? Is such portfolio assumed to be diversified or non-diversified in this instance? Explain.

2. What is the relevant measure of *systematic* risk of an asset or portfolio? Is such portfolio assumed to be diversified or non-diversified in this instance? Explain.

3. There are two methods used in developing a probability distribution to assist in the measurement of investment risk. What are these methods? Contrast one to the other.

4. What is Monte Carlo Simulation and when might it be used in the financial planning process?

5. If a lognormal probability distribution results, in which direction (left or right) does the mean fall with respect to the highest point of the curve? Practically, what is the implication of the mean positioned in this manner?

6. In investment planning, when would you typically expect a normal probability distribution to occur?

7. What does *skewness* measure? If a probability distribution is *negatively skewed*, what does this portend for the likely behavior of a risk-averse investor?

8. What does *kurtosis* measure and how does it interact with skewness in influencing the behavior of a risk-averse investor?

9. Assume that the standard deviation of a single asset is 15 and that its annual expected return is 10%. Assuming a normal probability distribution, what does this imply for the actual future investment return of the asset?

10. What does the *coefficient of variation* measure? Why might it be a more preferable method of analyzing total risk than that of standard deviation?

11. There is one additional measurement of risk that is critical in computing the standard deviation of a two or more asset portfolio. What is it and why is this measurement so important?

12. Unless the securities within a portfolio are all perfectly positively correlated, the standard deviation of the portfolio will be _____ than the weighted average standard deviation of the individual securities. Fill in the blank and explain why this occurs.

13. What is *semi-variance*? Why is it sometimes preferred instead of standard deviation in measuring the total risk of an asset or portfolio?

14. What characteristic of the *correlation coefficient* between two assets is an improvement upon that of merely finding their *covariance*? Asked another way, what aspect of covariance makes it particularly difficult to analyze and use in practice?

15. What types of correlated assets (low or high) are more useful in properly diversifying a portfolio to minimize total risk? Why?

16. What does the *beta coefficient* (beta) of an asset measure? How is beta computed (using what factors)?

17. Assume that a stock has a beta coefficient of 1.50. If the market increases by 10%, is this stock likely to increase or decrease and in what percentage?

18. Why might an investor wish to know the *weighted beta* of a portfolio?

19. What does the *coefficient of determination* (R^2) of an asset or mutual fund measure? If a fund has a relatively high R^2, what does this imply for the use of its beta coefficient as a reliable (or non-reliable) measure?

20. If a portfolio exhibits an R^2 of 0.65, what is the correlation between the dependent and independent variables?

SUGGESTIONS FOR ADDITIONAL READING

Tools and Techniques of Investment Planning, 2nd edition, Stephen R. Leimberg, Robert T. LeClair, Robert J. Doyle, Jr., and Thomas R. Robinson, The National Underwriter Company, 2006.

Investments: An Introduction, 9th edition, Herbert B. Mayo, Thomson/ South-Western, 2008.

Investment Analysis and Portfolio Management, 9th edition, Frank K. Reilly and Keith C. Brown, Thomson/South-Western, 2009.

The Wall Street Journal Guide to Money and Investing, 3rd edition, Kenneth M. Morris and Virginia B. Morris, Fireside Publishing, 2004.

CHAPTER TEN

Portfolio Management Theory and Behavioral Finance

• • •

Portfolio management theory is much in vogue these days, although likely by its more widely-known name of *modern portfolio theory (MPT)*. It builds on a foundation of investor behavior assumptions first introduced by Harry Markowitz in 1952. These assumptions are separately expanded upon in this chapter when discussing so-called *Markowitz portfolio theory*, but were further refined and developed by others, most notably William Sharpe, a Nobel Laureate finance professor and the author of the *Sharpe ratio*.

Upon completing this chapter, you should be able to:

- Explain Markowitz's portfolio theory, including the concepts of *efficient frontier* and the *optimal portfolio* for an investor
- Explain capital market theory
- Derive the *security market line* (SML) and discuss in what investment context it should be used
- Describe the underlying assumptions and forms of the *efficient market hypothesis* (EMH)
- Identify anomalies to the EMH
- Describe the basic principles of *behavioral finance* theory

BACKGROUND

A basic assumption of portfolio management theory is that an investor wants to maximize return from an investment for a given (or assumed) level of risk. Therefore, to truly optimize an investor's portfolio so as to achieve the highest possible return at the lowest possible risk, he or she must be open to the entire universe of investment choices. For example, less marketable investments such as coins, stamps, art, and antiques (broadly known by the term "collectibles") may also need to be included when diversifying a portfolio. In addition, the *relationship* between the returns on all these investments is also very important, since how they move in relation to one another (their *covariance*) is key to the proper diversification of a portfolio.

Portfolio management theory also assumes that investors are basically *risk-averse*, meaning that, given a choice between two assets with equal rates of return, they will select the asset with the *least amount of risk*. The purchase of an insurance policy to protect against potentially larger monetary losses in the future is evidence of the validity of this assumption. Further evidence of risk aversion is the difference in coupon rates demanded by investors as they accept greater risk in the form of a lower rated bond. For example, the coupon rate on bonds increases as an investor purchases speculative (or non-investment grade bonds) as compared to those bonds rated AAA or exhibiting little risk of issuer default. Accordingly, portfolio management theory assumes as a given that there is a *positive correlation* between expected return and total risk.

MARKOWITZ PORTFOLIO THEORY

Markowitz's approach to portfolio management was that an investor should evaluate investment options based on the investment's expected returns and total risk (as measured by standard deviation). He shows that the variance of the portfolio's rate of return (standard deviation of expected returns) was a meaningful measure of investment risk and, subsequently, derived the formula for computing the variance of a portfolio. This formula not only reflected the importance of diversifying investments to reduce the total risk of a portfolio, but also showed the investor *how* to go about achieving this result. Markowitz also was the first to derive the concept of an *optimal portfolio*, defined as one that exhibits the smallest *portfolio risk* for a given level of expected return or the *largest expected return* for a given level of portfolio risk.

The Markowitz portfolio management theory is based on several fundamental assumptions. They are as follows:

1. Investors consider each investment opportunity as being represented by a probability distribution of expected returns over a specified holding period.

2. Investors estimate the risk of the portfolio on the basis of the variability of expected returns.

3. Investors base decisions solely on expected return and risk, therefore their *indifference curves* are a function of expected return and the expected variance (or standard deviation) of returns only.

4. Investors base their indifference to alternative investments on the maximization of wealth over a specified period, and this indifference diminishes as they get beyond this period.

5. For a given level of risk, investors prefer higher returns to lower returns.

Accordingly, the Markowitz theory established the principle that a *single asset or portfolio of securities is considered to be efficient if no other asset or portfolio offers a higher expected return with the same or lower risk.*

The previous chapter presented the formula for the standard deviation of a two-asset portfolio. Markowitz was responsible for developing the standard deviation (total risk) of a portfolio formula and for proving that the resulting risk encompasses not only the variance of the individual assets but *also* includes the covariance between the pairs of individual assets in the portfolio. Under the theory, what happens to the portfolio's standard deviation when an investor *adds* a new asset or security to the portfolio? Specifically, one of the major effects when an asset is added is that the covariance changes between the returns of this asset and the returns of every other asset that is already in the portfolio. As a result, the relative weight of these numerous covariances is substantially *greater than* the additional asset's own variance of returns and, consequently, the critically important factor to consider is *not* the new asset's *own* variance but *its average covariance with all the other investments in the portfolio.*

Efficient Frontier

If we examined a number of asset combinations (as in the typical portfolio) and plotted their expected returns for every given level of risk assuming all the possible combined weights, we would develop a series of curves. The envelope curve that includes the best of these combinations is referred to as the *efficient frontier.* Specifically, this curve *represents that set of portfolios that has the maximum rate of return for every given level of risk.* In pictorial terms, the efficient frontier looks like this:

Figure 10-1

Every portfolio that resides on the efficient frontier has either a higher rate of return for equal risk or lower risk for an equal rate of return than another portfolio below or underneath the frontier. For example, in Figure 10-1, we would say that Portfolios A and B are both equally efficient and *dominate* Portfolio C. In other words, Portfolios A and B dominate Portfolio C because:

1. Portfolio A has an equal expected rate of return as Portfolio C, but with a significantly *lower* level of risk assumed by the investor; and

2. Portfolio B has an equal level of assumed risk by the investor as Portfolio C, but with a significantly *higher* expected rate of return.

Accordingly, Portfolio C may be said to be *inefficient;* it is *attainable,* but *not optimal.*

With respect to Portfolio D in Figure 10-1, it is said to be *unattainable.* That is, since it resides above the efficient frontier, it is arguably *efficient,* but the expected return is not *attainable* because it is located outside the universe of portfolios available to the investor. Point D also cannot exist for any extended period of time under the Markowitz assumptions.

Finally, because of the benefits of diversification to minimize total risk among imperfectly correlated assets, we would expect the efficient frontier to consist of portfolios or combination of assets rather than individual securities. However, there are two notable exceptions to this statement: each end point of the frontier represents (1) an individual security with the lowest total risk and (2) the highest expected rate of return, respectively. These are shown in Figure 10-1 as Assets x and y, respectively.

Optimal Portfolio

Per the Markowitz theory, the efficient frontier provides the investor with all possible sets of efficient portfolios (or possible choices); however, the frontier does *not* tell the portfolio manager the particular portfolio (or one choice) that the investor *should* construct. Rather, the specific portfolio chosen (or optimal combination of assets taking into account the investor's expected return and level of assumed risk) depends on the investor's *utility function* or how much risk the investor is willing to assume for a desired level of reward. This utility function is represented graphically by one or more investor *indifference curves.* Figure 10-2 below shows two sets of indifference curves plotted in combination with the efficient frontier.

Figure 10-2

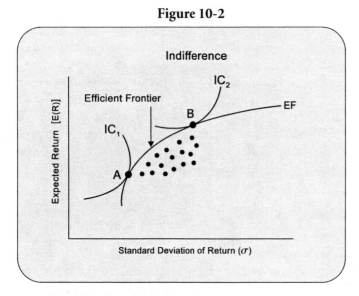

Two investors will choose the same portfolio only if their indifference curves are identical. Otherwise, the two portfolios will not be constructed the same.

Different investors typically have different indifference curves. If the investor is exceedingly risk-averse, his or her indifference curve tends to be *very steep,* indicating that a large amount of additional expected return is necessary to bear additional risk. This is shown in Figure 10-2 as IC_1. In contrast, if his or her indifference curve is relatively *flat,* the investor is less risk averse, meaning that only a small or modest amount of additional expected return is necessary to assume more risk. This type of curve is shown in Figure 10-2 as IC_2. In practical terms, an investor with an indifference curve of IC_1 would likely be characterized as having a conservative risk tolerance level and an investor with an indifference curve of IC_2 would be termed as having a moderate, perhaps aggressive, tolerance for risk.

Nevertheless, we are still left without an answer to our question: which particular portfolio will the investor choose? To know this, we analyze where the investor indifference curve *intersects* with that of the efficient portfolio. Although, in reality, each investor has a number of indifference curves, for purposes of illustration, we have shown only one. The point at which the indifference curve is tangent to (touches) the efficient frontier is referred to as the investor's *optimal portfolio*. In Figure 10-2, this is shown as Point A for the investor with the indifference curve IC_1 (the *more* risk-averse investor) and Point B for the investor with the indifference curve IC_2 (the *less* risk-averse investor). The *conservative investor's* highest utility point is at Point A, which represents a portfolio with less risk and a lower amount of expected return; the *more aggressive* investor's highest utility point is at Point B, which represents a portfolio with more risk and a commensurate higher amount of expected return.

One should also note that sometimes the optimal portfolio for an investor is known as his or her *mean-variance optimization*. This is because, as may easily be seen from the vertical and horizontal axis of Figures 10-1 and 10-2, the labels expected return (mean) and standard deviation (variance) are used.

CAPITAL MARKET THEORY

Capital market theory extends Markowitz's portfolio theory and develops a model for pricing all risky assets. The final product, referred to as the *capital asset pricing model* (CAPM) provides the portfolio manager (and investment advisor) with a basis for making an investment decision. That is, since CAPM generates the investor's *expected rate of return*, this may be compared to the investment's *market or required rate of return* to determine whether a purchase (or sale) of the risky asset should be made.

Since capital market theory builds on Markowitz portfolio theory (both theories constitute what we now know as *modern portfolio theory*), it requires the same assumptions concerning investor behavior, along with a few others. Accordingly, the assumptions underlying capital market theory are:

1. All investors are considered to be efficient investors whose objective is to target his or her *optimal portfolio*.

2. All investors have the same expectations; that is, they estimate identical (normal) probability distributions for future rates of investment return.

3. Investors can always borrow or lend money at the risk-free rate of return as represented by the yield on U.S. short-term securities, specifically, the 90-day Treasury bill..

4. All investors have the same one-period investment time horizon; a difference in this time period requires investors to derive minimization of risk strategies and invest in risk free assets that are consistent with their new horizon.

5. All investments are infinitely divisible, meaning that it is possible to buy or sell fractional shares of any asset or portfolio.

6. There are no taxes or transaction costs involved in buying or selling assets, meaning that these expenses are not relevant in investment decision-making.

7. There is no inflation or any change in market interest rates, or all changes in either investor-behavior factor are fully anticipated.

8. *Capital markets are in equilibrium,* meaning that all investments are properly priced taking into account the commensurate level of investor risk; thus, CAPM establishes a theoretical baseline by which to evaluate an investment's suitability for any investor.

Having noted all of these underlying assumptions, it now should be stated that the single major factor that permitted Markowitz portfolio theory to evolve into capital market theory was the concept of a risk-free asset. Indeed, the inclusion of a risk-free asset return in the CAPM formula was a major breakthrough allowing the portfolio manager a baseline figure from which to measure the amount of stock and market risk premium required by the investor to make a particular investment.

Capital Market Line (CML)

Using Markowitz portfolio theory, as we have seen, an investor develops a portfolio along the *efficient frontier* of all possible choices of investments. The macro aspect of capital market theory is represented by the development of a so-called *capital market line (CML)*. This line specifies the relationship between the risk and return on a portfolio when a risk-free asset is added.

Figure 10-3 The Capital Market Line

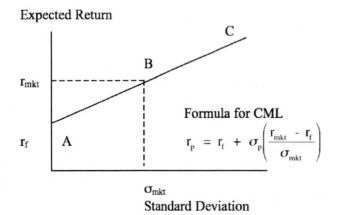

Figure 10-3 graphically represents the capital market line (CML). The Y-axis is the return and the X-axis is the risk as measured by the standard deviation (total risk). The Y-intercept (Point A) represents a portfolio 100 percent invested in Treasury securities earning the risk-free rate (r_f). Point B represents a portfolio 100 percent invested in a risky asset such as the S&P 500 index. The range BC represents a portfolio fully invested in the market plus additional leveraging at the risk-free rate.

The formula for the CML states that the expected return of a portfolio is a function of the risk-free rate plus the market risk premium per measure of market risk (represented by the standard deviation of the market) multiplied by the standard deviation of the portfolio.

Security Market Line (SML)

The second component of capital market theory is specification of the relationship between the expected return and the risk of an *individual asset or security*. At the *micro* level of the theory, this relationship is referred to as the *security market line (SML)*. The capital market line (CML) depicts the risk-return trade-off at the level of an overall market that is assumed to be in equilibrium. However, the CML applies only to efficient (or diversified) *portfolios* and *cannot* be used to assess the equilibrium expected return on a *single* security. Rather, this is the purpose of the SML. The SML, when using the capital asset pricing model (CAPM) as its applicable equation, indicates what should be the expected return on a risky asset and/or an inefficient (non-diversified) portfolio. Also, since the expected rate of return is determined under capital market theory to be in the context of a properly priced market (one that is in equilibrium), the expected return for any investment asset is implicitly equivalent to the market or required rate of return for the investor. Refer to Chapter 9 for the derivation of the SML.

In the security market line (SML), the vertical axis (as in that of the capital market line representation) is the investor's expected return. However, unlike the CML where the horizontal axis is represented by standard deviation, in the SML that axis uses the *beta coefficient (beta)* of the individual asset. In graphical terms, the SML with requisite formula looks like this:

Figure 10-4

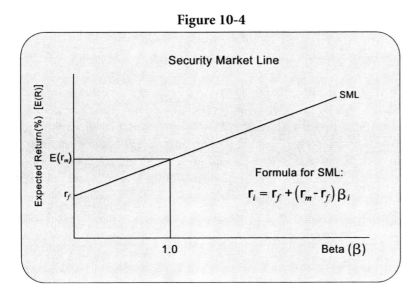

Security Market Line

Formula for SML:

$$r_i = r_f + \left(r_m - r_f\right)\beta_i$$

As previously noted, if security markets are in equilibrium, all individual assets (whether risky or not) should plot along the SML. However, what happens if investors determine that an asset does *not* fall on the SML (in other words, the asset is *not* priced at its intrinsic value)? In that case, let us now add two assets, X and Y, and plot each as either above the SML or below the SML as follows:

Figure 10-5

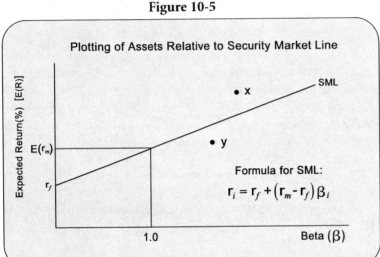

You should notice several very important implications as you analyze Figure 10-5:

1. Since Security X is plotted *above* the SML, it is *undervalued* because its market or required return is greater than the expected return, given its level of systematic risk as measured by beta. Why? To achieve the higher return, the price of Security X is depressed, driving up the yield. Accordingly, Security X will likely be purchased by value investors, subsequently driving *up* its price and lowering its yield. As more and more of Security X is purchased, its market or required return will be driven *down*, until, ultimately, it is at the level reflected by the SML.

2. Since Security Y is plotted *below* the SML, it is *overvalued* because it offers *less market or required* return than expected return, given its level of systematic risk as measured by beta. Accordingly, Security Y will likely be sold (or sold short) by investors, subsequently driving *down* its price. As more and more of Security Y is sold, its market or required return will be driven *up*, until, ultimately, it is at the level reflected by the SML.

A comment on return, CAPM is a model that determines the expected return of an asset, i.e., stock, with respect to its movement or correlation to a market portfolio of all risky assets. Although the proxy for this "market portfolio" is often the S&P 500 Index, the market portfolio is theoretical, i.e., it cannot be physically reproduced. Do not confuse market or required return with expected return. Market return is the return required by the market as reflected in its spot price (what an asset trades for on the open market). We will present how this return is derived from various valuation models in subsequent chapters. We will also discuss how to value individual assets using the capital asset pricing model (CAPM) in much greater detail in Chapter 14 of this text (Asset Pricing Models); however, here it is important to realize that:

1. The SML is the graphical representation of CAPM.

2. Individual assets are assumed to be "properly priced"; that is, the expected return of the investment is *equal* to the market or required rate of return when the asset lies on its SML.

3. If the market or required return of an individual asset is *greater* than its expected return according to CAPM (or plots above the SML), the asset is *undervalued* and, all other investment factors remaining equal, should be purchased.

4. If the market or required return of an individual asset is *less* than its expected return according to CAPM (or plots below the SML), the asset is *overvalued* and, all other investment factors remaining equal, should not be bought or, if already owned, should be sold (or, for the speculator, sold short).

Market and Stock Risk Premium

The *market risk premium* is the additional return required above the risk-free rate (RFR) for an asset. In CAPM, the market risk premium is the required return on the market portfolio of all risky assets, r_m less the RFR (r_m – RFR). The market return is often the historical return on a proxy, such as the S&P 500 Index. Generally, the RFR is a choice between the 30-day Treasury bill, the 90-day Treasury bill or the 10-year Treasury note (the benchmark Treasury security). The key is not so much the Treasury security selected but that it is consistently used as the intercept and in determining the market risk premium. To derive the *stock risk premium*, multiply the market risk premium by the stock's beta as follows:

Stock risk premium = $\beta(r_m - RFR)$

> **Example 10-1:** Assume that the return on the market is 10% and that the 90-day Treasury bill rate of return is 4.5%. Further, you have previously computed the beta coefficient of Stock X to be 1.20. Therefore, the stock risk premium associated with Stock X is 6.60% = 1.20 x [(0.10 - 0.045).

In turn, this means that an investor interested in purchasing Stock X would require an annual return of 6.60 percent in excess of what he or she could achieve simply by purchasing a risk free asset as represented by the 90-day Treasury bill rate. In other words, a combined or total return of 11.10% (4.5% + 6.60%) is required.

EFFICIENT MARKET HYPOTHESIS (EMH)

An *efficient capital market* is one in which security prices adjust rapidly to the arrival of new information and, therefore, the current prices of securities reflect all information known about the security. As a result of this premise, a well-known academic theory referred to as the *efficient market hypothesis* (EMH) has developed. This hypothesis suggests that investors cannot expect to outperform the overall market *consistently* on a risk-adjusted basis. Finally, day-to-day changes in the market prices of securities follow a *random walk* and cannot be predicted with any reliable degree of accuracy. Therefore, since prices move in this independent manner, any trading rules or security analysis (such as technical analysis) trying to find a pattern to this *walk* is considered to be of *no value.*

There are three basic assumptions underlying the premise of an efficient capital market. They are as follows:

1. A large number of profit-maximizing participants analyze and value securities on a daily (or close-to-daily) basis; therefore, it is fruitless to try to outperform such a large representation of time and intellect.

2. New information related to one security occurs independently from that of another.

3. Profit-maximizing investors adjust security prices rapidly to reflect the effect of new information; further, this price adjustment is unbiased, meaning that a potential investor cannot predict with any certainty where the market will over- or under-adjust the security's eventual trading value.

Finally, at the heart of an efficient capital market is a belief that the *expected returns inherent in the current trading value of a security reflect its systematic risk,* meaning that investors who buy securities at today's market price receive a rate of return consistent with the risk of investing in a diversified portfolio. Stated another way, all securities should lie on the security market line (SML) so that their expected returns are consistent with the assumption of systematic risk as reflected by their beta coefficient.

Most of the early academic research related to efficient capital markets was based on the *random walk hypothesis,* which argues that changes in stock prices occur without any predictable pattern. Extensive empirical analysis was performed, but little basic theoretical assumptions were ever stated. This changed in 1966 when Eugene Fama announced his *efficient market hypothesis* (EMH) and divided his empirical results into three sub-hypotheses or forms depending on the information that was received by the investor. Respectively, in order of their rigidity, the forms were named: (1) the *weak-form EMH;* (2) the *semi-strong form EMH;* and (3) the *strong- form EMH*

Weak-Form EMH

The weak form of the hypothesis assumes that current security prices fully reflect all *historical price data, but not data from outside the market* (such as that generated from analyzing company financial statements, the relevant industry, or the economy as a whole). Because it assumes that current market prices already reflect all security market information, the weak form implies that historical market data should have no relationship with future rates of return. As a result, technical analysis is of no use; however, credible fundamental analysis in security selection *may* achieve above-average risk-adjusted returns. In addition, those investors with access to insider information (though illegal) may also generate superior long-term performance.

The weak form does not incorporate the other forms of the hypothesis (strong or semi-strong), but remains *independent* of those forms, both as to its underlying assumptions and with respect to the market factors that are considered.

Semi-Strong Form EMH

The semi-strong form asserts that *only public information is considered* in stock prices. Therefore, an investor with access to insider information *may* outperform the market. Such public information includes all non-market information, such as earnings and dividends announcements, price-to-earnings (P/E) ratios, stock splits, news about the economy, and political views. This form suggests that investors who base their decisions on any important new information after it is public should not achieve above-average risk-adjusted profits from their transactions, since the security price already reflects such information. Neither fundamental nor technical analysis is accorded much credibility in the semi-strong variation.

The semi-strong form of EMH encompasses the weak form of the theory because all the market information considered by the weak form, such as security prices, rates of return, and market trading volume, has already been made public.

Strong-Form EMH

Essentially, the strong form of the efficient market hypothesis (EMH) assumes a *perfect market*, in which all information is cost-free and available to all investors at the same time. Specifically, the form holds that stock prices fully reflect *all information from public and private sources*. Therefore, even those investors with access to insider information are unlikely to consistently outperform the overall market. In addition, neither the fundamental nor technical analysis approach to security selection (see Chapter 15 of this textbook) will achieve superior performance.

The strong form encompasses both the weak form and the semi-strong form of the hypothesis and asserts that security prices adjust very rapidly to the release of new public information. Whether an investor fully understands the assertions of the strong form of the EMH, he or she who practices passive investment management by purchasing only index funds is tacitly agreeing with the validity of the strong-form EMH.

In summary, the three forms of the EMH, with the relevant information each considers in establishing security market prices, are as follows:

Form of EMH	Information Reflected in Price
Strong	Technical and fundamental analysis as well as insider information
Semi-Strong	Technical and fundamental analysis
Weak	Technical analysis

Given the assumptions of the EMH, if the information is already reflected in the security market price, it is of *no value* with respect to its potential to out-perform the broader market indexes.

Academic Studies Testing the Forms

As with most theories and/or hypotheses in investments, the academic evidence supporting the EMH is mixed. However, several studies have supported the assumptions of the EMH and, specifically, the *weak form* of the theory. As a result, it is likely fair to assert that credible fundamental analysis may generate superior risk-adjusted rates of return over time. In addition, experience also suggests that access to insider information will yield investor profits; otherwise, security laws restricting such access would not be in effect.

Nevertheless, still other studies have produced findings that do *not* support either the hypothesis or any of its forms. These are known as *anomalies* and, by definition, are in contrast to what would be expected if the market were indeed totally efficient. Some of these anomalies (with commentary on their implications for investors) are now discussed.

Anomalies to the EMH

1. *Price-earnings (P/E) effect*: This anomaly suggests that higher returns are attainable with portfolios consisting of securities with low price-earning (P/E) ratios. Indeed, considering the evidence, it does appear that firms trading at low price-to-earning multiples may generate higher rates of return over time than that of firms whose stock does not exhibit this characteristic. This is likely because growth companies enjoy high P/E ratios; the market tends to overestimate the growth potential of those companies and thus overvalues them, while simultaneously under-valuing low growth firms with low P/E ratios.

2. *Small-firm effect* (a.k.a. the *neglected firm effect*): This anomaly relates to the number of security analysts that follow smaller-sized companies. Specifically, with fewer analysts following a stock or security, the value of that stock may not be efficiently priced and may result in an undervalued offering. An example of this effect is foreign or international stocks where the opportunity for a significant price gain may be possible.

3. *The January effect*: This anomaly has been observed for decades and has, at its genesis, a unique trading rule for those investors interested in taking advantage of tax selling. Investors, particularly institutions, tend to engage in tax selling at the end of the calendar year, thereby harvesting capital losses on stocks that have declined in price. After the new year, the tendency is then to reacquire these stocks (after waiting for at least 30 days to avoid the *wash sale* tax rule) or to buy other stocks that look promising. Accordingly, this scenario generates negative (downward) pressure on stock prices in November and December of the previous calendar year and positive (upward) pressure in January of the subsequent calendar year.

4. *The Value Line enigma*: Value Line is a large well-known publication and advisory service that publishes financial information on over 1,700 stocks. A rank of "1" is the most favorable recommendation given by *Value Line* and "5" is the least favorable. Studies have shown that stocks rated "1" by *Value Line* tend to outperform the market and that stocks rated "5" significantly under perform the market. Hence, the enigma: this phenomenon should not occur if the EMH was valid.

5. *Analysts recommendations*: Finally, there is evidence in favor of the existence of superior security analysts who may possess private information. This evidence is provided by two studies finding that the price of stocks mentioned in the *Wall Street Journal* column entitled "Heard on the Street" experience a significant change on the day that the column appears.

Efficient Markets and Security Analysis

As should be appreciated by now, advocates of EMH do *not* attribute any validity to the technical analysis theory of attempting to determine future security prices. Indeed, the assumptions of technical analysis are directly *contradictory* to the belief that markets are inherently efficient. A basic premise of technical analysis is that stock prices move in predictable patterns over time. Furthermore, *technicians* believe that when new public information comes to the market, it is *not* immediately available to everyone; rather, such information is disseminated downward from professional investors and institutions to the greater mass of *uninformed* investors. Finally, the process of analyzing information and then acting on it takes time; therefore, stock prices move to a new *support level* in a gradual manner, causing trends in the direction of stock prices that persist over many years.

The belief in the pattern of price adjustments, as articulated by technical analysts, is anathema to EMH proponents who believe that security prices adjust to new information (public, private, or both, depending on which form of the hypothesis) *very rapidly*. EMH advocates do not assert that market prices adjust perfectly, which implies a chance of over- or under-adjustment (and an opportunity for inefficiency). Nevertheless, by the time information has been made public, this price adjustment has already taken place, so that a purchase or sale of a security using technical trading rules should not generate any abnormal rate of return beyond that of the overall market.

In contrast to technicians, *fundamental analysts* believe that, at any given point in time, there is a basic *intrinsic value* for the aggregate stock market, as a whole, and for an individual security. This value depends on underlying economic, industry, and company-specific factors that may be discerned from study and research. Therefore, if an investor can do a superior job of determining a security's intrinsic value, profit-making opportunities exist. As has been suggested, the weak form of EMH incorporates this result, with academic studies indicating some empirical support for its validity.

A Note on Technical Analysis

Technical charting implies three basic assumptions:

1. Markets discount the fundamentals;

2. Markets trend; and

3. Trends repeat over time.

Therefore, technical analysis assumes that, since the financial markets are forward-looking, the "fundamentals" in determining stock prices have already been discounted. Technical analysts view price trends as leading indicators of the fundamentals. In fact, the study of these price trends is what technical analysis is all about. The technical analyst's objective is to identify such trends early and trade in their direction (known as "the direction of least resistance"). These trends may be intraday or up to several months and even years.

Much of technical analysis is the study of market psychology. Investors are expected to respond to similar market situations in a consistent manner. This is why historical trends are followed closely and form the basis for why such trends repeat.

BEHAVIORAL FINANCE

We conclude our discussion of portfolio management theory by analyzing a recent branch of financial economics known as *behavioral finance*. This field of study argues that investors are not nearly as rational as traditional finance theory asserts. Rather, they may be motivated by psychological factors, such as the *herd effect* of not wanting to be left behind in the event of a market upturn. Accordingly, for investors that are curious about how emotions and biases influence security market prices, behavioral finance offers some interesting descriptions and explanations.

For example, studies have shown that if an individual is offered the choice of a sure $50 or, after the flip of a coin, the possibility of winning $100 (doubling his or her money) or winning nothing, the individual will most often choose the sure $50. Conversely, offer this same individual the choice between a sure loss of $50 or, after the flip of a coin, the possibility of losing $100 or nothing, and he or she will then likely choose the coin toss. Why is this so? Behavioral finance advocates explain this result by emphasizing the importance of *prospect theory*, which contends that investors *fear losses much more than they value gains.* Another psychological bias mentioned by *behaviorists* influencing investor behavior is that of *confirmation bias*. This means that investors tend to look for information that supports their previously established opinion and decision. As a result, they tend to overvalue the stocks of currently popular companies, such as a firm that has introduced a yet unproven technology. (Of course, this means that they also tend to undervalue the stocks of overlooked companies, as supported by the *neglected firm effect* anomaly to efficient market hypothesis as previously discussed.)

Other examples of behavioral finance in practice are so-called "frame dependence" and the tendency of investors to hold on to stocks that have lost value for far too long, while simultaneously selling *winning* stocks (that is, those that portend significant capital appreciation) much too soon. Frame *dependence* reflects the propensity of investors to make decisions based on how a question or issue is presented to them. For example, using a narrow frame of reference (such as short term gains or losses) can lead to irrational decisions. Alternatively, a broader frame of reference (such as the accumulation of long-term wealth) generally results in better investment decisions.

Finally, behavioral finance has also made analysts aware of an *escalation bias*. This bias causes investors to contribute more money into a failing stock or mutual fund than into investments that are outperforming the market average. This results in the relatively popular investment strategy of *averaging down* on a stock that has declined in value since its initial purchase, rather than selling it and admitting one's mistake. For example, if a particular stock was a good *buy* at $50, this same stock must now be a *real steal* once it has fallen in price to $30. Obviously, at this point, the investor should now reassess his or her motivations for buying the stock in the first instance. However, because of *escalation bias*, the investor tends to ignore any real, negative market forces weighing down the stock's value and focus only on any imaginary, false positives that cause him or her to buy even more of the same losing position.

In summary, advocates of behavioral finance have yet to come up with a coherent model that actually predicts the future rather than one that merely explains the past. Nevertheless, it does provide a new, additional factor to consider in portfolio management theory: that being the implication of psychological and economic principles for the improvement of financial decision making.

IMPORTANT CONCEPTS

Markowitz Portfolio Theory

Capital Market Theory

Modern Portfolio Theory (MPT)

Efficient frontier

Optimal portfolio

Indifference curve

Capital market line (CML)

Security market line (SML)

Capital Asset Pricing Model (CAPM)

Required rate of return

Market risk premium

Stock risk premium

Efficient Market Hypothesis (EMH)

Strong-form EMH

Semi-strong form EMH

Weak-form EMH

Anomalies to EMH

Price-earnings (P/E) effect

Small-firm (neglected firm) effect

January effect

Value line enigma

Technical analysis

Fundamental analysis

Behavioral finance

QUESTIONS FOR REVIEW

1. According to portfolio management theory, if an investor is given a choice between two assets with equal rates of return, but with different levels of risk, which asset will he or she choose? Why?

2. Define an *efficient portfolio* as first derived by Harry Markowitz.

3. What are the five fundamental assumptions of Markowitz portfolio management theory?

4. What portfolio management principle was first established by Markowitz?

5. What is the *efficient frontier*? Why should it be important for the average investor?

6. How does a portfolio manager theoretically go about selecting the *optimal portfolio* for his or her client?

7. Capital market theory extends Markowitz portfolio theory and develops a model for pricing all risky assets. What is the model and what is its importance for the portfolio manager?

8. What are three additional assumptions of capital market theory that build on Markowitz portfolio theory? (Note: Eight assumptions are listed in the text; choose the three that you consider to be the most important.)

9. What are the *macro* and *micro* components, respectively, of capital market theory? What is each attempting to measure?

10. If a security is plotted *above* the SML, what does this mean? What does it mean if a security is plotted *below* the SML?

11. How does one determinet the *stock risk premium* that is associated with the making of an investment?

12. What are the three basic assumptions underlying the premise of an efficient capital market?

13. What does the *efficient market hypothesis* suggest about capital markets and why might this be important to any investor?

14. Explain what market or non-market information is considered in each of the following forms of EMH:

   - Strong form
   - Semi-strong form
   - Weak form

15. According to academic studies, which form of EMH, if any, may have some validity?

16. Explain each of the following anomalies to the EMH:

   - Price-earnings (P/E) effect
   - Small-firm effect
   - January effect
   - Value line enigma

17. If an individual believes in the EMH, is technical analysis useful? Explain.

18. What is *behavioral finance* and what does it possibly add to portfolio management theory?

19. Define each of the following theories or concepts put forth by *behaviorists* (those who advocate behavioral finance in explaining investor behavior):

   - Prospect theory
   - Confirmation bias
   - Escalation bias

SUGGESTIONS FOR ADDITIONAL READING

Tools and Techniques of Investment Planning, 2nd edition, Stephen R. Leimberg, Robert T. LeClair, Robert J. Doyle, Jr., and Thomas R. Robinson, The National Underwriter Company, 2006.

Investments: An Introduction, 9th edition, Herbert B. Mayo, Thomson/ South-Western, 2008.

Investment Analysis and Portfolio Management, 9th edition, Frank K. Reilly and Keith C. Brown, Thomson/South-Western, 2009.

The Wall Street Journal Guide to Money and Investing, 3rd edition, Kenneth M. Morris and Virginia B. Morris, Fireside Publishing, 2004 .

CHAPTER ELEVEN

Measures of Investment Return

• • •

The second part of the risk/return tradeoff that is fundamental to investments is, of course, return. Indeed, the rate of return on an investment is often focused on the extent that it overshadows the first very important part of the tradeoff. In other words, how much risk does the investor need to assume in order to achieve the desired rate of return? Furthermore, return may be measured in many different ways and it is often difficult to know which method to select. That is the purpose of this chapter: to analyze the many different methods for measuring return and to use each method consistently in determining an appropriate investment vehicle, such as stocks, bonds, or mutual funds.

Upon completing this chapter, you should be able to:

- Calculate a specified measure of investment return
- Differentiate between those measures of return dealing primarily with stocks and mutual funds versus those dealing primarily with bonds
- Describe and compute certain portfolio measures of return, notably the Jensen (Alpha), Treynor, and Sharpe ratios

SIMPLE VS. COMPOUND RATES OF RETURN

The *simple annual rate of return* for an investment is computed by dividing its total return (its total gain or loss relative to the initial dollar investment) by the number of years that the investor has held the asset. For example, assume that the total return on an investment held for five years is 60 percent. The investor's simple annual rate of return is 12% (or 60 ÷ 5). If the investor has held the asset for less than a year, a corollary type of return known as the *annualized rate of return* is used. The example below describes this type of simple return.

Example 11-1: Jerry purchases a $10,000 3-month Treasury bill (91 actual-day maturity period) for $9,912. He therefore has an annual return of 3.51% calculated as follows:

$$\text{Annualized return} = \left[\frac{EV - BV}{BV}\right] \times \frac{360 \text{ days (bank discount basis)}}{\text{Actual number of days in period}}$$

$$\text{Annualized return} = \left[\frac{\$10,000 - \$9,912}{\$9,912}\right] \times \frac{360}{91} = 0.0351$$

Annualized return = 3.51%

Note: The conversion is on a bank discount basis of 360-days for Treasury bills (Treasury notes and bonds are on a market basis of 365 days).

In contrast to the simple annual rate of return, the *compound annual rate of return* assumes that the interest and principal on an investment is reinvested rather than always equated to a one-year holding period (compound return is also referred to as *interest on interest*). The compound annual rate of return for a given holding period is mathematically represented as:

$$\text{Compound holding period return} = \left[1 + \frac{EV - BV}{BV}\right]^{1/n} - 1 \quad , \text{ where}$$

EV = Ending value
BV = Beginning value
n = Number of periods in the holding period

Example 11-2 An investor purchased a bond at par ($1,000) with a six percent coupon payment (paid semiannually). At the end of three years, the investor sold the bond for $1,180 and earned total coupon interest (reinvested) of $189. The compounded annual holding period return is calculated as follows:

$$\text{Compound holding period return} = \left[1 + \frac{(\$1,180 + \$189) - \$1,000}{\$1,000}\right]^{1/6} - 1 = 0.0538 \text{ (semiannual)}$$

0.0538 x 2 = 0.1075 or 10.75%

The ending value consists of the sales price of the bond after three years plus the reinvested coupon payments over the holding period. Note that the bond pays coupon interest *semiannually*. The payment of semiannual interest is the norm for most U.S. bonds. The number of periods, "n," in the holding period is six (six semiannual periods in three years).

The financial calculator keystrokes (HP10BII) are:

1180[+]

189[=][-]

1000[=][÷]1000[=]

[+]1[=]

[SHIFT][y^x]0.1667[=]

1.0538[-]1[=]0.0538 (semiannual)

0.0538[x]2[= 0.1075

Answer: 10.75%

Which of these returns is better to use, the simple annual or compound annual rate of return? The answer to that question depends on how the investor intends to use the measurement.

If the objective of the investor is to estimate the future annual returns of an investment based on historical performance, the *simple* annual rate of return option is the preferable measurement. This is because the simple return is an unbiased estimate of future returns for a single year. However, if the investor is wishing to estimate the average annual rate at which his or her money would grow over a *period of years*, the *compound* annual rate of return is a better measure. In addition, since mutual funds quote the compound annual measurement in their advertisements and sales literature, the compound rate is also preferable when comparing the longer-term performance of one mutual fund against that of another mutual fund.

ARITHMETIC VS. GEOMETRIC AVERAGE ANNUAL RETURNS

The arithmetic average and geometric average were presented in Chapter 9. The *arithmetic average annual return* is similar in concept to the simple annual rate of return. It is computed by dividing the sum of a series of annual returns by the number of years of actual returns. For example, assume that an investment returned 12%, 16%, and a negative 6% over three years. This means that its arithmetic average annual return is 7.33%:

$$\text{Arithmetic Average Annual Return} \; = \; \frac{12\% + 16\% - 6\%}{3} = \frac{22\%}{3} = 7.33\%$$

The *geometric average annual return* takes into account the *interest on interest* in the same manner as does the compound annual rate of return. Unless the annual returns are all identical, the geometric average annual return will always be *smaller* than the arithmetic average annual return.

Example 11-3: Using the same returns as the example in the previous paragraph relating to the arithmetic return, we begin with the three annual returns of 12%, 16%, and a negative 6%. Accordingly, adding 1 to each return gives us 1.12, 1.16, and .94 (or 1-.06), which in turn yields a product of 1.2212:

$(1.12)(1.16)(0.94) = 1.2212$

We then take the third root of 1.2212 (since there are three returns) and subtract one. The third root is the exponent of 1/3 or 0.3333 when using a financial calculator. This results in a geometric average annual return of 6.89%:

$(1.2212)^{0.3333} - 1 = 1.0689 - 1 = 0.0689 \text{ or } 6.89\%$

Financial calculator keystrokes:
1.2212[SHIFT][y^x]0.3333][=]
1.0689[-]1[=]0.0689
Answer: 6.89%

If an investor wishes to ascertain the impact of time on a same-dollar type of investment (that is, with no additional contributions or periodic withdrawals), the *geometric average annual rate of return* calculation should be used.

TIME-WEIGHTED VS. DOLLAR-WEIGHTED RATES OF RETURN

The *time-weighted rate of return* is the geometric annual rate of return measured on the basis of the current year value of the investment asset. As noted, because the time-weighted method incorporates the geometric (not arithmetic) average, thereby taking into account a same-dollar type of analysis, it is the preferred method for analyzing the true annual performance of portfolio managers. Such managers have no control over either contributions to or withdrawals from the fund, which may distort the rate of return measurement accordingly. Therefore, if there are no interim cash flows (investor deposits or withdrawals) to a mutual fund, the time-weighted return, compounded annually, determines the true ending value of the investment asset.

Example 11-4 uses the time-weighted rate of return to determine the investor's effective return:

Example 11-4: An investor buys a share of XYZ mutual fund for $25. This share pays a dividend of $1.50 during the first year that the investor owns the fund. At the end of the first year, he purchases a second share for $30. At the end of the second year, these shares are still worth $30 and have not paid a dividend for that year. Now, assume that the investor sells the shares at the end of the second year. Accordingly, his time-weighted rate of return on the shares is 12.25%.

$$\text{Year 1 return} = \frac{\$30 + \$1.50 - \$25}{\$25} = 0.26 = 26\%$$

$$\text{Year 2 return} = \frac{\$60 - \$60}{\$60} = 0$$

$$\left[(1 + 0.26)(1 + 0)\right]^{1/2} - 1 = \left[(1.26)(1)\right]^{1/2} - 1 = 1.1225 - 1 = 0.1225 \text{ or } 12.25\%$$

In contrast, the d*ollar-weighted rate of return* is the compounded annual rate of return that discounts a portfolio's terminal value and interim cash flows back to an initial value. It is equivalent to the portfolio's *internal rate of return (IRR)*. However, the dollar-weighted rate of return has several weaknesses:

1. It assumes that the portfolio cash flows are *reinvested at the implied IRR*. In actuality, interim cash flows may be reinvested at different rates or not reinvested at all.

2. It may be misleading for purposes of portfolio performance return measurement since the method is influenced by the timing and presence of additional contributions (and/or investor withdrawals) that are beyond the control of the portfolio manager. Conversely, however, if investors wish to know the compounded annual rate of return on an investment where additional contributions and/or withdrawals have taken place, the dollar-weighted rate of return method should be used.

The dollar-weighted rate of return/internal rate of return method is typically used where there are a series of *unequal* cash flows, as is usual with most mutual funds that pay dividends. Example 11.5 incorporates the dollar-weighted rate of return method:

Example 11-5: Joe invested $10,000 in ABC mutual fund two years ago. The fund paid quarterly dividends of $200, $225, $175, $180, $160, $235, $245, and $220 at the end of each quarter, all of which were withdrawn on receipt. At the time of the last dividend payment, ABC mutual fund had grown to a value of $10,350. Accordingly, the dollar-weighted rate of return/internal rate of return for Joe's investment in the fund is 9.78%.

Create a time line of the cash flows:

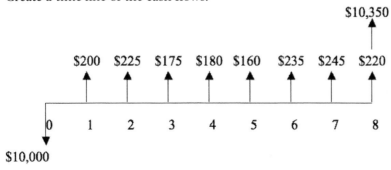

The internal rate of return is an iterative (trial and error) process without a financial calculator. However, if using a financial function calculator, such as the HP10B II, the IRR may easily be determined. In the above example, the HP 10 B II keystrokes are:

10000[±][CFj];200[CFj];225[CFj];175[CFj];180[CFj];160[CFj];235[CFj];...

...245[CFj];10570[CFj][SHIFT]IRR = 2.4455 (quarterly)

2.4455 x 4 = 9.7822 or 9.78%

Finally, because the negative returns in the dollar-weighted computation receive a greater weight than in the time-weighted formula (where such returns are weighted *equally*), the resulting dollar-weighted return will normally be *lower* than that of the time-weighted return. This is another reason why time-weighting of investor contributions is usually preferred in evaluating the long-term performance of portfolio and mutual fund managers.

NOMINAL VS. REAL (INFLATION-ADJUSTED) RETURNS

The *nominal rate of return* on an investment is simply its actual or stated rate of return (like the coupon rate on a bond) earned over a given period of time. The nominal rate is composed of the inflation rate and the real rate of return. An approximation of the nominal rate is: Nominal rate = Real rate + Inflation rate. This is an approximation because it does not account for the effect of compounding between the real rate and the inflation rate. The accurate mathematical relationship is:

$$(1 + \text{nominal rate}) = (1 + \text{real rate}) \times (1 + \text{inflation rate})$$

For example, if the real rate of return is 3.5% and the inflation rate is 4.5%, the approximate nominal rate is 8% (3.5% + 4.5%). The actual nominal rate is:

$$1 + r_{nom} = 1.035 \times 1.045 = 1.0816$$
$$1.0816 - 1 = 0.0816 \text{ or } 8.16\%$$

The approximation understates the actual nominal rate by 16 basis points (0.16%).

Re-arranging the variables solves for the real rate of return:

$$(1 + r_{real}) = \frac{(1 + r_{nom})}{(1 + r_{infl})}$$

Example 11-6: Mark has purchased a 10-year corporate bond with a coupon rate of 6.75%. Inflation has averaged 3.5% over this same time period. Therefore, Mark's real (inflation-adjusted) rate of return on the bond is 3.14% computed as follows:

$$3.14\% = \frac{1.0675}{1.035} - 1$$

After-Tax and After-Tax Inflation-Adjusted Rate of Return

A variation of both the nominal and real rate of return computation is that of the after-tax and the after-tax inflation-adjusted rate of return.

To compute the after-tax rate of return on an investment:

$$r_{after\text{-}tax} = r_{nominal} \times (1 - investor's\ marginal\ tax\ rate)$$

If the investor also pays state income taxes, a separate factor equal to (1 - state marginal income tax rate) is included in the computation. Then, to return to percentage terms, multiply the result by 100.

> **Example 11-7:** Susan is earning a before-tax (nominal) return of 15% on a recently purchased investment. She is in a 33% federal and a 4% state marginal income tax bracket. Accordingly, Susan's after-tax rate of return on the investment is 9.65% computed as follows:
>
> $$9.65\% = 15\% \times (1 - 0.33)(1 - 0.04)$$
>
> (Note: This computation assumes that Susan deducts state income taxes as an itemized deduction on her federal income tax return. If she does not itemize, the resulting after-tax rate of return is slightly less than shown.)

The computation for the after-tax inflation-adjusted rate of return incorporates both the real (inflation-adjusted) rate of return formula and that of the after-tax rate.

> **Example 11-8:** Continuing with the facts of Example 11-7 except Susan now resides in a state that does *not* impose income tax (total marginal tax rate is, therefore, only 33%). In addition, assume that inflation is currently running at a 3% annual rate. Therefore, Susan's after-tax inflation-adjusted rate of return on her investment is 7.81 percent computed as follows:
>
> $$\left[\frac{1.15}{1.03} - 1\right](1 - 0.33) = 0.0781\ or\ 7.81\%$$

It should be noted that the after-tax rate of return formula is only relevant where the earnings on the investment are currently subject to either federal or state income taxes or both. Since many investments are held in a tax-deferred account (like a qualified retirement plan or traditional IRA), the after-tax formula generally cannot be used until the date of the tax-deferred account's distribution. However, this is not the case with the real or inflation-adjusted rate of return formula. It may be used whenever inflation is present and where the planner is attempting to communicate the present value of future year dollars eroded by the loss of real purchasing power.

RETURNS DEALING PRIMARILY WITH STOCKS AND MUTUAL FUNDS

Total Return

The term *total return* is used by financial services professionals to mean the total gain or loss on an investment over a given time period as compared to the initial dollar investment expended by the investor (at the beginning of the time period). As such, this type of return consists of several components as follows:

1. The cash inflows to (or outflows from) the investment; a common example of a cash inflow is the payment of a dividend by the stock or mutual fund;

2. Any price or capital appreciation (gain) or capital loss on the investment; a common example is the increase in share value of a growth stock or growth mutual fund;

3. Any debt reduction (or increase); an example is debt repayment on residential or commercial real property owned by the investor; and

4. Any net tax savings (or additions) incurred by the investor; an example is the tax savings on interest and depreciation on rental real estate property.

The first two are the most common components of total return (and the ones most thought of by investors who understand the term). In turn, whether an investor values interest or dividends (income) or changes in the market value of the investment (capital gain or loss) depends primarily on his or her tax status and cash flow needs. For example, a retiree in a low tax bracket and with a relatively fixed income will likely value interest and dividends more highly than that of potential capital appreciation. Alternatively, a young wage-earner in a higher tax bracket will likely value growth-type investments (potential capital appreciation) more highly than those that generate taxable interest and dividends. Regardless, both are included in the *total return* generated by the investment.

Risk-Adjusted Return

The concept of a *risk-adjusted return* uses the inputs first introduced in the previous chapter on measurement of risk (chapter 9). Among these inputs are standard deviation (total risk) and beta coefficient (systematic risk). Accordingly, several popular methods exist to measure an investment's risk-adjusted return, with the final result dependent on whether standard deviation or beta is used as the denominator. However, whichever method is used, it should compare stocks or mutual funds of the same characteristics and peer group. For example, since beta relates a mutual fund's volatility to an accepted benchmark—usually the Standard & Poor's index of 500 stocks—it should *not* be used in a risk-adjusted return computation where a benchmark is not a relevant point of comparison.

To compute the risk-adjusted rate of return of a stock or mutual fund using beta in the denominator, divide the stock or fund's nominal rate of return by its beta coefficient. An example follows:

Example 11-9: JEM Mutual Fund has returned 6% annually over the course of the last year and features a beta of 0.50. Therefore, its risk-adjusted return is 0.12 (12%) (or 0.06 ÷ 0.50). This compares to KRF Mutual Fund that has returned 8% annually in the last calendar year but exhibits a beta of 0.80. Therefore, the risk-adjusted return of KRF fund is 0.10 (10%)(0.08 ÷ 0.80). Accordingly, on a risk-adjusted rate of return basis, JEM Mutual Fund has outperformed KRF Mutual Fund. This is the case, even though on an unadjusted basis, KRF Mutual Fund has a higher nominal annual rate of return.

Holding Period Rate of Return

We have introduced holding period return throughout this text as:

$$HPR = \left[1 + \frac{EV + I - BV}{BV}\right]^{1/n} - 1 \text{ , Where}$$

HPR = holding period return

EV = ending value of investment

BV = beginning value of investment

I = income (interest or dividends) received during period

n = number of periods in holding period

Rates of return should always be annualized. Taking (1 + HPR) to the 1/nth power results in the *periodic* compounded return. If "n" is expressed in years, this is the *annualized* compounded rate of return. If "n" is expressed as semiannual periods, the HPR must be multiplied by two to arrive at the annual rate.

The following example calculates the holding period rate of return over a four-year investment horizon:

Example 11-10: Joe purchases 200 shares of XYZ stock for $10,000. During the years that Joe has owned these shares, he has received dividend payments of $4,000. Yesterday, Joe sold all 200 shares for a total price of $20,000.

BV = $10,000

EV = $20,000

I = $4,000

n = 4 years

$$\text{HPR} = \left[1 + \left(\frac{EV + I - BV}{BV} \right) \right]^{1/n} - 1 = \left[1 + \left(\frac{\$20{,}000 + \$4{,}000 - \$10{,}000}{\$10{,}000} \right) \right]^{1/4} - 1 =$$

$$= \left[1 + (1.40) \right]^{1/4} - 1 = (2.40)^{1/4} - 1 = 1.2447 - 1 = 0.2447 \text{ or } 24.47\%$$

Note that 1.40 is the same as 140%, which is the return for the full four-year investment horizon.

Let's look at another example:

Example 11-11: Assume that Sara purchased 100 shares of stock during the previous calendar year at $50 per share and that a 3% dividend was declared on the stock for that same year ($1.50 per share). In the next year Sara sells the stock for $55 per share. Therefore, her HPR (total return) is 13% computed as follows:

BV = $50 x 100 shares = $5,000

EV = $55 x 100 shares = $5,500

I = $1.50 x 100 shares = $150

$$\text{HPR} = \frac{\$5{,}500 + \$150 - \$5{,}000}{\$5{,}000} = 0.13 \text{ or } 13\%$$

How is HPR computed if, for example, Sara had bought the shares of stock in a margin account established by the broker-dealer on her behalf? Intuitively, it would seem that, since she now has less money at risk, her holding period return should increase. However, let us expand on Example 11-11 in Example 11-12.

Example 11-12: Sara purchases the stock on 50 percent margin in a margin account established with her broker. Sara posts one-half of the beginning value in Example 11-11 ($5,000/2 = $2,500) and borrows the remaining $2,500 at a margin interest rate of 8%. The stock pays $1.50 in dividend per share for the year. Sara sells the stock after one year at $55 per share:

BV = $2,500 (Sara's equity investment)

EV = $5,500

I = $150

Loan repayment = $2,500 + $200 interest ($2,500 x 0.08 = $200)

$$\text{HPR} = \frac{\$5{,}500 + \$150 - (\$2{,}500 + \$200) - \$2{,}500}{\$2{,}500} = 0.18 \text{ or } 18\%$$

It should be noted that leverage (buying on margin) cuts both ways. Sara's loss would also be magnified if the stock price declined over the one-year holding period.

Finally, the after-tax HPR can be computed by adding Sara's marginal tax bracket (25%) into the analysis and then applying the after-tax formula of (1 – marginal tax rate). For example, using the information in Example 11-11, we can compute Sara's after-tax HPR to be 9.75% as follows:

HPR = 13% (from Example 11-11)

After-tax HPR = 13%(1-0.25) = 9.75%

This does not assume a capital gains tax rate may be applicable in the sale of the stock.

RETURNS DEALING PRIMARILY WITH BONDS

Current Yield

The *current yield* of a bond is the return represented by the amount of annual interest income received in relation to the market value of the bond. It is calculated by dividing the annual interest payment on the bond (as reflected in its *coupon rate* multiplied by the par value of the bond, normally $1,000) by the bond's current market price:

$$\text{Current yield (CY)} = \frac{\text{Annual coupon payment}}{\text{Market price of bond}}$$

Example 11-13 calculates the current yield.

> **Example 11-13:** Jeff has a bond with a coupon rate of 8.25% that is currently trading at 96.5% of par (par of $1,000). Therefore, the current yield on Jeff's bond is 8.55% computed as follows:
>
> $$CY = \frac{\$1,000(0.0825)}{\$1,000(0.965)} = \frac{\$82.50}{\$965} = 0.0855 \text{ or } 8.55\%$$

Note that in Example 11-13, the bond is trading at a *discount* to its par value. As a result, the bond's current yield will always *exceed* its nominal yield (as reflected by the bond's coupon rate of 8.25%). Conversely, if the bond were trading at a *premium* to its par value (that is, the market price was more than $1,000), the bond's current yield will always be *less than* its nominal yield (as reflected by the bond's coupon rate). The current yield on a bond is similar to the dividend yield on a stock.

Yield to Maturity

The *yield to maturity* (YTM) is the same as the dollar-weighted rate of return/internal rate of return concept that was discussed earlier, but in the context of a bond or fixed-income security. The YTM computation assumes that the investor reinvests all coupons received from the bond equal to the computed YTM. In effect, therefore, the computation assumes that the reinvestment rate is the yield to maturity. This, however, is not the case in actuality.

The yield to maturity formula is an iterative process (trial and error) as is the internal rate of return. However, the computation is facilitated with the use of a financial function calculator, like the HP 10BII, or with computer software. An example follows:

Example 11-14: Terry has purchased a market discount bond for $850 (par value of $1,000) with a coupon rate of 7%. The bond pays interest semi-annually and matures in 15 years. Therefore, the yield to maturity (YTM) on Terry's bond is 8.82% computed as follows and with keystrokes shown for the HP 10BII calculator:

First, identify the bond valuation variables:

Market value (PV) = $850

Coupon payment (PMT) = $70/2 = $35

Principal (FV) = $1,000

Market required return (I/YR) = YTM = ??

Periods (N) = 15 years x 2 = 30 semiannual periods

Calculator keystrokes:

30[N];850[+/-][PV];35[PMT];1000[FV][I/YR] = 4.4113 (semiannual)

4.4113 x 2 = 8.8226

The YTM is 8.82%

Note that the YTM should always be calculated as if the bond makes *semi-annual* interest payments (unless, of course, the facts of the problem specifically state that the bond returns interest payments annually). This same assumption is also to be made *even if* the bond is a zero-coupon bond and returns no (cash) interest payments on a periodic basis.

Yield to Call

Many corporate bonds, as well as some government bonds (with the exception of Treasury bonds), are callable. This means that, in times of falling interest rates, companies will choose to replace, or *call*, their old, more expensive bonds and issue new bonds in their place at the lower interest rate. The cost to the issuer for doing this is referred to as the *call premium* on the bond.

The actual formula for computing the *yield to call* (YTC) on a bond is the same as that for the yield to maturity (YTM) *except* that the principal value of the bond at its maturity date is replaced by the *call price* and the time to maturity is replaced by the time to first potential call date. In several situations, the calculated YTC is greater than the calculated YTM. However, remember the issuer *never* calls the bond on behalf of the bondholder. Reinvesting the callable bond proceeds at the lower market rate results in the adjusted internal rate of return being *less than* the YTM.

Like yield to maturity, the yield to call (sometimes referred to as *yield to worst* in the financial services marketplace) may be easily computed with the assistance of a financial function calculator. A sample computation using the HP 10BII calculator follows:

Example 11-15: Josh recently purchased a 20-year maturity, $1,000 par bond for $1,150 (a premium bond). The bond carries a coupon rate of 8% and interest is paid semi-annually. It has a call price of $1,050 and may be called in five years. Therefore, the yield to call (YTC) on Josh's bond is 5.42% computed as follows:

PV = $1,150

PMT = $40

FV = $1,050

I/YR = YTC = ??

N = 10

Note that the FV is the call price and N is the number of semiannual periods to first call.

Calculator keystrokes:

10[N];1150[+/-][PV];40[PMT];1050[FV][I/YR] = 2.7095 (semiannual)

2.7095 x 2 = 5.42%

Taxable Equivalent Yield

Finally, some bonds (such as municipal bonds) return tax-free income. As a result, investors need to have a method of comparing the yield (return) on these bonds to those that are fully taxable (a corporate issue). The formula that is used to make this comparison is the municipal bond's *taxable equivalent yield* (TEY) as follows:

$$\text{Taxable equivalent yield (TEY)} = \frac{\text{Tax - free yield}}{(1 - \text{tax rate})}$$

Again, after performing this calculation, the result is then multiplied by 100 to state the result in percentage terms.

Example 11-16: James is considering the purchase of a municipal bond with a coupon rate (nominal yield) of 5.5%. His marginal tax rate is 33 percent. James is also considering the purchase of a corporate bond with a coupon rate of 8.5 percent. Assuming all other factors equal, which bond should James purchase?

This may be approached in two ways, either by 1) calculating the TEY of the municipal bond or 2) calculating the after-tax yield of the corporate bond:

$$\text{TEY of municipal bond} = \frac{5.5\%}{(1 - 0.33)} = 8.21\%$$

After - tax yield of corporate bond $= 8.5\%(1 - 0.33) = 5.695\%$

Either approach results in the purchase of the corporate bond over the municipal bond.

PORTFOLIO MEASURES OF RETURN

Portfolio-return measures are scaled to provide comparison. The Jensen ratio or alpha, provides the added-value of the portfolio manager. The Treynor method provides the return per unit of systematic risk as measured by the portfolio's beta. The Sharpe ratio provides the return per unit of total risk as measured by the portfolio standard deviation.

Jensen Ratio (Alpha)

The Jensen ratio (also known as *alpha*) is a measure of the risk-adjusted value added by a portfolio manager. Specifically, alpha is measured as the portfolio's actual or realized return in excess of that predicted by the capital asset pricing model (CAPM). An alpha of *zero* indicates that the portfolio earned its expected rate of return given its level of assumed risk (as measured by beta). A *positive* alpha indicates that the portfolio manager has added value on a relative basis. Conversely, a *negative* alpha indicates that the portfolio manager has not performed as well as predicted by CAPM and in relation to his or her peers. Note that alpha (like the Treynor method) assumes a fully diversified investor portfolio since beta is included among its formula inputs.

The formula for the Jensen method of portfolio measurement (alpha) is:

Alpha, $\alpha = r_p - [r_f + \beta(r_m - r_f)]$

Where r_p is the portfolio's realized return and the remainder of the formula is the capital asset pricing model (CAPM).

Example 11-17: Assume that DEF portfolio has a realized rate of return of 17% over the last several years and a beta coefficient of 0.72. The realized rate of return for the overall market over this same time period is 18% and the risk-free rate is 6%. Accordingly, the alpha of the DEF portfolio is 2.36% computed as follows:

Alpha = 17% - [6% + 0.72(18% - 6%)] = 17% - 14.64% = 2.36%

The portfolio manager of DEF portfolio has a positive alpha of 2.36 percent, which means the manager has added value and has exceeded the portfolio return that would have been predicted by the capital asset pricing model (CAPM).

Treynor Ratio

Given our previous discussion of portfolio management theory (see chapter 10), we are aware that most investors are risk-averse. Therefore, portfolio performance is often evaluated on a risk-adjusted basis. In risk-adjusted measures, the portfolio return is compared to its assumed risk. The Treynor ratio evaluates this return premium in the context of an assumed diversified portfolio and measures any excess return relative to *systematic risk* (thereby using *beta* as its risk measurement). If the ratio/index number is relatively high, it indicates that the portfolio manager has achieved a return considerably *above* the portfolio's systematic risk. In addition, when comparing the index number obtained from the ratio against that of a benchmark index (such as the S&P 500 index of stocks), we can then determine whether the manager produced better or worse risk-adjusted returns than the benchmark.

The formula for the Treynor method of portfolio measurement is:

$$\text{Treynor } (T_p) = \frac{r_p - r_f}{\beta_p}$$

Where r_p equals the portfolio's realized return, r_f is the risk-free rate of return and β_p is the beta of the portfolio.

Example 11-18: LMN portfolio has a realized return of 16% over the last several years and a beta of 1.10. Three month Treasury bills (the proxy for the risk-free rate) are currently yielding 5%. The S&P 500 index has a realized return of 14% and a beta of 1.00. Compare the risk-adjusted return of LMN portfolio to the benchmark index.

$$T_{LMN} = \frac{16\% - 5\%}{1.10} = 10\%$$

$$T_{SP} = \frac{14\% - 5\%}{1.00} = 9\%$$

Accordingly, this means that the portfolio manager for LMN generated a *higher* risk-adjusted return than that of the benchmark.

Sharpe Ratio

Like the Treynor method, the Sharpe ratio evaluates risk-adjusted return, but (unlike Treynor) it does this in the context of an assumed *non-diversified* portfolio. Therefore, it measures any excess return produced by the portfolio manager relative to *total risk* (thereby using standard deviation as its risk measurement).

The formula for the Sharpe ratio of portfolio measurement is:

$$\text{Sharpe ratio } (S_p) = \frac{r_p - r_f}{\sigma_p}$$

Where r_p equals the portfolio's realized return, r_f is the risk-free rate of return and σ_p is the standard deviation of the portfolio.

> **Example 11-19:** Continue with the facts of Example 11-18, except now the risk-adjusted return of LMN portfolio is compared against the PLF sector fund with a realized return of 12% and a standard deviation of 4.5. In addition, assume that the standard deviation of LMN portfolio is 6.25.
>
> $$S_{LMN} = \frac{16\% - 5\%}{6.25\%} = 1.76$$
>
> $$S_{PLF} = \frac{12\% - 5\%}{4.5\%} = 1.56$$
>
> Thus, the portfolio manager for LMN also generated a *higher* risk-adjusted return than that of the benchmark, relatively non-diversified, sector fund.

Information Ratio

The *information ratio* uses a different hurdle rate for determining the amount of excess return generated by the portfolio manager. Specifically, the ratio uses the excess return of the portfolio over the benchmark return relative to the difference in the standard deviation of the portfolio and the standard deviation of the benchmark. A positive information ratio implies value-added performance by the portfolio manager.

The formula for the information ratio is:

$$\text{Information ratio } (IR) = \frac{r_p - r_B}{\sigma_p - \sigma_B}$$

Where r_p equals the portfolio's realized return, r_B is the benchmark's realized return, σ_p is the standard deviation of the portfolio and σ_B is the standard deviation of the benchmark.

Example 11-20: Continuing with the facts of both Examples 11-18 and 11-19, we observe that LMN portfolio has achieved a realized return of 16%. Further, we observe that the benchmark sector fund reports a realized return of 12%. Finally, the standard deviations of LMN portfolio and the benchmark sector fund are 6.25 and 4.5, respectively. Therefore, the information ratio of LMN portfolio is:

$$IR_{LMN} = \frac{16\% - 12\%}{6.25\% - 4.50\%} = 2.29$$

The positive information ratio is, thus, further evidence that the portfolio manager has been adding value beyond that possible simply by investing in the benchmark sector fund.

IMPORTANT CONCEPTS

Simple annual rate of return	Total return
Annualized rate of return	Risk-adjusted return
Compound annual rate of return	Holding period rate of return
Arithmetic average annual return	Current yield
Geometric average annual return	Yield to maturity (YTM)
Time-weighted rate of return	Yield to call (YTC)
Dollar-weighted rate of return	Taxable equivalent yield (TEY)
Internal rate of return (IRR)	Jensen ratio (alpha)
Nominal rate of return	Treynor ratio
Real (inflation-adjusted) rate of return	Sharpe ratio
After-tax rate of return	Information ratio
After-tax inflation-adjusted rate of return	

QUESTIONS FOR REVIEW

1. Contrast the simple annual rate of return to the compound annual rate of return. Which one of these two types of return will generate the greater percentage return and why?

2. If an investor has held an investment asset for less than a year, what measure is used to compute his or her return?

3. If an investor wishes to determine his or her percentage return on an investment asset without considering any additional contributions or periodic withdrawals, what type of return should he or she use? Explain why this is so.

4. What are the weaknesses inherent in the dollar-weighted rate of return computation? What is the preferred alternative to evaluate the performance of a portfolio manager?

5. When would you typically use the internal rate of return method to compute the return on an investment asset?

6. A corporate bond exhibits a coupon rate of 5.5% with semi-annual interest payments. What is this type of return called?

7. What is the formula for real (inflation-adjusted) rate of return and where might you use this type of return in the personal financial planning process?

8. Rick lives in New York City. His federal marginal tax rate is 25%, his New York State marginal tax rate is 7% and his New York City marginal tax rate is 2.5%. If he buys U.S. Treasury bonds with a 5% coupon rate, what is his after-tax rate of return?

9. What components make up an investor's *total return* on an investment asset? What are the two most common of these components?

10. What is the formula for *risk-adjusted return*? When should it be used in investment practice?

11. What is a major weakness of the *holding period rate of return* measurement?

12. If margin is used to purchase a stock and its price increases from the date of purchase, will the investor's holding period rate of return be more or less than if margin had not been used? Explain.

13. If a bond is trading at a premium to its par value, will the bond's current yield be more or less than its nominal yield? Explain.

14. Define what is meant by the term *yield to maturity* of a bond. What general rate of return concept is the same or similar?

15. When would a corporation be likely to call any previously issued bonds?

16. If a bond is selling at a discount to par, is its yield to call likely higher or lower than its yield to maturity? Explain.

17. Julie is the owner of a municipal bond with a nominal yield of 5%. She is in the 35% federal marginal income tax bracket only. What is the *taxable equivalent yield* (TEY) on Julie's bond?

18. Explain the input factors that are used in each of the following measures of portfolio return:

    • Jensen ratio (alpha)

    • Treynor ratio

    • Sharpe ratio

19. Assume that a mutual fund exhibits an alpha of negative two. Is this a positive or negative reflection on the performance of the portfolio manager? Explain why this is the case.

20. What is the hurdle rate used in the *information ratio* to determine whether value has been added (or lost) by the portfolio manager?

SUGGESTIONS FOR ADDITIONAL READING

Tools and Techniques of Investment Planning, 2nd edition, Stephen R. Leimberg, Robert T. LeClair, Robert J. Doyle, Jr., and Thomas R. Robinson, The National Underwriter Company, 2006.

Investments: *An Introduction,* 9th edition, Herbert B. Mayo, Thomson/ South-Western, 2008.

Investment Analysis and Portfolio Management, 9th edition, Frank K. Reilly and Keith C. Brown, Thomson/South-Western, 2009.

The Wall Street Journal Guide to Money and Investing, 3rd edition, Kenneth M. Morris and Virginia B. Morris, Fireside Publishing, 2004 .

CHAPTER TWELVE

Valuing Equity Securities

• • •

There are two general methods for valuing the theoretical price or trading value of an equity security (a stock): (1) those analytic formulas that attempt to determine the *intrinsic value* of the stock and (2) those market-based methods that attempt to estimate the *relative value* of the stock with reference to the value of other similar securities. There are several individual approaches under either general method, all of which are discussed in this chapter. However, in the intrinsic value approaches, two significant determinants of the value of the stock are the investor's *required rate of return* (sometimes referred to as the investor's *hurdle rate*) and the growth assumption. Think of the value of an asset as the present value of its future cash flows. The growth assumption determines the future cash flows and the required return is the discount rate used to calculate the present value of those future cash flows.

Upon completing this chapter, you should be able to:

- Compute the *intrinsic value* of a stock using a specified discounted cash flow model
- Describe the variations of the dividend discount model of stock valuation
- Determine the value of a stock or other asset using the discounted earnings (capitalized earnings) method of valuation
- Compute the *relative value* of a stock using a specified market-based model
- Define the *book value* of a company and determine how it is computed using an asset-based model of valuation

---

DISCOUNTED CASH FLOW MODELS/INTRINSIC VALUE

The *intrinsic value* of a stock is, by definition, the present value of its future cash flows discounted at the required return. However, unlike an option-free bond where the future cash flows are known (typically in the form of semi-annual interest payments promised the bondholder) the future cash flows from a stock are essentially unknown. Since cash flows from a stock consist primarily of discretionary dividend payments (as a proxy for expected earnings) on the part of the issuing corporation, they can, at best, only be estimated. However, dividends are not the only type of cash flow that may be used in a discounted cash flow (intrinsic value) approach. *Free cash flow to equity* may also be estimated. Free cash flow to equity is the excess of cash flow that the underlying corporation generates from operations in excess of the necessary capital investment in the corporation's assets. As a result, this free cash flow may or may not be distributed to shareholders in the form of dividends. (Note that dividends are a function of earnings, which may be accounting earnings, not cash earnings.)

There are four approaches to determining the intrinsic value of a stock. The first three of these approaches discount future cash flow in the form of *dividends*. They are: (1) the constant growth dividend discount model; (2) the multi-stage (variable) growth dividend discount model; and (3) the no-growth (perpetuity) dividend discount model. The fourth approach, the discounted free cash flow model, discounts *free cash flow to equity* and may be used to determine the intrinsic value of a stock where a dividend has not been paid, and is not expected to be paid.

Constant Growth Dividend Discount Model

The constant growth dividend discount model is used to determine the intrinsic value of a stock where its dividends are growing at a constant rate. The formula for the model is as follows:

$$V_0 = \frac{D_1}{r - g}$$

Where V_0 is the current intrinsic value of the stock, D_1 is the dividend paid for the next year (the first dividend to be paid in the future), r is the investor's required rate of return and g is the constant growth rate of the dividend payments. The numerator of the formula may also be rewritten as $[D_0 \times (1+g)]$ where D_0 is equal to the *current year's dividend* (the dividend that is paid now or was most recently paid) and g is the assumed constant growth rate of the dividends. In other words, you should note that $[D_0 \times (1+g)]$ is *equivalent* to D_1 when applying the constant growth dividend formula.

Example 12-1: Assume that ABC stock is currently paying a dividend of $2.00 and that the dividend is expected to grow at a constant rate of 6%. Further, assume that the investor's required rate of return is 10%. Therefore, under the constant dividend growth model, the intrinsic value of ABC stock to this investor is $53.00 per share computed as follows:

$$V_0 = \frac{D_1}{r - g} = \frac{\$2.00(1.06)}{0.10 - 0.06} = \$53.00$$

Two items need noting. First, make the distinction between a current dividend and an expected dividend. The example used a current dividend (or dividend just paid), which requires compounding by the growth rate to arrive at D_1. If the example would have used an expected dividend of $2.12, no adjustment is necessary. The other item is incorporating the next period's dividend to determine the current period's or prior period's intrinsic value. The next period's dividend, D_1, is used to find V_0. To find V_3, the intrinsic value at the end of Year 3, you need D_4. This is important as will be shown later in applying the multi-stage (variable growth) model.

As noted, the constant growth dividend discount model assumes that the growth rate of dividends declared by the issuing firm is constant. In practice, this is generally *not* the case; however, the average growth may be constant or near-constant. Nevertheless, the model is often used at least as a starting point in the proper valuation of a company's stock. As assumed by the model, the growth rate of the dividends (g) cannot be greater than the investor's required rate of return (r). If the investor's required rate is less than the dividend's growth rate, the model collapses and becomes meaningless since the denominator (and hence the intrinsic value of the stock) turns negative (stock prices are limited on the downside at zero). The model also assumes that the investor's required rate of return is known and never changes. This is likely *not* a realistic assumption either since this rate is highly dependent on the general level of current (and expected) market interest rates. Rather, the appropriate required return to use is not an average but the investor's current required return since the intrinsic value calculated is at the current or present time.

The model does permit a means of comparison to determine whether the stock should be purchased at its current trading value. For example, in Example 12-1, we determined the intrinsic value of ABC stock to be $53.00 per share. Therefore, if ABC were selling in the secondary market for $55.00 per share, and given the assumptions of the model, an investor likely should *not* purchase the stock since it would be considered to be *overvalued*. We can also determine what the expected return of the stock should be if we know the constant growth rate of its dividends and the market price of the stock. This is done by using a form of expected return formula relevant to the constant growth model as follows:

$$r = \left[\frac{D_0(1 + g)}{V_0} \right] + g$$

Where r is the market required return, D_0 is the current year dividend, g is the constant growth rate of the dividend, and V_0 (or P) is the current price or trading value of the stock.

Example 12-2: Continuing with the facts of Example 12-1, but assuming that the current price of ABC stock is $55.00, we determine the expected return of the stock to be 9.85% as follows:

$$E_r = \left[\frac{D_0(1+g)}{V_0}\right] + g = \left[\frac{\$2.00(1.06)}{\$55}\right] + 0.06 = 0.0385 + 0.06 = 0.0985 = 9.85\%$$

Since the market required return is 9.85 percent and the investor's expected return is 10 percent, the stock is over-valued to the investor and he should not purchase it (or sell it short, if the aggressive type).

In summary, with respect to the constant growth dividend discount model:

1. If the market *lowers* the required rate of return for a stock (for example, market interest rates decline), the value of the common stock will *increase*.

2. If the market *raises* the required rate of return for a stock (for example, market interest rates increase), the value of the common stock will *decrease*.

3. If investors decide that the expected growth rate in dividends will be *higher* (for example, the earnings prospects of the issuing company have become more favorable), the value of the common stock will *increase*.

4. If investors decide that the expected growth rate in dividends will be *lower* (for example, the earnings prospects of the issuing company have become less favorable), the value of the common stock will *decrease*.

Multi-Stage (Variable) Growth Dividend Discount Model

The multi-stage (variable) growth form of the dividend discount model assumes that the growth rate of the stock's dividend is *not constant, but rather changes* (either up or down). This is also known as trying to determine the intrinsic value of a stock with temporary supernormal or subnormal growth. To determine the value of such stock, you must combine time value of money techniques with the constant growth dividend discount model. Therefore, in analyzing the initial years of growth, you first compute the present value of the dividends of each year of the super or subnormal growth period. Next, you compute the remaining value of the stock using the constant growth model and discount this lump sum amount back to the present. (Remember, however, this is still only the case if the constant growth dividend rate is *less than* that of the investor's required rate of return). Third, sum all of the present values of the initial years of growth (Step 1) together with the present value lump sum amount, using the constant growth model (Step 2), to determine one final (combined) intrinsic value of the stock (Step 3).

The formula appears formidable but, when broken down, the variable growth period is nothing more than the sum of the present value of a series of lump sum dividends and the terminal value is the present value of the constant growth model. The formula is as follows:

$$V_0 = \sum_{t=1}^{n} \frac{D_0(1+g_S)^t}{(1+r)^t} + \frac{D_{n+1}}{r-g_L}\left(\frac{1}{(1+r)^n}\right)$$

Let us work through an example expanding on the ABC stock valuation first described in Example 12-1:

Example 12-3: As noted in Examples 12-1 and 12-2, ABC stock is currently paying (in year 0) a dividend of $2.00 per share. Now assume, however, that the dividend is expected to grow for three years at 6% and then at 7% thereafter. Further assume that the investor's required rate of return is 9%. Using the multi-stage growth dividend discount model, the intrinsic value of ABC stock to this new investor is $104.09 computed as follows:

Step 1: Compute present value of stock for each of the first three years individually and sum:

$$\frac{\$2.00(1.06)}{1.09} + \frac{\$2.00(1.06)^2}{(1.09)^2} + \frac{\$2.00(1.06)^3}{(1.09)^3} = \$1.945 + \$1.8914 + \$1.8394 = \$5.68$$

Step 2: Use the constant growth model to compute the terminal value of the stock at the end of Year 3 (beginning of Year 4) and discount back to present value:

$$V_3 = \frac{D_4}{r-g} = \frac{\$2.00(1.06)^3(1.07)}{0.09-0.07} = \$127.44$$

$$V_0 = \frac{\$127.44}{(1.09)^3} = \$98.41$$

Step 3: Add Step 1 and Step 2 present value amounts to determine the stock's final intrinsic value:

$$\$5.68 + \$98.41 = \$104.09$$

As noted earlier, the terminal value is calculated at the end of the non-constant growth period and is discounted back from that period. In Example 12-3, therefore, the Year 4 dividend (D_4) is used to calculate the terminal value at the end of Year 3. The terminal value is then discounted back three years. A common mistake is discounting the terminal value back four years. (Remember, the *next* period's dividend is used to calculate the previous period's price.)

In practice, it is generally atypical for companies to sustain constantly growing dividends. Indeed, it is much more probable that the future growth rate of dividends will *decline* over the years. In practice, companies tend to grow early in their life cycle, but as they mature their earnings growth rates tend to slow down, stop, or even decline. Company dividend payout rates then tend to follow suit.

Accordingly, the multi-stage model may be more relevant for practical use than that of the constant growth model. Nevertheless, the constant growth model is usually the focus of examination questions and does effectively communicate how the intrinsic value of a dividend-paying stock or mutual fund is actually derived.

No Growth (Perpetuity) Dividend Discount Model

There is yet a third form of the dividend discount model that assumes zero dividend growth. This is the perpetuity or no-growth dividend discount model, commonly used in determining the intrinsic value of preferred stock. The model is based on the formula for a perpetual annuity where the dividend is not increasing over time. To determine the value of this type of dividend stream, simply divide the dividend by the investor's required return:

$$V_0 = \frac{D}{r}$$

An example in applying the use of this form of the dividend discount model follows:

> **Example 12-4:** Assume that ABC stock *always* pays a $2.00 dividend and the investor's required rate of return is 10%. Therefore, the intrinsic value of ABC stock to this investor where there is zero growth of the dividends is $20.00 per share computed as follows:

$$V_0 = \frac{D}{r} = \frac{\$2.00}{0.10} = \$20.00$$

Discounted Free Cash Flow Model

What happens if a company's stock does *not* pay a dividend? In this case, *none* of the previous three forms of the dividend discount model will work. As a frequent alternative, a company's free cash flow to equity is then discounted to find the intrinsic value of its stock. Free cash flow to equity (FCFE) may be determined from a company's income statement or statement of cash flows:

From income statement:
FCFE = NI + Non-cash expenses – FC – WC + Net borrowing

Free cash flow to equity is the net income (NI) plus non-cash expenses such as depreciation less fixed capital costs (FC) less working capital (WC) plus net borrowing (debt that is available to equity owners).

From statement of cash flows:
FCFE = CFO – FC + Net borrowing

Free cash flow to equity is the cash flow from operations (CFO) less fixed capital costs (FC) plus net borrowing.

The FCFE model is mathematically equivalent to the constant growth form of the dividend discount model except that the current year's dividend (or D_0) or next year's dividend (D_1) is replaced by the FCFE on a per share basis. Therefore, the formula for the model may be written as follows:

$$V_0 = \frac{FCFE_1}{r-g} = \frac{FCFE_0(1+g)}{r-g}$$

Example 12-5: Frank Corporation has an estimated free cash flow to equity (FCFE) for next year of $4.00 per share. In addition, its FCFE is expected to grow at the rate of 3% per year for the next several years. Your client has a required rate of return of 12%. Therefore, the intrinsic value of Frank Corporation's stock to your client is $44.44 computed as follows:

$$V_0 = \frac{FCFE_1}{r-g} = \frac{\$4.00}{0.12-0.03} = \$44.44$$

As with the constant form of the dividend discount model, the FCFE model may be expanded for multiple or variable growth rates in the future simply by replacing dividends with FCFE per share. As a result, the FCFE model is also used to value closely held businesses where earnings are frequently manipulated by the owner for income tax or compensation-based reasons.

DISCOUNTED EARNINGS MODEL/CAPITALIZED EARNINGS

Each of the previous models has discounted cash flows, whether in the form of dividends or free cash flow to equity. However, there is still another way to determine the value of an investment asset, although it is most frequently used to compute the value of an *entire company* (or income property) rather than the individual shares of the company's stock. This method, known as the *capitalized earnings method*, discounts the value of the company's current earnings or income from property instead of its cash flows and is computed as follows:

$$V_0 = \frac{E_0}{R_c}$$

Where V_0 is the estimated value of the company (or property), E_0 is equal to the current annual earnings of that company (or property), and R_c is the capitalization or discount rate, encompassing both a required rate of return for the investor *plus an anticipated growth factor* for the subject asset.

Example 12-6: Reed is attempting to value a commercial real estate rental property that generated net operating (before-tax) earnings of $250,000 last year. Further, he has determined a capitalization rate of 8% to use in valuing this property. Accordingly, Reed values the property at $3,125,000:

$$V_0 = \frac{E_0}{R_c} = \frac{\$250,000}{0.08} = \$3,125,000$$

Of course, the *higher* the capitalization rate, the *lower* the amount that the investor is willing to pay for the company or property. This makes sense since the investor is essentially discounting the price (present value) of the company for a greater assumed risk or required rate of return. As a result, we can also analyze this risk factor by using a multiple of earnings approach or the *reciprocal* of the capitalization rate.

Example 12-7: In Example 12-6, we observed that Reed determined that a capitalization rate of 8% was appropriate in valuing the subject property. In turn, this equates to a multiple of earnings of 12.5 years (100 divided by 8) before Reed will recover his initial investment. Alternatively, if Reed had used a capitalization rate of 10%, the multiple of earnings would have been 10 years (100 divided by 10), thereby reflecting the additional risk that Reed believed that he was assuming and, accordingly, *reducing* the price that he would pay for the subject property to $2.5 million ($250,000 divided by .10).

Finally, in using this method to value the intrinsic value of a company, care must be taken to analyze its true or justifiable annual earnings. For example, a small closely held corporation may reduce its reportable earnings by paying out excessive salaries to the owner/employees and/or other forms of hidden compensation (such as paying rent to the owner/employees for the corporate use of personally owned property). They may do this, in part, to achieve a greater compensation or rental expense deduction for corporate income tax purposes. As a result, a potential investor will need to account for these differences in adjusting the earnings to a more realistic level, in turn impacting what he or she may be willing to pay for the targeted company.

MARKET-BASED MODELS/RELATIVE VALUE

In contrast to the various discounted cash flow models that attempt to estimate the *intrinsic value* of a stock, it is also possible to estimate the stock's *relative value* by comparing its price to that of other similar securities. This is done by referencing the stock's current trading value (price) to relevant variables that affect a stock's value, such as earnings per share, earnings growth, free cash flow, and sales. Accordingly, since they employ market-based data. the following are frequently referred to as market-based valuation models : 1) price to earnings per share (P/E); 2) price to earnings divided by growth (PEG); 3) price to free cash flow (P/FCF); and 4) price to sales (P/S). We begin with the P/E model, also known as the earnings *multiplier model,* since it is the most popular relative valuation measure.

Price to Earnings (P/E) Model

An alternative to the dividend discount model (intrinsic value) approach is the price to earnings (P/E) relative valuation method. As noted previously, none of the dividend discount model forms will work if the company does not pay (or does not expect to pay) a dividend. Therefore, one way investors may estimate the stock's value is by determining how many dollars they are willing to pay for a dollar of expected earnings (leading P/E). This estimation of value relies on the premise that the stock's value (market price) has some relationship to the earnings per share generated by the issuing company.

The P/E multiplier is derived from the discounted cash flow model. The P/E multiplier is also a function of earnings and growth:

$$P_0 = \frac{D_1}{r-g}$$

$$\frac{P_0}{E_1} = \frac{\frac{D_1}{r-g}}{E_1} = \frac{\frac{D_1}{E_1}}{r-g} = \frac{Payout_1}{r-g}$$

In theory, the P/E valuation model is determined by three factors as follows:

1. The expected dividend payout ratio of the stock (its dividends divided by its earnings);

2. The estimated required rate of return that all marketplace investors have determined for the stock (or the "r" that is included in the forms of the dividend discount model); and

3. The expected growth rate of dividends for the stock (or "g" as included in the dividend discount models).

Multiplying the expected earnings per share, E_1 by the stock's P/E multiplier results in a value estimation of the stock:

$$V_0 = E_1 \times \text{P/E multiplier}$$

Example 12-8: RDF stock is trading in the secondary marketplace for $50.00 per share. Its expected earnings per share over the next 12-month period are estimated to be $3.00 per share and a fundamental securities analyst has determined the relevant P/E ratio for the stock's peers to be 20. Therefore, using the P/E ratio approach, RDF stock should be trading for $60.00 per share ($3.00 times 20) and is *undervalued* in relation to its market peers.

The P/E multiplier offers an intuitive sense as to the impact of earnings growth on the price of a stock. For example, a P/E ratio of 60 implies that if the company maintained positive earnings with zero growth, it would take an investor 60 years to earn his or her initial investment earning the required return. During the dot.com bubble in the late 1990s, certain stocks were selling at a P/E of 190 or more! Obviously, the implied growth as dictated by the ratio was not possible.

Finally, as we have shown, the P/E ratio associated with a stock is primarily influenced by the investor's perception of risk (as measured by his or her required rate of return) and the expected dividend growth rate of the stock. There is an *inverse* relationship between investor risk and the anticipated P/E ratio. Therefore, *higher (lower) risk* relative to other companies should result in a *lower (higher) P/E ratio*. Conversely, there is a *direct* relationship between the expected dividend growth rate of the stock and the anticipated P/E ratio. Thus, *higher (lower) expected growth* relative to other companies should result in a *higher (lower) P/E ratio*.

Price to Earnings Divided by Growth (PEG) Model

The price to earnings (P/E) multiplier can also be expanded to compare a subject company's earnings growth rate to that of its peer companies. For example, if a subject company has a higher growth rate than that of its peers, perhaps it deserves a different relative measure of valuation where this superior rate of growth is recognized. Accordingly, another commonly used model is that of assessing a company's P/E ratio relative to its growth, also known as its *PEG* (price to earnings divided by growth) ratio. Specifically, this model's equation is written as follows:

$$PEG = \frac{P/E}{g}$$

Example 12-9: Continuing with the facts of Example 12-8 and RDF stock, we note that its value is estimated by referencing a P/E ratio of 20 for its marketplace peers. However, now assume that RDF Company estimates a growth rate of 10% in earnings for the next year. Accordingly, RDF's PEG ratio is:

$$PEG = \frac{P/E}{g} = \frac{20}{10.00} = 2.00$$

We may now compare RDF Company to its peers in terms of growth of earnings and determine: (1) whether the P/E ratio applied to value RDF is justifiable in relation to its peers and (2) whether its stock is a good value (again, relative to its peers). For example, if JAB Company (a marketplace peer of RDF) has an expected growth rate in earnings of 9%, and was valued using a P/E ratio of 18, then it would appear that the higher P/E ratio applied to value RDF stock was justifiable given its corresponding higher growth rate. However, if WLA Company (another peer of RDF) had an expected growth rate of 8% and was valued with a P/E ratio of only 14, then WLA stock would appear to be a better value in terms of price relative to earnings and growth (that is, WLA features a PEG ratio of 1.75—or 14 divided by 8—in comparison to RDF's PEG ratio of 2.0). Stocks with lower PEGs are more attractive than stocks with higher PEGs, all else being equal.

As with most valuation measures, there are also several caveats to be aware of when using the PEG model. First, any company's expected growth figures are normally available only for a short period of time (for example, no more than five years). As a result, companies with a lower growth rate, but whose growth rates are estimated over a longer period of time (say, 10 years), are penalized by use of the ratio. Second, the PEG ratio does not take into account the relative investor *risk* when investing in one company's stock versus another company's stock. Third and finally, the PEG equation assumes a linear or *lockstep* relationship between a company's growth and its applicable P/E ratio, which may or may not actually be the case.

Price to Free Cash Flow (P/FCF) Model

Another relative measure that may be used to value a company's stock is price to free cash flow (FCF). How one determines FCF will affect the results of the model. Free cash flow to equity (FCFE) was discussed earlier in this chapter. A major drawback of using FCFE is its volatility and possibly even a negative value. A general approximation of FCF is EPS plus depreciation, amortization, and depletion. Cash flow from operations (CFO) found in the statement of cash flows is also widely used. It is important with CFO that any cash flow from financing or investing activities is removed (since that cash flow is not generated from operational activities). Hence, the price of the stock is a function of the company's FCF, growth (g), and the investor's required rate of return (r). It may be written in formula as:

$$P_0 = \frac{(1 + g)FCF_0}{r - g}$$

Rearranging the variables results in price to free cash flow (P/FCF):

$$\frac{P_0}{FCF_0} = \frac{(1 + g)}{r - g}$$

Where P is the price of the company stock, FCF is the free cash flow of the company, g is the expected growth rate of the company's earnings, and r is the required rate of return of the potential investor.

> **Example 12-10:** Again, we continue with the performance numbers of RDF stock that we have noted so far in Examples 12-8 and 12-9. Specifically, RDF stock has an expected growth rate in earnings of 10%. Further, however, we now assume that the potential investor's required rate of return, considering an investment in RDF stock, is 14%. Thus, the price to free cash flow (P/FCF) ratio of the stock is 27.50:
>
> $$\frac{P_0}{FCF_0} = \frac{(1 + g)}{r - g} = \frac{1.10}{0.14 - 0.10} = 27.5$$

The price of the stock is 27.5 times its free cash flow.

Then, as with the other relative valuation measures, we compare this P/FCF ratio to that of RDF's marketplace peers to determine if its stock appears to be overvalued or undervalued. For example, if RDF was selling for $50 and exhibited a P/FCF ratio of 27.5 compared to BMG stock (its marketplace peer) selling for the same price, but with a P/FCF ratio of 25, the investor may well determine that RDF stock was a better buy (or is undervalued). In addition, the P/FCF ratio measure has the advantage that some consideration of investor risk in making the purchase is taken into account.

The price to free cash flow is another tool for valuing a firm. In this case the appropriate free cash flow is free cash flow to equity (FCFE):

$$V_0 = \frac{(1 + g)FCFE_0}{r - g}$$

This model should now look familiar. It is simply a variation of the constant growth dividend discount model discussed earlier in this text.

Price to Sales (P/S) Model

The final market-based method of relative valuation that we will consider is that of a company's stock price to its sales or more popularly known as the price to sales model. Sales are generally less subjected to distortion or manipulation than earnings per share. Also, a company may have negative earnings but still report positive sales (however, for a firm to be considered a going concern, it must eventually generate earnings and positive cash flow). Analysis of a company's revenue recognition practice is also important in determining sales. Finally, securities analysis generally considers annual sales of the company from the most recent fiscal year in the calculation: Total sales – returns – customer discounts. Accordingly, the price to sales ratio (P/S) is a function of profit margin, dividend payout, growth, and required return:

$$\frac{P_0}{S_0} = \frac{\text{Profit margin x Dividend payout x } (1 + g)}{r - g}$$

Where P is the price of the company stock, S is the company's annual sales, Profit margin is the company's earnings divided by its sales, Dividend payout is the percentage of its earnings paid out as dividends (dividend divided by earnings per share), g is the expected growth rate of the company's earnings, and r is the required rate of return of the potential investor.

Example 12-11: Continuing to build on our previous examples of 12-8, 12-9, and 12-10, now assume that RDF Company exhibits a profit margin of 30% (0.30) and a dividend payout of 50%

(0.50). The expected growth rate of 10% (0.10) and required rate of return of 14% (0.14), remain the same. Hence, the price to sales (P/S) ratio for RDF stock is 4.1250 computed as follows:

$$\frac{P_0}{S_0} = \frac{\text{Profit margin x Dividend payout x } (1 + g)}{r - g} = \frac{0.30 \times 0.50 \times (1.10)}{0.14 - 0.10} = 4.125$$

As with the other measures discussed to this point, the P/S ratio of RDF stock is then compared to its industry peers to determine whether the stock appears over- or undervalued relative to those peers. Again, similar to the P/E ratio analysis, a potential investor may wish to invest in a stock whose price to sales ratio is *low* in comparison to its peers with the expectation that this ratio will improve, thereby driving up the price of the underlying stock. However, and this is still a major warning, with any ratio analysis type of valuation, these are *relative* measures. Therefore, the industry peers against whom any stock is being compared may themselves be overvalued. As a result, an undervalued stock may simply be *less overvalued* than its industry peers. But, such stock may *still be overvalued* with respect to the aggregate market and may *not* be a good *buy*.

Figure 12-1 summarizes the intrinsic and relative valuation methods commonly used in determining expected stock prices.

Figure 12-1

Intrinsic Value Methods	Relative Value Methods
1. Constant Growth Dividend Discount Model 2. Multi-Stage(Variable) Dividend Discount Model 3. No Growth/Perpetuity Dividend Discount Model 4. Discounted Free Cash Flow Model	1. Price to Earnings(P/E) Ratio 2. Price to Earnings Divided by Growth (PEG) Ratio 3. Price to Free Cash Flow (P/FCF) Ratio 4. Price to Sales(P/S) Ratio

ASSET-BASED MODELS/BOOK VALUE

The *book value* of a company refers to the amount of equity available to its shareholders, that is, the amount that shareholders have invested over time in the company. Simplistically, book value is determined by subtracting company liabilities from company assets. However, many of these assets are reported on the company balance sheet at what the company paid for them (historical cost) less any accumulated depreciation, which often times does *not* reflect the current fair market value of those assets. As a result, most companies sell for *more than* their book or accounting value. Additionally, many companies operating as a *going concern* are more valuable in that capacity rather than simply by valuing the book value of their equity.

Price to book value (P/BV) incorporates balance sheet items, which makes this method attractive for valuing firms with zero or negative earnings.

Figure 12-2 schematically illustrates the interaction of the financial statements. First, company assets are used to generate revenues. Next, revenues are managed to generate income. Then, income is retained for internally financing new assets or is paid out in dividends. Income may also be generated externally through outside investments. Finally, external debt and equity financing is often necessary for additional purchases of new assets and the cycle repeats.

The calculation of book value may require adjusting to improve the comparability of P/BV across companies. Book value per share of equity is formally calculated as:

1. Shareholders' equity – Total value of senior claims to common stock = Common shareholders' equity
2. Common shareholders' equity/Number of common shares outstanding = Book value per share

Figure 12-2. Interaction of the Balance Sheet, Income Statement, and Statement of Cash Flow

(Source: Hal Lenhart, CFA 2002)

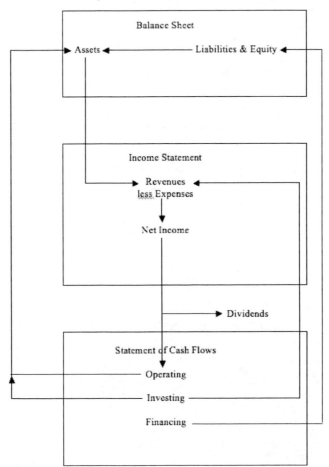

Below is a typical (abbreviated) company balance sheet for computing book value per share in Example 12-12.

Xeta Omega, Inc.
Corporate Balance Sheet
For Fiscal Year Ending December 31, 2009

Assets		Liabilities	
Cash	$1,500,000	Accounts Payable	$ 100,000
Inventory	$5,500,000	Notes Payable	$ 900,000
Equipment	$3,000,000	Total Liabilities	$1,000,000
Total Assets	$10,000,000		
		Stockholders' Equity	$7,500,000
		Preferred Shares	$1,500,000
		Total Liabilities and Equity	$10,000,000
		Shares Outstanding	150,000
		Market price per share	$16.35

Example 12-12: Using the information from the corporate balance sheet for Xeta Omega, Inc., we are now able to compute book value per share for the corporation as follows:

$7,500,000 - $1,500,000 = $6,000,000

$6,000,000/150,000 shares = $40/share

Xeta Omega's book value per share is $40.

Xeta Omega's P/BV = $16.35/$40 = 0.41

Finally, you should note the difference between a stock's market value, its intrinsic value, and its book value. All have been discussed in this chapter and are defined as follows:

1. A stock's *market value* is also known as its price or trading value, but is specifically the price of the stock as determined by investors in the secondary marketplace.

2. A stock's *intrinsic value* is its discounted present value based on future cash flows (or some other relevant factor) as determined by discounted cash flow (DCF) models.

3. A stock's *book value* is the amount of a company's common equity divided by the total number of common shares outstanding.

IMPORTANT CONCEPTS

Market value

Intrinsic value

Constant Growth Dividend Discount Model

Multi-Stage (Variable) Growth Dividend Discount Model

No Growth/(Perpetuity) Dividend Discount Model

Discounted Free Cash Flow Model

Discounted Earnings Model/Capitalized Earnings

Capitalization rate

Relative value

Price to Earnings (P/E) Valuation Model

Price to Earnings Divided by Growth (PEG) Valuation Model

Price to Free Cash Flow (P/FCF) Valuation Model

Price to Sales (P/S) Valuation Model

Book value

Price to book value (P/BV) ratio

QUESTIONS FOR REVIEW

1. What are the two general methods used to determine the *proper* price of a stock?

2. Define what is meant by the term *intrinsic value* of a stock.

3. What are the three forms of the dividend discount model?

4. What model should be used to determine the intrinsic value of a stock that does not pay (or expect to pay) a dividend?

5. With respect to the inputs of the constant growth dividend discount model, there is a basic assumption. What is it?

6. Using the constant growth dividend discount model, assume that you determine the intrinsic value of a stock to be $50.00 per share. If the stock is currently trading for $55.00 per share, what is your likely investment decision? Explain.

7. What is the reciprocal form of the constant growth dividend discount model and what is it that you are trying to determine?

8. Given the assumptions of the constant growth dividend discount model, if market interest rates increase, what happens to the intrinsic value of a share of common stock?

9. What are the three computational steps in determining the intrinsic value of stock if the multi-stage form of the dividend discount model is used?

10. Assume that a stock is expected to pay a $1.00 dividend in perpetuity. If the investor's required rate of return is 12%, what is the intrinsic value of this stock?

11. Define a company's *free cash flow*. Why might this determination be relevant?

12. If Investor A uses a capitalization rate of 15% in determining how much he would pay for a company and Investor B uses a rate of 12%, which investor is willing to pay more for the company? Explain why this is so.

13. What are four *relative valuation* methods used to determine what should be the market value of a stock?

14. In theory, what are the three factors that determine what price/earnings (P/E) ratio to use in estimating the market value of a stock?

15. If a stock has a lower expected dividends growth rate as compared to another company's stock, what is the corresponding effect on the P/E ratio that should be used?

16. Why might it be advisable to use the PEG ratio rather than the P/E ratio to determine the relative valuation of a stock?

17. What is an advantage of the P/FCF relative method of stock valuation?

18. A company's profit margin and dividend payout ratio is used in what method of stock valuation?

19. Why does a company often sell for more than its *book value*?

SUGGESTIONS FOR ADDITIONAL READING

Tools and Techniques of Investment Planning, 2nd edition, Stephen R. Leimberg, Robert T. LeClair, Robert J. Doyle, Jr., and Thomas R. Robinson, The National Underwriter Company, 2006.

Investments: An Introduction, 9th edition, Herbert B. Mayo, Thomson/ South-Western, 2008.

Investment Analysis and Portfolio Management, 9th edition, Frank K. Reilly and Keith C. Brown, Thomson/South-Western, 2009.

The Wall Street Journal Guide to Money and Investing, 3rd edition, Kenneth M. Morris and Virginia B. Morris, Fireside Publishing, 2004.

CHAPTER THIRTEEN

Valuing Debt Securities

• • •

We now proceed to methods used to value the other major class of investment securities, government and corporate debt obligations (bonds). Unlike stock, the valuation of an option-free bond is relatively easy since the future cash flows are contractually set. Indeed, in the basic valuation formula for a bond (reproduced below), the only unknown is the investor's required rate of return (r_B) necessary to make such a purchase. Subsequently, after introducing you to the bond rating agencies and some fundamental concepts used in bond valuation, the remainder of this chapter is devoted to measuring the change in the price of a bond given a respective change in market interest rates. Refer to Chapter 2 of this text for a review of bond fundamentals.

Upon completing this chapter, you should be able to:

- Explain bond ratings, including the definition of an *investment grade* bond
- Compute the intrinsic value of a bond using time value of money principles
- Discuss yield curves and the term structure of interest rates
- Apply the concepts of Macauley and modified duration in describing the interest rate sensitivity of a given bond
- Compute the estimated change in price of a bond using duration
- Define bond convexity and how it is used in the valuation of a bond
- Explain portfolio immunization
- State the basic principles of duration in bond portfolio management

BOND RISKS AND RATINGS

Bonds are subject to their own set of investment risks, as are all types of securities. As noted previously in Chapter 9, when discussing sources of investment risk, most of these constitute types of systematic risk that can only be minimized (not eliminated) if a bond investment is made. Among the types of systematic risk are reinvestment rate risk, interest rate risk, and purchasing power risk, which impact all forms of corporate, government, and municipal bond issues. However, U.S. government Treasury bonds do *not* possess another type of investment risk referred to as *default risk*, that is, the risk that a creditor may seize the underlying collateral of the bond (if any) and sell it to recoup the principal. In addition, government bonds do not possess *credit risk* or the risk that the issuer cannot make interest and principal payments.

The credit risk associated with a corporate bond may be minimized by investing in *investment grade* (or non-speculative grade) bonds. So how does one go about establishing the creditworthiness of a bond? This is the function of bond rating agencies, most notably the private firms of Standard & Poor's, Fitch's, and/or Moody's Investors Service (Moody's). Each of these firms rates a corporate bond issue and determines whether it is high or medium investment grade or, alternatively, speculative (non-investment) grade. Additionally, each firm assigns a rating to those bonds where the issuer has gone into default and is currently not able to make principal payments. Table 13-1 below provides a summary of all ratings currently used by the two major bond rating agencies, Standard & Poor's and Moody's.

TABLE 13-1

	Standard & Poor's	**Moody's**
Investment Grade:		
High Grade	AAA-AA	Aaa-Aa
Medium Grade	A-BBB	A-Baa
Non-investment Grade:		
Speculative	BB-B	Ba-B
Default	CCC-D	Caa-C
Overall Range	AAA-D	Aaa-C

Of course, it should be noted here that, like all entities whose job it is to make judgment calls, bond rating agencies are at times incorrect! For this reason, it is recommended that financial planners conduct their own due diligence with respect to the creditworthiness of bonds and use the rating agencies primarily as a crosscheck to or confirmation of their own conclusions.

BOND VALUATION

Straight (Option-Free) Bonds

Traditional Bond Valuation Model

As first presented in Chapter 2 of this text, the cash flows of a straight bond may be shown on a time line as:

Thus, the traditional bond valuation model is the sum of the present value of the coupon annuity and the present value of the principal lump sum at maturity.

The model can be expressed in formula form as:

$$V_0 = CP(PVIFA_{i/2,\,2n}) + P(PVIF_{i/2,\,2n}), \text{ where:}$$

V_0 = value of the bond
CP = coupon payment (semiannual)
P = principal or par value of the bond
i = required return (annual)/2 = semiannual
n = number of years/2 = number of semiannual periods
$PVIFA_{i/2,\,2n}$ = present value interest factor of an annuity
$PVIF_{i/2,\,2n}$ = present value interest factor of a lump sum

Example 13-1: Calculate the price of a bond with a six percent coupon (paid semiannually), 10 years to maturity, $1,000 par value, and the required return is (a) 6%, (b) 8%, and (c) 4%. First, identify the variables:

V_0 = ??

CP = $1,000 x 0.06/2 = $30 (paid every six months)

P = $1,000

i = (a) 6%/2 = 3%, (b) 8%/2 = 4%, (c) 4%/2 = 2%

n = 10 years x 2 = 20 semiannual periods

(a) V_0 = $30(PVIFA$_{6\%/2, 20}$) + $1,000(PVIF$_{6\%/2, 20}$) = $1,000

Rather than consult interest factor tables, use a financial calculator (HP10bII):

Keystrokes:20[N];3[I/YR];30[PMT];1000[FV][PV] = -1,000.00 (ignore sign) = $1,000

Note that the required return of 6% is equal to the coupon rate. The bond, therefore, sells *at par*.

(b) V_0 = $30(PVIFA$_{8\%/2, 20}$) + $1,000(PVIF$_{8\%/2, 20}$) = $864.10

Keystrokes:20[N];4[I/YR];30[PMT];1000[FV][PV] = -864.10 = $864.10

Note that the required return is now *greater than* the coupon rate. The bond, therefore, sells at a *discount* to par.

(c) V_0 = $30(PVIFA$_{4\%/2, 20}$) + $1,000(PVIF$_{4\%/2, 20}$) = $1,163.51

Keystrokes:20[N];2[I/YR];30[PMT];1000[FV][PV] = -1,163.51 = $1,163.51

Note that the required return is now *less than* the coupon rate. The bond, therefore, sells at a *premium* to par.

Example 13-1 illustrates the price-yield relationship of bonds. Bond prices move inversely to interest rates (yield) and the bond's price-yield curve is convex in shape. We will return to this relationship in the discussion of a bond's duration and convexity below.

The traditional bond valuation model is also used to calculate the yield-to-maturity (YTM or required return) of a bond.

Example 13-2: Calculate the YTM of a bond selling for 110-14 (percent of par in 32nds), six percent coupon, $1,000 par value, and eight years remaining to maturity.

V_0 = 110 and 14/32 percent of par = 1.104375 x $1,000 = $1,104.375

CP = $1,000 x 0.06/2 = $30 (paid every six months)

P = $1,000

i = YTM = ??

n = 8 years x 2 = 16 semiannual periods

Keystrokes: 16[N];1104.375[+/-] PV;30[PMT];1000[FV][I/YR] = 2.2179 (semiannual)

2.2179 x 2 = 4.44%

Since the bond is selling at a premium to par, the YTM is less than the coupon rate.

A variation of the traditional bond valuation models is used to calculate the yield-to-call (YTC) of a callable bond.

Example 13-3: Calculate the YTC of a bond selling at par with a 12 percent coupon, par value of $1,000, 15 years to maturity, call price of $1,120, and first available call in five years.

V_0 = $1,000

CP = $120/2 = $60 (paid every six months)

P = $1,120 (call price instead of par value)

i = YTC = ??

n = 5 years x 2 = 10 semiannual periods to first available call

Keystrokes: 10[N]; 1000[+/-] PV;60[PMT];1120[FV][I/YR] = 6.8737 (semiannual)

6.8737 x 2 = 13.75%

Note that this bond sold at par for a YTM of 12 percent. However, its YTC is 13.75%. Does this imply that the bondholder should desire the bond to be called? No. The bond issuer never calls a bond on behalf of the bondholder. Rather, interest rates must drop sufficiently for the issuer to re-finance the bond issue. If the bond is called, the bondholder must subsequently re-invest the proceeds in a bond paying lower coupons. The result over the remaining life of the issue is a YTM that is *less than* 12 percent.

An income yield measure of a bond is its *current yield*. The current yield (CY) of a bond is its annual coupon payment divided by the market price of the bond or:

$$\text{Current yield (CY)} = \frac{\text{Annual coupon payment of bond}}{\text{Market price of the bond}}$$

Hence, if a bond has a coupon of eight percent and is selling at 102-7/8 of par, the current yield is:

$$CY = \frac{(0.08)(\$1,000)}{1.02875(\$1,000)} = \frac{\$80}{\$1,028.75} = 0.0778 = 7.78\%$$

You should note that the current yield of a bond is similar to a dividend yield of a stock, since both are designed to measure the income return of the security.

Convertible Bonds

A convertible bond is like a straight or ordinary bond combined with an embedded option contract. An investor pays a *conversion premium* when he or she buys a convertible bond for the right to convert the bond into common stock. Let's explain through the use of Example 13-4

Example 13.4: Debbie owns a $1,000 par convertible bond with a coupon rate of 7 percent (with semi-annual interest payments). The bond matures in 10 years and the bond is convertible into the common shares of ABC Company at a conversion ratio of 27.5 shares. The current market price of ABC Company shares is $34 and the convertible bond is selling for $1,200 on the secondary market. Comparable debt currently yields 6 percent. Calculate the floor value and the conversion value of the convertible bond and comment on expectations supporting the premium market price of the convertible bond.

The floor value is the market value of the straight bond component of the convertible bond:

V_0 = ?? = $1,074.39
CP = $35 (semiannual coupon payment)
P = $1,000
i = 3% (semiannual)
n = 10 years x 2 = 20 semiannual periods

Keystrokes: 20[N];3[I/YR];35[PMT];1000[FV][PV] = -1,074.3874 = $1,074.39

The conversion value is the current market price of the stock ($34) multiplied by the conversion ratio of 27.5 shares or $935. However, this particular bond would *not* be converted. Rather, the current market price of $1,200 for the convertible bond reflects optimism in the expected price of the underlying stock.

The conversion premium ($125.61 in Example 13-4) is the difference between the floor value of the bond ($1,074.39) and its current market price ($1,200).

Zero Coupon Bonds

Zero coupon bonds (zeros) may also be valued using the traditional bond valuation model. Even though there is no semiannual coupon associated with the zero coupon bond, the bond's principal must still be discounted on a bond equivalent yield semiannual basis.

Exercise 13-5: A corporate zero coupon bond has a $1,000 face value and 10 years remaining to maturity. Market interest rates are currently eight percent. Calculate the expected price of the bond by setting up the model variables as follows:

V_0 = ?? =

CP = 0

P = $1,000

i = 8%/2 = 4%

n = 10 years x 2 = 20 semiannual periods

Keystrokes: 20[N];4[I/YR];0[PMT];1000[FV][PV] = -456.3869 or $456.39

YIELD CURVES/TERM STRUCTURE OF INTEREST RATES

The *term structure of interest rates* (or the *yield curve* as it is more popularly known) is a theory that relates the term of maturity of a sample of the same credit quality (or rated) bonds to their yield to maturity *at a given point in time*. Therefore, the theory represents a cross section of yields for a category of bonds that are comparable in all respects but their date of maturity. Different yield curves may be constructed for Treasury bonds, government agency bonds, municipal bonds, AAA rated corporate bonds, and so on. However, the accuracy of the yield curve will, ultimately, depend on the overall comparability of the bonds in the sample.

There are four basic types of yield curves that are pictured below:

Normal Yield Curve (A)
Yield

Inverted Yield Curve (B)
Yield

Maturity

Maturity

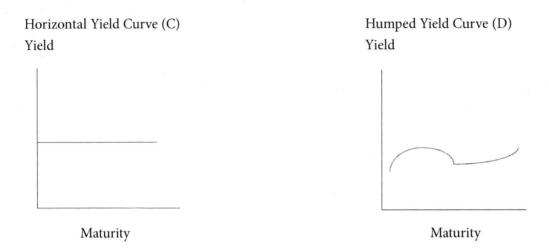

Horizontal Yield Curve (C)
Yield

Maturity

Humped Yield Curve (D)
Yield

Maturity

In most instances, the positive or normal yield curve (Curve A above) will predominate. This means that bond yields will increase as their maturity dates lengthen, making sense since, as maturities lengthen, investors will demand a premium for the extra risk (both interest rate and purchasing power risk) associated with *tying up* their money for longer periods of time. However, at times, any of the other types and shapes of curves may instead be present. For example, in the early 1980s when the Federal Reserve Board was tightening short-term credit (driving up interest rates) to slow the economy and combating inflation, the bond markets observed an inverted yield curve (Curve B above). During this period, short-term rates were greater than long-term rates as the Fed tightened credit on the short end. A horizontal yield curve (Curve C above) represents little, if any, differentiation of rates over maturities. Finally, a humped yield curve (Curve D above) represents a "blip" in yields. For example, a hump occurred around the three-year Treasury yield when the Treasury made a decision to stop issuing notes of that maturity.

Similar to the efficient market hypothesis (EMH) and its various forms discussed in chapter 10 of this textbook, the term structure of interest rates theory also has several iterations. Specifically, there are three different academic arguments about why yield curves mutate into one of the four basic shapes pictured above.

The first of these arguments is the most plausible and is known as the *expectations hypothesis*. According to this hypothesis, the shape of the yield curve results from the interest rate expectations of secondary market participants. More specifically, the hypothesis maintains that any long-term interest rate simply represents the geometric average or mean of the current and future one-year interest rates and should be expected to prevail over the maturity of the bond. In effect, the term structure consists of a series of intermediate and long-term interest rates, each of which is a reflection of the geometric average of current and expected one-year interest rates. Accordingly, the expectations hypothesis may help to explain the shape of *any* yield curve. As an example, investor expectations of increasing short-term future interest rates result in a positive or rising yield curve; conversely, investor expectations of declining short-term future interest rates will cause long-term rates to fall below current short-term rates, and the yield curve will turn negative (invert). Similar explanations may be proffered for the flat and humped yield curves.

The second argument for the shape of the yield curve is referred to as the *liquidity preference hypothesis*. This hypothesis holds that long-term bonds should provide higher returns than shorter-term obligations because investors are willing to sacrifice some yield to invest in short-term bonds to avoid the higher price volatility of longer-term issues. In other words, bondholders naturally prefer short-term loans to the government or corporate issuer and, to induce investors to lend money longer-term, it is necessary to offer higher yields. Furthermore, short-term bonds can more easily be converted into predictable amounts of cash should unforeseen market or economic events occur. As a result, the hypothesis argues that the yield curve should *always* slope upward and that any other shape is only a temporary aberration.

The third and final hypothesis, known as the *segmented market hypothesis*, is the least-plausible argument explaining why any yield curve assumes its given shape. Specifically, this hypothesis asserts that different institutional investors have different maturity needs that lead them to restrict their bond selections to only pre-determined maturity segments. That is, the shape of the yield curve is, ultimately, only a function of the investment policies of major institutional investors. In its strongest form, the segmented market hypothesis maintains that the maturity preferences of these investors are so fixed that they *never* purchase securities outside their preferred maturity range to take advantage of yield differentials. As a result, the short- and long-term maturity portions of the bond market are effectively segmented.

One final point: when long-term interest rates *increase* relative to short-term rates, the yield curve is said to be *steepening*. Conversely, when long-term interest rates *decrease* relative to short-term rates, the yield curve is said to be *flattening*.

BOND DURATION AND CONVEXITY

The *duration* of a bond is a risk measure of bond price volatility to changes in interest rates, similar to what beta is to stocks. Duration may be calculated as Macaulay duration, a time-weighted present value of the bond's coupon and principal periodic cash flows. The Macaulay duration is an *absolute* measure of the interest rate sensitivity of the bond. Alternatively, the modified duration is a *relative* measure for comparing different durations of bonds. The modified duration is the Macaulay duration relative to the bond's YTM. The Macaulay and modified durations apply only to option-free bonds. *Effective* duration is a price volatility measure that applies to *both* option-free bonds and bonds with embedded options.

The Computations of Bond Duration

The computation of the Macaulay duration uses the following formula:

$$\text{Macaulay duration} = \frac{\sum_{t=1}^{n} \text{PVCF}_t(t)}{V_0} \quad \text{Where,}$$

PVCF_t = present value of cash flow at period t

t = period

V_0 = market price of bond

Example 13-6 calculates the Macaulay duration.

Example 13-6: Calculate the Macaulay duration for a Treasury note paying a four percent coupon (semiannual) with three years to maturity and selling for 102-5/8 percent of par:

The note is selling for 1.02625 of $1,000 par or $1,026.25. The appropriate discount rate for the periodic cash flows is the YTM. Since the note is selling at a premium to par, the YTM is less than 4 percent; the YTM is:

V_0 = $1,026.25

CP = $40/2 = $20

P = $1,000

i = YTM = ??

n = 3 x 2 = 6

Calculator keystrokes:

6[N];1026.25[+/-][PV];20[PMT];1000[FV][I/YR][X]2[=]

I/YR = 3.08%

3.08% (annual)/2 = 1.54% is the appropriate semiannual periodic discount rate.

Period (t)	Cash Flow (CF)	PVCF (@1.54%)	PVCF x t
1	$20.00	$19.70	$19.70
2	$20.00	$19.40	38.80
3	$20.00	$19.10	$57.30
4	$20.00	$18.81	$75.24
5	$20.00	$18.53	$92.65
6	$1,020.00	$930.63	$5,583.78
Total		$1,026.17	$5,867.47

Note that the PVCF total is the market price of the note (difference due to rounding). The Macaulay duration is:

$$\text{Macaulay duration } = \frac{\$5,867.47}{\$1,026.17} = 5.72 \text{ (semiannual periods)}$$

$$\frac{5.72}{2} = 2.86 \text{ years}$$

As stated earlier, the Macaulay duration is an absolute measure. For bond price volatility, the modified duration is used and adjusts the Macaulay duration on a YTM basis. Referring to Example 13-5, the modified duration is calculated as:

$$\text{Modified duration} = \frac{\text{Macaulay duration}}{\left(1 + \dfrac{\text{YTM}}{2}\right)} = \frac{2.86}{1.0154} = 2.82$$

The modified duration is 2.82 years.

The effective duration can be applied to both option-free bonds and bonds with embedded options:

$$\text{Effective duration } = \frac{V_{(-)} - V_{(+)}}{2(V_0)(\Delta i)} \text{ , Where}$$

$V_{(-)}$ = Bond price to a decrease in interest rates

$V_{(+)}$ = Bond price to the same increase in interest rates

V_0 = Market price of the bond

Δi = Change in interest rate (interest rate shock)

Valuing bonds with embedded options is beyond the scope of this text, but involves developing a binomial interest rate tree and applying a pricing technique called backward induction. The effective duration may also be applied to option-free bonds. Again, referring to the note in Example 13-6, assume that the market rate (YTM) of 3.08 percent is shocked (up and down) by 100 basis points (1.0%). The results are as follows:

Shocking rates down 1 percent:

$V_{(-)} = ??$

CP = 2%

Principal = $1,000

i = 3.08% - 1.00% = 2.08% (annual) or 1.04% (semiannual)

n = 6

Calculator keystrokes:

6[N];1.04[I/YR];20[PMT];1000[FV][PV] = $1,055.56

V(-) = $1,055.56

Shocking interest rates up 1 percent:

$V_{(-)}$ = ??

CP = 2%

Principal = $1,000

i = 3.08% + 1.00% = 4.08% (annual) or 2.04% (semiannual)

n = 6

Calculator keystrokes:

6[N];2.04[I/YR];20[PMT];1000[FV][PV] = $997.76

V(+) = $997.76

The effective duration is:

$$\text{Effective duration} = \frac{V_{(-)} - V_{(+)}}{2(V_0)(\Delta i)} = \frac{\$1,055.56 - \$997.76}{2(\$1,026.25)(0.01)} = 2.82 \text{ years}$$

You can see that the effective duration on an option-free bond reconciles with the modified duration.

Several important relationships between duration and the various features of a bond can now be described as follows:

1. *There is an inverse relationship between the bond's coupon rate and its duration.* A bond with a larger coupon rate will have a shorter duration because more of its total cash flows come earlier in the form of interest payments.

2. *There is a positive or partially-direct relationship between the bond's term to maturity and its duration.* Therefore, a bond with a longer term to maturity will almost always have a higher duration. However, the relationship is *not totally direct* since, as the maturity date increases over time, the present value of the bond principal declines in value.

3. *A zero coupon bond will have a duration equal to its term to maturity.* Since no cash is received from a zero coupon bond until its maturity, the bond's maturity term and duration are the same.

4. *There is an inverse relationship between the bond's yield to maturity (YTM) and its duration.* Therefore, a bond with a higher yield to maturity will have a lower duration. This is because the higher yield will *discount* the future cash flows more deeply the further out from the present; in turn, the shorter-term cash flows will dominate the calculation, thereby leading to a shorter duration.

Estimated Change in Bond Price

To visualize the change in bond price to a change in yield, a bond's price-yield curve is presented below:

Price

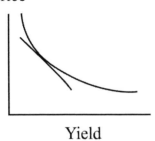

Yield

The price-yield curve is curvilinear (convex) rather than a straight line. This has important implications for bond price movement relative to changes in interest rates. Note the steepness of the curve on the left side and how it flattens moving downward to the right. What this implies is that an incremental decrease in interest rates results in a greater corresponding increase in the bond price as the same incremental increase in interest rates to a corresponding decrease in the bond price.

Duration is an approximation of the change in bond price relative to a change in market interest rates, which is the first derivative of the price-yield curve as measured by the slope of the tangent line:

$$\text{Duration} = \frac{\Delta \text{Price}}{\Delta \text{Yield}}$$

You can see, however, that the duration is only an approximation. Note that the tangent line *underestimates* the increase in price to decreasing interest rates and *overestimates* the decrease in price to increasing interest rates as shown in the gaps between the tangent line and the price-yield curve. Thus, to find the total change in bond price relative to a change in interest rates, the second derivative of the price-yield curve is required. This calculation results in the *convexity* of the bond.

Bond Convexity

Convexity is a measure of the curvature of the relationship between a bond's yield to maturity and its market price (value). Specifically, convexity helps explain the change in bond prices that is not accounted for simply by the bond's duration. Effective convexity is calculated by the formula:

$$\text{Effective Convexity} = \frac{\left(V_{(+)} + V_{(-)}\right) - (V_0)}{2(V_0)(\Delta i)^2}$$

The variables in the above formula are the same as seen previously in the calculation for effective duration.

Continuing with Example 13-6, the effective convexity is calculated as:

$$\text{Effective Convexity} = \frac{\left(V_{(+)} + V_{(-)}\right) - (V_0)}{2(V_0)(\Delta i)^2} = \frac{\$1,055.56 - \$997.76}{2(\$1,026.25)(0.01)^2}$$

$$\text{Effective Convexity} = \frac{\$57.80}{0.3341} = 4.87$$

Duration, together with convexity, measures the total change in price relative to a change in interest rates.

Change in price from duration:
%ΔP = -DMod x Δi x 100

%ΔP = Percentage change in price
D_{Mod} = Modified duration or effective duration
Δi = Change in interest rates (expressed in decimal form)

The negative sign before D_{Mod} implies the inverse relationship between bond prices and changes in interest rates.

Change in price from convexity:
%ΔP = Convexity x $(\Delta i)^2$ x 100

Example 13-7 applies the duration and convexity calculated for the Treasury note in Example 13-6.

Example 13-7: Calculate the total percentage change in bond price to a 200 basis points (2%) change in interest rates (increase and decrease) for the Treasury note described in Example 13-5.

200 basis points increase in interest rates:
%ΔP = -D_{Mod} x Δi x 100 = -2.82 x 0.02 x 100 = -5.64%
%ΔP = Convexity x $(\Delta i)^2$ x 100 = 4.87 x $(0.02)^2$ x 100 = 0.19%
Total %ΔP = -5.64% + 0.19% = -5.45%

Thus, the total change in bond price with a 200 basis point *increase* in interest rates is a decrease of 5.45%

200 basis points decrease in interest rates:
%ΔP = -D_{Mod} x Δi x 100 = -2.82 x -0.02 x 100 = 5.64%
%ΔP = Convexity x $(\Delta i)^2$ x 100 = 4.87 x $(0.02)^2$ x 100 = 0.19%
Total %ΔP = 5.64% + 0.19% = 5.83%

Thus, the total change in bond price with a 200 basis point *decrease* in interest rates is an increase of 5.83 percent.

You can see from this example that the price-yield curve favors the investor due to the steeper slope on the left side of the curve, as previously mentioned.

Finally, the relationships between convexity and bond attributes are the same as those of duration. That is:

1. *There is an inverse relationship between the bond's coupon rate and its convexity*; that is, a lower coupon means a higher convexity
2. *There is a direct relationship between the bond's term to maturity and its convexity*; that is, a longer maturity means a higher convexity
3. *There is an inverse relationship between the bond's yield to maturity (YTM) and its convexity*; that is, a higher yield means a lower convexity

PORTFOLIO IMMUNIZATION

The duration of a bond portfolio is the weighted average of the durations of the bonds included in the bond portfolio. This is illustrated by Example 13-8 as follows:

Example 13-8: Consider a three-bond portfolio. The portfolio consists of $100,000 of Bond A (8.2 duration), $250,000 of Bond B (2.48 duration), and $50,000 of Bond C (11.4 duration). The duration of the portfolio is:

Total value of portfolio = $100,000 + $250,000 + $50,000 = $400,000

Bond A weight = $100,000/$400,000 = 0.25

Bond B weight = $250,000/$400,000 = 0.625

Bond C weight = $50,000/$400,000 = 0.125

$D_{Port} = 8.2(0.25) + 2.48(0.625) = 11.4(0.125) = 5.025$

The portfolio duration (D_{Port}) is, thus, 5.025 years.

Portfolio immunization is an interest-rate management technique, which offsets interest rate risk against re-investment risk. Immunization is often used in pension fund management as pension liabilities come due. Rising interest rates result in a decrease in the value of the bond portfolio. However, rising interest rates also result in greater interest income from re-investing the bond portfolio's coupons. Conversely, decreasing interest rates increase the value of the bond portfolio, but decrease the interest income from re-investing the coupons. You can see how there is an offset between interest rate risk and re-investment risk. Full offset (or complete immunization from changes in interest rates) occurs when the duration of the portfolio equals the duration of the liability. Thus, when the duration of the portfolio is equal to the investor's horizon.

Immunization is not a fully passive strategy, however. Rather, the duration of the portfolio declines at an overall faster rate than that of the duration of the liability. Accordingly, periodic re-balancing of the portfolio is often necessary to bring the portfolio duration in line with the liability duration.

USING DURATION TO MANAGE BOND PORTFOLIOS

Building on the previous relationships discussed with respect to the impact of duration in bond portfolio management, we can now state the following:

1. *The smaller the bond's coupon rate, the greater its relative price fluctuation.*
2. *The longer the bond's term to maturity, the greater its relative price fluctuation.*
3. *The smaller the bond's yield to maturity, the greater its relative price fluctuation.*

In turn, these relationships lead us to some basic principles that are used to maximize a bond portfolio's rate of return when interest rates are expected to change. If the investor anticipates a *decline* in market interest rates, he or she should attempt to construct a portfolio of *long maturity bonds with low coupon rates*. This will provide the investor with a portfolio that has the *maximum interest rate sensitivity* to take advantage of the capital gains experienced by bonds from the decrease in market interest rates (in other words, letting price volatility work for the investor). Conversely, if the investor anticipates an *increase* in market interest rates, he or she should attempt to construct a portfolio of *short maturity bonds with high coupon rates*. This will provide the investor with a portfolio that has the *minimum interest rate sensitivity* to minimize the capital losses experienced by bonds from the increase in market interest rates.

IMPORTANT CONCEPTS

Default risk

Credit risk

Investment grade bond

Non-investment grade (speculative) bond

Present value of a bond

Par bond

Discount bond

Premium bond

Yield to maturity

Current yield

Coupon rate/nominal yield

Yield ladder

Yield curve/term structure of interest rates

Expectations hypothesis

Liquidity preference hypothesis

Segmented market hypothesis

Macauley duration/bond duration

Modified duration

Effective duration

Change in bond price using duration

Bond convexity

Effective convexity

Portfolio immunization

Interest rate risk

Reinvestment rate risk

Zero coupon bond

QUESTIONS FOR REVIEW

1. What are the three types of investment risk that impact all forms of bond issues?

2. How can the credit risk associated with a corporate bond be minimized?

3. When is a bond considered to be of *investment grade* and what does this mean in so far as the likely coupon rate offered by such bond in comparison to other bonds?

4. Is it easier to determine the present value (intrinsic value) of a stock or to determine that of a bond? Explain your reasoning.

5. KZZ $1,000 corporate bond has a 5-year maturity and carries a coupon rate of 8%. It pays interest semi-annually. The yield to maturity for similar quality bonds is 6%.

   Answer the following questions with respect to this bond:

   a) What is the present value of KZZ bond?

   b) Should the bond be selling at a discount or premium to its par value and why?

6. If a bond is selling in the secondary market at a discount to par, will its yield to maturity be more or less than its current yield? Explain.

7. Explain each of the four basic types of yield curves. Which one of these types is usually predominant and why?

8. What are the three academic arguments or hypotheses attempting to explain why the yield curve assumes its given shape? Which one of these arguments is likely the most plausible?

9. Define what is meant by the term *bond duration*. Why is this important?

10. What are the three inputs used in the computation of the bond duration formula?

11. Is the duration of a bond more or less than the bond's maturity date? Explain.

12. What are the four important relationships proved by Macauley in explaining the importance of duration to a bond investor?

13. How does modified duration differ from Macauley duration? In what formula is modified duration used?

14. Assume that the modified duration of JDD bond is 3.62 and that market interest rates increase by 50 basis points (1/2 of 1%). What is the estimated change in the value (market price) of JDD bond?

15. What concept is used to more closely approximate the change in the value of a bond given a respective change in market interest rates?

16. What are three relationships between the convexity of a bond and the attributes of that bond?

17. What is the objective of *portfolio immunization* and what is the operative characteristic in such an investment technique?

18. Is it more or less difficult to immunize a portfolio if the portfolio consists only of zero coupon bonds? Why?

19. What are the three basic relationships between the attributes of a bond and the bond's relative price fluctuation?

20. If market interest rates are expected to increase, what type of bond portfolio should be constructed by an investor? Why?

21. Which form of duration applies to bonds with embedded options?

SUGGESTIONS FOR ADDITIONAL READING

Tools and Techniques of Investment Planning, 2nd edition, Stephen R. Leimberg, Robert T. LeClair, Robert J. Doyle, Jr., and Thomas R. Robinson, The National Underwriter Company, 2006.

Investments: An Introduction, 9th edition, Herbert B. Mayo, Thomson/ South-Western, 2008.

Investment Analysis and Portfolio Management, 9th edition, Frank K. Reilly and Keith C. Brown, Thomson/South-Western, 2009.

The Wall Street Journal Guide to Money and Investing, 3rd edition, Kenneth M. Morris and Virginia B. Morris, Fireside Publishing, 2004.

CHAPTER FOURTEEN

Asset Pricing Models

• • •

This chapter covers several models that have been developed to arrive at an estimated price for assets or the derivatives of those assets. Specifically, four models are addressed, the first two of which may generally be used to value *any* investment asset or security. These are the capital asset pricing model (CAPM) and the arbitrage pricing theory (APT). In contrast, the other two models that are considered may only be used in the valuation of *options* (or the derivative of an asset). These models are the binomial option pricing model and the relatively well-known Black-Scholes valuation model.

The Capital Asset Pricing Model (CAPM) was introduced in Chapter 10 of this textbook. As such, we have learned that CAPM is the graphical representation of the security market line (SML) and may be applied in order to value individual securities by using the security's beta coefficient as the relevant measure of investor risk instead of standard deviation. CAPM also reflects what should be the expected return on any risky asset and is equal to the market or investor's required rate of return, given the model's assumption that capital markets are in equilibrium (or properly priced) at all times. Therefore, the purpose of the model is to quantitatively determine *the expected rate of return* of a security given its beta to the market portfolio of all risky assets.

Upon completing this chapter, you should be able to:

- Compute the investor's required rate of return using the Capital Asset Pricing Model (CAPM)
- Explain the factors involved in valuing a security using the Arbitrage Pricing Theory (APT)
- Describe how to value an option using the binomial option pricing model
- Describe the factors influencing the market price of an option under the Black-Scholes option valuation method

CAPITAL ASSET PRICING MODEL (CAPM)

The Capital Asset Pricing Model (a basic tenet of modern portfolio theory) asserts that the expected return of any individual security should be the risk-free rate of return that is currently available to an investor *plus* an applicable premium for the risk associated with that particular security. In formula terms, this may be written as follows:

$$r_e = r_f + \beta_i(r_m - r_f)$$

where r_e is the expected return of the security, r_f is the expected risk-free rate of return in the secondary marketplace (U.S. Treasury security yields such as the yield on the 90 day Treasury bill or the 10-year benchmark Treasury note), r_m is the expected rate of return of the market portfolio of all risky assets and β_i is the beta coefficient of the individual security. The market portfolio of all risky assets is theoretical and cannot be reproduced. A common proxy used for the market portfolio is the S&P 500 index of stocks. The *market risk premium* is the return on the market less the risk-free rate $(r_m - r_f)$. Multiplying the market risk premium by the stock's beta results in the *stock risk premium*.

The Capital Asset Pricing Model is a simple linear regression between the dependent variable, r_e and the independent variable $(r_m - r_f)$. The slope of the regression is the beta, β, and the y-intercept is fitted to the risk-free rate, r_f.

Transforming the Regression to the Security Market Line

CAPM is also a correlation model as depicted in the Security Market Line (SML). The Y-axis remains the security yield (% Security Y) but the X-axis becomes beta values (β). This is accomplished through correlation. The slope (β) represents correlation between the dependent variable and the independent variable since it is a measurement of "rise over run." If the market return is substituted for the dependent variable (Y), it would move perfectly with itself as the independent variable (X). Thus the correlation is 1.0 or the market's beta. The slope of the regression between Stock Y and the S&P 500 is the beta for Stock Y, a measure of its correlation to the market. The SML for Stock Y is shown graphically as follows:

Figure 14-1: The Security Market Line

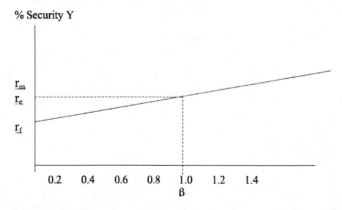

The SML visually shows the CAPM decision criteria. If the estimated or market yield matches the expected yield from CAPM, the stock will plot on its SML and be in equilibrium. If the estimated yield is *greater than* the expected yield from CAPM, the stock will plot *above* its SML and be UNDERVALUED. Specifically, the stock price is lower than expected driving up its yield. The reverse is true if the stock plots *below* its SML, which implies the stock is OVERVALUED. The stock price is higher than expected driving its yield lower.

The CAPM is a value stock model. If the stock's estimated yield plots above its SML, the stock is undervalued and should be purchased and held until the stock approaches equilibrium and plots on its SML.

> **Example 14-1:** Assume that the stock of Tour Tempo, Inc. has a beta coefficient of 1.2. Also assume that the expected return on the market is 8% and that the expected 90-day Treasury bill (T-bill) rate is 3.5%. Accordingly, CAPM, the expected return of the security is 8.90% computed as follows:

$$r_e = r_f + \beta(r_m - r_f) = 3.5\% + 1.2(8\% - 3.5\%) = 8.9\%$$

As anticipated, the expected return for Tour Tempo, Inc. (8.90%) is higher than the expected return on the overall market (8%). However, this makes sense given that the risk premium (specifically, the stock risk premium) is more than the market risk premium with a beta of the stock in excess of 1.0. Specifically, the stock risk premium to invest in Tour Tempo, Inc. is 5.40% [1.2 x (8% - 3.50%)] whereas the market risk premium is only 4.50% (8% - 3.50%).

The expected return found in Example 14-1 (or 8.90%) may be used as an input in the constant growth dividend discount model (see chapter 12) to determine the intrinsic value of Tour Tempo, Inc. stock. Thus, assuming that the expected growth rate of Tour Tempo's dividend payout is 5% and that the stock is currently paying a dividend of $1.50 per share, we determine the stock's intrinsic value to be $40.38 as follows:

$$\hat{P}_0 = \frac{D_0(1 + g)}{r - g} = \frac{\$1.50(1.05)}{0.089 - 0.05} = \$40.38$$

As noted in chapter 10, the CAPM does not reward the investor for unique or unsystematic risk, since theoretically, unique risk may be fully diversified leaving only systematic risk. Thus, the market portfolio of all risky assets represents a theoretical fully diversified portfolio. How a stock moves against this market portfolio is reflected in the stock's beta and represents the stock's systematic risk.

ARBITRAGE PRICING THEORY (APT)

As we have discussed, the CAPM is a simple linear regression, single-factor model. The expected return of a security is dependent on its movement against a theoretical market portfolio of all risky assets. The security's beta is the slope of the regression and measures the volatility of the security relative to the market.

In contrast, the APT model is a multiple regression as opposed to a simple linear regression for the CAPM. Thus, there are multiple independent factors in the APT, not a single independent factor, such as the market portfolio in the CAPM. Further, unlike CAPM, the independent factors that contribute to the return derived under the APT are *unexpected* and *not pre-specified*. While there may be many of these unexpected factors, academic research has identified four that are pre-eminent. These are:

1. Unexpected inflation (sometimes known as *inflation risk*)
2. Unexpected shifts in the risk premium that is sought by investors (*confidence risk*)
3. Unexpected changes in the investor's preference for short versus long-term investments (*time horizon risk*)
4. Unexpected changes in the overall level of the economy's industrial production (*business cycle risk*)

The generic form of the APT model or formula is written as follows:

$$r_i = a + b_1\,F_1 + b_2\,F_2 + b_3\,F_3 + b_4\,F_4 + \ldots\ldots b_n\,F_n$$

where r_i is the expected return of the asset or security, a is the constant or risk-free rate of return as in the CAPM, *b* is the sensitivity coefficient of the unexpected risk factor, and F is one of the unexpected risk factors (expressed in percentage terms or *price of risk*).

Note that the *sensitivity coefficient*, b, corresponds to beta of the CAPM. The sensitivity coefficient is essentially the slope of an independent factor when all of the remaining factors are held to zero. The CAPM is often criticized for its simplicity, but the APT is also not without its weaknesses. First, the independent factors used in the APT are not specified. Even though the market portfolio in CAPM is theoretical, nevertheless, it is identified and common proxies are used in the model. Another problem with the APT is the independency of the factors. For example, in the independent factors identified above, is inflation risk independent from time horizon risk?

Example 14-2: Continuing with the scenario first presented in Example 14-1, assume that you are attempting to determine the expected return for Tour Tempo, Inc. stock. However, you now wish to use the Arbitrage Pricing Theory (APT) and its associated inputs to determine the stock's expected return. As before, the current risk-free rate of return in the marketplace is 3.5% (as represented by the 90-day Treasury bill rate). In addition, the unexpected risk factors and the sensitivity correlation of Tour Tempo, Inc. stock to those factors are as follows:

Risk Factor	Sensitivity Coefficient (b)	Price of Risk (F)
Inflation Risk	-0.10	-3.00%
Confidence Risk	0.80	2.50%
Time Horizon Risk	1.20	-0.75%
Business Cycle Risk	1.50	4.00%

Therefore, the expected return for Tour Tempo, Inc. stock is 9.10% computed as follows:

$3.5\% + (-0.10 \times -3.0\%) + (0.08 \times 2.5\%) + (1.20 \times -0.75\%) + (1.50 \times 4.0\%) =$
$3.5\% + (0.0030) + (0.0020) + (-0.0090) + (0.06) =$
$0.035 + 0.0560 = 0.0910 \times 100 = 9.10\%.$

In turn, the expected return derived under the APT model may be compared to the expected return determined using CAPM, allowing the financial planner the opportunity to separately analyze the impact of the risk factors unique to APT. Again, it needs to be emphasized that the factors used in the APT are *unexpected*, which therefore permits an even greater *cushion* of risk that may be taken into account by the planner.

Finally, in the APT formula, if the particular risk is expected (rather than unexpected as is the normal assumption) the risk factor in the formula is represented by a *zero*. The deviation from each of the risk factors considered in the model is then measured against that base. Thus, by identifying additional risk factors that may impact the expected return of a security, the arbitrage pricing theory suggests an alternative valuation model that may be used to arrive at the risk-adjusted price of that security.

OPTION PRICING MODELS

Options are derivative contracts, that is, their values are derived from the underlying assets' values on which the contracts are written. The underlying assets may be real estate, stocks, bonds, interest rates, foreign currencies, or even other derivatives such as futures and swaps.

The holder of an option has the right, but not the obligation, to buy (a *call option*) or sell (a *put option*) the underlying asset at a given price (the *exercise* or *strike price*) within a given period of time (*American option*) or upon expiration (*European option*). The value of an option is implied in the right to buy or sell the underlying asset.

Option Contracts and Put-Call Parity

Put and call option pricing must be in parity to prevent arbitrage opportunities. An *arbitrage opportunity* is the ability to earn a riskless return without any investment of personal funds.

Put-call parity is the difference between the call price (c) and the put price (p) and equals the difference between the market price of the stock (S_0) and the present value of the exercise price continuously discounted at the risk-free rate (Xe^{-rt}). Mathematically, the parity is stated as follows:

$$c - p = S_0 - Xe^{-rt}$$

Where "e" is the natural log constant, approximately 2.7183

Note that a negative sign denotes selling. Buying a call and selling a put should equal buying the stock and shorting Treasury bills equal to the exercise price continuously discounted by the risk-free rate.

If this equality does not hold, an arbitrage opportunity exists. Arbitrageurs would swiftly enter the market, first selling the overpriced option and, subsequently, buying the underpriced option until parity is restored.

Assume the following:

Call	$2.85
Put	$0.57
Stock	$42.00
Exercise price	$40.00
Risk-free rate	6%
Time to expiration	90 days (on a bank discount basis of 360 days)

Does parity exist?

Applying the put-call parity equation:

$2.85 - $0.57 = $42 - $40e^{-0.06(90/360)}$

$2.28 = $42 - $40(0.9851)*$

$2.28 \neq $2.60 (\Delta-$0.32)$

*The continuous discount factor is easily calculated using a financial calculator. The calculator keystrokes (HP10B II) are:

0.06[+/-][X]90[=]

[÷]360[=]

[orange shift][e^x] = 0.9851

An arbitrage opportunity of $0.32 exists since the call is underpriced. To take advantage of this arbitrage opportunity, an arbitrageur would:

Buy the call	($2.85)
Sell the put	$0.57
Short the stock	$42.00
Invest in T-bills	($39.40)
Profit	$0.32

No personal funds were invested. The transaction is risk free because if the call is exercised, the holder will buy the stock for $40. This is funded through the maturity of the T-bills at $40. The put then expires worthless and the short sale on the stock is covered by the stock acquired through the call.

If the put is exercised, the call expires worthless. The stock is bought for $40, which is financed by the maturing T-bills. The stock subsequently acquired in the put is then used to cover the short sale.

If the call is overpriced, the arbitrage transaction entails selling the call, buying the put, buying the stock, and shorting the T-bills in the amount of the present value of the exercise price.

Option pricing models are based on European options, options that cannot be exercised until expiration (this does not mean, however, that European options cannot be traded in secondary markets).

The value of an option consists of (1) a time value, which decays to zero as the option approaches expiration and (2) an intrinsic value. The intrinsic value of a call option is:

$$\text{Value of call option} = MAX[0, S_T - X]$$

The value of a call option is the maximum of either zero or the price of the underlying asset (S_T) minus the exercise price of the option (X). If the price of the underlying asset is less than the exercise price of the call option, the holder would let the call option expire worthless, thus it has a zero value. The intrinsic value of a put option is:

$$\text{Value of put option} = MAX[0, X - S_T]$$

The value of a put option is the maximum of either zero or the exercise price minus the price of the underlying asset. If the price of the underlying asset is greater than the exercise price, the holder would let the put expire worthless.

If the holder of an American option elected to exercise the option before its expiration, the time value associated with the option would not be realized. Therefore, it is better to sell the American option on the secondary market, capturing both the time value and the intrinsic value, than to exercise the option early. This is why option-pricing models are based on European options, although variations of these models also apply to both European and American options.

Binomial Option Pricing Model

The Single-Period Binomial Model

The binomial model, as shown in Figure 14.2, consists of developing a binomial tree or lattice to reflect the initial state at time, t, and two possible, mutually exclusive outcomes at time, T (expiration):

Figure 14.2. Single-Period Binomial Tree

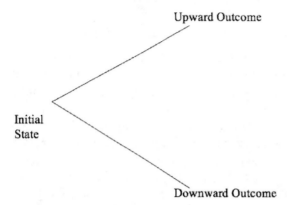

Let's apply this single stage binomial tree to valuing a stock call option with an exercise price of $100. If the current price of a stock is $100 and its price in one year may be $110 or $90, the binomial tree is shown in Figure 14.3:

Figure 14.3. Stock Outcomes

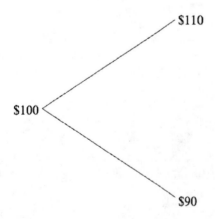

The value of a call at expiration, T, is either zero (letting the call expire worthless) or the difference between the stock price at expiration and the exercise price. Given an exercise price of $100, the binomial tree for the call option (C_t) shown in Figure 14.4 is:

Figure 14.4. Call Option

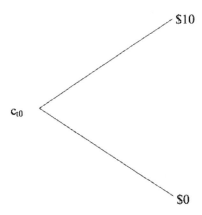

Therefore, if the stock price goes *up* (S_{TU} = $110), the price of the call at expiration, c_{TU}, is $10. If the price of the stock goes *down* (S_{TD} = $90), the price of the call at expiration, c_{TD}, is $0 (expires worthless).

Using the binomial option model, the call option can be valued using either the *portfolio replication method* or the *risk-neutral probability method*.

Portfolio Replication Method
Finding a portfolio that creates a synthetic European call (a portfolio that has the same value and payoff as the European call) will have the same initial value as the European call, c_0. Such a portfolio would consist of a stock and a short position in a risk-free bond. For the one-period binomial model:

$$c_0 = Port_0 = S_0 \Delta - (1+r_f)B_0$$

Where:

$Port_0$= the current value of the replicating portfolio
Δ= the delta neutral number of shares of stock
S_0= the current stock price
B_0= the current bond price
r_f= the risk-free rate

Continuing with the $100 stock and the binomial outcomes of $110 or $90 and a risk-free rate of six percent, the call is priced below using the portfolio replication method.

Set up simultaneous equations for each node working backward:

$110\Delta - 1.06B = \$10$

$\quad \$90\Delta - 1.06B = 0$

Subtract one from the other to cancel one of the variables:

$\$110\Delta - 1.06B = \$10$

$\underline{-\$90\Delta - 1.06B = 0}$

$\quad\quad \$20\Delta = \$10$

$\quad\quad \Delta = 0.5000$

Substitute into one of the equations:

$\$110(0.5000) - 1.06B = \$10$

$\quad\quad\quad\quad\quad B = \$42.4528$

Price of option at $t = 0$:

Upward node: $\$100(0.5000) - \$42.4528 = \$7.5472$

Downward node: $0 - 0 = 0$

$c_0 = \$7.55$

The binomial tree for the replicating portfolio as shown in Figure 14.5 is:

Figure 14.5 Replicating Portfolio

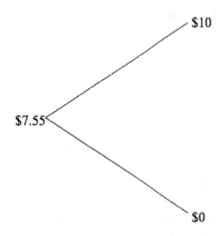

Risk Neutral Probability Method

The risk-neutral probabilities are:

$\pi = (1.06 - 0.90)/(1.10 - 0.90) = 0.80$

$1-\pi = 0.20$

The option prices at expiration are:

$c^+ = Max[0, \$110 - \$100] = \$10$

$c^- = Max[0, \$90 - \$100] = 0$

The option price today is:

$$c_0 = \frac{0.80\,(\$10) + 0.20\,(0)}{1.06} = \$7.5472$$

The probability of the stock price rising to \$110 is 80 percent and falling to \$90 is 20 percent. Thus, the expected value of the stock in one year is the weighted average or \$106 per share.

The single-period model suffers two defects. First, it holds for only a single period, whereas, options can expire over several periods. Second, assumptions concerning stock price changes are too simplistic and, thus, are likely unrealistic.

The Multi-Period Binomial Model

The principle behind the single-period binomial model also applies to the multi-period binomial model. In the single-period binomial model, there were two possible stock price outcomes. In a multi-period binomial model, there are 2^n possible stock price outcomes, where n equals the number of periods until expiration. Each terminal stock price has a call option with a specific value.

Black-Scholes Option Valuation Model

The binomial option pricing model is a *discrete* method for valuing options because it allows security price changes to occur in distinct upward or downward movements. However, it can also be assumed that security prices change *continuously* throughout time. This was the approach taken by Fisher Black and Myron Scholes in developing their relatively well-known model for valuing European-style options. Specifically, the model assumes that stock prices can be described by a statistical process known as *geometric Brownian motion*. Ultimately, this process is summarized by a volatility factor ascribed to the underlying security represented by the Greek symbol σ, like the standard deviation factor referenced in chapter 9 of this textbook.

While mathematically complex (beyond the scope of this book), the Black-Scholes model does help us to understand the value of a call option as it relates to the five following factors:

1. The current underlying security price
2. The option's exercise price
3. The time to expiration of the option
4. The risk-free rate of return
5. The volatility of the underlying security

Functionally, the model holds that the value of the option is dependent on all five factors. However, the first and fourth factors are observable market prices, while the second and third factors may be found by referencing the terms of the option contract. Therefore, as noted, the only variable that must actually be derived by the model itself is the volatility factor associated with (future price of) the underlying security. Fortunately, software exists that easily prices calls and puts using Black-Scholes.

Figure 14-6 below summarizes the relationship between the five factors in the Black-Scholes model and the value of the call option:

Figure 14-6: Factors Influencing Value of a Call Option using Black-Scholes Model

An Increase In The:	Results In The Call Value:
Underlying Security Price	Increasing
Option's Exercise Price	Decreasing
Option's Time to Expiration	Increasing
Risk-Free Rate	Increasing
Underlying Security Volatility	Increasing

The logic behind the first three of these relationships is straightforward. An increase in the underlying security price will *increase* the call's current value since the intrinsic value of the call is positive when the price of the underlying security exceeds the exercise price of the option. A larger exercise price will *reduce* the call's value since the price of the underlying security must increase more to be considered as "in-the-money". The *longer* that the option has until it expires, the *greater* the time value associated with the call option (this is also true with a put option). However, the last two relationships are not as apparent. Specifically, an increase in the risk-free rate of return will increase the value of the call option since it *reduces* the present value of the option's exercise price when discounted at a higher risk-free rate (that is, the greater the discount rate is, the smaller the present value of the exercise price). Similarly, when the volatility of the underlying security increases, the call becomes more valuable since this *increases* the probability that the option will be "in-the-money" at least sometime during the life of the option contract (this is also true with a put option).

The Black-Scholes option valuation model is popular with investors for at least two reasons: (1) it is computationally convenient (and may easily be programmed into one's computer) and (2) it produces reasonable values under a variety of circumstances. Nevertheless, academic studies have shown that the volatilities of the underlying securities on which the options were written tend to be overly *large* when the associated call options are in the money and are inordinately *small* when the call options are currently out of the money. This means that in-the-money call options are priced *higher* in the marketplace by investors than the Black-Scholes model would suggest and that out-of-the-money options are *not valued enough* per the terms of the model. In addition, the model assumes that the underlying stocks trade frequently. Therefore, stocks that trade less-frequently or are infrequently traded are *not* good candidates for the model. Finally, Fisher Black has commented that the model's assumptions of a constant risk-free rate and volatility level, until the expiration date of the call option, are almost certain to be violated in real life. As a result, the current option value derived by the model is best viewed only as an approximation.

The Black-Scholes model also does not apply to stocks paying dividends. Robert Merton modified the model to account for dividend-paying stocks. This modified model is known as the Black-Scholes-Merton model.

Finally, the binomial option pricing model, the Black-Scholes model and the Black-Scholes-Merton model are reconcilable with each other, theoretically arriving at consistent option prices.

IMPORTANT CONCEPTS

Capital Asset Pricing Model (CAPM)

Stock risk premium

Market risk premium

Systematic risk

Arbitrage pricing theory (APT)

Stock coefficient

Price of risk

American-style option

European-style option

Binomial Option Pricing Model

Portfolio replication method

Risk-neutral probability method

Black-Scholes Option Valuation Model

QUESTIONS FOR REVIEW

1. What is the purpose of the Capital Asset Pricing Model (CAPM)? What is the graphical representation of such model?

2. What is the *stock risk premium* associated with the purchase of a security? What is the *market risk premium* associated with that same security? Why is each of these important in investment theory?

3. Complete the following sentence: CAPM accounts only for the impact of _____ risk and does not consider _____ risk.

4. Assume that after using CAPM you have determined that an investment's expected return (determined from CAPM) is less than the market or investor's required rate of return. What is the likely course of action that you advise for this investor? Explain your conclusion.

5. What does the arbitrage pricing theory (APT) attempt to take into account that the CAPM does not consider?

6. What are the four unexpected factors that have been found to be pre-eminent in the calculation of an investment's expected return using arbitrage pricing theory?

7. If the risk factor in the APT formula is reflected as a zero, what does that mean?

8. What is the difference between an American-style and a European-style option?

9. If there is an increase in the exercise price of the option, what is the corresponding effect on the value of a call and put, respectively?

10. What is the assumption regarding the movement in the price of the underlying security in each of the following option valuation models:

The Binomial Option Pricing Model

The Black-Scholes Option Valuation Model

11. Why is the Binomial Option Pricing Model sometimes referred to as the *two state option pricing model?*

12. What is used as the discount rate in determining the value of an option under the Binomial Option Pricing Model?

13. What are the five factors or variables considered in the Black-Scholes Option Valuation Model? Which one of these factors has an *inverse* relationship to the value of a call option?

14. If the volatility of the underlying security increases, why does the call option become more valuable?

15. What are three problems with using the Black-Scholes Option Valuation Model to value a European-style call option?

SUGGESTIONS FOR ADDITIONAL READING

Tools and Techniques of Investment Planning, 2nd edition, Stephen R. Leimberg, Robert T. LeClair, Robert J. Doyle, Jr., and Thomas R. Robinson, The National Underwriter Company, 2006.

Investments: An Introduction, 9th edition, Herbert B. Mayo, Thomson/ South-Western, 2008.

Investment Analysis and Portfolio Management, 9th edition, Frank K. Reilly and Keith C. Brown, Thomson/South-Western, 2009.

The Wall Street Journal Guide to Money and Investing, 3rd edition, Kenneth M. Morris and Virginia B. Morris, Fireside Publishing, 2004.

CHAPTER FIFTEEN

Investment Strategies

• • •

This chapter considers the subject of investment strategies, whether unique to the investor or investment advisor or part of generally accepted practices. The chapter begins with a discussion of the importance of implementing a written investment policy statement to guide future investing and ends with a brief analysis of the popular theories of value and growth investing.

Upon completing this chapter, you should be able to:

- Explain the importance of an investment policy statement
- Identify common and appropriate benchmarks in evaluating investment performance
- Describe common strategies used in formula investing, including *dollar cost averaging*
- Explain types of bond swaps
- Identify strategies involving the timing of investment purchases and sales
- Describe short selling and how it may be effectively used by an investor
- Differentiate forms of security selection and security analysis
- Compute a margin call and the required equity amounts necessary in the use of leverage
- Contrast the basic principles underlying value investing to those of growth investing

INVESTMENT POLICY STATEMENTS

Possible investment strategies that should be pursued by an investment advisor on behalf of his or her client begin with the formulation of a complete and thorough investment policy statement. Such a statement should be developed in accordance with the client's investment goals and objectives, but it should also list the constraints or limitations that bear on those goals. Specifically, the *objectives* portion of the statement should include the desired return requirements of the investor's portfolio as well as a recitation of the level of risk that a client is willing and able to take. Of course, many clients do not know the level of risk that they are willing to assume, so it is up to the investment advisor to assist them in accurately expressing this risk. Because of this, many advisors have developed a risk tolerance questionnaire that they ask the client to complete before proceeding with the formal development of the investment policy statement.

The investor's desired rate of investment return and risk tolerance should be complementary. In other words, if the investor expresses little to no tolerance for risk, an investment in aggressive growth-type mutual funds is likely not appropriate. Furthermore, the desired rate of return should be achievable by the client and investment advisor. In this regard, many advisors will consult the historical rate of return of asset classes as guidance for what is possible. However, if they do so, they must quickly caution the client that the historical rate of return is no guarantee of the same or similar performance in the future (as indicated in the market meltdown of 2008). As a result, many advisors will also include in the investment policy statement an appropriate *benchmark* by which to measure the performance of their investment recommendations in the future. The choice of which benchmark(s) to use is the focus of the next section in this chapter.

Finally, the constraints or limitations that could possibly impede the achievement of the client's desired rate of return should be listed in the second major part of the investment policy statement. Specifically, many advisors use the following five constraints as a part of any statement:

1) The time horizon of the investor (the investor's investment life cycle)

2) The liquidity needs of the investor during this time horizon

3) The tax status of the investor's portfolio or accounts within the portfolio

4) Any laws and regulations that may bear on the investor's portfolio; and

5) Any unique circumstances of the investor, such as a possible upcoming inheritance (cash inflow) or substantial financial withdrawal (cash outflow)

Of these constraints, the liquidity needs of the investor during the stipulated time horizon of the statement is likely the most important. For example, if the investor would like to purchase a vacation home during the stipulated time horizon, the need for cash to do so must be factored into the statement. Similarly, if the client must allow for withdrawals to send his or her children to college (while, perhaps, also in the process of saving for his or her own retirement), this fact should also be considered.

APPROPRIATE BENCHMARKS

Although many investors use comparisons to other portfolio managers as a measure of performance, benchmarks should really include certain independent characteristics.

Among these characteristics are the following:

1) The benchmark selected should be unambiguous, with the composition and weighting of assets within the benchmark clearly stated.

2) The benchmark should be measurable, that is, it should be possible to monitor and calculate the benchmark's rate of return on a relatively frequent basis.

3) The benchmark should be consistent with the manager's investment style; for example, if the portfolio manager invests primarily in growth stocks, the selected benchmark index should also reflect this.

4) The benchmark should be reflective of current investment practice.

5) The benchmark should be selected *before* the beginning of the investment period or investor's time horizon.

Finally, if desired, the benchmark should also be *investible*. This means that the investor should be able to invest in the benchmark as an alternative to employing the particular investment advisor or portfolio manager. However, there should be a level of comfort that runs both ways. Not only should the investor be given the option to invest in the benchmark as an alternative, but the investment advisor should also be comfortable that the benchmark used is indeed appropriate as a measuring device.

So what are some examples of what should be used as an appropriate benchmark? Appropriate *value weighted indexes* include the Standard & Poor's 500 index of the largest U.S. capitalization stocks, the Russell 2000 index of small capitalization stocks, and the Wilshire 5000 index of stocks used to measure overall U.S. market conditions. In addition, the European and Far East (EAFE) Index may be used to compare international stock performance. (Note that a value weighted index is the sum of the current market capitalization values of the securities within the index divided by the sum of those securities' market capitalization values in a designated base year.)

An appropriate *price weighted index* may be any of the Dow Jones indexes, including the widely watched Dow Jones Index of 30 industrial stocks. (Note that a price-weighted index is the sum of the current prices of the securities within the index divided by a previously announced adjusted divisor.)

FORMULA INVESTING

The term *formula investing* essentially means that an investor does not actively trade or manage his or her portfolio, but instead follows a certain set of automatic rules regardless of market conditions. The most commonly-known type of formula investing is so-called *dollar cost averaging*, but there are other forms as well. We will now consider each.

Dollar Cost Averaging

Using dollar cost averaging, an investor decides to purchase additional shares of stock or shares in a mutual fund at regular intervals and, usually, in equal dollar amounts. Often, this is accomplished through the use of an automatic withdrawal plan at the investor's bank or other financial institution. The purchase is made at the appropriate interval, no matter what the price of the investment may be at that time. In turn, since the dollar amount is typically the same regardless of market conditions or market prices at the time, this technique is referred to as *dollar cost averaging*.

The effect of this technique is to *increase* the number of shares gradually over a long period of time. In the event that the current price of the stock or mutual fund is less than or below that of the previous price, the investor has succeeded in purchasing more shares of the investment. Because more shares are acquired when the price of the stock or mutual fund declines, this has the result of *reducing* the average cost of a share. Subsequently, if the stock or mutual fund share price increases, the investor will earn more profits on currently held lower-priced shares, thereby increasing his or her dollar-weighted rate of return.

Let us look at an example wherein an investor uses the dollar cost averaging strategy to purchase additional shares rather than a lump sum purchase of all shares at one time.

> **Example 15-1:** Kent purchases $10,000 of the ABC mutual fund shares in January, 2009 when its share price is $25.00. He therefore purchases a total of 400 shares ($10,000 divided by $25.00) with a cost basis of $25 per share. Now, instead, assume that Ken uses this same amount of $10,000 to make 10 separate purchases of $1,000 each over the next ten months when the price of ABC mutual fund shares is fluctuating as follows:

Month	Share Price	# of Shares Purchased ($1,000/share price)
1/2009	$25.00	40.00
2/2009	$27.00	37.04
3/2009	$22.00	45.45
4/2009	$20.00	50.00
5/2009	$18.00	55.55
6/2009	$21.00	47.62
7/2009	$23.00	43.48
8/2009	$26.00	38.46
9/2009	$25.00	40.00
10/2009	$27.00	37.04
Total		**434.64**

Accordingly, as may be seen and computed, when using dollar cost averaging over the 10-month period, Kent has now purchased 434.64 shares of ABC mutual fund with a cost basis of only $23.00 per share ($10,000 divided by 434.64 shares). Because Kent was able to take advantage of market fluctuations, he therefore ends up with 8.66% more shares and associated market value.

It should be noted that dollar cost averaging works best when markets are declining or fluctuating, as Example 15-1 illustrates. It does *not* work well when the market is steadily increasing, since in that event, the investor would be better off buying as many shares as possible up front when the price per share is lower. In addition, even in a declining market, the investor should not automatically assume that the market price of the stock or mutual fund will eventually increase. Rather, a stock or mutual fund that is declining in price may result from an underlying corporate earnings problem or a weakness in that particular market sector. If this is the case, the investor needs to consider the ongoing expenditure of funds as a fixed cost that should not influence the purchase of any additional shares.

Share Averaging/Averaging Down

Some investors do not like to make periodic purchases of stock or mutual fund shares. Instead, they prefer to purchase additional shares only when the price of the shares *declines*. Accordingly, these investors are following a strategy of *averaging down*. This is a method by which the investor reduces the cost basis of an investment in one security by buying more shares as the price of that security decreases. As with dollar cost averaging, the investor is rewarded if the price of the security subsequently increases. Of course, by only buying "on the dips" in the market, the investor may also miss out on buying into a bull market, wherein share prices tend to move upward for a significant period of time. Finally, a variation of the averaging down strategy occurs when the investor purchases the same number of shares every time. If the investor does this, he or she is said to be following a policy of *share averaging*.

With dollar cost averaging, there is a *greater* total reduction in the average cost of shares than there is with share averaging. When the investor *dollar cost averages* the amount spent is held constant, but the number of shares purchased varies. Conversely, when the investor *share averages* the number of shares purchased is held constant, but the dollar amount varies. Since the investor purchases a fixed number of shares with share averaging, regardless of how low the price falls, the average cost of the overall shares is *not* reduced to the extent that it is with dollar cost averaging. Share averaging is also, by definition, not as easy to automate (for example, by way of automatic monthly investing) as dollar cost averaging, since the amounts invested using share averaging are seldom the same.

Dividend Reinvestment Plans (DRIPs)

Dividend reinvestment plans (DRIPs) are offered by many large companies/stock issuers as a service to their shareholders. With such plans, dividends are automatically reinvested into the company's stock. If the dividends are reinvested, the investor purchases additional shares of company stock without contacting a broker/dealer, who may charge a commission if these shares were purchased directly.

There are two general types of dividend reinvestment programs. The first (and less popular) type exists when a bank acts on behalf of the company and all shareholders. The bank collects the cash dividends for the shareholders, pools all of the shareholder monies or contributions, and then purchases the additional shares in the open market. In the second (and more popular) type of plan, the company issues new shares of stock in lieu of a cash dividend, with the money then reinvested by the company to satisfy future capital needs. While this latter type of plan was initially offered only by utility companies, it is now the standard DRIP for most other types of companies and/or mutual funds.

Bond Ladders, Barbells, and Bullets

Bond ladders are a popular strategy for staggering the maturity of a client's bond investments and, subsequently, for establishing a schedule for reinvesting the proceeds as the bonds mature. For example, a $50,000 portfolio of bonds could acquire $5,000 worth of bonds that mature for each of the next 10 years. Therefore, when interest rates change, the prices of the bonds with the shorter terms to maturity will fluctuate less then the prices of the bonds with the longer terms to maturity (recall the discussion of duration in chapter 13). This has the effect of minimizing the impact of the price changes in the bonds due to interest rate fluctuations. As shorter-term bonds mature, their principal may subsequently be reinvested at higher market interest rates.

Ladders are popular among investors who want bonds as part of a long-term investment objective, such as seeking predictable income for retirement needs, or saving for a young child's college tuition. However, investors should be aware that laddering may require the commitment of substantial investment assets over time.

Bond barbells are a strategy for buying short-term and long-term bond issues. The long-term end of the barbell allows the investor to lock attractive long-term interest rates, while the short-term end ensures that the investor will have the opportunity to invest in other assets if the bond market experiences a downturn in value. For example, if the investor has $100,000 to invest, he or she might expend $50,000 to purchase notes with maturities of two to three years and the other $50,000 to purchase bonds with a 10-year maturity date. As a result, if interest rates change, the investor needs to replace only half of his or her bond portfolio. Expectations of lower interest rates would mean selling the short-term bonds (since their price is closer to par value) and investing the proceeds in longer-term bonds. If higher rates are anticipated, the investor would do the opposite: sell the longer-term bonds and reinvest the proceeds in shorter-term maturity bonds.

Bond bullets are a strategy for having several bonds mature at the same time and minimizing the interest rate risk when the investor buys the bonds. For example, assume that an investor wants all her bonds to mature in 10 years, but is very concerned about the interest rate risk associated with such a purchase. Therefore, using the bond bullet strategy, she buys two bonds immediately, two bonds two years from now, and two more bonds four years from now. Accordingly, the bonds purchased immediately have a maturity date of 10 years, the bonds purchased two years later have maturity dates of eight years, and the bonds purchased four years later carry a maturity date of six years each. The bond bullet strategy is useful when the investor knows that she will need the proceeds from the bonds at a specific date, such as when a child begins college, but wants to protect bond principal at the same time.

BOND SWAPS

Bond swapping is the process of selling one debt instrument (a bond) and replacing it with another. Such swapping is done to save on income taxes, increase the yield to maturity (YTM) or current yield of the bond, or reduce the overall interest rate risk of the bond portfolio. As an example, a *tax swap* is an exchange that is motivated solely by current tax law considerations. To illustrate such a swap, assume that an investor purchases a $1,000 par value bond now trading in the secondary market for $800. If he swaps that bond for a similar quality bond selling for $800, he now has that same amount of money to invest, plus he is entitled to claim a capital loss of $200. If he is currently in a 25% marginal income tax bracket, he generates an additional $50 ($200 × 0.25) in cash by virtue of the allowable capital loss. In addition, he can use the sale proceeds to repurchase the swapped bond for $800 and hold that bond until its scheduled maturity date.

Other additional forms of bond swaps are as follows:
1) *Substitution swap*: This form of swap involves exchanging bonds with similar characteristics selling for different prices. It is done to increase the current yield of the bond.
2) *Inter-market spread swap*: This form of swap involves the exchanging of similar bonds with different coupon rates. It is done to increase the overall rate of return from the bond.
3) *Rate anticipation swap*: This swap attempts to take advantage of expected changes in interest rates. If rates are expected to increase, long-term bonds are swapped for short-term bonds (decreasing bond duration). If rates are expected to decline, short-term bonds are swapped for long-term bonds (increasing bond duration) to take advantage of the expected price increases for the longer-term issues and to lock in higher coupon rates.
4) *Pure yield pickup swap*: Here, a lower yield-to-maturity (YTM) bond is exchanged for a higher yield-to-maturity (YTM) bond. The new bond that replaces the old bond is either a longer-term bond or a lower-quality bond sufficient to generate a higher overall yield to maturity.

TIMING OF INVESTMENT PURCHASES AND SALES

Investment strategies also include the timing of the purchase of securities and their subsequent sale. A so-called *passive investor* actually does not try to time investment purchases and sales at all; rather, he or she practices what is known as a *buy-and-hold* strategy, remaining optimistic that over the long term a considerable profit will be generated, if historical performance is any guide. We now consider the buy-and-hold strategy as well as other timing methods.

Market Timing

Market timing is an attempt to predict the overall direction of the secondary securities market and take advantage of changes in the prices of those securities, either up or down. In the purest form of the strategy, the investor evaluates possible alternatives to the securities market, including real estate, and allocates his or her money accordingly. However, most commonly, the market timing strategy refers to when an investor times his or her purchases of securities, while staying fully (or predominately) invested in the secondary market.

There are various trends in the economy and security markets to use in assessing when the investor should be in or out of the market. Many of these trends are integrated into computer software that may be used to assist in the market timing process. The technical analysis method of security selection is also sometimes used in the process. However, historical studies have shown that an investor's rate of return is dramatically *reduced* if he or she is out of the market for the best 20 to 30 days of market performance. Further, to pinpoint exactly when these days will occur is exceedingly difficult to determine (even for long time investment advisors and/or money managers). Therefore, an investor that practices market timing should proceed carefully and realize that such a strategy has not, to date, been proven successful over the long term.

Finally, the market timing strategy should not be confused with the portfolio rebalancing strategies that are currently practiced by many portfolio managers. Portfolio rebalancing is done by portfolio managers to keep the investor's asset allocation consistent with that allocation originally agreed upon between the investment advisor and the client. Over time, given market fluctuations in value, the investor may "drift" from his or her original asset allocation and need to be repositioned. Thus, portfolio rebalancing is done to comply with investor goals and risk tolerance and does not depend on attempting to time the market to generate possible profits. Indeed, rebalancing primarily reflects a mechanical "buy low, sell high" strategy, wherein the assets that have appreciated the most are exchanged for assets that have appreciated the least. As such, portfolio rebalancing is predicated on the premise of *regression/ progression to the mean*, in which those assets that have performed well will tend to under-perform in the future, whereas those assets that have not performed well will tend to over-perform in the future.

Buy-and-Hold

Passive portfolio management is essentially a long-term *buy-and-hold* strategy. The attractiveness of this strategy is supported by the efficient market hypothesis (EMH). As we have previously learned, in its strongest form, this hypothesis maintains that the current market prices of securities reflect all information (public or private) presently available to investors and that it is pointless to try to achieve superior portfolio performance.

A pure buy-and-hold strategy has several advantages. First, the investor minimizes his or her transaction costs in the acquisition and trading of securities. Over a longer period of time, this can add up to sizeable savings. Second, such a strategy can assist in managing an investor's income tax obligations. Specifically, if securities are held for more than one year from their date of purchase, they are entitled to long-term capital gain treatment. Currently (in the year 2009), the maximum long-term capital gain rate is 15%, as compared to an *ordinary income* maximum rate of 35%. Therefore, a tax savings of 20% occurs by investing in this manner. Finally, a buy-and-hold strategy ensures that an investor will *not* be out of the securities market during an upturn in prices. As we have learned, this also means that the investor does not have to pursue the historically fruitless attempt to time the market.

Passive Investing/Indexing

In addition to the buy-and-hold strategy, passive portfolio management is characterized by a belief that a portfolio's return will be unable to beat a relevant market index, such as the S&P 500, over time. Therefore, *indexing* or investing in index mutual funds is characteristic of an investor who believes in passive management. The purpose of an indexed portfolio is not to beat the targeted index, but merely to match its long-term performance, less any management fees and/or transaction costs. One way to construct a passive or indexed portfolio is to simply buy-and-hold the securities in the index, at their appropriate weightings. This method is known as *replication*, and is characterized by a low tracking error with the actual index that is targeted. A second method of constructing such a portfolio is *stratified sampling*, whereby several securities are chosen to be representative of identified sectors in the overall index.

In contrast, *active* portfolio management is an attempt by the portfolio manager to outperform the benchmark portfolio or index on a risk-adjusted basis. Active portfolio management strategies include such approaches as *sector rotation*, which emphasizes investment in certain economic sectors or industries in response to the next market upturn, and *earnings momentum*, whereby a search for companies with above-average growth of earnings is practiced. When deciding whether to pursue an active management strategy, the investor must weigh its higher costs (fees and expenses) against the possibility of a higher risk-adjusted rate of return than that of passive indexing. Not surprisingly, academic studies have also shown that the benefits of indexing (passive management) *decline* as the investment expertise of the portfolio manager *increases*. There is also evidence that certain market segments (for example, small capitalization stocks and international stocks, to name two) may, in fact, benefit from active management. This would indicate that some market segments are less efficient than others.

SHORT SELLING

An investor who owns a security is said to be *long* as it relates to that security. Conversely, an individual who does not own the security and borrows it from a third party (normally, a broker-dealer) is said to be *short*. Therefore, a short-selling strategy involves the sale of securities *borrowed from* the investor's broker-dealer.

There are several requirements that must be met before an investor may engage in short selling. These are as follows:

1) Short sellers must have a margin account with the broker/dealer.

2) While maintaining their short position, short sellers must reimburse the broker-dealer for any dividends or interest paid on the borrowed securities.

3) Short sales have historically been permitted only with rising prices of the underlying security, referred to as an *uptick*; in other words, the short seller can only sell the borrowed security if the last trade price was less than the current trade price. (You should note that this rule was repealed by the SEC in July, 2007, but is, as of this writing, under re-consideration by the SEC. Specifically, the SEC is investigating what role the repeal of the "uptick rule" played in the market collapse of 2008 and whether it should be re-instituted.)

4) The net proceeds from the short sale, plus the required margin, are first held by the broker-dealer before being disbursed to the short seller.

Why would an investor sell short and what are the mechanics involved in doing so? An investor sells short because he or she believes that the market (and particular security *shorted*) will *decline* in price, and a profit can be made from the short sale and subsequent repurchase of the security at a lower price. Mechanically, when the price declines, the short seller instructs his or her broker-dealer to sell the borrowed security, then to repurchase the security at the lower price and, finally, to cancel (or *cover*) the short position by replacing the borrowed security with the real security. The short seller profits by the difference between the price at which the borrowed stock was sold and the price at which it was repurchased. This difference constitutes either short-term or long-term *capital gain*, depending on the length of time (*holding period*) that the short seller owned the repurchased security. If the short seller closes out the short position by purchasing the securities after they have appreciated in value, he or she incurs either a short-term or long-term *capital loss*.

An alternative to engaging in short selling is simply to purchase a put option on the targeted security, thereby permitting the investor to sell the security at its exercise price if its market price declines. In the event that the price of the security instead increases, the investor only sacrifices the premium paid for the put option. Therefore, an individual who sells short *incurs more risk* than the investor who simply buys a put. The loss associated with holding a put option is limited to the premium paid for the put option. The potential loss in a short sale, however, can be considerably higher than holding a put option, since the appreciation in the security sold short is theoretically unlimited when covering the short sale (note that there is no time limit on when a short sale must be closed out).

Example 15-2: Calculate the realized return on a short sale of MEJ stock given the following information:

- Sold short 100 shares at $35 per share on a 40 percent margin
- Broker fees on the short sale were $125
- Broker loan rate was 8 percent
- Bought shares back to cover short sale one-year later at $25 per share
- Broker fees on purchase were $135
- Stock paid $1.00/share in dividends during the year held.

Solution: Following is an accounting of the transaction.

Short sale receipt ($35 x 100 shares)	$3,500
Margin posted (40%)	$1,400
Broker loan amount	$2,100
Broker fee on short sale	($125)
Dividends paid broker ($1.00 x 100 shares)	($100)
Buyback of stock ($25 x 100 shares)	($2,500)
Broker fees	($135)
Interest on broker loan ($2,100 x 0.08)	($168)
Net receipt	$472
Realized return ($472/$1,400 equity)	33.71%

Short Selling Against the Box

Investors use short sales for *hedging purposes* (to limit the risk of investment loss) when they sell short *against the box*. (Note that additional hedging strategies are the subject of the next chapter, Chapter 16, in this textbook). Selling short against the box means that an investor sells short securities that they also own (or are *long*) in their portfolio. This technique offers perfect negative correlation of securities because gains or losses that the investor holds in the long position are matched by gains or losses in the short position. As a result, the economic value of the investor's position does not change.

Originally, short selling against the box was used primarily for income tax reasons. That is, an investor who had an appreciated position in a security that he or she wanted to sell, but did not want to incur a taxable gain for income tax purposes, would enter into such a strategy. As a result, the strategy permitted the investor to defer the tax bill until the position was closed (perhaps to a later year when he or she was in a lower marginal tax bracket), while eliminating all economic risk as if the position had been sold. However, under current tax law, short sales against the box are now treated as *constructive sales*, meaning that a tax gain on the appreciated long position must be recognized in the tax year in which the investor enters into the short sale. Accordingly, investors must now increase the basis of their long position by the amount of their realized gain, just as if they had actually sold and repurchased the securities, and begin a new holding period for income tax purposes.

SECURITY SELECTION AND ANALYSIS

An individual who practices active portfolio management is involved in active security selection. As such, this selection is made using the *fundamental analysis* of securities, the *technical analysis* of securities or, sometimes, both.

Fundamental Analysis

Fundamental analysts consider both particular company fundamentals and broader economic trends, although the order in which they do so (and the emphasis they place on each) depends on their orientation as either a *top down* or *bottom up* analyst.

With respect to particular company fundamentals, a fundamental analyst concentrates on three critical financial statements: 1) the company balance sheet; 2) the company income statement; and 3) the company statement of cash flows. The *balance sheet* reflects the resources of the company (assets) and the claims against those resources (liabilities). The difference between the two represent the common equity of the company, equivalent to the net worth of an individual on his or her statement of financial position. A part of this common equity is the retained earnings of the company. The amount of retained earnings is critical since it represents a source of internal financing for the future growth of the company. In addition, certain other ratios of interest to the fundamental analyst may be determined from analysis of the company balance sheet. The company *income statement* shows how profitable company operations were during a given period of time (usually quarterly). Typically, three years of statements are provided for the analysis by the fundamental analyst. Finally, the third important statement, *the statement of cash flows*, presents the actual cash received and paid out during the reporting period. Cash flow is important because it ultimately reflects the amount necessary to pay employees/workers, vendors, creditors, and company stockholders. The statement is normally divided into operating cash flows, investing cash flows, and financing cash flows.

With respect to economic trends, a fundamental analyst researches such factors as the gross domestic product (GDP), the unemployment rate, the consumer price index (CPI), and the producers price index (PPI). His or her goal in researching these factors is to predict the future direction of the economy and, therefore, the possible future direction of price movements in the stock of the particular company or industry sector that is being reviewed. In addition to the above macro economic factors, the fundamental analyst pays close attention to the actions of the Federal Reserve Board (the Fed) as it is in charge of the monetary supply and targets the overall interest rate reflected in the economy. Indeed, the Federal Reserve Open Market Committee (FOMC) that conducts open market operations on behalf of the Fed is a closely-watched barometer of Fed sentiment and the likely direction of future interest rates. If the FOMC is pursuing an *expansionary* monetary policy, it will *buy* U.S Treasury securities, ultimately driving market interest rates *down*; whereas, if pursuing a *contractionary* monetary policy, it will *sell* U.S. Treasury securities, ultimately forcing market interest rates *up*.

1. Top-Down Analysis

Top-down fundamental analysts begin with researching the overall economy and current state of the secondary market. Specifically, the analyst examines the overall economy and selects an industry that he or she believes will perform best over an upcoming time frame (for example, one to three years). The analyst then screens a database of securities to find acceptable companies in this industry. Finally, depending on his or her investment orientation (for example, a value or growth investor), the analyst narrows down (*targets*) the list of companies in the industry by focusing on companies that have the preferred characteristics. For example, a fundamental analyst that is following a *value* approach will target companies that have a low stock price relative to its earnings. An analyst that is pursuing a *growth* approach will be more interested in companies that exhibit a potential for superior earnings growth with the current stock price being of less consequence.

2. Bottom-Up Analysis

Bottom-up fundamental analysts often call themselves *stock pickers*. This is because they attempt to identify the best securities to buy (and the right price at which to buy them) *regardless* of the market sector or industry. A bottom-up analyst typically begins, first, with an examination of the company fundamentals, often by screening large databases of securities. Once identifying securities of interest, he or she then considers the prospect for the company, the sector or the industry and, ultimately, the overall economy. Like the top-down analyst, the bottom-up analyst will select securities (*stock pick*) based on his or her investment orientation and then report the chosen securities to the field or company representatives via a periodically scheduled research letter.

3. Ratio Analysis

As noted, fundamental analysts employ ratio analysis in analyzing the financial strengths or weaknesses of a company. These ratios are used to compare the financial performance and position of one company to another and, then, to make an investment decision regarding the purchase or non-purchase of its stock. The general categories that the ratios fall into are those that show the company's liquidity and solvency (leverage); assets, and profitability.

Likely the most important of the *liquidity and solvency ratios* is the company's *current ratio* as determined from the company's balance sheet. The current ratio is found by dividing the company's current assets by its current liabilities and reflects the ability of the company to pay its short-term liabilities or obligations to employees, suppliers, and creditors.

$$\text{Current ratio} = \frac{\text{Current assets}}{\text{Current liabilities}}$$

While there is no rule of thumb for what is an appropriate ratio, at least to creditors, the higher the current ratio the better, as it reflects the overall solvency of the company. Practically, the current ratio should be higher than one, but not so great as to indicate that company resources are being used inefficiently. Other liquidity and solvency ratios include a company's *debt ratio* (total liabilities divided by total assets), debt/equity (long-term debt divided by common equity), and the *times interest earned ratio*, computed by dividing the company's earnings before interest and taxes (EBIT) by its interest expense.

$$\text{Debt ratio} \; = \; \frac{\text{Total liabilities}}{\text{Total assets}}$$

$$\text{Debt/equity} \; = \; \frac{\text{Long - term debt}}{\text{Common equity}}$$

$$\text{Times interest earned} \; = \; \frac{\text{EBIT}}{\text{Interest expense}}$$

Asset ratios illustrate how effectively the company is managing its business operations. Accordingly, various turnover ratios are used, including the company's *accounts receivable turnover* (sales divided by average accounts receivable), its *inventory turnover* (cost of goods sold divided by average inventory), and the *total asset turnover* (sales divided by average total assets). Certainly for a manufacturing corporation (such as an automobile company), its inventory turnover is critical since it measures how often the company depletes its current inventory and must generate more. A longer-than–normal time period of days of inventory on hand may indicate that a company is not being very efficient in its operations..

$$\text{Accounts receivable (AR) turnover} \; = \; \frac{\text{Sales}}{(\text{AR beginning} + \text{AR end})/2}$$

$$\text{Inventory turnover} \; = \; \frac{\text{Cost of goods sold}}{(\text{Inventory beginning} + \text{Inventory end})/2}$$

$$\text{Total asset turnover} \; = \; \frac{\text{Sales}}{\text{Average total assets}}$$

Profitability ratios measure the amount of earnings a company generates from operations. Generally, any company (whether manufacturing or service-related) will strive to have as high a *net profit margin* (net income divided by sales) as possible. Another frequently analyzed profitability ratio is a company's *return on equity (ROE)*, found by dividing its net earnings by common equity.

$$\text{Profit margin} = \frac{\text{Net income}}{\text{Sales}}$$

$$\text{Return on equity} \; = \; \frac{\text{Net income}}{\text{Common equity}}$$

A more intuitive measure of ROE is the three-stage DuPont ROE, which incorporates a firm's profit margin, total asset turnover, and financial leverage:

$$\text{DuPont ROE} = \frac{\text{Net income}}{\text{Sales}} \times \frac{\text{Sales}}{\text{Total assets}} \times \frac{\text{Total assets}}{\text{Common equity}}$$

The DuPont ROE reduces to the conventional ROE of net income over common equity.

Technical Analysis

Both fundamental and technical analyses attempt to anticipate price movements based on the balance of supply and demand. The **fundamental analyst** anticipates the future direction of a firm's earnings and uses the forecast to determine the intrinsic value of the stock. Hence, as a matter of orientation. the fundamental analyst looks for undervalued stocks.

Alternatively, the technical analyst approaches the task from analyzing the price movement itself. The technical analyst assumes that the price already reflects the fundamentals and that these fundamentals are what ultimately cause prices to trend. The process of "charting" captures this trend. However, one does not need to ignore the fundamentals in performing technical analysis. After all, the fundamentals are the foundation for trends. Therefore, technical analysis is useful for timing the entry and exit points of buying and selling securities.

Premise for Technical Charting
Technical charting implies three basic assumptions:

1. Markets discount the fundamentals.

2. Markets trend.

3. Trends repeat.

Technical analysis assumes that since the financial markets are forward-looking, the fundamentals have already been discounted in the price. Technical analysts view price trends as leading indicators of the fundamentals. In fact, the study of these price trends is what technical analysis is all about. The technical analyst's objective is to identify trends early and trade in their direction (known as "the direction of least resistance"). Trends may be intraday or up to several months and even years.

Much of technical analysis is the study of market psychology. Investors are expected to respond to similar market situations in a consistent manner. This is why historical trends are followed closely and form the basis for why trends repeat.

Basics of Charting
Price charts come in a variety of forms—bar charts, candlestick charts, and point and figure charts. Our focus will be on bar charts. Bar charts represent the open, high, low, and close (settle) prices in

the trading interval (hourly, daily, weekly, monthly, etc.). The top and bottom of the vertical bar represents the high and low respectively. The left-side nick represents the open price and the right-side nick the closing price:

A series of these bars form a charting pattern of price action for a given trading period. Charts provide a visual representation of trends from which trendlines, support lines, and resistance lines may be drawn.

Trends

Trends indicate the direction of the market. The *greater* is the duration of the trend, the *more significance* is given to the trend. Charts are prepared from following trends. An upward trendline is drawn on the periodic lows. The downward trendline is then drawn on the periodic highs. Figure 15.1 graphs an upward and downward trendline.

Figure 15.1. Trendline, Resistance, and Support

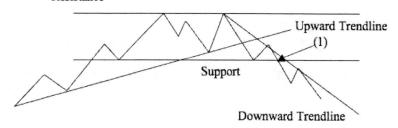

From trendlines, support and resistance price levels may be identified. These price levels imply buying and selling psychology. Thus, a main objective of technical analysis is to spot new trends and trend reversals.

Support and Resistance

Figure 15.1. also shows support and resistance levels. The *support level* is synonymous with demand. When the price of the security or market reaches the support level, demand forces tend to move the price up. Conversely, resistance levels are synonymous with supply. When the price reaches the resistance level, supply forces tend to move the price down. Price action between the resistance level and the support level indicates equilibrium or near equilibrium conditions in supply and demand.

When the price breaks out of the resistance level, demand exceeds supply and an upward trend may be forming. Likewise, when the price breaks through the support level, excess supply causes prices to fall, indicating that a downward trend may be forming.

Resistance levels form when sellers realize they are wrong and wish to get out at prices that allow them to break even. Reverse psychology occurs in the formation of support levels. Buyers are happy to see the security rise. As the security price retraces from the resistance level, buyers will buy more when the price reaches their original buying price. You can see that a continuation of these patterns results in a sideways or consolidation of trading activity. This consolidation may continue for some time before the market corrects for a fundamental change and resumes or reverses a prior trend. Point (1) in Figure 15.1. marks a support price breakout that indicates a trend reversal. It is important to make note of the volume associated with the price breakout. Higher volume confirms the direction. Volume is a more important indicator when associated with a price breakout through the resistance level. Falling prices have a tendency to gain momentum on their own. A prior resistance level becomes the new support level and a prior support level becomes the new resistance level on corresponding price breakouts.

Chart Patterns
Charts are not merely trendlines and support and resistance levels. In analyzing price charts, the analyst looks for distinctive patterns (which may not be so distinctive to other analysts) that signal potential future price movements. As mentioned above, the technical analyst strives to identify new trends or trend reversals.

Double Top/Double Bottom
The most common type of reversal pattern is the *double top or double bottom*. This pattern may be observed on charts covering a few days or weeks to months or years. The longer the pattern takes to form, the greater its significance. A double top pattern is characterized by two prominent peaks and represents a possible reversal of the upward trend. Figure 15.2. illustrates a *double top* pattern.

Figure 15.2. Double Top Reversal Pattern

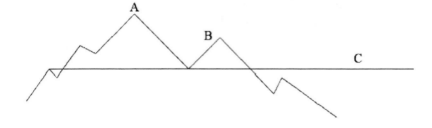

The reversal pattern is implied by the following observations:
1. The double heads are identified by the letters A and B.
2. B is lower than A.
3. The trendline breaks through line C, which becomes a new resistance level.

The *double bottom* is the reverse of the double top and is illustrated in Figure 15.3.

Figure 15.3. Double Bottom Reversal Pattern

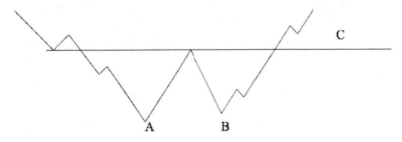

The *double bottoms* are identified as A and B. A is lower than B and the up trendline breaks through line C. Line C thus becomes the new support level.

In analyzing double tops and double bottoms, it is important to verify that new resistance and support levels are indeed formed. Otherwise, the double top or double bottom may not be a reversal but a consolidation of trading activity. Higher volume associated with the breakout reinforces a reversal pattern.

Head and Shoulder Reversal
The *head and shoulders pattern* consists of three prominent peaks. The left and right peaks are the shoulders and the higher (or lower) middle peak is the head. For a reversal to occur, the trendline must break through the neckline, which is the tangent line to the shoulder peaks. Figure 15.4. illustrates a head and shoulder reversal for both an upward and a downward trend.

Figure 15.7 4. Head and Shoulder Reversal Patterns

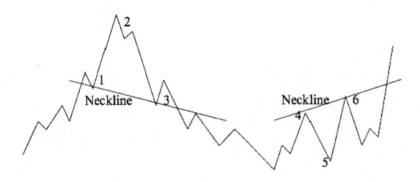

Peaks 1 and 3 are the shoulders and peak 2 is the head in the reversal pattern to the upward trend. Note that peak 3 (the right shoulder) falls below peak 1 (the left shoulder). Hence, the price trendline breaks through the neckline (which forms a new resistance level) and continues falling.

Conversely, peaks 4 and 6 are the left and right shoulders and peak 5 is the head in a reversal pattern to a downward trend. Here, the right shoulder (peak 6) is higher than the left shoulder (peak 4). The neckline forms a new support level). Higher volume confirms the breakouts and if a true reversal is indeed occurring.

> **Exercise:** Go to the charting site www.bigcharts.com and input a stock symbol. Click on "Quick Chart" and look for possible head and shoulder reversal patterns.

Price Gaps

Price activity is not continuous. *Price gaps* occur when the market jumps from one price to another leaving an opening (gap) in the price chart. Price gaps can only be observed on bar charts since the opening and closing prices of a security or market are necessary. An upside gap is a positive indicator (*bullish*) and a downside gap is a negative indicator (*bearish*).

Price gaps fall into three categories: (1) breakaway gap, (2) measuring gap, and (3) exhaustion gap. A *breakaway gap* breaks out of the resistance or support level and indicates a significant price move. A *measuring gap* occurs about halfway through the trend. Finally, an *exhaustion gap* takes place towards the end of the trend.

Price gaps may or may not be partially filled. A breakaway gap on the upside, accompanied by heavy volume, may be a strong buy signal. Waiting for the gap to be filled or partially filled before buying may result in a lost opportunity. Prices may move upward without looking back. The heavier the volume when the gap occurs, the less likely that it will be filled (or partially filled). Downside gaps follow the same principles as upside gaps. Figure 15.5. illustrates the three categories of gaps.

Figure 15.5. Price Gaps

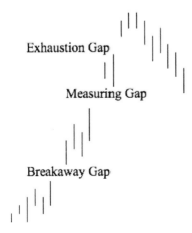

Gaps occur more often in low volume markets and are less significant than gaps occurring in high volume markets.

Triangles
Unlike the double top/double bottom and the head and shoulder reversal patterns, *triangles* represent continuation patterns, suggesting the current trend is simply consolidating for a period of time. The sideways movement is obvious.

An *ascending triangle* is bullish and characterized by a horizontal upper line and an ascending lower line. The indication is an upward trend once prices break out of the consolidation pattern. The ascending lower line is a result of higher lows during the consolidation period.

A *descending triangle* is bearish and characterized by a descending upper line (decreasing highs) and a horizontal lower line. The indication is a downward trend once prices break out of the consolidation pattern.

A *symmetrical triangle* is a neutral indicator and is characterized by a descending upper line and an ascending lower line. A symmetrical triangle indicates that the trend prior to consolidation will most likely continue on the breakout. A variation of the symmetrical triangle is the *wedge*. The wedge may represent a continuation pattern or a reversal pattern and is characterized by converging upper and lower lines. However, unlike the symmetrical triangle, the wedge has a definite slope. It is the slope that indicates the market psychology. A rising wedge is a *bearish* signal and a falling wedge is a *bullish* signal.

Figure 15.6. illustrates the ascending triangle, descending triangle, and symmetrical triangle.

Figure 15.6. Consolidation Patterns

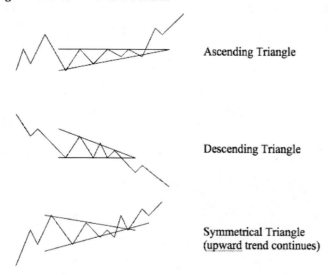

Ascending Triangle

Descending Triangle

Symmetrical Triangle
(upward trend continues)

Volume and Open Interest

Volume is probably the second most important indicator behind price. In fact, many technical analysts use volume as a leading indicator of price. Volume usually diminishes as the pattern forms and then increases noticeably on the breakout. As mentioned above, volume is especially important during resistance breakouts.

Volume is the total amount of trading activity for the security or commodity market that day. It may be the total number of commodity contracts, bonds, or stock traded during the day. The volume is indicated on price charts as a series of bars at the bottom of the chart. Such presentation does not always provide the precision necessary in detecting significant shifts in volume flows and subsequent analysis of buying and selling pressure.

A simple volume indicator, which is actually a volume trendline is the *on-balance volume (OBV)* line developed by Joseph Granville. The direction of the OBV line (its trend) is more important than the actual volume measurement. For example, a downtrend in prices with a flat OBV may indicate that support is forming in the market and it may not be wise to be "too bearish."

Open interest is the total number of outstanding futures or option contracts that have not expired, been offset, or exercised at the end of the day. One only needs to count one side of the contract since for every long position there must be a short position.

Finally, there are also certain theories used by technical analysts to describe overall market trends. Among these are:

1) *The Dow Theory*: According to this theory, the primary trend in a bull market is a series of higher highs and higher lows. In a bear market, the primary trend is a series of lower highs and lower lows. Daily fluctuations in the market are considered irrelevant in predicting future behavior.

2) *The Odd-Lot Theory*: Typically, small investors engage in odd-lot (less than 100 shares at once) trading. Adherents of the odd-lot theory believe that investors invariably buy and sell at the wrong time. Therefore, when odd-lot traders buy (sell), odd-lot analysts are bearish (bullish).

3) *The Short Interest Theory*: Short interest refers to the number of market shares that have been sold short (see previous discussion on short selling). Therefore, because short positions must eventually be *covered*, some technical analysts believe that short interest reflects market demand. A high amount of short interest is considered bullish and a low amount of short interest is considered bearish.

4) *The Mutual Fund Cash Position Theory*: If a mutual fund portfolio manager is holding a great amount of cash (that is, if he or she remains relatively un-invested in the securities market), it is considered a bullish signal to the technical analyst. This is because, ultimately, this cash will find its way to the market and be used to buy outstanding shares of stock. Conversely, a low amount of cash is considered bearish to the analyst since the portfolio manager is already relatively fully invested in the market.

5) *Investment Advisory Opinions*: Many technical analysts believe that, if a large proportion of investment advisory services are pessimistic (bearish), this signals the approach of a market trough and the onset of a bull market. Specifically, the technician's market trading rule resulting from this theory is that a 60 percent bearish sentiment among investment advisory services indicates a major market *bottom*, while a 60 percent bullish sentiment suggests a major market *top*.

6) *Barron's Confidence Index*: Published by *Barron's* financial newspaper, the Confidence Index is the ratio of Barron's average yield on 10 investment-grade bonds divided by the yield on the Dow Jones average of 40 lower-grade bonds. Technical analysts believe that the ratio is a bullish indicator when investors are investing in lower-quality bonds for the added yield, therefore causing the yield spread to decline and the Confidence Index to increase. Conversely, when investors are bearish, they avoid investing in lower-quality bonds, therefore causing the yield spread to increase and the Confidence Index to decline.

USE OF LEVERAGE (MARGIN)

Leverage involves the use of borrowing by investors to enhance return on their equity. With respect to securities investing, leverage commonly translates to the use of *margin* and the establishment of a margin account by the investor with his or her broker-dealer. Therefore, a margin account permits an investor to borrow from the broker-dealer using stocks and other securities as security (collateral) for the loan. However, certain financial requirements must be met by the investor before he or she is allowed to engage in market trading involving the use of margin.

As with all security transactions, there are both advantages and disadvantages associated with the creation of a margin account by the investor. Likely, the major advantage of such an account is the ability of the investor to increase the size of his or her return on invested equity beyond that possible if only personal funds are used.

Example 15-3: Assume that Brad purchases 1,000 shares of CDO stock at $30 per share using $30,000 of his own money. Further assume that CDO stock appreciates to $40 per share when Brad sells all of his shares one year later. Brad would realize a return of:

$$\text{Annual return} = \frac{\$40,000 - \$30,000}{\$30,000} = 0.3333 \text{ or } 33.33\%$$

Now assume Brad buys the stock on 50 percent margin. The broker loan rate is 8 percent. Brad's original $30,000 equity would now buy 2,000 shares of CDO stock borrowing $30,000 from the broker. One year later Brad sells 2,000 shares of CDO stock at $40 per share realizing $80,000. After paying off the loan ($30,000) plus $240 in interest ($30,000 x 0.08), Brad would realize a return of:

$$\text{Annual return (with leverage)} = \frac{\$80,000 - \$30,240 - \$30,000}{\$30,000} = 0.6587 \text{ or } 65.87\%$$

There are also a number of disadvantages that investors need to consider before deciding to establish a margin account. These major disadvantages are as follows:

1) Investors can lose more funds than they deposit in the margin account. As we shall see in the upcoming Example 15-5, a decline in the value of securities purchased on margin may require investors to provide additional monies to the broker-dealer making the loan in order to avoid the forced sale of those securities.

2) The broker-dealer may sell the margined securities without contacting the investor. If the investor's equity in the margin account falls below the maintenance margin percentage required by the broker-dealer, the firm can sell the securities in the account and the investor has no legal recourse.

3) Investors are not entitled to a grace period or any other extension of time to satisfy a *margin call* (request from broker-dealer to deposit additional funds). While, as a practical matter, most broker-dealers will provide an extension of time for the investor to deposit additional monies, by law they are *not required* to do so.

Computation of Margin Call and/or Required Investor Equity

To understand the subsequent examples and computations, it is first necessary that you understand certain commonly-used terms with respect to margin trading. These are as follows:

- *Initial margin requirement*: The percentage of the original price of purchased securities that must be provided by the investor. This amount is established by the Federal Reserve Board pursuant to Regulation T of the Securities Act of 1934 and is currently 50%.

- *Maintenance margin percentage*: The level at which the investor will be required to add additional funds to the margin account established by his or her broker-dealer. This percentage is usually set at 35% of the current fair market of the margined securities but may differ among broker-dealers (for example, it could be as low as 25 or 30 percent of the current fair market value of the margined securities).

- *Debit balance*: The amount owed to the broker-dealer by the investor, including the original amount borrowed plus any interest accrued and due.

- *Equity/Actual Equity*: The current fair market value of the margined securities less the debit balance.

Accordingly, in applying several of these terms, the formula for determining when a margin call to the investor by the broker-dealer will occur is:

$$\text{Margin call} = \left[\frac{1 - \text{Initial margin requirement}}{1 - \text{Maintenance margin requirement}} \right] \times \text{Purchase price of stock}$$

You should also note that the numerator of this formula is equal to the amount owed to the broker-dealer and constitutes the debit balance of the investor (after accounting for any interest accrued and due).

Example 15-4: Jason buys 100 shares of Tripedia Company stock, currently trading at $40 per share, using a margin account with a 50% initial margin requirement. Jason posts $2,000 as initial margin and borrows an additional $2,000 from his broker-dealer. Jason is now concerned, however, about when he might receive a margin call. Assuming a 35% maintenance margin percentage, calculate the stock price below which Jason will receive a margin call.

$$\text{Margin call} = \left[\frac{1 - 0.50}{1 - 0.35} \right] \times \$40 = \$30.77$$

Example 15-5: Assume the same facts as in Example 15-4, but that the stock price of Tripedia company stock declines to $25.00. How much money is Jason now required to deposit with his broker-dealer so as to avoid a forced sale of the previously-purchased securities?

Required Equity		Actual Equity	
Stock Value	$25.00	Stock Value	$25.00
Equity %	35%	Debit Balance	($20.00) [$2,000/100]
Required Equity	$ 8.75	Actual Equity	$ 5.00

Therefore, Jason will be required by the broker-dealer to deposit an additional $3.75 per share ($8.75 less $5.00) or a total dollar amount of $375 ($3.75 × 100 shares purchased) to maintain the equity position of 35%. In other words, the actual equity position must be compared to the required equity position to determine if there is a deficit or additional deposit that is due by Jason.

Finally, funds that are borrowed from a bank by the broker-dealer, and which are based on the firm's account balances, are referred to as *call loans*. The applicable rate charged on such loans by the bank (known as the *call loan rate*) is published in numerous financial websites and in various financial publications such as the *Wall Street Journal*.

VALUE VS. GROWTH INVESTING

This chapter concludes with a brief look at the two primary styles of investing used by many investors today, value and/or growth investing.

Value and growth investing are really just different sides of the same "investment coin." In this case, however, the investment coin is the price/earnings (P/E) ratio of stocks. *Value investing* is a strategy that tends to concentrate on the *numerator* of that ratio (or price), while *growth investing* focuses on the *denominator* of that ratio (or earnings). Specifically, value investing assumes that the current P/E ratio is *below* its natural level and that an efficient market will soon recognize this and drive the stock price upward. Value investors are disciples of the late Benjamin Graham (of whom Warren Buffet is the most prominent), who looked for stocks that sold for two thirds or less of their net current assets and stocks with high dividend yields and low P/E ratios. In contrast, growth investors assume that the P/E ratio will remain *constant* over the near term and the stock price in an efficient market will increase as the forecasted earnings growth of the issuing company is realized. Such investors look for *growth stocks*, that is, stocks of a company that have a significant ability to make capital investments earning a return greater than the firm's cost of capital. These stocks usually have a superior rate of earnings growth, low dividend payouts, and an above-average price to earnings ratio.

As with investment strategies generally, there is no one correct answer regarding which investment style—value or growth—is best. It is fair to assert, however, that an investor should consider both strategies in constructing his or her portfolio and, perhaps, weight the portfolio with a combination of each active-management strategy.

IMPORTANT CONCEPTS

Investment policy statement

Benchmark

Value-weighted index

Price-weighted index

Dollar cost averaging

Averaging down

Share averaging

Dividend reinvestment plans (DRIPs)

Bond ladder

Bond barbell

Bond bullet

Bond swap

Market timing

Buy-and-hold

Passive portfolio management

Indexing

Active portfolio management

Short selling

Short selling against the box

Fundamental analysis of securities

Top-down analysis

Bottom-up analysis

Liquidity and solvency (leverage) ratios

Current ratio

Asset ratios

Profitability ratios

Return on equity

DuPont three-stage return on equity

Technical analysis of securities

Dow Theory

Odd-Lot Theory

Short Interest Theory

Mutual Fund Cash Position Theory

Investment advisory opinions

Barron's Confidence Index

Leverage

Margin account

Margin call

Initial margin percentage

Maintenance margin percentage

Value investing

Growth investing

QUESTIONS FOR REVIEW

1. What are the two major components of a complete and thorough investment policy statement?

2. List five constraints that should be part of any investment policy statement.

3. What are the characteristics of an appropriate *benchmark* by which to judge investment performance?

4. What is the difference between a value-weighted and a price-weighted index? Give an example of each type of index.

5. What is the most common type of *formula investing*? Explain this technique and its practical importance for an investor.

6. When does *dollar cost averaging* work best? When does it *not* work well?

7. What is *share averaging* and how does it differ from *dollar cost averaging*?

8. Who offers dividend reinvestment plans (DRIPs) and why should an investor consider such a plan?

9. Describe the following types of investment strategies involving the periodic purchase of bonds:

- Bond ladders

- Bond barbells

- Bond bullets

10. Why does an investor (or portfolio manager) engage in a bond swap?

11. Describe the following types of bond swaps and when each might be used by a fixed-income investor:

- Substitution swap

- Intermarket spread swap

- Rate anticipation swap

- Pure yield pickup swap

12. What is *market timing*? How does it compare to the *portfolio rebalancing strategy* currently practiced by many portfolio managers?

13. What type of investment theory or hypothesis is inherently being followed by a pure *buy-and-hold* investment strategy? Explain.

14. What are three advantages of the *buy-and-hold* investment strategy?

15. *Indexing* is a primary method of what type of portfolio management strategy? What is the goal of this type of portfolio management strategy?

16. Complete the following sentence: "_____ portfolio management is an attempt by the portfolio manager to outperform the benchmark portfolio or index on a risk-adjusted basis." Then list and describe several examples of this type of portfolio management.

17. What is *selling short* and what are the technical requirements that must be met before an investor may engage in this strategy?

18. Why does an investor *sell short* and what are the mechanics involved in doing so? Specifically, how does the investor profit from such activity?

19. What is an alternative to selling short and is it more or less risky? Explain.

20. What is meant by the term *short selling against the box* and why was it originally used? Now, what is the taxable result of such strategy?

21. Contrast the fundamental analysis of securities to the technical analysis of securities. Which of these two approaches uses company financial statements?

22. Assume that an investment advisor first examines the overall economy and selects an industry that she believes will outperform the market over the upcoming time period. She then screens a database of companies in whose stocks to invest. What type of security selection is she practicing?

23. What are four general categories of ratios that may be used in selecting securities based on ratio analysis?

24. If you divide a company's earnings available for common shareholders by the company's book value, what ratio is derived? What is a complementary ratio that may also be determined if ascertaining the company's earnings available for common shareholders?

25. What is a *head and shoulders formation* and what type of analyst uses this concept?

26. Explain the following types of theories used by a technical analyst:

- The Dow Theory

- The Odd-Lot Theory

- The Short Interest Theory

- The Mutual Fund Cash Position Theory

- Investment Advisory Opinions

- *Barron's* Confidence Index

27. Why does an investor engage in *leveraging* techniques? What is the most common form of this technique used in the securities industry?

28. List three disadvantages associated with the establishment of a margin account by an investor.

29. Define the terms *initial margin requirement* and *maintenance margin percentage* and explain how they are used in the computation of when an investor may expect to receive a *margin call.*

30. Contrast the focus of a value investor to that of a growth investor. What kinds of stocks are of interest to each type of investor?

SUGGESTIONS FOR ADDITIONAL READING

Tools and Techniques of Investment Planning, 2nd edition, Stephen R. Leimberg, Robert T. LeClair, Robert J. Doyle, Jr., and Thomas R. Robinson, The National Underwriter Company, 2006.

Investments: *An Introduction,* 9th edition, Herbert B. Mayo, Thomson/ South-Western, 2008.

Investment Analysis and Portfolio Management, 9th edition, Frank K. Reilly and Keith C. Brown, Thomson/South-Western, 2009.

The Wall Street Journal Guide to Money and Investing, 3rd edition, Kenneth M. Morris and Virginia B. Morris, Fireside Publishing, 2004.

CHAPTER SIXTEEN

Hedging and Options Strategies

• • •

For examination purposes, CFP Board of Standards, Inc. is interested in you, the student, understanding the definition of *hedging* versus *speculation*. Furthermore, as a financial planner, you should attempt (presuming suitability requirements are met) to have your client *hedge* (not *speculate*) if concerned about minimizing his or her risk of investment loss. This chapter addresses certain popular hedging techniques, including the use of derivative or alternative investments. Alternative investments were previously introduced in chapter 7 of this textbook.

Upon completing this chapter, you should be able to:

- Contrast hedging techniques to those used primarily for speculation
- Explain the primary characteristics of a futures contract
- Describe basic option transactions
- Analyze a given situation in using options to protect or *hedge* an investor position
- Describe multiple option transactions
- Identify types of non-equity options and their use as a hedging technique
- Discuss the income tax rules that apply to equity option transactions

HEDGING VS. SPECULATION

A *speculator* is an investor (sometimes referred to as a *trader*) that does not typically own the underlying asset in which he or she is trading.. The speculator trades the derivatives contract only. Speculators are often cited as not providing any social contribution to the markets, yet speculators are necessary for providing the other side of a hedge trade and in bringing equilibrium to the markets.

On the other hand, a *hedger* is an investor who typically does own the underlying asset in the derivatives contract. The hedger has positions in both the derivatives market and the cash market. The derivatives contract is similar to an insurance policy since it is designed to cover risks associated with investment loss. To hedge, the investor takes opposite positions in the cash and derivatives markets. For example, if a manager of a stock portfolio that tracks the S&P 500 index is concerned about a temporary loss in the portfolio value, he or she can hedge with S&P index futures. The manager is *long* the stock portfolio (owns the stocks) and, therefore, would take a *short* position (sell) in S&P index futures contracts. A full hedge would theoretically insure the portfolio from any loss (the loss in portfolio value is perfectly offset by the gain in the futures position). Such a perfectly hedged portfolio would earn the investor a risk-free rate of return and have a standard deviation of zero.

Hedging includes both investment strategies and investment tools. In terms of *strategies,* a hedger follows the basic principles of sound investing, which includes: 1) portfolio diversification and management theory and 2) proper asset allocation. The investment *tools* of a hedger involve the use of derivative securities, notably 1) futures contracts, 2) the buying and selling (writing) of options, and 3) a combination of option contracts that are variations of the basic forms. The hedger's tools are the focus of the remaining sections of this chapter.

FUTURES CONTRACTS

A *futures contract* is an agreement between a buyer, seller, and some third party exchange (such as a commodity exchange) for the future delivery of an asset at a specified date and for a specified price. You should note that the same goal may be achieved between private parties without the involvement of the third-party exchange. However in this case, the agreement is known as a *forward contract.*

There are essentially three types of futures contracts, those involving: 1) commodities, 2) financial instruments, or 3) foreign currencies. Since the emphasis of this text is financial planning and investing, we will concentrate on financial instruments. The carrying cost of financial derivatives is simply the risk-free rate as opposed to storage, insurance, and transportation costs associated with commodities. Foreign currencies are generally traded in the forward markets.

An investor may become involved in the futures market when he or she desires a high degree of leverage in investing. This leverage derives from the low margin requirements of the futures market. For example, compared to initial margins of 50% on most securities (see chapter 15), initial margins on futures are extremely minimal. Specifically, an investor can likely finance up to 95% of the value of the futures contract at the time of purchase, meaning that a small cash deposit of only 5% needs to be made initially. In addition, unlike margin accounts for the purchase of securities that are interest bearing, the investor pays *no* interest on the unpaid balance in a futures contract. In essence, the initial margin is a security deposit. Credit risk associated with futures contracts is managed through maintenance margins and variation margins (refer to Chapter 7 of this text).

Operationally, an investor may also take part in a so-called *managed futures* program with a broker-dealer. Under this arrangement, the broker-dealer has the discretionary power to trade in the futures market for the investor's account. An additional characteristic of this program is that the broker may participate in the profits earned for the account in addition to any commissions that may be generated through the trading activity within the futures market.

A futures contract may be settled (*closed out*) by either delivery or offset. *Delivery* means the actual transfer of the asset to the other party (normally, a speculator). Since delivery often proves to be impractical, most futures contracts are settled by offset. With the exception of index futures contracts, the ability to deliver the underlying asset, such as stocks or Treasury bonds supports the integrity of the contract, In an *offset*, the buyer of the futures contract sells his or her position sometime prior to the date of actual delivery of the commodity and the seller of the contract buys that position. The initial trade and subsequent offset is referred to as a "round trip."

> **Example 16-1:** Assume it is the beginning of the fourth fiscal quarter and a bond portfolio manager of a pension plan anticipates an upcoming distribution of pension benefits at the beginning of the next fiscal year. To hedge against possible loss in the value of the portfolio, the manager would sell December interest rate futures (Treasury bond contracts). Come December, the manager would offset his or her position in the futures by buying the same amount of December contracts. Note that the initiation of the hedge reflects a long position in the bond portfolio (owns the bonds) and a short position in the futures contracts. If interest rates *rose* during the fourth quarter, the loss in value of the bond portfolio would partially be offset by the gain of the short position in the futures market. If interest rates *fell* during the quarter, the hedge would have reduced the gain in the portfolio by the amount lost in the futures position. Regardless, the hedge is an insurance policy against unacceptable loss and the cost of the hedge should be considered as the insurance policy premium.

This example illustrates the offsetting positions that are fundamental to the concept of hedging and the attempt to minimize the risk of investment loss. Accordingly, you should analyze hedging transactions based on: 1) what position does the hedger already occupy (that is, is he long or short in the cash or spot market)?; and 2) what *opposite* position from his or her cash or spot position does the hedger need to assume? If one follows these steps, trying to understand what may at times seem like an extremely complex set of transactions will be less confusing.

BASIC OPTION TRANSACTIONS

Similar to futures contracts, options contracts involve transactions for a specified property (usually securities) at a specified price for possible delivery within or at the end of a specified time. Unlike futures contracts, only the party writing the contract (seller) has the obligation to perform if the holder of the option (buyer) elects to exercise his or her option right. This is referred to as an *asymmetrical payoff* in options contracts. The seller's gain is limited to the premium received for writing the option and the buyer's loss is limited to the premium paid for the option. Both parties are obligated to perform in a futures contract and, therefore, the payoff is considered symmetrical.

There are four basic positions in the options market. They are:

1) Purchasing or buying a call
2) Selling (*writing*) a call
3) Purchasing or buying a put
4) Selling (*writing*) a put

However, any of these may be combined with another position to form a multiple option transaction, as we shall learn.

The amount that an investor (or speculator) pays for an option is called the option's *premium*. An option's premium reflects two types of value:

1) The option's *intrinsic* value or the amount by which the option is *in the money* (see chapter 7 in this text); and
2) The option's *time value* or the market's perceived worth of the time remaining to the expiration date of the option.

Example 16-2: Assume that a February 35 call option (option contract expires in February and has an exercise price of $35) on MAD stock carries a premium of 4 ½. From chapter 7, you will recall that a call option has intrinsic value whenever the stock's market price (S_T) exceeds the exercise price (X) of the option ($S_T - X$). Therefore, if the market price of MAD stock closed yesterday at 37 7/8, the intrinsic value of the stock is 2 7/8:

$S_T - X = \$37.875 - \$35 = \$2.875$ or 2 7/8

We then also know that the time value of the call option is 1 5/8 since the option's intrinsic value (2 7/8) when added to its time value (1 5/8) must equal the option's premium (4 ½):

Option premium = Intrinsic value + time value
$4.50 = $2.875 + $1.625 (or 1 5/8)

Accordingly, an option has time value anytime the option's premium *exceeds* its intrinsic value. Time value represents the time remaining before the expiration of the option and the more time that remains, the greater the chance for a change in the underlying stock price. More distant option expirations, of course, have greater time value. Since there is no intrinsic value when the market price of the underlying stock and the exercise price of the option are equal, the time value of the option is at its maximum at this point and, indeed, constitutes the *entire value* of the option's premium.

The factor with the greatest impact on the premium of an option, related to its intrinsic value component, is the *volatility* of the underlying stock. A stock that is highly volatile has the potential to experience greater price changes. However, as we have learned, this same stock also has the possibility for the greatest investor reward or profit. If the market price for such a stock falls from one day to the next, the premium for a *call* (or option right to buy) would *fall* and the premium for a *put* (option right to sell) would *rise*.

Buying Calls

An investor will buy a call option in hopes that the underlying stock will *increase* in value. In other words, he or she is *bullish* on the prospects for the underlying stock. By purchasing or buying a call option, an investor can profit from an increase in the stock price while investing only a relatively small amount of money (the option's premium). As a result, the maximum gain available to the call buyer or owner is, theoretically, *unlimited* with his or her maximum loss limited only to the option's premium (recall the asymmetrical payoff).

Other reasons for buying a call are:

1) *Deferring a decision:* An investor can buy a call on a stock and lock in the purchase price until the option expires. In turn, this also permits him or her to postpone making a financial commitment, other than the cost of the premium, until the expiration date of the option.

2) *Diversifying holdings:* With limited funds, an investor can buy calls on a variety of stocks, therefore diversifying his or her portfolio.

3) *Speculation:* Investors can speculate on the upward price movement of the stock by paying only the premium, whereas purchasing the actual stock outright would require a far greater investment.

4) *Protect (hedge) a stock position:* Investors can use calls conservatively to act as an insurance policy against adverse market performance. For example, if a portfolio manager was anticipating new funds in the near future and wanted to take advantage of a bullish market, he or she could purchase call options to benefit from the higher market.

Selling or Writing Calls

An investor would sell—or write—a call in hopes that the underlying stock price will *decline* or at least stay the same. In other words, he or she is *bearish* on the prospects for the underlying stock. A call option is usually written on a stock that may have achieved a new high in price and is part of a trend that is not expected to continue. If the call is *uncovered* or *naked* (that is, if the seller does *not* already own the underlying stock on which the option is written), the seller's maximum gain is the premium received. His or her maximum loss is, however, theoretically *unlimited*, since the seller could be forced to buy the stock at a potentially infinite price if the option is exercised by the holder.

Other reasons for selling or writing a call are:

1) *Receipt of income:* Income may be earned for a portfolio from premiums received by writing calls. Investors then hope for expiration of the calls (that is, the underlying stock price does not rise), so that they can keep the premium income without any offsetting loss.

2) *Locking in a stock price:* If an investor has already made a paper profit from holding a stock and is interested in selling it, a call can be written at an exercise price that will ensure that the profit is realized.

3) *Speculation:* By writing calls an investor can profit if the underlying stock's price falls below or remains at the exercise price. The profit is the amount of the premium collected for the call.

4) *Protect (hedge) a stock position:* The premium that is collected from writing the call may be used to offset any loss if the underlying stock price rises. Note that writing a call should be a covered call only and never a naked call since the writer is exposed to the additional risks of buying high and selling low if the call is exercised.

Buying Puts

An investor will buy a put option in hopes that the underlying stock will *decline* in value. In other words, he or she is *bearish* on the prospects for the underlying stock. By purchasing or buying puts an investor can profit from a decrease in the stock's price while investing a relatively small amount of money (the put premium). As a result, the maximum gain available to a put buyer is the exercise price of the option less the premium paid for the option. However, his or her maximum loss is limited to the amount of the premium paid for the put option.

Other reasons for buying a put are:

1) *Deferring a decision:* An investor can buy a put on a stock and lock in a sales price until the option expires. This allows him or her to postpone a selling decision until the expiration date of the option.

2) *Speculation:* Investors can speculate on the downward price of a stock that is not owned by paying only the premium for the option. (Note that this is akin to selling a stock *short*, but with much less risk, given that the loss to the put buyer is limited to the premium paid, whereas the short seller's loss is potentially much greater.)

3) *Protect or (hedge) a stock position:* Investors can use puts conservatively to act as an insurance policy against adverse market performance. For example, if a portfolio manager anticipates a distribution in a falling market, he or she can buy puts on the stock or benchmark index for the portfolio to hedge against the loss of value in the portfolio (this strategy is known as "a protective put").

Selling or Writing Puts

An investor would sell or write a put in hopes that the underlying stock price will *increase* in value. In other words, the investor is *bullish* on the prospects for the underlying stock. Puts are usually written on stocks that have recently experienced a new market low in price and is part of a trend that is not expected to continue. If the put is not exercised, the put writer's maximum gain is the premium received. His or her maximum loss is the put option's exercise price less the premium received and occurs when the underlying stock price drops to zero.

Other reasons for selling or writing a put are:

1) *Receipt of income:* Income may be earned for a portfolio from the premiums received by writing puts. Investors then hope for the expiration of the puts (that is, the underlying stock price does not decline), so that they can keep the premium without any offsetting loss.

2) *Speculation:* By writing puts, an investor can profit if the underlying stock's price rises or remains at or below the exercise price. The profit is the amount of the premium collected for the put.

3) *Buying stock below its current price:* The premium received from writing puts may be used to offset the cost of the stock when and if the put is exercised (the writer must purchase the stock at the exercise price). Accordingly, the writer buys the underlying stock at a price that is reduced by the premium received.

A summary of the maximum economic gain and loss with respect to basic option positions is shown in Figure 16-1 below.

Figure 16-1

Options Gains and Losses		
	Max Gain	**Max Loss**
Buy Call	Unlimited	Premium
Buy Put	Exercise Price - Premium	Premium
Sell Call	Premium	Unlimited
Sell Put	Premium	Exercise Price - Premium

Using Options to Protect or Hedge a Position

An investor with an established stock position may use options to help protect (hedge) against the risk of that position. If the investor has a *long* stock position (that is, he or she already owns the underlying stock), he or she hopes for the price of the stock to *increase*. The risk of the position, a market price decline, may be offset by either buying a put (known in options language as a *protective put or portfolio insurance*), or by selling a call *(a covered call and* not *a naked call)*. The more conservative hedge is a protective put. If the investor has a *short* stock position (that is, he or she does not own the underlying stock), he or she hopes for the price of the stock to *decline*. The risk of the position, a market price increase, may be offset either by buying a call or by selling a put. The more conservative hedge is buying a call. Note that writing options entails additional risk beyond only the loss of the premium as associated with buying options.

The above paragraph and concepts are shown graphically in Figure 16-2 below

Figure 16-2

Using Options to Protect a Position

	Buy = Long	Sell = Write = Short
CALL	↑ (Right to Buy)	↓ (Obligation to Sell)
PUT	↓ (Right to Sell)	↑ (Obligation to Buy)

If an investor is *long*, the risk is that the market will fall, which is a downward arrow. Therefore to hedge the position, select a position with a downward arrow. Accordingly, this is a *long put* or a *short call*. If the investor is short, the risk is that the market will rise, which is an upward arrow. Therefore to hedge the position, select a position with an upward arrow. Accordingly, that is a *long call* or a *short put*.

Sometimes, an investor may hedge his or her downside risk on a long position of stock by not expending any immediate out-of-pocket cash. This is known as a *cashless collar*. In this strategy, the investor sells an out-of-the-money covered call and uses the premium received to offset the cost of an out-of-the-money put option. The maturity date of this collar may range from several months to a number of years, and both options may be written to expire simultaneously. The concept behind the cashless (or *zero cost*) collar is to protect a gain on the underlying stock without the cost of purchasing a put option on the stock.

Example 16-3: Assume that an investor is long 100 shares of WLA stock that is currently trading at $50.00 per share. He enters into a cashless collar by buying a put (long put) with an exercise price of $45.00 per share at $3 (or $300 per contract since each contract is for a round lot of 100 shares of stock) and selling a call (short covered call) with an exercise price of $60.00 per share at $3 (or an offsetting $300). Therefore, his net cost of the option is zero. If the stock should decline below $45, the investor can *put* the stock to the writer of the option at $45.00 per share:

Premium received from selling call (1 contract)	$300
Cost of put (1 contract)	($300)
Call expires worthless	0
Gain from exercising put ($50 - $45)	$500
Loss in stock value	($500)
Net gain	$ 0

However, his upside potential is limited to $1,000:

Premium received from selling call (1 contract)	$300
Cost of put (1 contract)	($300)
Put expires worthless	0
Gain from call being exercised ($60 - $50)	$1,000
Net gain	$1,000

Also note that, should the stock price fall between $45 and $60 per share, both the put and call expire worthless and the value of the stock holdings would be the same as if there were no collar.

MULTIPLE OPTION TRANSACTIONS

Investors can also simultaneously buy or sell more than one option contract on the same or opposite sides of the market. Generally, these transactions are known as *spreads, straddles,* or *combinations* and, like basic option transactions, may be used either by traders (speculators) to speculate on a security's price movement or by hedgers to limit position costs and risks. Our focus, of course, will be on the use of multiple option transactions as a *hedging* (not speculative) strategy.

Spreads

A *spread* is the simultaneous purchase of one option and sale of another option on the *same* side or position within the market. For example, a *call or bull spread* is the purchase of a call at one exercise price (a long call) and the sale of a call at a higher exercise price (a short call) at the same time. The premium received from selling the higher exercise call is used to offset the premium paid for the lower exercise price call. Similarly, a *put* or *bear spread* is the purchase of a put at one exercise price (a long put) and the sale of a put at a lower exercise price (a short put) at the same time. Again, the premium received from writing one put is used to offset the premium paid in buying the other put.

Straddles

A *straddle* is the simultaneous purchase of one option and sale of another option on *opposite* sides or positions within the market. For example, a *long straddle* is the simultaneous purchase of a call option and a put option with the same exercise price, usually at-the-money. Similarly, a *short straddle* is the simultaneous selling of a call option and a put option for the same exercise price; again, usually at-the-money.

A long straddle is a bet on *high* volatility. The long straddle makes money if the stock price moves significantly either up or down. A short straddle is a bet on *low* volatility. The short straddle makes money as long as the stock price does not change too much.

> **Example 16-4 *(long straddle)*:** Assume that an investor/hedger buys an RCC November 50 call at 3 and an RCC November 50 put at 4. The current market price of RCC stock is $44.00 per share. Therefore, her maximum potential gain on this long straddle is unlimited on the call option and is $4,400 per contract on the put option, if the stock price falls to zero. (Note, however, that the amount of total gain will be reduced by the $700 of premiums paid for the options.) The maximum loss is, therefore, $700 or the total of the premiums paid for both the call and put ($300 + $400).

> **Example 16-5 *(short straddle)*:** Continue with the facts of Example 16-4 and RCC stock, but now assume that the investor/hedger sells an RCC November 45 call at 4 and an RCC November put at 5. (Again, note that the current market price of RCC stock is $44.00 per share.) Therefore, her potential maximum gain is $900 or the total of the premiums received for both the call and put ($400 + $500). The maximum loss on this short straddle is unlimited on the call option and is $4,400 per contract on the put, if the stock price falls to zero.

Combinations of Calls and Puts

A *combination* is composed of a call and a put option with *different* exercise prices and/or dates of expiration. Combinations are similar to long straddles in investor strategy. That is, the investor/hedger will use a combination if he or she expects substantial volatility in the price of the underlying stock (on which the options are written), but is not certain of the direction in which its price will actually move. Sometimes, the investor/hedger will use a combination rather than a long straddle because a combination is less expensive to establish if both the call and put option are currently out-of-the-money.

NON-EQUITY OPTIONS

An investor/hedger will use non-equity options for much the same reason as options purchased or written on equities—to offset the magnitude of his or her loss if the market value of the underlying asset declines. However, because the underlying asset is not a share of stock, non-equity options have different characteristics. We will briefly discuss three types of non-equity options, including 1) index options; 2) interest rate options; and 3) options purchased or written on foreign currencies.

Index Options

Options purchased or written on indexes allow investors to hedge against market swings. These options may be based on the movement of broad-based or narrow-based indexes. Broad-based indexes are representative of the entire market and include the S&P 500, the Russell 2000, the Wilshire 5000 and the AMEX (American Stock Exchange) Major Market Index (MMI). Narrow-based indexes track the movement of market sectors, such as technology or health care.

There are some unique features of index options. Among them are:
1) *The multiplier:* Index options typically use a multiplier of $100 both to calculate the option's cost and the exercise price of the option.

2) *Exercise and settlement:* Index options settle in *cash* rather than in the delivery of a security (as do equity options). If the option is exercised, the writer of the option delivers cash equal to the intrinsic value of the option to the buyer or holder.

3) *Settlement price:* When index options are exercised, their settlement price is based on the closing value of the index on the day of exercise, *not* on the value at the time of exercise. For example, if an investor exercises an option at 9 AM Eastern time, the settlement price is based on that day's later closing price (typically 4:30 PM Eastern).

4) *Position limits:* Unlike equity options that typically have "position limits"(or the sum of all like option contracts held with various brokers) that may be assumed either by the buyer or by the writer, there are currently *no* position limits established for index option contracts.

An example of the exercise of an index option, and the resulting profit or loss to the investor/hedger, follows:

Example 16-6: Assume that an investor is long an XMI January 410 call at 8 ½. At the expiration date of the call, the XMI option is at 430. Accordingly, because this call is in-the-money by an index amount of 20, it would be exercised. The writer of the option must then deliver cash equal to the intrinsic value (in-the-money) amount to the holder. Thus, the amount that must be delivered is $2,000 (the 20 point spread times the $100 multiplier). The holder has a profit of $1,150, since the $2,000 cash received must be reduced by the $850 premium paid (8 ½ times $100) for the call option.

Like equity options generally, if an investor/hedger believes that the market will decline in value, he or she can either buy an index put or sell (write) an index call. If the investor/hedger believes that the market will rise, he or she can either buy an index call or sell (write) an index put.

Interest Rate Options

Interest rate options permit an investor/hedger to protect against fluctuations of interest rates. There are two types of interest rate options: price-based options and yield-based options. *Price-based* options are options on U.S. Treasury securities and allow investors to protect against changes in the price of those securities because of interest rate changes. *Yield-based* options are also based on U.S. Treasury securities, but allow investors to protect against changes in yield, instead of changes in price. Yield-based options have a *direct* relationship to interest rates versus price-based options that have an *inverse* relationship to such rates (recall that bond prices move inversely to interest rates).

> **Example 16-7:** A yield-based option with an exercise price of 45 reflects a yield of 4.5%. If an investor buys this option at a premium of 2 1/2, and interest rates *increase* to 5.5%, he receives cash equal to the intrinsic value amount of 10 points. Since the multiplier for yield-based options is also $100 (like index options and Example 16-6), 10 points of intrinsic value multiplied by $100 totals $1,000. Therefore, the investor will profit in the amount of $750 ($1,000 less the $250 premium cost to buy the option).

With respect to *price-based* options, an investor/hedger who expects interest rates to increase would buy a put or write a call on U.S. Treasury securities, since the price of the securities would fall with rising interest rates.. If interest rates are expected to fall, an investor/hedger would buy a call or write a put on U.S. Treasury securities, since the price of the securities would rise with falling interest rates.

With respect to *yield-based* options, if the investor/hedger anticipates that interest rates will fall, he or she would purchase a yield-based put. Conversely, if the investor/hedger anticipates interest rates to rise, he or she would purchase a yield-based call.

Foreign Currency Options

Foreign currency options (FCOs) allow investors/hedgers to protect themselves against fluctuating currency exchange rates. Currency options are available on Canadian and Australian dollars, the British pound, the Euro, and the Japanese yen, among others. Importers and exporters frequently also use these options to hedge against currency exchange rate risk. The exercise prices for most of these options are quoted in U.S. cents. Thus, an exercise price of 180 British pounds means that the Pound must be bought or sold for 180 U.S. cents ($1.80) if the option contract is exercised. Japanese yen are quoted in one-hundreth of one cent. Therefore, Japanese yen trading at ¥120 per dollar would be quoted at 83 ($0.0083).

Finally, you should note that an *inverse* relationship exists between the exchange rate of the U.S. dollar and that of a foreign currency. Thus, if an investor/hedger believes that the value of a foreign currency is going to *rise*, he or she should buy a call option or sell (write) a put option on that currency. If the investor/hedger believes that the value of a foreign currency is going to *fall*, he or she should buy a put option or sell (write) a call option on that currency.

Example 16-8: A U.S. importer must pay for Japanese television sets in the Japanese yen currency within three months. In the meantime, the importer is concerned that the value of the U.S. dollar will *fall* relative to the yen (and the value of the Japanese yen will rise costing him more U.S. dollars). Therefore, the importer should purchase a call option on the Japanese yen to lock in the purchase price of the amount of yen needed at the end of the three months.

It is important to remember the inverse relationship between foreign currencies and the U.S. dollar. If the U.S. dollar is *rising (strengthening)*, the value of the foreign currency is *falling* in relative terms, so the investor/hedger should buy a *put* option (write a call) on that foreign currency. If the U.S. dollar is *falling (weakening)*, the value of the foreign currency is *rising*, so the investor/hedger should buy a *call* option (write a put) on that currency.

INCOME TAX RULES FOR OPTIONS

There are three possible practical consequences of an investor/hedger that enters into an equity option transaction:

1) The option can expire unexercised (in other words, the option is out-of-the-money and has no intrinsic value). If this happens, the buyer of the option loses the premium and the seller profits from the receipt of the premium.

2) The option can be exercised. If this happens, the investor/hedger either buys or sells the underlying stock depending on his or her position within the market.

3) The option may be *closed out*. This means that if the investor/hedger has *purchased* an option, he or she can *sell* the option prior to its expiration. If the investor/hedger has *sold* an option, he or she can *purchase* the option prior to its expiration. Notice that when *closing out*, the second transaction is always the *opposite* of the first transaction. In turn, whether the investor/hedger makes or loses money depends on the respective prices of the premiums paid or received initially.

For income tax purposes, options are considered to be *capital assets*, thus capital gain or loss treatment applies to the three practical consequences just described. Furthermore, the exercise of an option does *not* generate a capital gain or loss until a subsequent purchase or sale (a *closing* transaction) of the underlying stock takes place. Finally, the IRS does not allow the use of the normal nine-month option to postpone the sale of stock in order to generate long-term capital gains treatment. As you should surmise by now, the type of options that result in the sale of stock are long puts and in-the-money calls. If, at that time, the underlying stock has been held 12 months or less prior to the purchase of the put or sale of the call, the resulting gain is classified as *short-term* in nature.

While the tax consequences of options will be discussed further in chapter 18 of this text entitled the "Taxation of Investment Vehicles," Table 16-1 below summarizes the tax implications of option strategies in accordance with each of the three possible practical consequences.

Table 16-1

Strategy	Option Expires	Option Exercised	Option "Closed Out"
Buy a call	Capital loss	Cost Basis = Exercise Price + Premium Paid	Capital gain or loss
Sell a call	Capital gain	Sale Proceeds = Exercise Price + Premium Received	Capital gain or loss
Buy a put	Capital loss	Sale Proceeds = Exercise Price – Premium Paid	Capital gain or loss
Sell a put	Capital gain	Cost Basis= Exercise Price – Premium Received	Capital gain or loss

IMPORTANT CONCEPTS

Hedging/hedger	Uncovered/ naked
Speculation	Protective put
Futures contract	Cashless collar
Commodities	Spread
Offset	Bull spread
Long position	Bear spread
Short position	Straddle
Call option	Long straddle
Put option	Short straddle
Option premium	Combination of call and put
Intrinsic value of an option	Index option
Time value of an option	Interest rate option
Bullish	Price-based option
Bearish	Yield-based option
Buyer/holder	Foreign currency option (FCO)
Seller/writer	*Closing out* position
Covered call	Capital assets

QUESTIONS FOR REVIEW

1. What is the difference between an investor who is *speculating* and an investor who is *hedging?* Which strategy is designed to *reduce* investor risk?

2. What are the three investment tools of an investor/hedger?

3. What is a *futures contract* and how does it differ from a *forward contract*?

4. What are the three primary types of futures contracts?

5. How does a futures contract differ from a securities transaction that is executed via the use of a margin account?

6. What is the primary method of settling (*closing out*) a futures contract?

7. If a farmer is long his crop, what does he do to "hedge" in the commodities market? Explain.

8. In the options market, which party has the obligation to buy or sell the underlying security? How does this differ from the futures market?

9. There are four basic positions in the options market. What are these positions?

10. What two types of values are reflected in the premium charged for an option? Explain each value.

11. Complete the following sentences: If an investor buys a call option, he or she is _____ on the prospects for the underlying stock. If an investor sells or writes a call option, he or she is_____ on the prospects for the underlying stock.

12. What are four reasons why an investor would *purchase* a call option? What are four reasons why an investor would *sell* a call option?

13. Complete the following sentences: If an investor buys a put option, he or she is _____ on the prospects for the underlying stock. If an investor sells or writes a put option, he or she is _____ on the prospects for the underlying stock.

14. What are three reasons why an investor would *purchase* a put option? What are three reasons why an investor would *sell* a put option?

15. What are a *protective* put and a *covered call* and why is each used by an investor?

16. What is a *cashless* or *zero cost collar* and why is it used by an investor?

17. Contrast a *spread* to a *straddle*.

18. If an investor is fairly certain that the market will not decline, but nevertheless wants to limit his or her amount of possible loss, what types of hedging strategies might he or she use? Explain.

19. If the investor is fairly certain that the market will not increase, but nevertheless wants to limit his or her amount of possible loss, what types of hedging strategies might he or she use? Explain.

20. When does an investor use a *long straddle*? In what circumstances is a *short straddle* used?

21. If a *combination of calls* and *puts* is used, what does this mean? When will such a strategy be used by an investor?

22. List three types of non-equity options.

23. What are four unique features of an index option?

24. What is the difference between a *price-based* and a *yield-based* option?

25. If an investor expects the U.S. dollar to strengthen against the Japanese yen, and he wants to protect against exchange rate risk, what should he do? Explain.

26. There are three practical consequences in any option transaction. What are they?

27. For purposes of federal income taxation, an option is considered what kind of asset? As a result, how are all gains or losses taxed?

SUGGESTIONS FOR ADDITIONAL READING

Tools and Techniques of Investment Planning, 2nd edition, Stephen R. Leimberg, Robert T. LeClair, Robert J. Doyle, Jr., and Thomas R. Robinson, The National Underwriter Company, 2006.

Investments: An Introduction, 9th edition, Herbert B. Mayo, Thomson/ South-Western, 2008.

Investment Analysis and Portfolio Management, 9th edition, Frank K. Reilly and Keith C. Brown, Thomson/South-Western, 2009.

The Wall Street Journal Guide to Money and Investing, 3rd edition, Kenneth M. Morris and Virginia B. Morris, Fireside Publishing, 2004.

CHAPTER SEVENTEEN

Asset Allocation and Portfolio Diversification

• • •

This chapter takes up the topics of asset allocation and portfolio diversification. There is likely no more important single factor contributing to the long-term investment performance of a portfolio than one that is structured using proper asset allocation principles. Further, diversification has been shown to be a key determinant in eliminating the unsystematic (unique) risk of a portfolio.

Upon completing this chapter, you should be able to:

- Explain the primary determinants of portfolio performance
- Describe the types of asset allocation
- Identify forms of asset allocation implementation strategies, including the use of a mathematical optimizer
- Identify strategies for managing concentrated investment portfolios
- Discuss factors that should be considered in the construction of a tax-efficient portfolio
- Summarize how asset allocation and portfolio diversification principles may assist in the tax efficiency of a portfolio

BACKGROUND/DETERMINANTS OF PORTFOLIO PERFORMANCE

What factors determine portfolio performance? A considerable amount of academic research has been conducted attempting to answer this question. Perhaps the most notable of these studies is a 1986 article in the *Financial Analyst Journal* by Gary P. Brinson, L. Rudolph Hood, and Gilbert L. Beebower, otherwise known as the (first) "Brinson study." This study uses a database of 91 corporate portfolios, ranging in size from $700 million to $3 billion in assets, over a 40-quarter time frame from the years 1974 through 1983. All portfolios were separated into three traditional asset classes: cash/cash equivalents, bonds (debt), and common stock (equity).

As a premise, the authors of the study hypothesized that there are only three fundamental decisions that a portfolio manager makes that have a discernable impact on portfolio performance. These decisions are as follows:

1. *Security selection:* This is an outgrowth of the *active management style* of portfolio management; that is, to what extent does actively selecting a specific security within the three asset classes contribute to overall portfolio performance.
2. *Weighting/timing:* This is the active decision by a portfolio manager to over- or underweight a specific asset class relative to the manager's *normal* or long-term asset allocation. It is also related to a market timing strategy since this weighting takes place according to changing market conditions.
3. *Investment policy:* An allocation among asset classes (and their respective weights) is a part of any credible investment policy. Such a policy is not really optional, since an investor has either implicitly (by default) or explicitly (in writing and as part of an investment policy statement) adopted some form of investment policy and asset allocation strategy.

After framing the study with the above decisions, the authors then ran a sophisticated quantitative analysis technique, known as *regression analysis*, to determine the contribution of each decision to the actual ending performance of a model portfolio. The results were quite striking, although discouraging to those portfolio managers who practice either active security selection or over- or underweighting among asset classes. Specifically, the Brinson study discovered that active security selection *reduced* the ending returns below a strictly passive portfolio by 0.36 % and weighting/timing also *lost* another 0.66 % from the portfolio's ending returns. Together, these two decisions resulted in an *underperformance* of the portfolio by 1.02 % as compared to passive management and a sound investment policy.

Instead, the Brinson study found that *over 93 % of the variation* in the actual portfolio ending performance could be traced to the *investment policy and, by extension, the asset allocation decision.* To quote the conclusion of the study:

> "Although active investment strategy may result in significant returns in some instances, these are dwarfed by the return contributions from investment policy, that is, the selection of appropriate asset classes and their normal weighting deriving from that policy."

Further, in 1991, Brinson updated his study based on data from 82 large pension (institutional) plans for the period between 1977 and 1987. This (second) updated study reconfirmed Brinson's earlier research and concludes :

> "For our sample of pension plans, active investment decisions by plan sponsors and managers, both in terms of security selection and timing, did little to improve performance over the 10-year period from December 1977 to December 1987."

As a result, it is critical to recognize that the initial asset allocation decision (staying within the original weighting percentages deriving from this decision) is likely the *single most important factor* that determines actual portfolio performance over an extended period of time.

TYPES OF ASSET ALLOCATION

Strategic Asset Allocation

Strategic asset allocation is used to determine the long-term asset class weights in a portfolio. Typically, long-term historical average asset rates of return, risk, and covariance are used as estimates of future risk-adjusted performance. Efficient frontiers are generated using this historical rate of return information and the investor then decides which asset mix is appropriate given his or her risk tolerance and financial goals (over a pre-determined time horizon). As a result, a *constant-mix* (or weighting) asset allocation is determined with periodic rebalancing done to adjust the portfolio to the specified weights subsequent to actual performance.

Rebalancing is used in strategic asset allocation only in response to changes in the investment life cycle of the client or to reestablish the initial asset mix. Unlike in tactical asset allocation (discussed next), rebalancing is *not* done in strategic allocation to capture additional return due to changing market conditions. Rather, the portfolio manager determines the long-term asset allocation that is best suited for the particular investor by utilizing information from both the secondary market and from that investor. However, once the asset mix is established, the manager does not attempt to constantly adjust it in an effort to take advantage of market swings or overall investor sentiment.

Life-cycle 401(k) mutual funds are an example of rebalancing that is done in the context of a strategic asset allocation orientation. In these types of funds, portfolio managers vary the initial asset allocation based on the client's advancing age and/or associated risk tolerance (for example, safety of principal becomes more important as the investor approaches retirement), but market conditions or timing does *not* play a part. The life-cycle adjustment that takes place is based on tried-and-true characteristics of investors, proven over the years to generate the optimal risk-adjusted rate of return possible. An investor's life cycle consists of four phases: (1) growth, (2) consolidation, (3) spending, and (4) gifting. Each phase typically coincides with the investor's age, professional career, and retirement.

Tactical Asset Allocation

In contrast to the strategic approach, *tactical asset allocation (TAA)* continuously adjusts class mix in the portfolio in an attempt to take advantage of changing market conditions and overall investor sentiment. With TAA, these adjustments are driven *solely* by perceived changes in the relative values of the three traditional asset classes (cash/cash equivalents, bonds, and common stock). In effect, TAA is a *market timing approach* to portfolio management that is intended to increase exposure to a particular asset class when its performance is anticipated to be above average (and decrease exposure to this class when its performance is expected to be less than average).

Tactical asset allocation is fundamentally based on the concept of *mean reversion* which maintains that, whatever a security's actual historical performance, the security will eventually revert or regress to its long-term average or mean value. This analysis is normally done by comparing the performance of one asset class to another. Therefore, for example, assume that the ratio of common stocks' historical return to that of bonds is 1.25. This means that stocks are perceived to have approximately 25% more long-term return than that of bonds. However, if in the most recent investment year, common stock returns exceeded those of bond returns, the tactical investor or portfolio manager might determine that bonds are now undervalued relative to common stock. In response, the manager would then overweight (or re-adjust) the bond component of the portfolio from an initial 60-40 % stock-to-bond mix to a 50-50 % stock-to-bond asset allocation.

Finally, you should note that tactical asset allocation is characterized by a fundamentally *contrarian* approach to investing. As a result, the investor or portfolio manager will always be buying a traditional asset class—cash/cash equivalents, stocks, or bonds—that is *not* being purchased "by the herd" or the majority of marketplace investors.

Insured Asset Allocation

A third form of asset allocation strategy that is sometimes used is that of *insured asset allocation*. This form of asset allocation (like tactical asset allocation) results in continuing adjustments to the initial portfolio mix, but does so as the result of changes in the investor's *wealth position*. For example, increasing portfolio values increases the investor's wealth and, consequently, should accentuate his or her ability to handle risk. In turn, this means that the investor should be able to increase his or her exposure to risky assets. Conversely, a decrease in the overall value of the portfolio reduces the investor's wealth, meaning that his or her ability to handle risk should also decrease and the investor would likely reduce his or her exposure to risky assets.

Selection of a Type of Asset Allocation

The type of asset allocation that will be used likely depends on the investor's or manager's portfolio management style. Certainly, an investor or manager who believes in *active portfolio management* (and, thus, that the market is inherently *inefficient*) will tend towards *tactical asset allocation*. Alternatively, an investor or manager who adopts more of a long-term *buy-and-hold* strategy (passive management style) will find *strategic asset allocation* to be preferable. Finally, an investor who is very wealth-management oriented may find *insured asset allocation* to best meet his or her investment-planning goals. Regardless, as the Brinson studies show, a thoughtful analysis of which asset allocation technique to adopt, and subsequent adherence to this technique throughout the investor's time horizon, is critical, since the mix of an investor's assets constitutes the primary factor impacting long-term portfolio performance.

ASSET ALLOCATION IMPLEMENTATION STRATEGIES

There are a number of practical strategies that investors or portfolio managers may wish to adopt to assist in implementing the asset allocation selected. Among these are model portfolios, judgmental intuition, multiple scenario analysis (MSA), and/or mathematical optimizers.

Model Portfolios

Perhaps the simplest solution for the investment advisor or portfolio manager is to adopt the use of a portfolio model to develop and implement an appropriate asset allocation. Such a model is often provided by the sponsors of an investment product or family of products. Specifically, the investment advisor uses a questionnaire to determine the client's risk tolerance and, after answering a few additional standard questions provided by the model, inputs the answers and risk tolerance into a *black box* that, in turn, generates the appropriate allocation. For example, an individual who is 48 years old, is just beginning to save for retirement, is self-supporting and has a moderate risk tolerance, may find an asset allocation of 50 percent growth stocks, 20 percent income stocks, 20 percent investment grade bonds, and 10 percent cash equivalents to be appropriate.

However, there are several limitations on the use of any of these models, including:

1. The lack of specific customization to a client's particular financial goals and current cash flow situation;
2. The prevalence of a *one size fits all* mentality; for example, when using a standardized model, the investment advisor may have no real appreciation of the specifics of the model's underlying assumptions, such as its expected returns, standard deviations, and correlation coefficients;
3. The relevance of the *asset class benchmark* used by the model, tailored to the advisor's own investment style; for example, if the advisor has a pre-conceived bias against the use of corporate bonds, using the Lehman Brothers Bond Index as an appropriate *benchmark* may be impractical; and
4. The lack of tax efficiency of some models wherein they either ignore or do not properly attribute the impact of income tax factors involved in the construction of an optimal asset allocation.

Judgmental Intuition

This is an approach that, while acknowledging the necessity of an asset allocation strategy, develops a solution based on all art and no science. In other words, historical qualitative data plays little, if any, role, in determining the proper asset allocation and, instead, the advisor or manager implements his or her investment *hunches*. As an extension of this approach, sometimes an investment committee or investment club will try to determine the turning point in the performance of the traditional asset classes and thereby try to be "in the right (market) place at the right time." However, you should be aware that investing on emotions is *never* a wise investment model.

Multiple Scenario Analysis (MSA)

This is an approach familiar to financial planners and investment advisors. In fact, a variation of the approach, Monte Carlo Simulation, was first discussed in chapter 9 of this textbook. In its most abbreviated form, Multiple Scenario Analysis (MSA) is based on projecting a best-case and worst-case analysis using a number of what-if scenarios and, from within that number, selecting a most probable or likely outcome.

The problem with the MSA approach is the overwhelming amount of data that is generated and then, because of this fact, the tendency of portfolio managers to put an unfounded degree of confidence in the results. Furthermore, because MSA is so time consuming and expensive when generating this data, there is a bias *against* any short-term changes to the input factors. This, of course, makes the outcomes only as valid as the inputs used or, pejoratively, illustrates the dangers of a "garbage in-garbage out" strategy.

Mathematical Optimizers

A *mathematical optimizer* is the use of a computer software program that is designed to allocate investment assets and construct the optimal portfolio. It is analogous to the black box used by model portfolio providers to specify an appropriate asset allocation. Depending on the belief of the investment advisor or the portfolio manager, such a tool is either the solution to the asset allocation problem or the problem itself.

The benefits of mathematical optimizers are as follows:

- They are exact.
- They provide solutions for an infinite number of efficient portfolios.
- They provide a mechanism for controlling the various components and sources of investment risk.
- They permit the manager to determine the portfolio's sensitivity to changes in expectations of market risk and return.
- They assist in the design of a procedurally prudent investment policy statement.

Nevertheless, mathematical optimizers may generate a result that is subject to *misleading exactness*. That is, the inputs may be subject to significant statistical errors and are, thus, fundamentally flawed. In addition, the conclusion of the optimizer may be counter-intuitive to the portfolio manager based on his or her knowledge of quantitative concepts and/or portfolio management theory. Another weakness is *over-optimization* where the optimal fit to historical trends and data do not reflect the actual market.

STRATEGIES FOR DEALING WITH CONCENTRATED PORTFOLIOS

Currently, this is one of the most vexing problems of portfolio managers, particularly those who manage money for corporate executives. Specifically, many executives hold a disproportionate percentage of their investment portfolio in their own employer's stock. As a result, this exposes them to considerable unsystematic (business) risk. While this risk may be significantly minimized by diversification of the portfolio into other stocks or securities, many executives are reluctant to dispose of their employer's stock, believing strongly that their own efforts will increase the stock's future market value.

Therefore, strategies for dealing with a concentrated portfolio are both important and difficult to implement. Nonetheless, there are some basic strategies that may be used to manage such a portfolio, including the sale or gifting of some or all of the position, the use of options, variable prepaid forward contracts, a charitable remainder trust (CRT), and/or an exchange fund. Each is now briefly discussed.

Sale of Some or All of the Position

There are various forms of sales that may be used to minimize the unsystematic risk of the concentrated portfolio. Of course, the simplest of these is the outright sale of all or some of the executive's stock position. However, beyond the practical problem of obtaining the executive's agreement to do this, his or her basis in the employer shares is typically *very small*. Accordingly, there will be a significant capital gains tax liability associated with the sale of the shares, a fact that encourages the executive to continue retaining the shares.

An alternative to the outright sale is the installment sale or, sometimes, the private annuity. However, the former (the installment sale) will also result in income tax consequences during the executive's lifetime, as well as potentially disadvantageous estate tax consequences should the executive die during the term of the installment contract. In turn, while the disadvantageous estate tax consequences may be eliminated by executing a self-canceling installment note (SCIN), additional income tax liability results to the executive's estate with the implementation of the SCIN (consider the forgiveness-of-debt income tax rule). Finally, entering into a private annuity with a family member may prove a viable option for the executive, but the obligor of the annuity must be trusted longer-term to make good on the annuity payments due the annuitant, since such a contract may not be *collateralized* with the underlying employer stock.

Gifting of Some or All of the Position

This alternative does avoid the income tax consequences associated with a sale of employer stock (since the making of a gift is excluded from the definition of gross income). Nevertheless, unless proceeding carefully and with the advice of a competent tax advisor, gifting of the stock to others (likely family members) may result in the imposition of sizeable federal and/or state gift taxes. In addition, the income tax basis associated with a lifetime gift is usually *carried over* to the donee, meaning that he or she is ultimately responsible for the payment of income taxes due on sale. Therefore, unless the donee is in a lower marginal income tax bracket than the donor, this could result in a greater income tax liability being paid on the position than if the stock had remained in the name of the executive.

The Use of Options

The use of options and derivatives has been discussed in previous chapters in this textbook and will not be reiterated here. However, the executive who uses options to minimize the investment risk of a concentrated position is now acting as a hedger, given the common understanding of that term. Specifically, he or she is taking an offsetting short position to the already-established long position generated by owning the employer stock. As a result, techniques such as the purchase of a protective put option or the selling of a covered call option to minimize the executive's downside risk of the employer stock decreasing in market value may prove valuable.

Variable Prepaid Forward Contracts

When using a variable prepaid forward contract, the executive agrees to sell a variable number of shares at some point in the future, typically between one and five years, in return for receiving an up-front cash advance. This cash advance is usually between 75 and 90 percent of the stock's current fair market value, and does not have to be repaid. Therefore, the executive can immediately reposition these funds to work in a diversified portfolio. The contract is then settled at expiration by delivery of a portion of all of the shares pledged in the contract, to be determined by the stock price at expiration. Taxes are also deferred until the contract's expiration, at which time the executive pays capital gains taxes on the difference between the proceeds from the cash advance and his or her cost basis (if any) in the employer shares.

The variable prepaid forward contract is structured similarly to an option collar (see chapter 16) such that the executive's *downside exposure* is protected by a floor amount and the appreciation potential is capped by a ceiling. The executive also retains ownership of the underlying employer shares and retains the right to any dividend payments from the shares, although the dividend is considered to be *non-qualified* for income tax purposes (i.e., does not qualify for preferential tax rates).

Charitable Remainder Trust (CRT)

A charitable remainder trust (CRT) is fundamentally an estate planning strategy and is best left for a detailed discussion in an estate planning textbook. But when a CRT is established and assets are transferred to its trustee, a charitable income tax deduction becomes available that may be used to offset currently taxable income. In addition to the charitable deduction that is created, the asset transferred to the trust may be sold without any income tax liability since the CRT is a non-taxable (tax-free) entity. The proceeds from the sale of employer stock can then be reinvested to diversify the concentrated portfolio and generate income for the executive. As such, the CRT may prove to be the solution for the corporate executive who is looking to diversify out of a portfolio heavily invested in employer stock while, at the same time, affording the executive the right to the income from the stock that would be available if he or she retained some or all of the shares.

Exchange Fund

Some financial institutions offer so-called *exchange funds* that may be used in the management of a concentrated portfolio. Specifically, these funds permit the corporate executive (or any investor, for that matter) to contribute shares of his or her publicly-traded employer stock to the fund. In exchange, the executive receives a percentage income interest in the overall fund. Because the exchange is tax-free for income tax purposes, there are no immediate income tax consequences to the executive. In addition, because the fund also owns numerous securities other than the executive's employer stock, the executive receives an interest in a diversified fund.

There are some drawbacks, however, to the use of an exchange fund. Such fund is inherently illiquid; for example, investors must generally hold the shares of the fund for seven years to avoid incurring a tax liability. Further, federal income tax law mandates that 20 percent of the fund's assets be invested in relatively illiquid assets like real estate. Finally, the portfolio that the executive eventually owns may not be optimal, providing inefficient diversification plus a less-than-probable expected rate of return.

CONSTRUCTION OF A TAX-EFFICIENT PORTFOLIO

One of the goals of any financial planner in creating a properly constructed and diversified portfolio should be to ensure that it is tax-efficient. That is, while it is imprudent in most instances to establish a completely tax-free portfolio (for example, a portfolio consisting entirely of municipal bond funds), it is a realistic goal to strive to maximize the amount of after-tax income possible from the portfolio. Accordingly, several variables and assumptions make up the foundation of any tax-efficient portfolio.

Variables and Assumptions in Portfolio Tax Management

A number of variables and assumptions impact the after-tax return of an investment portfolio. These include:

1. *The marginal income tax bracket of the investor:* Most academic studies divide taxpayer/investors into low and high income tax brackets when evaluating the after-tax rate of return of a particular investment. The maximum marginal income tax rate is currently 35% and the lowest is 10% (a spread of 25%). Historically, the spread between the highest and lowest rates is relatively small, but there is no doubt that a taxpayer in a higher marginal income tax bracket benefits proportionately more from a tax-free or tax-deferred investment than does the lower-bracket investor. This is shown in our previous discussion when computing the *taxable equivalent yield* (TEY) of a municipal bond. Accordingly, the marginal income tax bracket of the taxpayer/investor should be an important factor in portfolio development and analysis.

2. The *holding period of the investor:* This is simply the length of time a particular investment is likely to be owned without a significant change or repositioning of the portfolio. Currently, an investment (or *capital asset* for income tax purposes) needs to be owned by the taxpayer for a period of one year and a day in order for it to be eligible for preferential tax treatment as a *long-term* asset. As a result, any gains from the sale of the investment will qualify for either a 15% or 5% tax rate depending on the taxpayer/investor's marginal income tax bracket (a taxpayer in the 25% or higher marginal tax bracket pays capital gains taxes at the rate of 15% and a taxpayer in the 10 or 15% marginal tax bracket receives the 5% rate – a zero rate in 2009 and 2010). The eligibility for this lower potential tax rate should, of course, be considered when analyzing whether to sell an investment. However, this consideration should *not* override the economic determination that a stock that has otherwise performed poorly should likely be sold.

3. *Relative interest, dividends, and capital gains:* The term *relative* here refers to the assumption that is made with respect to the income tax components of the investment's total return. Specifically, each of these three components (interest, dividends, and capital gains) receives different tax treatment. For example, interest is taxable as ordinary income and so-called *qualifying dividends* are taxable as ordinary income but are entitled to a preferential rate. Likewise, capital gains derive a tax advantage from the sale of a capital asset (like a stock or bond). Therefore, an investment's return in the form of its taxable component(s) needs to be analyzed carefully by the investor or portfolio manager. Indeed, one of the fundamental principles of effective tax management is to *convert income* from an ordinary income form (such as interest) to that of capital gains (deriving from the sale or disposition of a capital asset).

4. *Turnover of assets:* This variable primarily applies to assets that are *pooled* or combined together. The most common example is that of the open-end investment company or mutual fund. Generally, the *more frequently* that the assets within a pooled fund experience *turnover* (the more frequently they are bought and sold within a given period of time), the *less tax-efficient* is the fund. That is, if the mutual fund portfolio manager frequently sells or disposes of the investments within the fund, there is often a greater income tax consequence to the mutual fund shareholder. This is because, by law, a mutual fund must *pass through* its

tax gains or losses to its shareholders to avoid certain disadvantageous tax consequences at the fund level. Accordingly, a mutual fund investor that is interested in a tax-efficient fund should look closely at its *turnover ratio* of assets. The *greater* this ratio, the *less* income tax efficient is the fund.

Timing of Capital Gains and Losses and the Netting Process

As most financial planners and investment advisors are aware, a *netting* process occurs with respect to the reporting of capital gains and losses. That is, gains or losses are first grouped according to whether they are short term (an asset sold after being owned for only one year or less) or long term (an asset sold after being owned for more than one year). Next, short-term capital losses are applied to reduce short-term capital gains, resulting in a net short-term capital gain or loss for the year. The same procedure then applies with the application of long-term capital losses against long-term capital gains.

Taxpayers who have capital losses (whether short term or long term) that exceed the capital gains in a given year must follow a special set of rules. Specifically, losses from the sale of capital assets are allowed *only* to the extent of an individual's net capital gains for the year of sale *plus* up to $3,000 of excess losses. If the net capital loss for the year exceeds $3,000, the taxpayer may carry forward the excess amount to future years until it is completely depleted. Any capital loss that is carried forward retains its original short-term or long-term character in that year. Finally, when both a net short-term capital loss *and* a net long-term capital loss exist, the allowable $3,000 net capital loss is first treated as an offset to the short-term capital loss.

> **Example 17-1:** Assume that during the taxable year 2009, Joseph incurs a short-term capital loss of $1,000 and a long-term capital loss of $12,000. Based on this assumption, Joseph's total net capital loss for the year 2009 is $13,000. Of this amount, $3,000 is available to offset Joseph's other or *ordinary* income. Since the first $3,000 offsets the short-term capital loss, Joseph will fully utilize all of his short-term capital loss in the year 2009. He will then apply $2,000 of long-term capital loss in 2009 and will carry forward a $10,000 long-term capital loss to the next taxable year, 2010, and beyond.

Because of these special rules, it is very important that the taxpayer/investor consider the *time* at which he or she sells (or otherwise disposes of) an investment. A major advantage of investing in most securities is that the choice of this time is within the discretion of the investor. That is, there is no taxable event recognized unless the taxpayer chooses to incur one. For example, if the taxpayer is a pure *buy-and-hold* investor, it is unlikely that he or she will ever incur a capital gain or loss of his or her own choosing (since the *pass-through* tax treatment of mutual funds may apply) during his or her lifetime. Rather, assuming that the security appreciates in value, the taxpayer's heirs will likely receive a *step up* in the basis of the security, free of any capital gain taxation. It will then be up to the taxpayer's heirs to either continue to postpone recognition of a taxable event with respect to the inherited securities or to sell the investments at some future date.

Remember, the critical time frame for the taxpayer/investor to keep in mind is that of the *more-than-one-year* period mentioned earlier. If the taxpayer has owned (held) the investment asset for at least this amount of time, he or she will be entitled to a tax preference in the form of a reduced tax rate on any gains resulting from the sale of the asset. Alternatively, if the taxpayer has not yet held the asset for at least this time period prior to its disposition, ordinary or regular income tax treatment will apply. As noted, depending on the taxpayer's marginal income tax bracket, the sale of an investment prior to a *year and a day* may mean an additional tax rate of 20% (35% less 15%). Further, when translated to dollar terms across the broader portfolio, the taxable impact of multiple asset sales that are considered *long term* in nature may be significant.

Wash Sale Rule

Under the so-called *wash sale rule*, a taxpayer who realizes a loss on the sale or other disposition of stock or securities and also purchases those same securities during a prescribed time period may *not* claim the loss as a tax deduction. Specifically, this rule operates to disallow the claiming of a tax loss on the sale of the stock *if* the investor/taxpayer purchases "substantially identical" stock within a period beginning 30 days before the date of the sale and ending 30 days after the date of sale. Similarly, a loss realized on the closing of a short sale of stock or securities is disallowed if, within 30 days before or after the closing, substantially identical stock or securities are sold or another short sale of substantially identical stock or securities is entered into. The term *substantially identical* is defined in the Treasury Regulations, but is based on a test of facts and circumstances that takes into account the characteristics of one security as compared to the security with which it is replaced. Bonds or preferred stock are not ordinarily considered substantially identical to the common stock of the same issuer; however, they may be considered as such when the bonds or preferred stock are convertible into the common stock of the same corporation.

> **Example 17-2:** Sarah buys 200 shares of XYZ stock for $10,000. She sells all of these shares for $7,500 on December 2, 2009 and on December 30, 2009 she purchases 200 more shares of XYZ stock for $8,000. Therefore, because Sarah purchased *substantially identical* stock, she cannot deduct her loss of $2,500 on the sale of XYZ shares on her 2009 personal income tax return. (Note that the result would be the same if Sarah had purchased a $10,000 convertible bond issued by XYZ Corporation and had converted the bond into the 200 shares mentioned and had then sold--and repurchased--those shares in the same time frame.)

When a loss is disallowed because of the wash sale rule, the disallowed loss is subsequently *added to* the cost of the replacement stock or securities. The result is that the investor/taxpayer acquires a new adjusted basis in the reacquired stock or securities. Accordingly, this adjustment effectively operates to postpone the loss deduction until the sale or disposition of the replacement stock or securities beyond the prohibited time frame.

Example 17-3: Continuing with the facts of Example 17-2, Sarah subsequently adds the disallowed loss of $2,500 to the cost of the new 200 XYZ shares that she purchased. As a result, her adjusted basis in the new shares is $10,500 ($8,000 original cost plus the $2,500 loss she could not claim under the wash sale rule loss prohibition). Then, as long as Sarah does not sell the replacement shares prior to January 30, 2010 (and once again reacquire substantially identical shares), she can recognize the originally disallowed loss on a subsequent sale of the XYZ shares.

Finally, when there has been a wash sale, the holding period of the replacement securities *includes* the period that the taxpayer held the securities on which the loss was not deductible. This may result in the transformation of a short-term holding period into that of a long-term period, thus, qualifying the shares for preferential tax treatment.

Qualified Dividend Income

A dividend is the most common type of corporate stock distribution and is a distribution to the shareholder of either cash (a cash dividend) or property (a stock dividend) payable from the C corporation's current or accumulated earnings and profits. A dividend distribution is considered ordinary income to the investor/taxpayer and is *not* deductible by the distributing corporation. Therefore, *double taxation* of the corporation's earnings and profits occurs, first at the corporate entity level and next at the shareholder/investor level. However, effective January 1, 2003, *qualifying dividend income* to the shareholder/investor is taxable at a preferred rate of 15% or 5%, depending on the shareholder's marginal income tax bracket. Shareholders who are in the 25% or greater marginal income tax bracket receive a preferred flat rate of 15% on qualifying dividends, while those shareholders in the 10% or 15% bracket are eligible for the 5% flat rate (zero in the years 2009 and 2010). The 5% and 15% tax rates also apply to stocks that are held for more than one year before being sold at a taxable gain (the so-called *long-term capital gain preference*).

So what requirements must be met before a dividend is considered to be *qualified* for these favorable rates? For purposes of these rules, qualified dividend income is that received by a shareholder during the taxable year from both domestic and qualified foreign corporations. A qualified *foreign* corporation is one that is incorporated in a U.S. possession (such as Puerto Rico) or that is eligible for benefits of a comprehensive income tax treaty with the United States. In addition, corporations whose shares are traded as American Depository Receipts (ADRs) on an established U.S. securities market also are qualified foreign corporations. Qualified foreign corporations do *not* include foreign holding companies or those companies that are incorporated outside the U.S or a U.S. possession solely for purposes of investment (and not as an ongoing operating concern).

Most dividends payable from real estate investment trusts (REITs) are *not* eligible for the reduced or favorable rates that apply generally to qualified dividends. This is because most REITs do not pay corporate income taxes and, instead, are only *pass-through* entities (like an S corporation) to its shareholders. Nevertheless, a small number of dividends paid by REITs may be qualified and are eligible for the preferential rates. These exceptions include dividends paid by a REIT that are attributable to dividends received from a non-REIT corporation, such as a taxable REIT subsidiary, and income that was subject to tax at the REIT entity level when it distributes less than 100 percent of its taxable income.

Finally, in order to be a *qualified* dividend for income tax purposes, a separate holding period applies. Dividends received from a stock or mutual fund are not eligible for the reduced rates if the shareholder does not hold the share of stock for more than 61 days during the 121-day period beginning 60 days before the ex-dividend date of the stock. The ex-dividend date is the date following the record date on which the issuing corporation finalizes the list of shareholders who will receive the dividend. In the case of preferred stock, this holding period is extended to more than 91 days during the 181-day period beginning 90 days before the ex-dividend date. In turn, the ex-dividend date is defined as the first date following the declaration of a dividend on which the purchaser of the stock is not entitled to receive the *next* dividend.

Tax-Exempt Income

The best of all possible results is to not have the income from an investment taxed *at all*. This is referred to as *tax-exempt income*. Unfortunately, there are not many of these types of investments available. There are, however, several forms of debt instruments (bonds) that do generate income that is tax exempt for either federal, state, or local income tax purposes (and sometimes all three).

The first of these types of investments is a municipal bond issued by a state or local government. As discussed previously in chapter 2 of this text, these bonds usually come in one of two forms: either a *general obligation* (G.O.) bond used to finance the everyday operational needs of the state or local government or a *revenue* bond that is floated to finance the expense of a specific project, such as an airport. In both instances, the interest income earned on these investments is excluded from the recipient's taxable income for regular income tax purposes. This exclusion usually applies for both federal and state income tax purposes if the bondholder is also a resident of the state or local government issuing the bond. (You should note, however, that the interest from certain types of state or local government bonds issued for a private business purpose, such as the construction of an office park, is potentially subject to the federal alternative minimum tax (AMT). These are sometimes referred to as *private activity bonds* or, more colloquially, *AMT bonds*.)

There is also a second form of debt instrument that will produce tax-exempt income for some taxpayers. These are obligations issued by the U.S. Treasury in the form of Treasury bills, notes, and bonds (see chapter 2 of this text). While the interest earned on all of these obligations is subject to federal income tax, this same interest is exempt from income taxes levied by any state or local government. In common parlance, this result occurs because of a theory known as the *doctrine of reciprocity*. In other words, certain obligations issued by the federal government are taxable only at that level and not by the state. Conversely, certain obligations, such as a municipal bond investment that is purchased by a non-resident, may be taxable by the state, but not by the federal government.

Finally, before investing in tax-exempt issues, the taxpayer/investor should be aware that (due to the tax advantage) the nominal rate of return on such issues is often *less than* that of taxable obligations. However, in computing the tax-equivalent yield for individuals who would otherwise incur tax (particularly those in the higher marginal income tax brackets), the after-tax return of tax-exempt issues may well be *greater* than that of taxable issues.

TAX EFFICIENCY AND ASSET ALLOCATION

The frequency with which Congress changes marginal income tax rates is very familiar, particularly to financial planners and portfolio managers. Certainly, the most obvious impact of an increase in marginal tax rates is a reduction in the after-tax return on most investments. But, what about the impact of the rate increase on the relative desirability of bonds (as a proxy for a fixed-income type of investment) versus stocks (or a capital-appreciation type of investment)? It would seem clear that if a portfolio manager, in response to an increase in marginal tax rates, recommends an increase in the percentage of stocks, he or she is also recommending a higher risk portfolio. However, is this really the case? A particular study, commissioned by SEI Investments Company in July 1993, attempted to provide a definitive answer to this question.

The SEI study developed a ratio that measures the *rate of return to risk* for stocks and bonds. Accordingly, this ratio, referred to here as the *SEI ratio*, subtracted the inflation rate from the rate of investment return for the portfolio (for both the before- and after-tax return of stocks and bonds) and divided the result by the investment's standard deviation (or measure of absolute risk). Then, SEI calculated the *SEI advantage factor (SEI factor)*, a measure of the real rate of return of the investment per each unit of risk, as: SEI Ratio for stocks less SEI Ratio for bonds. The results are as shown in the following Table 17-1 below:

Table 17-1: Rate of Tax Return to Risk

	Before Tax Return		After Tax Return (Current)[1]		After Tax Return (New)[2]	
	Equity	Bonds	Equity	Bonds	Equity	Bonds
Real Rate of Return	6.50%	2.50%	3.35%	0.55%	3.35%	-0.10%
Risk (S.D.)	21.00	7.00	14.70	4.90	14.70	4.20
SEI Ratio	0.31	0.36	0.23	0.11	0.23	-0.02
SEI Factor	-0.05		0.12		0.25	

[1] For current after-tax rates, assumes a combined 30% ordinary and capital gains tax rate

[2] For new after-tax rates, assumes a 40% ordinary income tax rate (capital gains tax rate is unchanged)

Table 17-1 shows the relative advantage of stocks (or equity) over bonds in terms of a resulting before- and after-tax return. However, the startling fact about the findings of the study is that, as the table demonstrates, an increase in tax rates not only reduces the total investment return of stocks, but also reduces the total *risk* associated with such investment (from a standard deviation of 21.00 to one of only 14.70). In addition, the relative advantage of stocks over bonds (as measured by the *SEI advantage factor*) increases as the assumed ordinary income tax rate becomes greater (for example, from 0.12 with an assumed 30 percent ordinary and capital gains rate to 0.25 with an assumed 40% combined rate). Of course, this makes sense given that the interest return from bonds (or fixed-income types of investments) is taxable as ordinary income, so that the *higher* the ordinary income rate, the *less* the relative tax advantage of bonds as compared to stocks.

While the goal of portfolio income tax management is often debated (Is the goal to maximize the after-tax rate of return of the portfolio or to avoid as much tax liability as possible?), there is little doubt that taxes are the greatest artificially imposed impediment to wealth accumulation. As such, the financial planner that specializes in investment management and portfolio asset allocation ignores the impact of annual taxes only at the risk of his or her client's potential, total dollar loss. In addition, if the client assumes this income tax risk without being informed by the planner of the basic taxation of investments, the long-term relationship of planner to client is likely to be severely jeopardized.

IMPORTANT CONCEPTS

Asset allocation

Brinson study

Strategic asset allocation

Rebalancing

Tactical asset allocation

Insured asset allocation

Model portfolio

Multiple Scenario Analysis (MSA)

Mathematical optimizer

Concentrated portfolio

Charitable Remainder Trust (CRT)

Exchange fund

Tax-efficient portfolio

Asset turnover

Netting process

Holding period

Wash Sale Rule

Qualified dividend income

Tax-exempt income

Doctrine of Reciprocity

SEI study

QUESTIONS FOR REVIEW

1. What are three decisions that a portfolio manager could make that would have a discernable impact on portfolio performance? Which of these decisions have academic studies shown is likely the most important?

2. What is the conclusion of the Brinson study with respect to the asset allocation decision?

3. In *strategic* asset allocation, what is the role of portfolio rebalancing? Give an example of a type of mutual fund that uses these principles.

4. In *tactical* asset allocation, are the financial goals more important or are changing market conditions more important? Explain.

5. Define *insured* asset allocation and explain how it differs from both strategic and tactical asset allocation.

6. There are four types of asset allocation implementation strategies discussed in the chapter. What are they and what are several limitations on the use of any of these strategies?

7. Explain the following sentence: "Mathematical optimizers may generate a result that is subject to 'misleading exactness.'"

8. What is usually meant by the term *concentrated portfolio*? List six strategies that may be used in managing such a portfolio.

9. How is a charitable remainder trust (CRT) used in minimizing the unsystematic risk that is inherent in a concentrated portfolio?

10. What is an *exchange fund* and how does it differ from an *exchange traded fund*? (Note: See chapter 4 of this textbook to review the application of an *exchange traded fund*.)

11. What are four underlying variables and assumptions that impact the after-tax rate of return of an investment portfolio?

12. How is each of the following components of investment return taxed?

- Interest
- Dividends
- Capital appreciation

13. Complete the following sentence: The _____ the *turnover* of assets within a mutual fund, the _____ income-tax efficient is the fund. Explain your sentence completion.

14. What is meant by the phrase "netting of capital gains and losses"?

15. What is the *holding period* that applies before an investment sold at a gain qualifies for favorable income tax treatment? Then, what tax rates apply in such a situation?

16. What is the practical effect of an investment loss tax deduction being disallowed because of the so-called *wash sale rule*? What triggers the application of this rule?

17. What requirements must be met before a dividend distribution is considered to be *qualified* for favorable income tax treatment? Then, what tax rates apply in such situation?

18. What are two types of investments that generate tax-exempt income?

19. What is the *doctrine of reciprocity* and why is it important in the taxation of investments?

20. What was the conclusion of the *SEI study* and why is it important in portfolio tax management and asset allocation?

SUGGESTIONS FOR ADDITIONAL READING

Tools and Techniques of Investment Planning, 2nd edition, Stephen R. Leimberg, Robert T. LeClair, Robert J. Doyle, Jr., and Thomas R. Robinson, The National Underwriter Company, 2006.

Investments: An Introduction, 9th edition, Herbert B. Mayo, Thomson/ South-Western, 2008.

Investment Analysis and Portfolio Management, 9th edition, Frank K. Reilly and Keith C. Brown, Thomson/South-Western, 2009.

The Wall Street Journal Guide to Money and Investing, 3rd edition, Kenneth M. Morris and Virginia B. Morris, Fireside Publishing, 2004.

CHAPTER EIGHTEEN

Taxation of Investment Vehicles

• • •

This textbook concludes with a discussion of the taxation of investment vehicles. While much of this is best reserved for a formal textbook on income taxation and income tax planning, because of its importance to the financial planner, the basic principles involved in tax planning with investments are presented here.

Upon completing this chapter, you should be able to:

- Identify the basic concepts of our income tax system, including types of income
- Describe how to take advantage of tax-advantaged accounts in investing
- Explain the income tax treatment of investment interest expense
- Define personal interest expense and why it is important for investment tax planning
- Describe how distributions from a mutual fund are taxed
- Explain the general rules associated with the taxation of a stock or bond
- Identify characteristics of the taxation of insurance-based investment products
- Explain the three basic forms of real estate ownership and their taxable consequences
- Identify the taxation principles that apply to the sale or disposition of collectibles
- Describe the taxation of derivative investment vehicles, most notably options and/or futures

BASIC CONCEPTS

A fundamental income tax strategy is the conversion of ordinary income into capital gains income. However, to do this, the taxpayer first needs to invest in a *capital asset*. Fortunately, the majority of assets held for investment purposes easily fall within the Internal Revenue Code's definition of a capital asset and, therefore, typically qualify for preferential tax treatment. (The most notable exception to the definition of a capital asset is a life insurance product, which generates ordinary income for tax purposes.) In addition, for this preferential treatment to occur, a capital asset must be owned or held for a specified period of time, referred to as the *holding period* for the asset. Currently, this period is more than 12 months or one year, commonly referenced as *one year and a day*. Accordingly, if a capital asset (investment) is held for more than the required 12-month holding period, it becomes a *long-term asset* and is subject to lower income tax rates (either a flat rate of 5% [0% for 2009 and 2010] or 15% depending on the taxpayer/investor's marginal ordinary income tax bracket).

Additional income tax management or strategies include the avoidance of income and/or its deferral to a subsequent year. Avoidance techniques are best left to a course or textbook on income tax planning and will not be further discussed here. However, deferral techniques take advantage of tax-exempt trusts or accounts to postpone the recognition of taxable income from the current taxable year to a year or years into the future. Likely, the most notable of deferral techniques is an employer-sponsored, *qualified* retirement plan or a taxpayer's individual retirement account (IRA). In recent years, other deferral-of-income techniques, such as the Roth IRA, have also been added to the Internal Revenue Code to encourage individuals to save for their own retirement. All of these techniques operate from the basic tax principle that it is better to defer taxable income into a future year and use the magic of compound interest to accumulate as many before-tax dollars as possible before mandatory minimum distribution rules apply.

TYPES OF INCOME

As noted, for income tax purposes, there are two basic types of income that are possible: ordinary income and income from capital gains. However, three additional types of income are defined in the Treasury Regulations accompanying the *passive loss rules* and the taxpayer should be aware of them. These types of income are referred to as:

1. Active income
2. Portfolio income
3. Passive income.

Certainly, *passive income* is the most important for purposes of the passive loss rules, as only that type of income may be used to offset losses that are *passive* in nature, such as those deriving from a limited partnership investment. However, the definition of *active* income and *portfolio* income may also help us understand the difference between ordinary and capital gain income for tax purposes.

Active income, by definition, is any income that is *not passive*, or income from an investment activity in which the taxpayer *materially participates* (as defined in the Treasury Regulations). But, more specifically, active income includes a taxpayer's salary and wages or any income from a trade or business. Roughly, this also equates to *ordinary income* for tax purposes, whereby withholding also applies, as does taxability at the taxpayer's highest marginal tax rate under the progressive tax system.

On the other hand, *portfolio* income includes interest, dividends, annuities, and royalties, as well as gain or loss from the disposition of investment property that is *not* derived in the ordinary course of the taxpayer's trade or business. Roughly, this equates to income from investments or *capital gain income*, although we often need to go further and classify the kind of return that is generated in order to determine the precise tax treatment. For example, interest and dividend income from a security are taxed at ordinary income rates whereas gain on disposition of that security (or capital appreciation) will enjoy capital gains rates.

As noted previously, gains (or losses) from investment property may be either long term or short term in nature. Only long-term gains, however, receive a preferential rate of taxation. Generally, the maximum rate on long-term capital gains for investment property sold during 2009 and 2010 is 0 percent for taxpayers in the 10- or 15% marginal income tax brackets and 15%, to the extent that he or she is taxed at higher marginal rates (currently, through the year 2010, either 25%, 28%, 33%, or 35%). These rates are used for computing the regular income tax. Finally, short-term gains retain their character as capital-gain income (and, thus, must first be used to offset any capital losses), but are taxed at the same marginal rates as if the income were *ordinary* in nature.

DEFERRAL OF INCOME/TAX ADVANTAGED ACCOUNTS

Assume that, as a financial planner, you are advising a client who holds individual stocks and bonds in addition to both taxable and tax-deferred or tax-advantaged accounts, such as a traditional deductible or Roth IRA. What type of account do you recommend that the client use to position these individual stocks and bonds? Conventional wisdom suggests that the client should position his or her stock holdings in the taxable accounts and bonds in the tax-advantaged accounts for several reasons:

1. The highest ordinary income-generating investments (or here, bonds) should be protected from current taxation by placing them in the tax-advantaged account.

2. The lowest yielding investments (or here, stocks generating capital gains or qualifying dividends at lower rates) should be placed in the taxable account.

3. Capital gains may be deferred at the discretion of the taxpayer/investor. In other words, because the imposition of the taxable event at the date of sale is chosen by the taxpayer, he or she should position currently taxable income in the type of account with the least tax exposure to the investor.

As enticing as this wisdom is in theory, however, its practical implementation is often the subject of considerable discussion and analysis.

Some financial planners and portfolio managers argue that this approach to tax-efficient investing overlooks two very important points: 1) the economic goal of attempting to achieve the *maximum* possible total return for the investor, and 2) the existence of tax-free alternatives in the investment marketplace. With respect to the first point, the goal of any portfolio manager should be to maximize the efficient use of the tax-advantaged account. This may be accomplished by positioning the investments generating the *highest* taxable return in the tax-advantaged account (and not the lowest return as the conventional wisdom theory maintains). Further, the second point addresses the choice in the investment world between bonds that pay taxable income and bonds that do not (for example, municipal bonds). There is no similar choice for equities. Therefore, some planners and portfolio managers argue that the real choice is between sheltering income from *stocks*, whose qualifying dividends and capital gains are taxed at the same low rates, and *municipal bonds* whose return is in the form of tax-free income.

Tax-Advantaged Account Investing

While the positive impact of tax deferral through tax-advantaged accounts likely cannot be understated, this advantage comes at a price. Specifically, in most instances, when achieving tax deferral through the accumulation of investment wealth in a tax-advantaged account (including an employer-sponsored retirement plan) potential capital gain income is converted *back* into the ordinary-income form. In other words, investment income that may otherwise be taxed to an investor as capital-gain income (like stocks or mutual funds) is now taxable at potentially higher ordinary income marginal rates. This point is important to realize when the planner is doing both investment and retirement planning.

There is one major exception to this dilemma, however. This is the concept of *net unrealized appreciation (NUA)*, which applies in the case of lump-sum distributions made from certain types of qualified employer plans where employer securities are part of the distributable assets. These types of distributions are normally made in stock bonus types of retirement plans, including the well-known *employee stock ownership plan (ESOP)*. In these types of plans, the appreciation in the value of employer securities while held in the retirement plan trust is not taxable to the recipient at the time of *distribution*, but rather at the time of subsequent *sale* of the stock. The appreciation is, thus, *unrealized* for income-tax purposes and, accordingly, non-taxable. Further, once the employer stock is sold and the taxpayer/investor chooses to incur a taxable event, the previously untaxed appreciation in the stock *retains* its character as capital gain rather than as ordinary income. As a result, this is a significant tax-related reason why employer stock is an attractive component of any retirement portfolio, although investors do need to pay attention to prudent investment practices, such as the proper diversification of the retirement asset portfolio.

An example of the application of the net unrealized appreciation (NUA) concept follows:

> **Example 18-1:** Bruce participates in his employer's employee stock ownership plan (ESOP) and has recently received a lump-sum distribution of employer stock valued at $500,000. The market value of the employer stock that was contributed to Bruce's account over the years was $100,000 (basis to

the qualified plan trust). Therefore, at time of distribution of the stock, Bruce has net unrealized appreciation in the stock of $400,000 ($500,000 less $100,000). This appreciation is not taxed to Bruce until he subsequently sells the shares of employer stock in the secondary market, with any resulting gain taxable to Bruce at capital gains rates and on the excess of the amount realized upon sale over his basis in the stock. The amount of basis to the qualified plan trust ($100,000) is taxable to Bruce as ordinary income at the time of distribution.

Finally, you should note that, if the employer stock appreciates after the time of distribution to Bruce, the net unrealized appreciation portion of his gain is *always* taxed at long-term capital gain rates, regardless of his actual holding period. (In Example 18-1, this would be the $400,000 amount.)

INVESTMENT INTEREST EXPENSE

Investment interest expense (such as margin interest) on an investor's individual income tax return (IRS Form 1040) is deductible only to the extent of *net investment income*. *Net investment income* means the excess of investment income over investment expenses (not including investment interest expense). Investment income is gross income from property held for investment including: (1) property that produces interest, dividends, annuities, or royalties that are not derived in the ordinary course of a trade or business; (2) property that produces gain or loss not derived in the ordinary course of a trade or business from the sale or exchange of property that either produces item 1 types of income or that is held for investment (not including an interest in a passive activity); and (3) an interest in a trade or business activity that is not a passive activity and in which the taxpayer did not materially participate. Investment income, for purposes of computing the investment interest deduction, generally does not include net capital gain from the disposition of investment property. However, individuals may elect to treat all or any portion of such net capital gain as investment income by paying tax on the elected amounts at their ordinary income rates. The taxpayer may elect similar treatment for qualified dividend income. Thus, the taxpayer loses the benefit of the otherwise applicable maximum capital gains tax rate with respect to the elected amount. The election must be made on IRS Form 4952, Investment Interest Expense Deduction, on or before the due date of the tax return for the tax year in which the net capital gain or the qualified dividend income is recognized.

Having determined the amount of gross investment income, one needs to then deduct the allowable investment expenses (other than investment interest) to arrive at net investment income. An individual may deduct ordinary and necessary expenses paid or incurred for the production or collection of income or for the management, conservation, or maintenance of property held for the production of income, as long as they are proximately related to these purposes and reasonable in amount. These types of investment expenses are considered a miscellaneous itemized deduction on Schedule A of IRS Form 1040 and are tax-deductible only to the extent that they exceed two percent of an individual's adjusted gross income (AGI). [Note: Expenses attributable to property held for rents or royalties are deductible from gross income and are not subject to the two percent of AGI limitation. In addition, no deduction is allowed for interest on indebtedness incurred or continued to purchase or carry obligations earning fully tax-exempt interest or other exempt income.) Investment expenses include such items as investment counsel fees, custodian fees, fees for clerical help, office rent, state and local transfer taxes, and similar expenses paid or incurred by individuals in connection with their investments.

> **Example 18-2:** Andy and his wife Carol have earned income of $90,000 this year. They also have portfolio income of $10,000, consisting of $4,000 of interest from their certificates of deposit (CDs), $3,500 of dividends, and $2,500 of royalties. Their adjusted gross income (AGI) is $100,000. They also have incurred $20,000 of margin interest expense and $5,000 of other investment expenses. Accordingly, they may deduct only $3,000 of the other investment expenses ($5,000 less 2 percent of AGI, or $2,000). This results in net investment income of $3,500 ($6,500 gross investment income less $3,000 tax-deductible other investment expenses) and, accordingly, this is the maximum amount of investment interest expense deductible in this year. However, if they elect to treat the dividend income of $3,500 as ordinary income (that is, if they *elect out of* the qualifying rates), they could deduct up to $7,000 of investment interest expense (because their gross investment income would be increased to $10,000 and their net investment income to $7,000.)

You should note that if, in Example 18-2, Andy and Carol had incurred net short-term gains of $4,500 and net long-term gains of $5,500 (with their portfolio income thereby equaling a total of $20,000 gross investment income), they could only elect to use the net-long term gains of $5,500 as gross investment income for purposes of calculation of the investment interest expense deduction if they elected not to use the preferential long-term tax rates. This would mean that they would have to use ordinary income tax rates on *both* the dividends and on the long-term gains if they want to be able to increase their gross investment income to $20,000 and, accordingly, obtain an investment interest expense deduction of $17,200 ($20,000 less $2,800 tax-deductible other investment expenses—$5,000 less 2 percent of revised AGI of $110,000 = $2,800). Otherwise, the net investment income of $9,000 ($3,500 of dividend income and $5,500 of net long-term gains) would reduce their investment interest expense deduction this year and result in a carry-forward to future years.

The planner should work closely with a tax advisor to determine when it is preferable to opt out of the reduced rates and tax dividend income or long-term capital gain income at the higher ordinary income rates.

PERSONAL INTEREST EXPENSE

Individuals are also *not* generally permitted to deduct any personal interest paid or accrued during the taxable year. Most often this means that individuals are not allowed to deduct interest paid on credit card debt or automobile loans. However, like most everything else associated with income taxes and the Internal Revenue Code, the definition of what is and what is not personal interest is not nearly so straightforward.

Specifically, personal interest is defined to include all types of interest *except*:

1. Interest incurred in connection with the conduct of a taxpayer's trade or business;

2. Investment interest expense (as just discussed);

3. Interest expense taken into account in computing a taxpayer's income or losses from passive activities;

4. Qualified residence interest; and

5. Interest on qualified educational loans.

Likely, the most important of these exceptions is the exception for *qualified residence interest*, since this includes both home mortgage *acquisition-indebtedness* interest and interest incurred as a result of a home equity loan or line of credit. Indeed, home mortgage interest will probably make it more advantageous for taxpayers to elect to itemize their deductions rather than claim the standard deduction available for their filing class (for example, married filing jointly). However, the details of this exception are beyond the scope of this text and best reserved for discussion in an income tax textbook, such as Kaplan University's text entitled *Individual Income Tax Planning, 3rd edition* by Mershon and Fevurly.

MUTUAL FUNDS TAXATION

Investors in a mutual fund typically receive annual income in one of three forms: 1) ordinary taxable dividends; 2) exempt interest dividends (for example, dividends from a municipal bond fund); and 3) capital gain distributions. Shareholders who receive either short-term or long-term capital gain distributions from the fund report these distributions on Schedule D of IRS Form 1040 (dividends are reported on Schedule B of this same form). Occasionally, shareholders will also receive a distribution that is a tax-free return of capital arising out of a sale of shares by the fund; these will be labeled as non-taxable distributions on their Form 1099-DIV. Finally, mutual fund investors often have a dividend reinvestment option under which dividend income and capital gain distributions are used to purchase additional shares for the investor's account. See chapter 15 of this text discussing *dividend reinvestment plans (DRIPs)*. While the investor receives no cash payments for these shares, he or she is, nevertheless, in *constructive receipt* of the dividends reinvested on his or her behalf and must pay income tax on this distribution. The same concept applies with respect to the receipt of reinvested capital gain distributions; that is, they are currently taxable.

You should note that while dividends paid from a tax-exempt fund (such as a municipal bond fund) are non-taxable annually, a sale or exchange of shares from such fund *does* result in a taxable event. However, to the taxpayer's benefit (consistent with the general tax rule applying to taxable funds), the original cost basis of tax-exempt fund shares is *increased* by the amount of any reinvested dividends. This rule applies even though the distribution is considered as an exempt-interest dividend and is not otherwise reportable in the taxpayer's annual income.

Taxable distributions are one of the biggest drawbacks to investing in mutual funds (compared to owning stocks or bonds directly). When a taxpayer buys a stock or bond, no taxes are currently owed (except for those on declared dividends or taxable interest) until he or she sells the security. Therefore, the taxpayer controls the timing of the taxable event with an individual stock or bond. This is *not* the case with mutual funds. The law requires that gains from the sale of securities within the fund—those remaining after taking offsetting losses—*must* be distributed by December 31st of the taxable year. Some funds can, and often do, take steps to minimize taxable distributions to shareholders by practicing buy-and-hold strategies or by taking whatever losses they can early in the taxable year.

However, taxpayers are generally at the mercy of the mutual fund manager in the timing and implementation of these strategies. Accordingly, this means that the taxpayer's best strategy is to find out about the timing of these potentially taxable distributions *before* they occur. Another strategy is to avoid those mutual funds that historically buy and sell their holdings frequently (referred to as mutual fund *turnover*) and instead invest in more stable funds.

Of course, if a taxpayer/investor sells shares of a mutual fund, there is income tax due on any gain. This gain is measured by the sale price received for the shares (after deducting any expenses of sale) less the investor's basis (adjusted cost) in the shares. The calculation of the shareholder's total basis in the shares sold is relatively complicated, particularly if, as is often the case, these shares have been accumulated at different times over different years. In this instance, there are three methods the taxpayer/investor may use to calculate basis: 1) the specific identification method; 2) the average cost method; and 3) the first-in-first-out (FIFO) method.

Generally, when analyzing the three methods, the specific identification method will prove *most favorable* for the investor (that is, result in the *highest* basis and, therefore, the *least* amount of income tax due upon sale of the shares), assuming a steadily appreciating secondary market in share prices. However, this method requires extensive taxpayer record keeping. Conversely, the FIFO method is usually the *least favorable* alternative for computing mutual fund shareholder basis and is the method used by the IRS when the taxpayer/investor cannot identify the actual shares sold. Finally, the average cost method is typically the most frequently-used means of computing shareholder basis. In this method, the taxpayer pools all of his or her purchased shares in one account and divides its total cost by the number of shares held. Accordingly, all shares have the *same* unit cost or basis for purposes of computing any gain (or loss). Many mutual funds provide the average cost basis of shares to their investors as part of the fund's shareholder services.

STOCKS

Consistent with the general rules previously discussed, when an investor sells individual shares of stock, he or she recognizes a capital gain or loss. Whether such gain is long term (thus qualifying for preferential tax treatment) or short term depends on how long the investor has owned the shares before selling them. When shares of stock are sold, the amount of gain or loss is the difference between the net sales price of the shares (referred to in tax language as the *amount realized*) and the shareholder's basis in the shares. If these shares were a one-time purchase, the shareholder should have little difficulty in establishing his or her cost basis. However, similar to the mutual funds problem in identifying which shares were actually sold, basis determination becomes more problematic when the shares were acquired at different times and prices. In these situations, the shareholder will need to adequately identify the *round lot* (100-share increment) from which he or she acquired the shares or will need to rely on the FIFO method and attribute the basis of the shares to the earliest of the lots purchased or acquired.

A *dividend* is the most common type of publicly-traded corporate stock distribution (closely held stock normally does *not* return a dividend) and is a distribution to the shareholder of either cash or property out of the corporation's current or accumulated earnings and profits. Such a distribution is treated as ordinary income to the taxpayer/investor (not capital gains) and is also not deductible by the distributing corporation. However, effective January 1, 2003, and as previously discussed, so-called *qualifying* dividend distributions are eligible for the same 5% [0%] or 15% rates as long-term capital gains if they meet certain conditions.

If a corporation *redeems* its stock (buys the shares back), it may be treated as an exchange of the stock (rather than as a dividend) if the transaction satisfies one of four tests. The significance of this *sale and exchange* treatment to the shareholder is that he or she is entitled to recover his or her basis in the shares and pay capital gains only to the extent of any excess corporate distribution. However, this treatment is not easy to achieve and is generally available only if one of the four following situations exists:

1. The redemption is substantially disproportionate with respect to the shareholder;
2. The redemption terminates the shareholder's *entire* interest in the corporation;
3. The redemption is not substantially equivalent to a dividend; or
4. The redemption consists of stock held by a non-corporate shareholder and is made in a partial liquidation of the redeeming corporation.

When a corporation distributes shares of its own stock as a dividend, the distribution is referred to as a *stock dividend* and, unlike a cash distribution, is generally *not* taxable. However, the planner should distinguish between a stock dividend, which *may be* taxable in some instances (for example, if the shareholder had the option of receiving stock or taxable cash), from that of a stock split, which is *never* taxable. A stock split is not considered a distribution of a corporation's current or accumulated earnings and profits and, thus, does not carry with it any taxable consequences to the taxpayer/investor.

BONDS

One of the three major categories of bonds—municipal bonds—and its primary form of return have already been discussed in connection with tax-exempt income (see Chapter 17). Accordingly, only government issues (U.S. Treasury securities) and corporate bonds are relevant to our discussion here.

U.S. Treasury Securities

As you should be aware by now, there are three basic types of U.S. Treasury securities: bills, notes, and bonds. Treasury *bills* (with a maturity date of one year or less) are issued at a discount from face value and are redeemable at the bill's face value at maturity. Unless an investor chooses to accrue the amount of this discount daily and include it in his or her income, the amount of this acquisition discount is taxable in full at the maturity date of the bill. Therefore, an investor holding the bill as of the date of maturity includes the amount of the discount as ordinary income at that time. A taxpayer/investor who sells the Treasury bill prior to its maturity includes as ordinary income only the portion of the acquisition discount proportionate to the total time he or she has held the bill.

The taxation of Treasury *notes* (with maturity dates of more than one year up to 10 years from date of issue) and Treasury *bonds* (more than a 10-year maturity date) to a taxpayer/investor is much more complex than that of Treasury bills. If the bond or note was originally issued at a discount (that is, at a price below its face value) after July 1,1982, any investor who did not pay more than the face value of the obligation must include in his or her income each year a calculated share of this *original issue discount(OID)*. This calculation is very complicated and will not be dealt with here, but you should note that the taxpayer/investor is paying tax on income that he or she has not yet received in the form of cash (so-called *phantom income*). The taxpayer's basis is then increased by the amount of OID he or she includes in income each year.

If the Treasury note or bond is subsequently sold prior to its maturity date (the usual case), proceeds from the sale must then be segregated into the following components:

- An amount equal to the taxpayer's adjusted basis in the note or bond is recovered income tax free; this amount is usually the purchase price of the obligation plus the addition of any accrued OID.

- If the sale occurs prior to the interest-reportable date of the note or bond, the seller receives from the buyer an amount separately stating interest accrued on the obligation, but not yet due; this amount is reported by the seller as accrued-interest income on his or her income tax return for the year of sale.

- The excess (deficiency) of any sale proceeds received over the seller's basis and accrued interest is treated as capital gain (or loss) per the previously discussed general rules applying to capital assets.

Finally, any interest received from Treasury bills, notes and bonds is subject to federal income tax at ordinary income rates. However, under the *doctrine of reciprocity,* this same interest is entirely exempt from all state and local taxes.

Corporate Bonds

The taxation rules regarding corporate bonds are somewhat similar to those of U.S. Treasury securities, but probably even more complex. This is because of another type of discount (or premium) that is commonly associated with the buying and selling of corporate obligations. For income tax purposes, this discount (or premium) is known as *market discount or market premium.*

As we know, bond prices in the secondary market fluctuate as the level of interest rates changes and as the issuer's bond rating varies. Therefore, bonds may be purchased at a discount from the face or par value of the bond because of an increase in interest rates subsequent to the bond's issue. A bond *acquired* at a discount in the secondary market (as contrasted to one *issued* at a discount) is known as a *market discount bond.* The corporate bond that is issued at a discount is taxed similarly to that of a U.S. Treasury bill. That is, the discount is *accreted* or accrued annually over the term of the bond.

However, the amount attributable to a market discount is generally *not* includible in the taxpayer/investor's income until the sale or disposition of the bond. That portion is subsequently treated as ordinary income with any sale price excess over and above the bond's par value treated as capital gain. Instead of recognizing interest income (the portion attributable to the market discount) at the date of sale, the taxpayer may elect to include the market discount annually, using either the so-called *ratable accrual method* or the *constant interest* method. However, once this election is made, it applies to *all* market discount bonds acquired during and after the tax year of the election.

> **Example 18-3:** Assume that George has purchased two $1,000 par value five-year corporate bonds at a discount in the secondary market for $965 each. He sells both these bonds prior to their maturity for $1,020 each. Therefore, in the year of sale, George must report interest income of $35 on each of the two bonds ($1,000 less $965) and pay capital gains on the $20 excess of the sale price over the par value of the bonds ($1,020 less $1,000). Note that if George had elected to include the market discount of $35 annually using either the *ratable accrual* or *constant interest* method, he would have had to apply this method to both of the bonds and not just one. However, this method would have *increased* his basis in the bonds and thereby lowered the amount of interest income that he would have had to report at the time of sale. George might choose to ratably accrue the market discount if he anticipated being in a higher marginal income tax bracket in the future. In such event, George would pay more tax today, but less in the future at his anticipated higher marginal tax rate.

When a bond owner has paid a *premium* over the par or face value of the bond, he or she has the option of 1) amortizing the premium until the maturity date of the bond and reducing his or her basis in the bond by the amortized amount or 2) not amortizing and treating the premium as part of the bond's basis. Most investors will elect to amortize the premium annually, using a constant yield method. See the Treasury Regulations to IRC Section 171. This is because investors pay tax at their ordinary income marginal brackets as the interest is paid on the bond, but have to wait until they sell the bond to recover the amount of the premium. As a result, if investors hold the bond until its date of maturity, redeeming it at par, they must treat the amount of the premium as a long-term capital loss. In addition, instead of offsetting ordinary interest income, this loss usually must offset capital gains that are generally taxable at a more-favorable (lower) tax rate. Consequently, investors will typically recover *less* in tax benefits than they have already paid on the portion of the interest payments attributable to the bond premium.

Finally, although an investor may elect to amortize the premium on a *taxable* corporate bond, any premium paid on a *tax-exempt* bond (such as a municipal bond) may *not* be amortized. Instead, such premium must reduce the taxpayer/investor's basis at the time of purchasing the bond. However, this makes sense when remembering that the interest from a municipal bond is not subject to taxation annually and must be recovered as ordinary income upon sale of the bond.

INSURANCE-BASED PRODUCTS

In recent years, the life insurance industry has implemented products with less of an insurance orientation and more of an investment focus. Nonetheless, the tax treatment of life insurance is considerably different than that of a security. For example, the cash value increases resulting from investment income on a life insurance policy are *not* subject to current taxation. These increases in cash value remain exempt from income tax if the policy terminates in a death claim. In addition, dividends payable from a life insurance policy are typically considered a return of premium by the policyholder and are also not taxable. This tax-free accumulation each year is known as the *inside buildup* in the policy and is unique to life insurance. In contrast, if an individual invests in security products in a taxable account, interest, dividends, and recognized capital gains are all currently taxable and generally *not* deferrable.

Because of the tax-favored treatment of life insurance, Congress has adopted certain rules to ensure that a life insurance policy is what it says it is; most notably, in 1984, several tests known as the *cash value accumulation* test and the *cash guideline and premium corridor* test were adopted to define an insurance policy. These tests were expanded in 1988 with the implementation of the *modified endowment contract (MEC)* rules designed to curb the use of single premium life insurance policies masquerading as insurance (versus security) products. The major taxable consequence of the application of the MEC rules is that loans or withdrawals from a single premium life insurance policy (or any other policy that has failed the so-called *7-pay test* which is part of the 1988 rules) are *immediately taxable* as ordinary income. In other words, the taxable earnings within a MEC policy are treated as having been distributed *first*, which is the opposite of the general rule where a loan or withdrawal from a life insurance policy is considered to be drawn, at least initially, from the policyholder's non-taxable basis.

Another form of life insurance product that may serve as an investment is an annuity. Individuals purchase annuity contracts from commercial insurance companies to protect themselves from the risk of *superannuation* or the risk of outliving one's money during lifetime. The owner of the contract makes one or more payments to the insurance company; in return, the owner is provided with the professional money management skills of the company and the guarantee of a periodic payment during lifetime. This payment may begin immediately or may be deferred to some point in the future. If deferred, tax is postponed until the owner starts to receive the periodic payments, which, in turn, represent the beginning of the *distribution stage* (versus *accumulation stage*) of the annuity.

On receipt of the annuity payments over the chosen time period (referred to as "annuitizing" the annuity), the portion of each annuity payment representing an accumulation of the deferred earnings is taxable as ordinary income. The portion representing the return of the owner's after-tax investment (if any) is treated as a non-taxable return of capital. In determining the amount of the annuity payment that is *not* taxable annually, a so-called *exclusion ratio* is used. This ratio is established by dividing the amount of the owner's after-tax investment (in the form of premiums paid under the terms of the annuity contract) by his or her *expected return* on the contract. This percentage is then multiplied by the amount of the annuity payment to determine the income-tax free portion of each payment. An example of the application of the ratio follows:

Example 18-4: Assume that Joan, age 60, purchases an annuity contract from an insurance company for $120,000 that will begin to pay her a fixed amount of $1,500 per month at age 65. Her life expectancy at that age (or when she begins to *annuitize* the annuity) is 20 years. Therefore, her *expected return* in the contract is 20 × $1,500 × 12 or $360,000. Since Joan's investment in the contract is $120,000, the applicable exclusion ratio is .3333 or 33.3%. When multiplying this ratio by the monthly payment of $1,500, we determine that $500 of the payout is income tax free (and that the remaining $1,000 of the monthly payout is taxable). Should Joan outlive her projected life expectancy, the annuity payments are fully taxable once she has fully recovered her basis in the contract.

The above example illustrates the taxable consequences of a so-called *nonqualified annuity* that was annuitized by the owner of the annuity contract. However, less than 10% of non-qualified annuities are actually paid out in this manner. The remaining majority are either taken in a lump sum or random withdrawal by the annuity owner or left to the owner's beneficiaries at his or her death. If withdrawn in a lump sum or random withdrawal, *last-in, first-out (LIFO)* taxation rules apply, resulting first in taxability of the earnings portion of the annuity (as ordinary income) and second, in recovery of the owner's non-taxable basis/after tax contributions. If the annuity owner dies while still owning the annuity, the greater of either the contract's cash value or the guaranteed death benefit, less withdrawals, is payable to the owner's beneficiary(ies); in either case, income tax consequences result from the selected payout or distribution of the annuity contract.

REAL ESTATE

As previously discussed in chapter 6 of this textbook, real estate may be owned either directly or indirectly; for example, through ownership shares in a real estate investment trust (REIT). However, the Internal Revenue Code (IRC) does not distinguish between forms of real estate ownership and, instead, taxes real estate according to the character of its income. We will now briefly consider the three basic forms of real estate ownership and the taxable consequences of each.

Undeveloped Land

This form of investment does not usually generate significant current taxable income or cash flow to the investor. Rather, the primary tax advantage to the owner/investor is that the capital appreciation (if any) in the market value of the land is not recognized as income until the owner disposes of the land in a taxable transaction (note: it is possible to do a non-taxable *like-kind exchange* with undeveloped land). At such time, any capital appreciation in the land's value, from the time the owner purchased the property, is taxed as capital gain. The primary exception to this taxable treatment is if the owner is also considered to be a *dealer* in real estate by the I.R.S., in which case ordinary income tax treatment will result.

Finally, the payment of real estate taxes on undeveloped land is normally tax-deductible by the owner during the entire period of his of her ownership.

Rental Real Estate

Unlike undeveloped land, in rental real estate ownership, current income is typically received by the owner in the form of rents. Accordingly, these rents are taxable to the owner as ordinary income and any net profit (after deductible expenses) is reported on Schedule E of the owner's IRS Form 1040. Since an annual depreciation deduction is also afforded the owner who invests in either residential or commercial rental real estate, he or she may recoup some of the investment dollars expended through claiming such a deduction. However, you should note that the depreciation allowance is only a tax benefit and does not impact the actual before-tax cash flow generated from the rental real estate to its owner. This effect was observed when performing the *net operating income (NOI)* computation in chapter 6, leading to an estimated intrinsic value of the rental property and the basis for an appropriate investment decision with respect to possible purchase by the investor.

REIT Ownership

In this form of indirect ownership of real estate, the investor/shareholder is taxed very similarly to that of other mutual fund investors. Notably, all distributions in the form of dividends are taxable as ordinary income unless these distributions are specified otherwise by the REIT entity. In addition, as mentioned earlier, dividends generated from the REIT normally do *not* constitute a qualifying dividend for income tax purposes and the preferential 5% [0% in 2009 and 2010] or 15% rates.

A REIT is required to distribute 90% of income, therefore making such investment very similar to that of a mutual fund. However, unlike a mutual fund, losses from a REIT investment may not be passed through to the shareholder. In contrast to this treatment, losses from a direct investment in real estate (either in undeveloped land or in rental property) may be passed through to investors, although limitations may exist in the case of rental real estate.

Finally, assuming that the REIT distributes at least 90% of its income to shareholders, there is no corporate-level entity tax. In turn, this permits REIT shareholders to enjoy the benefits of limited liability with respect to their real estate investment, while avoiding the disadvantageous consequences of double taxation associated with corporate ownership.

COLLECTIBLES

Unless the investor is considered a dealer, an individual who invests in collectibles (art, coins, stamps, and the like) is normally purchasing a capital asset. Therefore, any gain on the sale of a collectible is subject to long-term capital gain treatment, assuming it is owned for the requisite *one year and a day* period from the date of purchase. However, there is a special flat tax rate accorded to the sale of a collectible; currently, this rate is either 15% or 28% (depending on the taxpayer's highest ordinary income marginal tax rate) and constitutes an exception to the normal lower capital gains rates imposed on the sale of other capital assets. Nonetheless, any loss on the sale of a collectible is treated as a long-term or short-term capital loss and must first offset any other long-term or short-term capital gain without separate treatment.

Like stocks generally, there is no maturity date on a collectible. Accordingly, this makes it possible for the investor to time the recognition of a taxable event and postpone any gain into a year in which he or she has experienced losses on a collectible or, alternatively, when his or her total income is low. Of course, the investor pays no income tax on the annual gain from the collectible (if there is any) until he or she chooses to sell.

DERIVATIVES (OPTIONS AND FUTURES)

The taxation of futures and options is a very complicated area of the Internal Revenue Code (IRC). While the taxation of options was discussed previously in Chapter 16 of this textbook, no mention has yet been made of the taxable consequences of a futures contract. Specifically, futures contracts are referred to in the IRC as a *Section 1256 contract* and enjoy their own unique set of tax provisions known as the *marked-to-market rules*. A detailed explanation of these very complex rules will not be attempted here, except to state that futures contracts are generally treated as a capital asset and are taxed at their fair-market value at the end of any given year of ownership (as if the futures contract had been sold). This is the case even if the contract is not yet complete or the maturity date has not yet arrived. Under the marked-to-market rules, 60% of the gain or loss from a regulated futures contract is treated as long-term capital gain or loss and 40% is treated as short-term gain or loss on the last business day of the taxable year when the contract is owned. This treatment occurs *regardless* of the actual holding period of the contract and underlying property.

In the taxation of options, an investor realizes *no* taxable gain or loss on the purchase of a put or call. As noted in chapter 16, both puts and calls are capital assets, so that if either of these options is sold prior to exercise or expiration, capital gain or loss will result. To figure out the taxable consequences, however, the planner must first differentiate whether his or her client is the *holder (buyer)* of the option or is its *writer (seller)*. In this regard, it is also helpful to review the tax consequences to either position owner as outlined in the previous Table 16-1.

If a taxpayer/investor *writes (sells)* the option, the amount received for doing so is not taxable at the time of receipt. Rather, the amount received is carried in a deferred account until the obligation expires, or the writer sells (in the case of a call option) or buys (in the case of a put option), the underlying stock when the option is exercised. If the option expires unexercised, the amount received for writing the option is short-term capital gain. If a *call* is exercised, and the writer sells the underlying stock, he or she *increases* the amount realized on the stock sale by the amount of the call premium. If a *put* is exercised, and the writer buys the underlying stock, he or she *decreases* his or her basis in the stock by the amount of the put premium.

For the *holder (buyer)* of the option, if the option expires, it is considered sold at the end of the standard nine-month period and a short-term capital loss is created. If the holder exercises a *call* option, its cost or premium paid is added to the basis of the underlying stock purchased. This means the premium paid may be treated as a long-term capital gain if the underlying purchased security was held more than 12 months (otherwise, the premium paid is treated as a short-term capital gain). In exercising a *put* option, the holder is obligated to sell the stock to the writer of the put. Therefore, it is the sale of the underlying stock (not the put option) that is taxed. Accordingly, in order to determine his or her gain or loss on the sale of the stock, the holder of the put offsets the total option premium paid against the price received for the stock to arrive at the net amount realized. If this net amount realized exceeds the holder's basis in the stock sold, the excess is capital gain and, like the call option, is considered as either a short-term or long-term capital gain depending on how long the underlying stock has been held prior to sale.

IMPORTANT CONCEPTS

Capital asset

Holding period

Capital gain or loss

Ordinary income

Active income

Portfolio income

Passive income

Tax deferred or tax advantaged account

Net unrealized appreciation (NUA)

Investment interest expense

Net investment income

Personal interest expense

Constructive receipt of income

Specific identification method

Average cost method

First-in-first-out (FIFO) method

Cash dividend

Stock dividend

Stock redemption

Stock split

Original issue discount (OID)

Market discount bond

Market premium bond

Inside buildup

Modified endowment contract (MEC)

Annuitization

Exclusion ratio

Expected return of contract

Last-in-first-out (LIFO) taxation

Capital appreciation

Rental income

REIT

Collectibles flat rate of taxation

Marked-to-market rules

Taxation of options

QUESTIONS FOR REVIEW

1. For income tax purposes, how is an investment generally classified and why is this important?

2. What is the time period that an investment must be owned for it to qualify as a *long-term* asset?

3. What are the three types of income for purposes of the passive loss rules and to what general type of income (ordinary or capital) is each roughly equivalent?

4. What does conventional wisdom suggest as to where an investor should position an investment in stocks versus bonds? Why do some financial planners disagree with this approach?

5. When can an investor take advantage of the *net unrealized appreciation* (NUA) income tax concept? What is the benefit to the investor in applying this concept?

6. Complete the following sentence: Investment interest expense may be deducted to the extent of _____.

7. What items typically constitute *net investment income*? Which one(s) of these items may or may not be included at the discretion of the investor?

8. Is personal interest expense always non-deductible? Explain.

9. How (in what form) do mutual fund investors typically receive annual income? If they participate in a *DRIP*, are distributions from that plan currently taxable? Why or why not?

10. How does a taxpayer/investor potentially minimize taxable annual distributions from a mutual fund?

11. What are the three methods for calculating a taxpayer's basis in mutual fund shares? In a rising secondary market, which one of these is the most favorable to use?

12. How is a dividend distribution from a stock generally taxed? How is this different from a distribution that constitutes a stock redemption?

13. Contrast the potential tax treatment of a stock *dividend* to that of a stock *split*.

14. How does the concept of *original issue discount* enter into the resulting taxation of a U.S. Treasury bill?

15. If a U.S. Treasury bond or note is sold prior to its maturity date, how must the proceeds from the sale be segregated for income tax purposes?

16. Explain the taxable significance of a corporate bond that is selling in the secondary marketplace at a discount to its par value.

17. If a corporate bond is selling in the secondary marketplace at a premium to par value, how do most investors choose to account for this premium for income tax purposes? How does this differ in the case of a municipal bond that is selling at a premium?

18. Contrast the taxable consequences of the annual accumulation of earnings within a life insurance policy to that of an annual return from a security. Which one is taxed more favorably? Explain.

19. What is a proxy for application of the *modified endowment contract (MEC) rules* to an insurance product? What is the practical consequence of the MEC rules?

20. How is the distribution of an annuity taxed to the investor if he or she chooses to *annuitize* the payout? How does this taxable treatment differ from a lump sum or random withdrawal from an annuity?

21. Contrast the income tax treatment to a taxpayer from each of the following three types of real estate investments:

    • Undeveloped land

    • Rental real estate

    • Shareholder in a real estate investment trust (REIT)

22. What is the special flat tax rate that applies if a collectible is sold at any time?

23. What unique tax concept applies in the taxation of a futures contract?

24. Summarize the tax consequences to the *writer* of an option in each of the following circumstances:

    • The option expires unexercised

    • The option is exercised

25. Summarize the taxable consequences to the *holder* of an option in each of the following circumstances:

    • The option expires unexercised

    • The option is exercised

SUGGESTIONS FOR ADDITIONAL READING

Individual Income Tax Planning, 3rd edition, Jeffrey B. Mershon and Keith R. Fevurly, Kaplan, Inc., 2007.

U.S. Master Tax Guide, most recent annual edition, CCH Editorial Staff Publication, CCH Incorporated

Index

• • •

A

Account executives, 96

Accounts receivable (AR) turnover, 252

Accredited investors, 39

Accumulation phase, annuities, 67, 316

Active income, 307

Active portfolio management
earnings momentum, 247
features of, 247
mutual funds, 53
rental property, 78
sector rotation, 247

After-tax inflation-adjusted rate of return, 171–172

After-tax rate of return, 171

Against actuals, 99

Against the box, short selling, 249

Aggressive investments
growth funds, 51
Markowitz portfolio theory, 151
and risk, 117

Agricultural futures, 99–100

Alpha (Jensen ratio), 178–179

Alternative investments
collectibles, 108–109
derivatives, 92, 94–95
forward contracts, 92–93
futures, 93–100
gold, 109
natural resources, 110–111
options, 44, 94, 101–107

Alternative minimum tax, tax preference, and private purpose bonds, 20

American Depository Receipts (ADRs), 45–46, 121–122

American options, 101, 102, 227

AMEX (American Stock Exchange), 279

Amount realized, 312

AMT bonds, 300

Analyst recommendations, 159

Annualized rate of return, 166

Annuitant, 68

Annuities, 67–70
annuitization, defined, 67, 316
equity-indexed annuities (EIAs), 70
fixed annuities, 68–69